Holy arte thou...

thou Holy arte

Thou arte the lorde god of hostes.

Heauen and earthe are fulfilled wᵗ the glorie of ᵗᵱ magestie

The glorious company of apostelle praise the

The godly felowshippe of the prophetes worship the

The faire felowshippe of martere praise the.

The holy congregacion of...

...ndes desyre you and as a christian call vppon god to quicken... ...wes to quicken you in his waye...

The Sisters Who Would Be Queen

Leanda de Lisle

❖

The Sisters Who Would Be Queen

❖

The Tragedy of
Mary, Katherine &
Lady Jane Grey

Harper
Press

HarperPress
An imprint of HarperCollins*Publishers*
77–85 Fulham Palace Road
Hammersmith, London W6 8JB
www.harpercollins.co.uk

Visit our authors' blog: www.fifthestate.co.uk

First published in Great Britain by Harper*Press* in 2008

Family trees © HarperCollins*Publishers*,
designed by HL Studios, Oxfordshire

1

Leanda de Lisle asserts the moral right to
be identified as the author of this work

A catalogue record for this book
is available from the British Library

HB ISBN 978-0-00-721905-6
TPB ISBN 978-0-00-728043-8

Typeset in Minion with Fairfield LH display by
G&M Designs Limited, Raunds, Northamptonshire

Printed and bound in Great Britain by
Clays Ltd, St Ives plc

Mixed Sources
Product group from well-managed
forests and other controlled sources
www.fsc.org Cert no. SW-COC-1806
© 1996 Forest Stewardship Council
FSC

FSC is a non-profit international organisation established to promote the
responsible management of the world's forests. Products carrying the FSC
label are independently certified to assure consumers that they come
from forests that are managed to meet the social, economic and
ecological needs of present or future generations.

Find out more about HarperCollins and the environment at
www.harpercollins.co.uk/green

For Peter, Rupert, Christian and Dominic, with love

'Such as ruled and were queens were for the most part wicked, ungodly, superstitious, and given to idolatry and to all filthy abominations as we may see in the histories of Queen Jezebel'

THOMAS BECON 1554

Contents

Part Four: *Lost Love*

List of Illustrations

PLATE SECTION I

Mary Tudor and Charles Brandon, Duke of Suffolk, after Clouet ©
By kind permission of His Grace the Duke of Bedford and the
Trustees of the Bedford Estates

The tomb at Westminster Abbey of Frances Grey (née Brandon),
Duchess of Suffolk © The Dean and Chapter of Westminster

The ruins of Bradgate Manor, Leicestershire © Leicester Mercury
Media Group

Thomas Seymour of Sudeley by Nicholas Denizot (1545–49) ©
National Maritime Museum, Greenwich, London

Catherine Parr attributed to Master John (*c*.1545) © The National
Portrait Gallery, London

Edward Seymour by Hans Holbein the Younger © The Trustees
of the Weston Park Foundation, UK/The Bridgeman Art
Library

Katherine Brandon (née Willoughby), Duchess of Suffolk, by Hans
Holbein © Grimsthorpe and Drummond Castle Trust

Henry Brandon, Duke of Suffolk, by Hans Holbein the Younger
(1541) © The Royal Collection 2007 Her Majesty Queen
Elizabeth II

Charles Brandon by Hans Holbein the Younger (1541) © The Royal
Collection 2007 Her Majesty Queen Elizabeth II

William Parr, Marquess of Northampton, by Hans Holbein the
Younger (*c*.1540) © The Royal Collection 2007 Her Majesty Queen
Elizabeth II

Edward VI by Unknown Artist (*c*.1547) © The National Portrait
Gallery, London

Jane Dormer, Duchess of Feria, aged 29, by a follower of Claudio
   Coello © Private Collection. Photograph courtesy of Antonia
   Deutsch.
Edward VI's 'Devise for the Succession' © By kind permission of The
   Masters of the Bench of the Inner Temple. Photograph courtesy
   of Ian Jones.
Lady Jane Grey by Lavina Teerlinc (c.1545–47) © Yale Center for
   British Art, Paul Mellon Collection, USA/The Bridgeman Art
   Library
A document signed by 'Jane the Quene' © By kind permission of
   The Masters of the Bench of the Inner Temple. Photograph
   courtesy of Ian Jones.
Tower of London © The Society of Antiquaries of London
'The Execution of Lady Jane Grey' by Paul Delaroche (1834) © The
   National Gallery, London

PLATE SECTION II

Stephen Gardiner, Bishop of Winchester, by Unknown Artist ©
   Corpus Christi College, Oxford, UK/The Bridgeman Art Library
Mary I by Hans Eworth © Society of Antiquaries of London,
   UK/The Bridgeman Art Library
Lady Katherine Grey by Lavina Teerlinc (c.1555–60) © V&A Images,
   Victoria and Albert Museum
Lady Dacre and son by Hans Eworth (1559) © Private
   Collection/The Bridgeman Art Library
Queen Elizabeth I by Unknown Artist (c.1558) © Philip Mould Ltd
Mary Queen of Scots after François Clouet (1560) © Bibliothèque
   Nationale, Paris, France, Giraudon/The Bridgeman Art Library
Robert Dudley, Earl of Leicester, by Steven van der Meulen
   (c.1560–65) © Wallace Collection, London, UK/The Bridgeman
   Art Library
Katherine Grey as Countess of Hertford with her son Edward, Lord
   Beauchamp, by Lavina Teerlinc (c.1562) © Belvoir Castle,
   Leicestershire, UK/The Bridgeman Art Library

Sir William Cecil, later Lord Burghley, by Arnold van Brounckhorst
(c.1560) © The National Portrait Gallery, London

Lady Mary Grey, as Mrs Keyes, by Hans Eworth © By kind
permission of The Trustees of the Chequers Estate/The
Bridgeman Art Library

The East Front of Chequers © By kind permission of The Trustees
of the Chequers Estate, Mark Fiennes/The Bridgeman Art Library

Effigies at Salisbury Cathedral of Lady Katherine Grey and her
husband Edward Seymour, Earl of Hertford © Photograph
courtesy of Dr John Crook

Map of London, from 'Civitates Orbis Terrarum' by Georg Braun
(1542–1622) and Frans Hogenburg (1635–90), c.1572 © Glasgow
University Library, Scotland/The Bridgeman Art Library

ENDPAPERS

Lady Jane Grey's prayerbook © British Library Board. All rights
reserved. Harley 2342, ff74v–75.

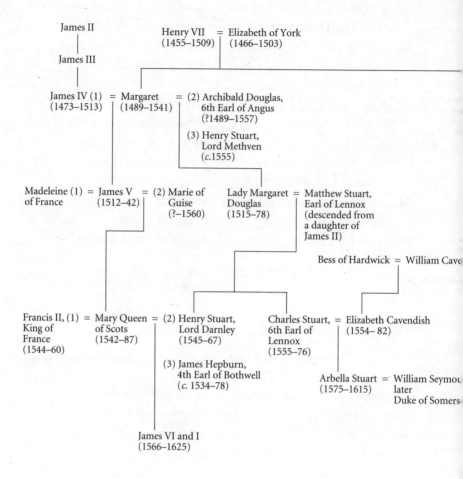

James II
|
James III
|

Henry VII = Elizabeth of York
(1455–1509) (1466–1503)

James IV (1) = Margaret = (2) Archibald Douglas,
(1473–1513) (1489–1541)   6th Earl of Angus
                               (?1489–1557)

                          (3) Henry Stuart,
                              Lord Methven
                              (c.1555)

Madeleine (1) = James V = (2) Marie of   Lady Margaret = Matthew Stuart,
of France   (1512–42)   Guise   Douglas   Earl of Lennox
                              (?–1560)   (1515–78)   (descended from
                                                            a daughter of
                                                            James II)

                                            Bess of Hardwick = William Cave

Francis II, (1) = Mary Queen = (2) Henry Stuart,   Charles Stuart, = Elizabeth Cavendish
King of   of Scots   Lord Darnley   6th Earl of   (1554– 82)
France   (1542–87)   (1545–67)   Lennox
(1544–60)   (1555–76)

                              (3) James Hepburn,
                                  4th Earl of Bothwell   Arbella Stuart = William Seymou
                                  (c. 1534–78)   (1575–1615)   later
                                                                          Duke of Somers

                    James VI and I
                    (1566–1625)

The Descendants of Henry VII

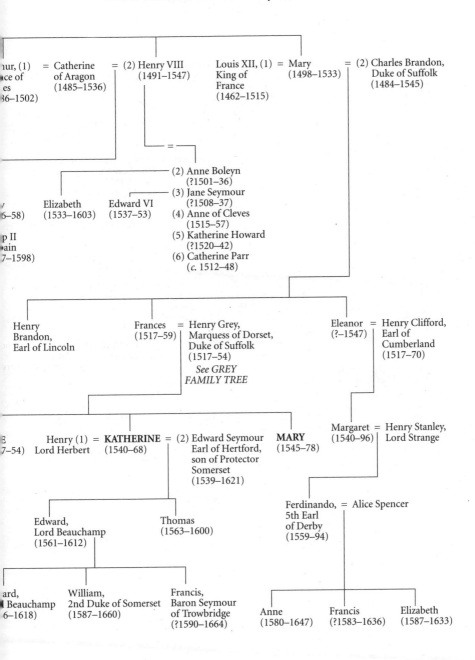

ur, (1)　=　Catherine　=　(2) Henry VIII　Louis XII, (1)　=　Mary　=　(2) Charles Brandon,
ce of　　　of Aragon　　　(1491–1547)　King of　　　(1498–1533)　Duke of Suffolk
es　　　　(1485–1536)　　　　　　　France　　　　　　　　　　(1484–1545)
36–1502)　　　　　　　　　　　　　　(1462–1515)

=

(2) Anne Boleyn
(?1501–36)

Elizabeth　Edward VI　(3) Jane Seymour
(1533–1603)　(1537–53)　(?1508–37)
(4) Anne of Cleves
(1515–57)
(5) Katherine Howard
(?1520–42)
(6) Catherine Parr
(c. 1512–48)

Henry　　　　Frances　=　Henry Grey,　　　　　Eleanor　=　Henry Clifford,
Brandon,　　　(1517–59)　Marquess of Dorset,　(?–1547)　Earl of
Earl of Lincoln　　　　Duke of Suffolk　　　　　　　Cumberland
　　　　　　　　　　　　(1517–54)　　　　　　　　　　　(1517–70)
　　　　　　　　　　　See GREY
　　　　　　　　　　　FAMILY TREE

Henry (1)　=　**KATHERINE**　=　(2) Edward Seymour　**MARY**　　　Margaret　=　Henry Stanley,
Lord Herbert　(1540–68)　　　Earl of Hertford,　(1545–78)　(1540–96)　Lord Strange
　　　　　　　　　　　　　　son of Protector
　　　　　　　　　　　　　　Somerset
　　　　　　　　　　　　　　(1539–1621)

Edward,　　　　　Thomas　　　　　　　　　　Ferdinando,　=　Alice Spencer
Lord Beauchamp　(1563–1600)　　　　　　　　5th Earl
(1561–1612)　　　　　　　　　　　　　　　　of Derby
　　　　　　　　　　　　　　　　　　　　　(1559–94)

ard,　　William,　　　　　　Francis,　　　　　　　Anne　　　Francis　　　Elizabeth
Beauchamp　2nd Duke of Somerset　Baron Seymour　　　(1580–1647)　(?1583–1636)　(1587–1633)
6–1618)　(1587–1660)　　　　of Trowbridge
　　　　　　　　　　　　　　(?1590–1664)

The Grey Family Tree

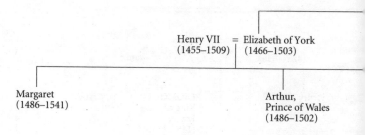

Henry VII = Elizabeth of York
(1455–1509) | (1466–1503)

Margaret
(1486–1541)

Arthur,
Prince of Wales
(1486–1502)

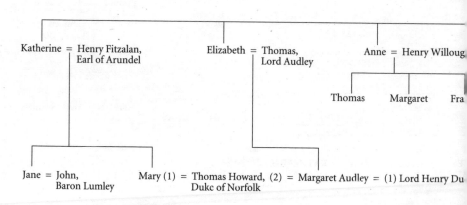

Katherine = Henry Fitzalan,
Earl of Arundel

Elizabeth = Thomas,
Lord Audley

Anne = Henry Willoug

Thomas   Margaret   Fra

Jane = John,
Baron Lumley

Mary (1) = Thomas Howard, (2) = Margaret Audley = (1) Lord Henry Du
Duke of Norfolk

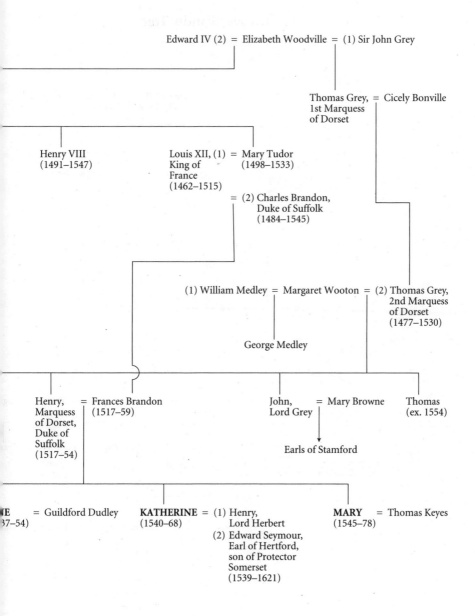

Edward IV (2) = Elizabeth Woodville = (1) Sir John Grey

Thomas Grey, = Cicely Bonville
1st Marquess
of Dorset

Henry VIII
(1491–1547)

Louis XII, (1) = Mary Tudor
King of   (1498–1533)
France
(1462–1515)

= (2) Charles Brandon,
    Duke of Suffolk
    (1484–1545)

(1) William Medley = Margaret Wooton = (2) Thomas Grey,
                                           2nd Marquess
                                           of Dorset
                                           (1477–1530)

George Medley

Henry,   = Frances Brandon
Marquess   (1517–59)
of Dorset,
Duke of
Suffolk
(1517–54)

John,   = Mary Browne
Lord Grey

Thomas
(ex. 1554)

Earls of Stamford

ᴇ   = Guildford Dudley
37–54)

KATHERINE = (1) Henry,
(1540–68)   Lord Herbert
            (2) Edward Seymour,
                Earl of Hertford,
                son of Protector
                Somerset
                (1539–1621)

MARY   = Thomas Keyes
(1545–78)

The Dudley Family Tree
Showing the claim of Henry, Earl of Huntingdon, to the English throne

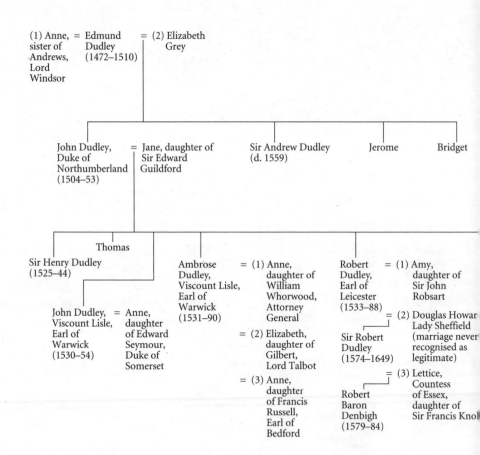

(1) Anne, = Edmund = (2) Elizabeth
sister of   Dudley   Grey
Andrews,   (1472–1510)
Lord
Windsor

John Dudley,   = Jane, daughter of   Sir Andrew Dudley   Jerome   Bridget
Duke of   Sir Edward   (d. 1559)
Northumberland   Guildford
(1504–53)

Thomas

Sir Henry Dudley
(1525–44)

Ambrose   = (1) Anne,   Robert   = (1) Amy,
Dudley,   daughter of   Dudley,   daughter of
Viscount Lisle, William   Earl of   Sir John
Earl of   Whorwood,   Leicester   Robsart
Warwick   Attorney   (1533–88)
(1531–90)   General   = (2) Douglas Howard
                                 Sir Robert   Lady Sheffield
             = (2) Elizabeth,   Dudley   (marriage never
                   daughter of   (1574–1649)   recognised as
                   Gilbert,   legitimate)
                   Lord Talbot
                                             = (3) Lettice,
             = (3) Anne,   Robert   Countess
                   daughter   Baron   of Essex,
                   of Francis   Denbigh   daughter of
                   Russell,   (1579–84)   Sir Francis Knol
                   Earl of
                   Bedford

John Dudley,   = Anne,
Viscount Lisle, daughter
Earl of   of Edward
Warwick   Seymour,
(1530–54)   Duke of
                 Somerset

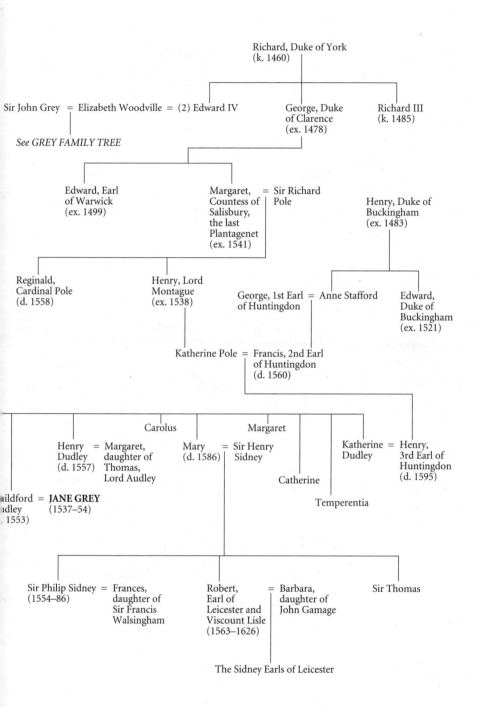

Richard, Duke of York
(k. 1460)

Sir John Grey = Elizabeth Woodville = (2) Edward IV

See GREY FAMILY TREE

George, Duke
of Clarence
(ex. 1478)

Richard III
(k. 1485)

Edward, Earl
of Warwick
(ex. 1499)

Margaret,
Countess of
Salisbury,
the last
Plantagenet
(ex. 1541)

= Sir Richard
Pole

Henry, Duke of
Buckingham
(ex. 1483)

Reginald,
Cardinal Pole
(d. 1558)

Henry, Lord
Montague
(ex. 1538)

George, 1st Earl = Anne Stafford
of Huntingdon

Edward,
Duke of
Buckingham
(ex. 1521)

Katherine Pole = Francis, 2nd Earl
of Huntingdon
(d. 1560)

Carolus

Margaret

Henry = Margaret,
Dudley   daughter of
(d. 1557) Thomas,
          Lord Audley

Mary = Sir Henry
(d. 1586) Sidney

Katherine = Henry,
Dudley   3rd Earl of
            Huntingdon
            (d. 1595)

Catherine

ildford = **JANE GREY**
dley   (1537–54)
1553)

Temperentia

Sir Philip Sidney = Frances,
(1554–86)   daughter of
             Sir Francis
             Walsingham

Robert,   = Barbara,
Earl of   daughter of
Leicester and   John Gamage
Viscount Lisle
(1563–1626)

Sir Thomas

The Sidney Earls of Leicester

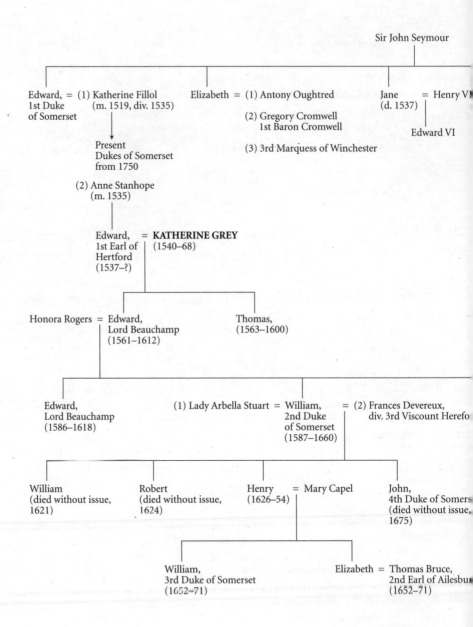

Sir John Seymour

Edward, = (1) Katherine Fillol   Elizabeth = (1) Antony Oughtred   Jane   = Henry V‖
1st Duke   (m. 1519, div. 1535)   (d. 1537)
of Somerset

                                 (2) Gregory Cromwell
                                     1st Baron Cromwell   Edward VI

Present   (3) 3rd Marquess of Winchester
Dukes of Somerset
from 1750

(2) Anne Stanhope
   (m. 1535)

Edward,   = **KATHERINE GREY**
1st Earl of   (1540–68)
Hertford
(1537–?)

Honora Rogers = Edward,   Thomas,
           Lord Beauchamp   (1563–1600)
           (1561–1612)

Edward,   (1) Lady Arbella Stuart = William,   = (2) Frances Devereux,
Lord Beauchamp   2nd Duke   div. 3rd Viscount Herefo‖
(1586–1618)   of Somerset
                                           (1587–1660)

William   Robert   Henry   = Mary Capel   John,
(died without issue,   (died without issue,   (1626–54)   4th Duke of Somers‖
1621)   1624)   (died without issue,
                                                             1675)

William,   Elizabeth = Thomas Bruce,
3rd Duke of Somerset   2nd Earl of Ailesbu‖
(1652–71)   (1652–71)

The Seymour Family Tree

mas, 1st Baron = Catherine Parr   Henry   John   Dorothy   Anthony   Margery
nour of Sudeley
8–ex. 1548)

Francis,
Baron Seymour of Trowbridge
(?1590–1664)

Algernon Seymour,
7th Duke of Somerset
(1684–1750, died
without male issue)

Prologue

God, the Prime Mover, brought peace and order to the darkness of the void as the cosmos was born. Everything, spirit or substance, was given its place according to its worth and nearness to God. Above the rocks, which enjoyed mere existence, were plants, for they enjoyed the privilege of life. Each plant also had its appointed rank. Trees were higher than moss, and oak the noblest of the trees. Superior even to the greatest tree were animals, which have appetite as well as life. Above the animals, mankind, whom God blessed with immortal souls, and they too had their degrees, according to the dues of their birth. This was the great Chain of Being, through which the Tudor universe was ordered, and at its top, under God, stood Henry VIII. It was a place he held convincingly. As he prepared for the joust on a spring day in 1524 he was still the man described by a Venetian ambassador as 'the handsomest Prince in Christendom'. Tall and muscular with a fine complexion, the thirty-two-year-old monarch had ruled England for fifteen years and was in the prime of life. He had just had some new armour made and was looking forward to testing it at the tilt.

Henry was considered the finest jouster of his generation and the watching crowd had high expectations of the sport ahead. Attending the King on foot was his cousin, Thomas Grey, the 2nd Marquess of Dorset: his diamond and ruby badge of a Tudor rose testified to his skills as an athlete. Henry's opponent, his brother-in-law, Charles Brandon, Duke of Suffolk, was, however, still more renowned. His father had been killed in 1485, holding the standard of Henry VII at the battle of Bosworth Field, where the Tudor crown was won. He had been raised at court and had married Henry's younger sister, Mary, the beautiful widow of Louis XII of France. But Suffolk was also the King's closest friend. The two men even looked alike and at great court tournaments dressed often in identical armour.

As Henry reached his end of the tilt, Suffolk was informed that the King was in place. The duke, however, was having trouble with his new helmet. 'I see him not,' Suffolk shouted out; 'by my faith for my headpiece blocks my sight.' Thomas Grey of Dorset, hearing nothing above the stamping of the horses, then fatefully handed the King his lance. Henry's visor was still fastened open as he readied himself, but Suffolk's servant, mistaking the signal warned the duke, 'Sir, the King is coming.' Suffolk, blinded by his helmet, spurred his horse forward. Immediately the King responded, charging with his blunted spear down the sandy list. In the crowd people spotted the King's bare face and there were desperate shouts of 'Hold! Hold!'; but 'the duke neither saw nor heard, and whether the King remembered his visor was up or not, few could tell'. The thundering of hooves was followed by the clap and crack of impact. Suffolk had struck the King on the brow and his shattered lance filled the King's head-piece with splinters. As the horses pulled up, the King still in the saddle, some in the crowd looked set to attack the duke, while others blamed Dorset for handing the King his spear too soon. Henry, in response, protested loudly that no one was at fault and, taking a spear, ran a further six courses to prove he was unhurt. But the deepest fears of the spectators still lingered.

The battle of Bosworth had followed a long period of violent disorder, fuelled by rival claimants to the throne. The eventual victor, Henry VII, had ensured the peace England now enjoyed by bequeathing his crown to an adult son, Henry VIII, who was his undisputed heir. But what would have happened if that son, the King, was now killed, or died suddenly? The fear of a return to the violence of the past was visceral. It was believed that disorder had been brought into the universe when Lucifer, the Angel of Light, had rebelled against God, and into the world by sin, when that fallen Angel tempted Eve in the Garden of Eden. Ever since, Lucifer had remained watchful for any opportunity to set loose anarchy, intending eventually to engulf earth and the heavens in chaos of unimaginable horror and evil. In the shadow of Armageddon, the question of what would happen if the King died was of vital interest – and the answer was a troubling one. Henry's only legitimate heir was a little girl, his still carefree eight-year-old daughter Mary. Under English law it was possible for a woman to inherit the crown. Her mother, Catherine of Aragon, assumed that one day she would. But England had not yet had a Queen regnant, who ruled in her own right, and it was uncertain one could survive long.

Women were believed the weaker sex, not only in terms of their physical strength. More significantly, they were also judged to be, like Eve, morally frail – a belief so deeply held that it has underpinned attitudes to women and power into modern times. While reason and intellect were associated with the male, women were considered creatures of the body: emotional, irrational and indecisive. As such they ranked below men in the Chain of Being. Although a servant might owe obedience to his mistress by reason of her place in the social hierarchy, sisters took second place to their brothers in the inheritance of property, and wives were subject to their husbands in marriage. It did not seem fitting to Henry that a woman – by nature inferior to men – should sit at the apex of power, as a monarch did. Nor did he believe it really possible.

Henry feared that even if ambitious warrior nobles did not overthrow the unsoldierly Mary, her husband would be the true ruler. England might even be absorbed into a foreign empire through a marriage treaty. His wife's Hapsburg relations were infamous for extending their territory by this means. And, in any case, what did it say about his virility that he could only provide his dynasty with second best: a girl?

Henry had accepted that, at thirty-eight, Catherine of Aragon was too old to have more children, and he stopped visiting her chambers that year. But as he considered the fate of his country, and his dynasty, Henry remained determined to settle his kingdom on a male heir. His pursuit of this goal would bring him more power than any of his medieval predecessors had possessed, but in doing so he would tear unwittingly into the myths from which royal authority was drawn. He broke with the Papacy in Rome to claim a royal authority over spiritual and temporal affairs, placing himself above English law and using Parliament to seize the right to nominate his heirs. But the breach with Rome placed the crown at the heart of a religious struggle, and in bringing Parliament into the divine process of the succession he had introduced the mechanism of consent. As the new Protestant beliefs brought fresh life to the old prejudices against women holding power, two generations of Tudor princesses and three Queens would struggle to survive the coming storms. Amongst them the granddaughters of the King's two jousting companions: Lady Jane, Katherine and Mary Grey.

Dynastic politics, religious propaganda and sexual prejudice have since buried the stories of the three Grey sisters in legend and obscurity. The eldest, Lady Jane Grey, is mythologised, even fetishised, as an icon of helpless innocence, destroyed by the ambitions of others. The people and events in her life are all distorted to fit this image, but Jane was much more than the victim she is portrayed as being, and the efforts of courtiers and religious factions to seize control of the succession did not end with her death. Jane's sisters would have to tread carefully to survive: Lady Katherine Grey, as the forgotten rival Queen Elizabeth feared most, and Lady Mary Grey, as the last of the sisters who were heirs to the throne. Each, in turn, would play their role in the upheavals of a changing world, and bear the costs of the continued demands for royal sons. It would be left to Katherine's grandchild, the heir to a lost English dynasty, to see the circle close. Standing at Henry's opened tomb he would bear witness to where the King's determination to control the future ended, and how efforts to deny women the absolute power of the crown helped bury absolutism in England.

PART ONE

❖

Educating Jane

❖

'Is the Queen delivered?
Say Ay and of a boy.'

'Ay, ay my liege,
And of a lovely boy: the God of heaven
Both now and ever bless her: 'tis a girl
Promises boys hereafter . . .'

Henry VIII, Act V scene i
William Shakespeare

Chapter I

Beginning

Frances, Marchioness of Dorset, prepared carefully for the birth of her child. It was an anxious time, but following the traditions of the lying-in helped allay fears of the perils of labour. The room in which she was to have her baby had windows covered and keyholes blocked. Ordinances for a royal birth decreed only one window should be left undraped and Frances would depend almost entirely on candles for light. The room was to be as warm, soft and dark as possible. She bought or borrowed expensive carpets and hangings, a bed of estate, fine sheets and a rich counterpane. Her friend, the late Lady Sussex, had one of ermine bordered with cloth of gold for her lying-in, and, as the King's niece, Frances would have wanted nothing less.

The nineteen-year-old mother-to-be was the daughter of Henry's younger sister, Mary, Duchess of Suffolk, the widow of Louis XII and known commonly as the French Queen. She was, therefore, a granddaughter of Henry VII and referred to as 'the Lady Frances' to indicate her status as such. The child of famously handsome parents, she was, unsurprisingly, attractive. The effigy that lies on her tomb at Westminster Abbey has a slender, elegant figure and under the gilded crown she wears, her features are regular and strong.[1] Frances, however, was a conventional Tudor woman, as submissive to her father's choice of husband for her as she would later be to her husband's decisions.

Henry – or 'Harry' – Grey,[2] Marquess of Dorset, described as 'young', 'lusty', 'well learned and a great wit', was only six months older than his wife.[3] But the couple had been married for almost four years already. The contractual arrangements had been made on 24th March 1533, when Frances was fifteen and Dorset sixteen.[4] Amongst commoners a woman was expected to be at least twenty before she married, and a man older, but of course these were no commoners. They came from a hereditary elite and were part of a ruthless political culture. The children of the nobility were political and financial assets to their families, and Frances's marriage to Dorset reflected this. Dorset came from an ancient line with titles including the baronies of Ferrers, Grey of Groby, Astley, Boneville and Harrington. He also had royal connections. His grandfather, the 1st Marquess, was the son of Elizabeth Woodville, and therefore the half-brother of Henry VIII's royal grandmother, Elizabeth of York. This marked Dorset as a suitable match for Frances in terms of rank and wealth, but there were also good political reasons for Suffolk to want him as a son-in-law.

The period immediately before the arrangement of Frances's marriage had been a difficult one for her parents. The dislike with which Mary, Duchess of Suffolk, viewed her brother's then 'beloved', Anne Boleyn, was well known. It was said that women argued more bitterly about matters of rank than anything else, and certainly Frances's royal mother had deeply resented being required to give precedence to a commoner like Anne. For years the duke and duchess had done their best to destroy the King's affection for his mistress, but, in the end, without success. The King, convinced that Anne would give him the son that Catherine of Aragon had failed to produce, had married her that January and she was due to be crowned in May. It seemed that the days when the Suffolks had basked in the King's favour could be over; but a marriage of Frances to 'Harry' Dorset offered a possible lifeline, a way into the Boleyn camp. Harry Dorset's father, Thomas Grey of Dorset, had been a witness for the King in his efforts to achieve an annulment of his marriage to Catherine of Aragon. He had won his famous diamond and ruby badge of the Tudor rose at the jousting tournaments that had celebrated Catherine's betrothal to the King's late brother, Arthur, in 1501. In 1529, the year before Thomas Grey of Dorset died, he had offered evidence that this betrothal was consummated. It had helped support Henry's arguments that Catherine had been legally married to his brother and his own marriage to her was therefore incestuous.[5] Anne Boleyn remained grateful to the family, and Harry Dorset was made a Knight of the Bath at her coronation.

From Harry's perspective, however, the marriage to Frances – concluded sometime between 28th July 1533 and 4th February 1534 – also carried political and material advantages to his family.[6] His grandfather, the 1st Marquess, may have been Henry VII's brother-in-law, but by marrying a princess of the blood he would be doing even better; and the fact he had only the previous year refused the daughter of the Earl of Arundel may be an early mark of his ambition. Through Frances, any children they had would be linked by blood to all the power and spiritual mystery of the crown. It was an asset of incalculable worth – though it would carry a terrible price.

Over three years later, it was sometime before the end of May, 1537, that Frances's child was to be born.[7] Harry Grey of Dorset was in London and Frances would surely have been with him at Dorset House, on the Strand.[8] It was one of a number of large properties built by the nobility close to the new royal palace of Whitehall. There was a paved street behind and, in front – where the house had its grandest aspect – there was a garden down to the river with a watergate on to the Thames. Travelling by boat in London was easier than navigating the narrow streets and foreigners often commented on the beauty of the river. Swans swam amongst the great barges while pennants flew from the pretty gilded cupolas of the Tower. But there were also many grim sights on the river that spring. London Bridge was festooned with the decapitated heads of the leaders of the recent rebellion in the north, the Pilgrimage of Grace: men who had fought for the faith of their ancestors and the right of the Princess Mary to inherit her father's crown. For all Henry's concerns about the decorum of female rule, the majority of his ordinary subjects had little objection to the concept. That women were inferior as a sex was regarded as indisputable, but there was room for exceptions. The English were famous in Europe for their devotion to the Virgin Mary, the second Eve, born without the taint of the first sin, and who reigned as Queen of Heaven. It did not seem, to them, a huge leap to accept a Queen on Earth. Just as the Princess Mary's rights were under attack, however, so were their religious beliefs and traditions.

When the Pope had refused to annul Henry's marriage to Catherine of Aragon, he had broken with Rome and the Pope's right of intervention on spiritual affairs in England had been abolished by an act of Parliament on 7th April 1533. With the benefit of hindsight this was a definitive moment in the history of the English-speaking world, but at the time most people had seen these events as no more than moves in a political game. Matters of jurisdiction between King and Pope were not things with which ordinary people concerned themselves, and the aspects of traditional belief that first came under attack were often controversial ones. Long before Henry's reformation in religion there had been debate for reform within the Catholic Church, inspired in particular by the so-called Humanists. They were fascinated by the rediscovered ancient texts of Greece and Rome, and in recent decades Western academics had, for the first time, learnt Greek as well as Latin. This allowed them to read earlier versions of the Bible than the medieval Latin translations, and to make new translations. As a change in meaning to a few words could question centuries of religious teaching so a new importance came to be placed on historical accuracy and authenticity. Questions were raised about such traditions as the cult of relics, and the shrines to local saints whose origins may have lain with the pagan Gods. It was only in 1535 when two leading Humanists, Henry's former Lord Chancellor, Thomas More, and the Bishop of Rochester, John Fisher, went to the block rather than accept the King's claimed 'royal supremacy' over religious affairs, that people began to realise there was more to Henry's reformation than political argument and an attempt to reform religious abuses. And even then many did not waver in their Catholic faith. These 'Henrician' Catholics included among their number the chief ideologue of the 'royal supremacy', the Bishop of Winchester, Stephen Gardiner. For the bishop, as for the King, papal jurisdiction, the abolished shrines, pilgrimages, and monasteries, were not intrinsic to Catholic beliefs.[9] The Holy Sacraments, such as the Mass, remained inviolate and they argued that although the English Church was in schism in the sense that it had separated from Rome, it was not heretical and in opposition to it.[10]

Those who disagreed, and opposed Henry's reformation, felt his tyranny to full effect, as the heads displayed at London Bridge and other public sites bore silent witness. One hundred and forty-four rebels from the Pilgrimage of Grace were dismembered and their body parts put on show in the north and around the capital. Even if Londoners avoided the terrible spectacle of these remains, they would not miss the other physical evidence of the King's reformation. Everywhere the great religious buildings, that had played a central role in London life, were being destroyed or adapted to secular use. Only that month, the monks from the London Charterhouse who had refused to sign an oath to the royal supremacy, were taken to Newgate prison, where they would starve to death in chains.

Inside Frances's specially prepared chamber at Dorset House, however, the sights, sounds and horrors of the outside world were all shut out. She was surrounded only with the women who would help deliver her baby. When the first intense ache of labour came it was a familiar one. Frances had already lost at least one child, a son who died in infancy, as so many Tudor children did. Nothing is recorded of his short life save his name: Henry, Lord Harington.[11] Contemporary sources focus instead on the children born to Anne Boleyn: her daughter, Elizabeth, born on 7th September 1533, at whose christening Dorset had borne the gilded salt;* and the miscarriages that had followed – the little deaths that had marked the way to Boleyn's own, executed on trumped-up charges of adultery on 19th May 1536. The King's second marriage was annulled and

---

* Salt was used in Catholic baptism until the 1960s: a small amount was placed on a baby's lips as a symbol of purity and to ward off evil.

an act of Parliament had since declared both the King's daughters, Elizabeth and Mary, illegitimate and incapable of succession.[12] This raised in importance the heirs of the King's sisters in the line of succession, and both King and kingdom had already shown sensitivity to the implications. The rebels of the Pilgrimage of Grace had expressed their fear that England would pass on Henry's death to the foreigner, James V of Scots, the son of his elder sister, Margaret. Meanwhile her daughter by a second marriage to the Earl of Angus, Lady Margaret Douglas, a favourite of the English court, was currently in prison for having become betrothed without the King's permission. Her lover, Anne Boleyn's uncle, Thomas Howard, would die in the Tower that October. But while Frances's child would, inevitably, hold an important place within the royal family, the King remained determined his own line would succeed him. The pressure on her to produce a male heir was therefore of a different order to Henry's wives. Dorset wanted a son, as all noblemen did, but he and Frances were still young and, when a girl was born, their relief that she was strong and healthy would have outweighed any disappointment in her sex.

A servant carried the newborn child immediately to a nearby room and handed her to a nurse. It was usual for fathers to be at hand when their children were born and Dorset would have been one of the first to visit the dimly lit nursery where his daughter was being fed and bound in swaddling, to keep her limbs straight and prevent her from scratching her face. Her spiritual welfare was of still greater concern to her parents and her christening was arranged as soon as possible, though this meant Frances could not attend. New mothers were expected to remain in bed for up to a month, and some did not even sit up for a fortnight. Frances played a role, however, in helping choose as her daughter's godmother, the King's new wife, Jane Seymour, after whom the little girl was named.[13]

With her pursed lips and sandy eyelashes, Jane Seymour seems a poor replacement for Anne Boleyn, whose black eyes, it was said, 'could read the secrets of a man's heart', but like her predecessor, Jane Seymour was a ruthless seductress.[14] Her betrothal to Henry was announced only the day after Anne was executed. Having got her king it was her performance as a brood mare that was now important. In this too, however, she was showing marked success. A pregnancy had been evident for weeks and on 27th May the rumours were confirmed with a Te Deum sung at St Paul's Cathedral 'for joy of the Queen's quickening with child'.[15] It remained to be seen whether Jane Seymour would give the King the son he wanted, but in choosing her as godmother to their new daughter, Frances and Harry Dorset had offered a vote of confidence, and although they could not know it, the Seymour family would remain closely linked to their own, one way or another, thereafter.

About a fortnight after the christening, Frances had her first day out of bed and dressed in one of her finest nightgowns for a celebratory party. The royal tailor advised damask or satin, worn with an ermine-trimmed bonnet and waistcoat, allowing the wearer to keep warm as well as look good, for visiting female friends and relations. Frances had a younger sister, Eleanor, married to Lord Clifford, and an equally young stepmother. Frances's mother had died on Midsummer's Day in June 1533, and her father had wasted little time before remarrying. The bride he had chosen was his fourteen-year-old ward, the heiress, Katherine Willoughby. He was then forty-nine, and the muscles of the champion jouster, like those of his friend the King, had begun to turn to fat. Frances would doubtless have wished her father had waited longer and made a different choice: the new Duchess of Suffolk had been raised alongside her like a sister since the age of seven. But Frances had accepted what she could not change and remained close to her childhood friend, who was now pregnant with the second of Frances's half-brothers, Charles Brandon. After the party was over, Frances could venture beyond her chambers to the nursery and other rooms in the house, until the lying-in concluded at last when Jane was about a month old with the 'churching' – a religious service of thanksgiving and purification that ended with Frances being sprinkled with holy water. 'Purge me with hyssop, and I shall be clean,' she prayed; 'wash me, and I shall be whiter than snow.' Frances then was ready to return to Henry's court.[16] Here, the care and blessings, showered on most new mothers, were in stark contrast to the treatment Henry had meted out to the Queens who had borne his children. If his third wife, Jane Seymour, had any fears about the future, however, there was little sign of them before her own lying-in began. She made her last public appearance on 16th September at Hampton Court. There was a grand procession into Mass at the royal chapel (which still survives, the ceiling a brilliant blue, studded with golden stars), and afterwards the court gathered in the vast space of the Watching Chamber (which also remains) to enjoy cold, spiced wine. There had been months of building work carried out in anticipation of the royal birth, and the heady scents of clove and cinnamon mixed with those of burnt brick and newly hewn wood. Once Jane Seymour disappeared to her chamber, however, so most of the court left the palace. There had been an outbreak of plague that summer and they were encouraged to go home.

There persists a myth that Lady Jane Grey was born during the subsequent three weeks of the Queen's confinement, at the Grey family's principal seat of Bradgate Manor in Leicestershire. Dorset's mother, the dowager marchioness, was, however, installed at Bradgate until January 1538 and Frances was busy enjoying herself, not lying in bed. On 11th October 1537, when news reached her that Jane Seymour was in labour, she was being entertained at the house of a friend and her husband was on their estate at Stebbing in Essex.[17] Dorset left immediately for London, where a procession was already being organised for priests and clerks, the mayor and aldermen, to pray for the Queen. It seemed their prayers were soon answered. At two o'clock the following morning, on the eve of the feast of St Edward, Henry VIII's longed-for son, soon also to be christened Edward, was born. By 9 a.m. on that pivotal morning, Dorset was with the large crowd at the door of the medieval church of St Paul's, singing the Te Deum. When the great hymn of thanks was finished volleys of gunfire were shot from the Tower and hogsheads of wine were set out for the poor to drink. The long-term security and peace of the nation hinged on having an undisputed succession and people of all religious persuasions now rejoiced at the birth of their prince.[18]

As the nation celebrated in the days ahead, Frances joined Dorset and together they made frantic efforts to arrange for permission to be at court for Edward's christening. It was an event the entire nobility and royal family wished to attend, and Frances's father had been invited to be godfather at the confirmation that followed immediately after the baptism. But, to their frustration, they found that they were not to be allowed back to Hampton Court. There had been several plague deaths in Croydon, where Dorset's mother had a property. They hadn't visited her recently, but no chances were being taken with the possible spread of disease to the palace.[19]

Such precautions would not save the Queen. Days later Jane Seymour suffered a massive haemorrhage, probably caused by the retention of part of the placenta in her womb. She was given the last rites two days after her son's christening and died on 24th October. Frances was bequeathed several pieces of the Queen's jewellery, pomanders and other trinkets,[20] and while she and Dorset had missed the royal baptism, they took leading parts in the state funeral in November. Dorset, his father-in-law the Duke of Suffolk, and four other courtiers, rode alongside the horse-drawn chariot that bore Jane Seymour's coffin in procession to Windsor. It was surmounted by her effigy, painted to look lifelike and dressed in robes of state, with her hair loose, and rings on her fingers set with precious stones: the wooden dummy of a woman who had served her purpose. Riding immediately behind it, on a horse trapped in black, was the King's elder daughter, the Princess Mary, who acted as chief mourner. The child who, thirteen years earlier, when her father was almost killed at the joust, had been his undisputed heir, was now a grown woman, twenty-one and pretty, with his pink and white complexion, and a painfully thin frame. She had seen her late mother humiliated in her father's quest for a son, and Parliament brought into the divine process of the succession to deny her her birthright. But the vagaries of fate are uncertain. Under the Act of Succession of the previous year, Henry had been granted the right to nominate his heirs, and Mary knew she could yet be restored in line to the throne, despite having been declared illegitimate.

Behind Mary, sitting in the first of the chariots bearing the great ladies of the court, sat Frances, dressed in black and attended by footmen in demi-gowns.[21] The procession then continued with the mourners in descending order of precedence so that at its very end even the servants walked according to the rank of their masters. 'The heavens themselves, the planets and this centre, Observe degree, priority and place,' Shakespeare wrote later in *Troilus and Cressida*;

> *Take but degree away, untune that string, And hark, what discord follows ... Strength should be lord to imbecility, And the rude son should strike his father dead. This chaos, when degree is suffocate, Follows the choking.*[22]

Chapter II

First Lessons

Some of Jane Grey's first memories must have been of the magnificent family seat at Bradgate Manor in the Midlands, even if she was not born there.[1] It was the first unfortified house in Leicestershire, a palace of rose-red brick patterned in diamonds of deep lilac, that Dorset's father and grandfather had built as an airy replacement for the ancient castle whose stones still lay nearby. The peace and order heralded with the advent of the Tudors meant everything about the house could be done with an eye to beauty or pleasure. In place of thick walls pierced by narrow openings, large mullioned windows let in the light and its towered wings marked the outer points of a welcoming U-shaped courtyard.

The family's private rooms, including Jane's bedchamber, and the cot she slept in as an infant, were in the west wing. There was a chapel where, as she grew older, she said her prayers, and a small kitchen. The west wing housed the servants' hall, a bakery, brewery and the main kitchen, which was constantly busy. Her father entertained here generously and when he was in residence the house was packed with at least three dozen of his retainers as well as visitors and members of the extended family. For the most part the household ate together in the great hall, an 80-foot-long room in the centre of the house, kept warm by a large fireplace. There was a dais at one end, where the family ate in state and a gallery the other end where music was played.

Jane reached what was, in religious tradition, the age of reason, when she was seven. She was small for her age, but with a fiery character to match her reddish hair and a quick, articulate intelligence. She was said later by a contemporary to be her father's favourite daughter.[2] She was certainly proving every inch his child. It was a time for her adult education to begin and a year later, in 1545, an impressive new tutor arrived to oversee her studies. John Aylmer had been introduced to Dorset when he was still only a schoolboy and the marquess had paid for his education until he graduated from Cambridge that year. He was a brilliant academic and had been picked by the marquess for his post over several other clever young men of whom he was patron.

Jane had also, by now, two younger sisters, whose adult education had yet to begin. The middle sister, Katherine, turned five that August, the same month their grandfather, Charles Brandon, Duke of Suffolk, died.[3] Affectionate and golden-haired, Katherine preferred her pets to Jane's books, but she was the beauty of the sisters. In the limnings, or miniatures, painted by the court artist Lavina Teerlinc she resembles her lovely grandmother, the King's late younger sister, Mary Tudor, the French Queen.

The youngest of the three sisters, Mary Grey, was still only a baby at this time and it may not yet have been apparent that there was anything wrong with her. But Mary was never to grow normally. As an adult she was described as the smallest person at court, 'crook backed' and 'very ugly'. It has even been conjectured that she was a dwarf. Whatever the truth, Mary Grey had something of the best qualities of both her sisters, with Katherine's warmth and Jane's intelligence, as well as the strong spirit they all shared. If her parents were disappointed with her in any way, there is no record of it.[4]

Life at Bradgate was idyllic for the sisters. There were extensive gardens for them to play in, as well as the great park, which was the glory of the house. A medieval village had been destroyed to create the illusion of a perfect wilderness covering several square miles at the edge of Charnwood Forest. Here was a place 'more free from peril than the envious court', where you could find 'tongues in trees, books in the running brooks, Sermons in stones, and good in every-thing.[5] The children could walk their father's prize greyhounds, or accompany their mother and her friends as they hunted deer with longbow and arrows.[6] On rainy days there were also other amusements inside.

Dolls were popular toys of the period and the types the sisters enjoyed are described in a later inventory of items in Jane's possession. 'Two little babies in a box of wood, one of them having a gown of crimson satin, and the other a gown of white velvet.'[7] Their parents were careful, however, not to spoil them. Over-indulgence was believed to make children physically and morally soft, with potentially disastrous results. Loving parents instilled discipline early with good manners considered essential. The girls were taught to stand straight and show respect to their elders, to speak only when they were spoken to and to respond promptly to commands. They had to eat nicely, observe the correct precedence at table and show gratitude for any praise they were given. At night, if their parents were at home, they would go to them to say goodnight and kneel to ask their blessing.

The duty of obedience was considered a particularly useful lesson for girls since they were expected to remain submissive to their husbands after they had left the care of their fathers. But the thinking on what women were capable of was changing. Baldassare Castiglione's bestselling *Book of the Courtier* argued that women were as intelligent as men, and suggested they could learn to control their 'emotional' natures through the exercise of will and reason. A Grey family friend later translated the book into English.[8] In the meantime, other Englishmen such as Richard Hyrde were already promoting female education, and for a brief period that would end with the generation of the Grey sisters, the education of women remained fashionable.[9] Both Frances and Dorset were determined that their daughters would be given the opportunity to develop practical and intellectual skills of the highest order.

Of the former, the humble business of cooking and sewing remained important. Even noblewomen were expected to know something about the more expensive dishes created in their kitchen and to be able to make clothing. Frances sewed shirts and collars as New Year gifts for the King and her friend Lady Lisle's quince marmalade was amongst her best-received presents to Henry, who liked it 'wondrous well'.[10] As future courtiers the sisters also received regular lessons in dance and music: the lute, the spinet and the virginal were all popular choices of instrument for girls destined for court. But it was in the sisters' academic studies that Lady Jane Grey, in particular, was to excel, with strong encouragement from her father.

Dorset had received a brilliant education in the household of the King's illegitimate son, the late Henry Fitzroy, Duke of Richmond. He had learnt eloquent Latin from a pupil of Erasmus, and French from John Palsgrave, the greatest scholar of the language in England. It had left Dorset with a love of scholarship that was renowned during his lifetime and which he was determined to pass on to his children. As soon as his daughters had learned to read, write and understand basic mathematics they made a start in French and Italian. Over half a century later Dorset's youngest daughter, Lady Mary Grey, still kept copies of Palsgrave's French grammar and dictionary in her library, along with the *Book of the Courtier* and an Italian grammar.[11] By the age of eight Jane, and later Katherine, were also learning Latin and Greek, subjects that Aylmer was particularly well qualified to teach. A visitor to Bradgate, the radical divine Thomas Becon, described him as 'singularly well learned in both'.

But Aylmer was much more than a mere language teacher. The point of education in the sixteenth century was not simply to learn to read, write and understand ancient languages. It was about moulding good subjects of God and the King. Jane and Katherine's Greek and Latin were a means to help reinforce lessons of moral, social and religious truth indoctrinated from the cradle – literally so. The visitor, Becon, insisted that as soon as a child was capable of speaking in sentences they should be taught phrases such as: 'Learn to die ...'.[12] Jane would, years later, repeat the phrase in her last letter to Katherine and reflect on its meaning. This was to be a good Christian in this world, and so to achieve the reward of absolute happiness with God in the next. Unfortunately, what it was to be a good Christian, and where the path to eternal life lay, remained a matter of lethal debate. Since Jane's birth in 1537 new divisions had arisen between those, like the ideologue of the royal supremacy, Bishop Gardiner, who adhered to Henry's Church but remained conservative in his core beliefs, and those who saw the King's reformation as the gateway to more drastic change.

The term Protestant only began to be used in England in the mid-1550s.[13] The more usual term for those we would now think of as Protestant was 'evangelical'. They were so named because they wished to return to the 'evangelium' or 'good news' of the gospel, stripping away Church traditions they believed had no biblical basis in favour of a more fundamental reading of Scripture. There was no real orthodoxy within the English evangelicals, with individuals adhering to beliefs of varying degrees of radicalism, and people were careful not to express their views openly if they did not accord with the King's. Dorset's were later regarded, however, as being at the more radical end of the spectrum and Frances shared her husband's beliefs. The ground was being prepared for an ideological struggle in which the Grey sisters, members of the first generation to be raised as evangelicals, were being groomed to play a significant role.

For Jane, being the elder of three sisters did not mean merely doing things first. She was the most important in rank. It was Jane in whom the Dorsets invested the lion's share of their time and money, and to whom everyone else paid the most attention. While Jane was growing up – and until her death – the younger sisters remained in the shadows. They were at home, therefore, playing with their pets and learning their prayers, waiting for their own turn in the spotlight, when Jane, at nine, took her first steps on to the great national stage that was the King's court.

In 1546, Jane's mother was serving as a Lady of the Privy Chamber to Henry's sixth wife, Catherine Parr. From time to time she could, therefore, bring Jane to court with her, to prepare her for a role as a Maid of Honour, serving the Queen. The court was the hub of political, cultural and social life in England. For a young girl such as Jane, however, it must have been often a confusing place. She could never be sure what lay behind a smile, or if what was said was what was meant, but amongst the gossiping courtiers and scheming bishops, the Queen, at least, struck a sympathetic figure. Catherine Parr was warm-hearted and intelligent, with a calm manner that invited confidence and respect. She was also a highly sensual woman: the kind that most attracted Henry. She wore gorgeous scarlet silks, bathed in milk baths, scented her body with rose water, and her breath with expensive, cinnamon lozenges. Beside this delicious vision, the fifty-five-year-old King appeared monstrous. It must have been difficult for Jane to imagine Henry as the 'perfect example of manly beauty' he had been described as in his youth. Pallid and obese, he was almost unable to walk on legs ruined by injuries acquired hunting and jousting. He spent most of his time in his private lodgings suffering fevers, but occasionally would emerge to be wheeled down the corridors of the royal palaces on chairs of tawny velvet; his eyes pinpoints of pain.

Henry did not have long to live, and with Edward only in his ninth year, it was apparent that all the blood spilled to secure the future of the Tudor dynasty could prove wasted. In the end he had exchanged the unknown consequences of female rule only for the familiar weaknesses of a royal minority. A young boy could not hope to fill the shoes of the old tyrant. Others would wield power on Edward's behalf when he became King, and a ferocious struggle for that power had already begun. Although Jane was too young to grasp the subtleties of the shifting circles of interests manoeuvring around her, she surely understood that the most important battle lines concerned her faith. She knew too that the Queen was the leading evangelical at court. Catherine Parr had been wed twice before to old men and, still only in her early thirties she found in religion a passion that was absent in her marriages. She made energetic efforts to spread the new teaching in the universities and every afternoon evangelical chaplains preached to her ladies and their friends at court. Afterwards the women would sit with their guests and discuss what they had heard.

There was a frisson of danger to this, for any divergence from the King's beliefs risked accusations of heresy. And just how deadly that could be, Jane Grey's family was soon to witness.

A group of religious conservatives on the Privy Council were plotting that summer to bring down their evangelical rivals. They intended to do so through an attack on their opponents' wives. The means was to be a twenty-five-year-old gentlewoman called Anne Askew. A witty and articulate poet and evangelical, Askew had broken a taboo by disobeying her husband and quarrelling with him over religion. He had thrown her out, and she had subsequently been arrested for preaching that Christ was not really present in the consecrated bread and wine of the Mass. In June 1546 she had been condemned to death for heresy. But as Askew waited for sentence to be carried out, rumours leaked that she had allies in the Queen's Privy Chamber. They were said to include the wives of leading evangelical Privy Councillors. According to an Elizabethan Jesuit, the conservatives learned that Askew had even been introduced to the Queen and the King's 'favourite nieces', Frances Grey and her sister Eleanor.[14] The most likely person to have achieved such a coup was Frances's widowed stepmother and childhood friend, the young Katherine Suffolk.

Blonde, blue-eyed, and charming when she wished to be, Katherine Suffolk was one of the most remarkable women of her time. Her temper and caustic wit were legendary. One of her contemporaries called her rages, 'the Lady Suffolk heats'.[15] In the superficial world of the court, however, her contemporaries found her unusual directness and honesty both unnerving and attractive. She said what she thought, and what she thought was usually interesting and sometimes shocking. Although her Spanish mother had been Catherine of Aragon's favourite lady-in-waiting, Katherine Suffolk despised the religion in which she was raised and was considered by foreign ambassadors to be 'the greatest heretic in the kingdom'. She had huge influence with Catherine Parr and connections to Askew. The condemned woman's brother-in-law, George St Poll, was a member of her household.

Askew was brought from Newgate to the Tower, where she was repeatedly tortured on the rack by two Privy Councillors in an effort to get her to name her court contacts. In the long and terrible history of the Tower no other woman is recorded as having been so treated. Askew was asked specifically about any connections she had to Katherine Suffolk, and it must have been a highly anxious time for the Grey family, as they wondered what Askew would reveal. But despite being torn apart 'until the strings of her arms and eyes were perished' Askew admitted only that a number of anonymous women had sent her money.[16] The news that a gentlewoman had been put to the rack then reached the public. That a gentlewoman should have been tortured at all appalled people, but that Askew was already a condemned prisoner, outraged them. In an effort to calm the public mood Askew was offered the opportunity to recant her views and receive a pardon. She refused and on 16th July 1546 was brought to Smithfield for execution by burning. Her body was so badly broken by the rack she had to be tied to the stake in a chair. The Queen's cousin, Nicholas Throckmorton and two of his brothers, were there to shout out their support for her as she burned and died. Most of the ordinary people looking on were horrified at the cruelty, but they saw it often enough, meted out both to traditional Catholics burnt for 'treason' and radical evangelicals – 'heretics' – such as she.

Jane, Katherine and Mary Grey would have all learnt eventually the details of Askew's death. The gentlewoman's links to Katherine Suffolk, their step-grandmother, made her death almost a family matter. Her writings and the story of her life were soon, in any case, to be immortalised in a new evangelical cult of martyrdom, and they would have become familiar with Askew's recorded words and actions in her last months. It underpinned the lesson with which they were inculcated: 'Learn to die . . .'.[17] But it was Jane, being that much older, who was most deeply affected by Anne Askew's example, and many of her later writings echoed Askew's spirited and combative attacks on conservative beliefs.

According to the mid-sixteenth-century martyrologist John Foxe, however, the attempt to expose heresy in the Queen's Privy Chamber was just a prelude to a direct attack on the Queen herself: and one in which Lady Jane Grey would, in the nineteenth century, be given a walk-on part. Foxe claimed that Bishop Stephen Gardiner, the new intellectual leader of religious conservatism, was desperate to get rid of Catherine Parr and end her influence with the King. He convinced Henry that her efforts to urge him to religious reform amounted to an attack on his place as head of the Church in England. Henry rose to the bait and, after a heated discussion with his wife on matters of religion, announced he wished to be rid of her, just as he had been rid of Anne Boleyn. Foxe described how articles for the Queen's arrest were drawn up, but that as Henry's temper cooled he allowed one of his doctors to warn Catherine she had stepped over the mark. Terrified, Catherine went to the King that night, 'waited upon only by the Lady Herbert, her sister, and the Lady Jane [Grey] who carried the candle before her'.[18] In the King's chamber Catherine worked hard to soothe her husband, submitting herself to his will in a speech that strongly resembles that made later by Shakespeare's Kate in *The Taming of the Shrew*. When Henry accepted her assurances that she only wished to be his good wife, Catherine knew she was safe – or so we are told. 'Lady Jane' is a Victorian misreading of 'Lady Lane', and there is very little truth even in Foxe's original story.

There were rumours in 1546 that Henry had already tired of Catherine, but, contrary to Foxe's account his disillusion had nothing to do with the Queen's reformist fervour. It was believed that he wanted to replace her with the alluring young Katherine Suffolk, who could have become a more formidable opponent to the conservatives than Parr. Foxe's version of the events of 1546 placed Catherine Parr close to the ranks of the martyrs he admired, and perhaps also helped counterbalance the most difficult elements of Askew's story for sixteenth-century readers: her disobeying her husband, her preaching, and her arguing with her male superiors. The martyrologists liked their female saints weak and tender, like good children, if also brave and steadfast.[19] Foxe's picture of an unpredictable King and a court riven by deadly religious rivalries, however, is accurate enough, even if the details are not. And because we know something of what follows, the later image of Jane Grey on the cusp of the new reign remains a haunting one – a young girl walking into the darkness, carrying her candle before her.

Chapter III

❖

Jane's Wardship

King Henry VIII's death, at fifty-six, was announced on 31st January 1547. For over a fortnight afterwards, wherever Jane turned at court, she saw black. Thirty-three thousand yards of dark cloth and a further eight thousand yards of black cotton, shrouded the floors and ceilings of all the royal chapels, was hung throughout the royal apartments, over the royal barges, carriages and carts. But as soon as the King was interred in Jane Seymour's tomb at Windsor, on Wednesday 16th February, the cloth was taken down, the rich unveiled tapestries and brilliantly painted walls heralding the reign of Edward VI, her cousin and contemporary.

That Sunday, the coronation began with the nine-year-old King processing before a cheering crowd from Whitehall to Westminster Abbey, the court following in line of precedence. Catholic ambassadors described Edward as 'the prettiest child you ever saw', and they had little reason to flatter him. A slight boy with corn gold hair and pink cheeks, he looked angelic – his father before the fall. Always anxious to please the adults around him, Edward managed not to stagger once under the weight of the heavy robes of red velvet and ermine. But the adults, concerned whether he could cope with the rigours of the day-long rituals, had taken care to shorten the ceremonies by several hours and arrangements had been made for rest periods. When he reached his throne on the dais in the church,

Edward also found two extra cushions had been placed on it to give him extra height. His health and strength reflected the vitality of the new regime and it was important Edward not appear vulnerable.

Henry had appointed sixteen executors of his will, whom he had envisaged acting as co-rulers until Edward came of age, but these decrees had been buried even before he was. The executors had established themselves as the Privy Council on the same day as his death was announced, three days after Henry had drawn his last breath. The Council was traditionally a large administrative body (it had forty members by the end of Edward's reign). At its core were the King's advisers, currently the sixteen executors, who had promptly elected Edward's elder uncle, the evangelical Edward Seymour as 'Lord Protector of England'. A country so used to being governed by the will of one man was not ready for an oligarchy of sixteen. In line with his position, the Lord Protector had also been granted the title 'Duke of Somerset'. The ambassadors were now invited to the coronation to witness the revolutionary political and religious programme the Protector, and his allies, intended.

Since 1375 the so-called *Liber Regalis* had laid down how Kings of England were to be crowned, and it dictated the format of the ceremonies ahead. But for Edward's coronation several significant modifications were made. The first became apparent as the Archbishop of Canterbury, Thomas Cranmer, presented Edward to the three estates – the Lords, Commons and bishops – in the congregation beneath him. Instead of asking their assent to his crowning, Cranmer demanded they swear their service to Edward. The significance of this became apparent in the coronation oath, which the archbishop had also rewritten. The ancient promise to preserve the liberties and privileges of the clergy was struck out, and Edward, instead of agreeing to accept laws presented by his people, swore that the people were to accept *his* laws: in reality the Council's laws presented under his authority. Henry VIII had regarded his claimed 'royal supremacy' over religious affairs his greatest achievement. The arguments used in its support placed him above not only the Pope's laws, but England's also. He was the superior legislator who 'gave' the law and exercised his '*imperium*', or 'command', over Church and state.[1] But this authority was now in the hands of politicians and prelates he had assumed were his lapdogs. Their power, through the boy King, was absolute and would be wielded for a specific purpose. Cranmer's sermon explained that Edward was to be a new Josiah, the biblical king and destroyer of idols. It was a Year Zero in which a new religious ideology was to be imposed on his people and England's Catholic past rooted out of his subjects' hearts and churches.

At the conclusion of the rituals, Jane's father, Dorset, and her young uncle, the eleven-year-old Henry, Duke of Suffolk, stepped forward. Together they helped Edward hold his sceptre and 'the ball of gold with the cross' and presented him to the congregation as their King.[2] Propped up like a living doll he represented more than anyone else the central place children now held in the brutal world of adult politics. But Jane, along with her teenage cousin the Princess Elizabeth, would soon join Edward as the tools of ambitious men.

The future for Lady Jane Grey and her sisters was to be dominated by one document: King Henry's will. Parliament had given Henry the right to bequeath the crown by testament and when he had called for it, on 26th December 1546, he was prepared to use that power. Lying sprawled on the vast state bed at Whitehall, with its gilded frame and rich hangings, the ailing monarch had worked at his revisions for four days. The period between Christmas Day and New Year is a strange hiatus, a time caught between the past and the future, appropriate, perhaps, for the birth of such a document. The seasonal celebrations did not disturb him, but Henry's councillors and confidants had buzzed around him like flies until, on the 30th, he approved the final changes.

The principal provisions of the will had been confirmed already under the third Act of Succession in 1544. Edward was bequeathed the throne followed by any children Henry had with Catherine Parr. The crown then passed to Edward's illegitimate half-sisters, Mary and Elizabeth. At that point, however, there was a dramatic change in the line of succession. Just as Henry had ignored in 1544 the common laws on inheritance that excluded illegitimate children from the throne, so he had now refused to be bound by the tradition of primogeniture. The entire Stuart line of his eldest sister, Margaret of Scotland, was excluded from the succession. In the event of the death of his children without heirs, the crown was settled instead on the descendants of his younger sister, Mary Brandon, Duchess of Suffolk. At the stroke of his pen her granddaughters, Lady Jane, Katherine and Mary Grey were named the heirs to Elizabeth.

Henry never chose to explain why he had excluded the Stuarts in favour of the Brandon line. The Kings of Scotland had, however, been enemies of England for generations. Henry had hoped to find a solution to their centuries of warfare in betrothing the infant Mary Queen of Scots to Edward. When the Scots rebuffed him, Henry was faced with the prospect of their Queen being married to a European prince or a Scottish nobleman, and, either way, he did not want to risk England falling into foreign hands. It was to that end that he had made his daughters' inheritance provisional on their taking a husband in accordance with the wishes of the Privy Council. Curiously, his will did not insist on a similar rule for the Grey sisters. Perhaps he assumed that Frances would have a son or grandson by the time his line was extinct. It would explain why her name was overlooked in the will. It is also possible, however, that Henry's decision was influenced by his mistrust of her husband.

Harry Dorset was described by a contemporary, as 'an illustrious and widely loved nobleman', much admired for his learning and his patronage of the learned.[3] But as the rich husband of a royal wife, Dorset did not need to work hard for the status he held, and he had grown lazy and uncompromising. Although he had fought for the King in the wars with France, he had done little more than the minimum required of a nobleman. He preferred to leave the business of fighting to his younger brothers, Lords John and Thomas Grey. Nor was he suited to the snake pit of court politics. Remembered in the seventeenth century as 'upright and plain in his private dealings', he hated the dissembling that was part of court life. He had all the arrogance of the ideologue and an imperial ambassador described him a few years later as being without sense. He was happiest with his books, or in the company of 'good fellows', men who enjoyed a day's hunting and a game of cards. This was not the kind of man Henry respected and the new Protector Somerset had no more use for him than the late King had had.[4]

Somerset was a successful soldier-politician, on whom Henry had relied heavily in the last years of his reign. He was also emerging as a high-minded evangelical, and became known later as 'the good duke'. Unfortunately this was how he saw himself. The portrait in which he sports a white suit and golden beard, like some heavenly princeling, encapsulates his self-image perfectly. Harry Dorset was not, however, the only member of the extended royal family, to resent Somerset's power and arrogance. King Edward's younger uncle, Thomas Seymour, was already looking to Dorset for a political alliance against his older brother. Described by his servant, Sir John Harington, as a fine soldier and a dashing courtier, Thomas Seymour had a magnetic voice, 'strong limbs and manly shape'. Women fell for him, and men admired him: indeed, once they had succumbed to his charm they never forgot him. Even thirty years after his death his former entourage was bound in friendship by his memory, and 'the best of them disdained not the poorest'.[5] In common with the protagonists of Greek tragedy, however, Thomas Seymour also possessed a fatal flaw: greed and of the most dangerous kind – the greed for power. Somerset had tried his best to engage Seymour's support for his Protectorship. The younger brother had been brought on to the Privy Council, given the title Baron Seymour of Sudeley, and made Lord Admiral. What the new Baron Sudeley had hoped for most, however, was the post of Governor of the King's Person, which would have allowed him to share the power of the Protectorship. And in this he was thwarted. Few others wished to see such a division of authority, and so in March, a month after the coronation, Somerset took the post for himself. A furious Sudeley was now determined to block any further advance by his brother, while continuing to seek power for himself. But to achieve this he needed first to raise his profile within the royal family.

Since January Jane and her sisters had seen a new and increasingly regular visitor to Dorset House on the Strand. Jane would have recognised him as a man about court: he was Sudeley's gentleman servant, John Harington. A landowner and man of considerable subtlety and intelligence, Harington had been sent to prepare the ground for what Sudeley called a 'friendship' with Dorset.

Sudeley, meanwhile, was wooing Henry VIII's widow. Catherine Parr had been in love with Sudeley before she had married Henry and now she was free to make her own choice she clearly found him irresistible. Within weeks of the King's death the handsome Lord Admiral had the Queen dowager 'under the plummet [duvet]' at her manor in Chelsea. They married in secret in May 1547, shortly after she was given the care of her stepdaughter, the Princess Elizabeth. Over the following weeks, as Sudeley saw the huge influence his new wife had over Elizabeth, it struck him that the wardship of the next in line to the throne, Lady Jane Grey, would also be valuable. Notably, Edward's heirs were all female. The entire political system, the stability of England depended on a series of women and girls and, whether adult, like Catherine Parr and the Princess Mary, or children, like the Princess Elizabeth and Lady Jane Grey, they were, to Sudeley, beings to be used and manipulated.

Sudeley had often noticed Jane Grey about the court. She appeared rather small, but her dark brows and eyes, which were 'sparkling and reddish brown in colour', suggested a lively spirit. He now began to watch her with closer interest, observing her playing and talking with the new King. An audience with Edward was always a formal affair, but as Jane Grey's cousin, Jane Dormer, recalled, it was still possible to spend many happy hours with him, 'either in reading, playing or dancing'. Edward was universally considered 'a marvellous, sweet child, of very mild and generous condition', and Dormer recalled how he would call her 'my Jane', and, when she lost at cards, he would comfort her: 'Now Jane, your king is gone, I shall be good enough for you.'[6]

As similar scenes were played out under Sudeley's gaze, he realised that Lady Jane Grey, with her royal blood, could one day be more than a playmate for Edward. She could become the King's wife, a possibility that served his purposes well. Sudeley knew, or suspected, that Somerset hoped to see Jane Grey married to his eight-year-old son, Edward Seymour, the Earl of Hertford.[7] He hoped that if he could persuade Jane's father to make her his ward, he would be able to thwart his brother's ambitions in this regard and gain some control over whom Jane did marry. There would be many powerful people who would want her as a bride – all useful allies in the struggles ahead.

As Sudeley knew, Dorset had not been treated well by the Protector. When Catherine Parr's courtly brother, William, had been made Marquess of Northampton it was said it had been done not so much to promote Northampton as to demote Dorset, who was, until Northampton's election, the only marquess in England. This view appeared to be confirmed in March, when Northampton had been raised to the Privy Council, and Dorset had not. Harington was instructed to assure Dorset that, as the King's second uncle, Sudeley was well placed to do him the favours the Protector denied him.[8] When, during one of his subsequent visits to his London home, Dorset confirmed his willingness to be Sudeley's friend and ally, Harington seized his opportunity. The most appropriate mark of this future friendship, he said, would be if Dorset were to send Jane to live in Sudeley's household as his ward. At that, however, Dorset balked.

It was usual for aristocratic families to send a daughter approaching adolescence to live with a well-connected family. The tradition served a number of useful purposes, binding, as it did, parents as allies and children as friends. The contacts made were used often in the arrangement of a future marriage. For a girl of noble birth it was virtually unthinkable that her marriage should be left to chance, but Jane, at ten, was rather young to be 'put out', as it was termed. And there were other considerations. We do not know the precise timing of Harington's visit, but if it took place before Sudeley's marriage to Catherine Parr became public, Harington was asking Dorset to send his daughter to the household of an unmarried man. If, as is more likely, it took place after, then it was to a man whose marriage was considered a scandal. Catherine Parr had destroyed her reputation by marrying so soon after the King's death. Virtue, in a woman, was associated almost entirely with chastity, that is, unimpeachable sexual morality and continence. It was believed that the female sex drive was stronger than the male (since women were creatures of feeling rather than reason) and therefore the likely explanation for Catherine Parr's behaviour was assumed to be unbridled lust. Sudeley, meanwhile, was judged guilty of selfish ambition. If his wife became pregnant it would be uncertain whose child it was. This was potentially dangerous to the stability of the country. Since Henry VIII had introduced a law requiring the monarch's assent to any royal marriage, their actions might even have been judged treasonous, had Sudeley not persuaded Edward to write a letter that made it appear the marriage was made at his suggestion.

Harington had anticipated that Dorset's reaction to the proposed wardship might not be favourable and assured Dorset that Sudeley would see to it that Jane was placed in a most advantageous marriage. 'With whom?' Dorset demanded. 'Marry,' Harington replied, 'I doubt not but you shall see him marry her to the King; and fear you not but he will bring it to pass.' Dorset was stunned by Harington's remark. He listened, however, as Harington continued, describing how Sudeley, watching Jane about court, had declared that she was 'as handsome a Lady as any in Christendom, and that, if the King's Majesty, when he came to age, would marry within the realm, it was as likely it would be there than in any other place'.[9] Dorset began to consider the possibilities: maybe Sudeley's idea was not an unrealistic one? Henry VIII had taken English wives. His daughter was an intelligent, highly educated, evangelical princess: the perfect bride for Edward. For the Greys, it would also be a better match than either his grandfather, or he himself, had made. Dorset agreed to discuss the matter of Jane's wardship with Sudeley as soon as possible.

While the royal children played their innocent games, the adults began moving the pawns on the political chessboard. Within a week of Harington's approaches, Dorset was at Seymour Place along the Strand, talking with Sudeley in the privacy of his garden. The banging and clattering of builders echoed across the hedges and herb beds. Next door, the Protector was clearing the local parish church of St Mary and the Holy Innocents to make way for a vast Italianate palace. It was the first building of its kind in England, a suitable monument to Somerset's burgeoning status as alter rex (another king).[10] Above the noise Sudeley repeated to Dorset that he believed Jane would make the King a fine Queen. But he offered also substantial proof of his friendship: several hundred pounds towards an eventual payment of £2,000 for Jane's wardship. Dorset was impressed. Sudeley's 'fair promises' and eagerness to be his friend were in stark contrast to the treatment he had received at Somerset's hands. Convinced that an alliance with Sudeley was an honourable way forward he sent for his daughter immediately.

Dorset's actions have since been characterised as those of a heartless parent selling his daughter for profit. As Jane watched her bags being packed and kissed her sisters farewell, this, however, was surely not how she saw it. It was usual for money to change hands in matters of wardship. Her father's had been bought twice over, by the late Earl of Arundel and Duke of Suffolk, and for double the figure Sudeley was prepared to pay for Jane. It was not the money that had appealed to Dorset. By placing his daughter with Sudeley, he would open the greatest possible prospects for her, which in turn could bring glory to the family name. Jane would have understood this, for noble children were part of a family network that extended to kin and beyond, in which each was expected to play their part for the good of the whole. Jane's mother, Frances, appears to have had her doubts, however, about the wisdom of the scheme. Her friend and stepmother Katherine Suffolk disapproved of Sudeley and was shocked by his hasty marriage to their friend, the Queen dowager, Catherine Parr. But although Frances later made strenuous efforts to keep Jane at home, away from Sudeley, she saw it as her duty to support her husband in his decisions – and from this time forward he was determined that his favourite child would one day be Queen.

The ten-year-old was installed with her guardian at Seymour Place as soon as the necessary arrangements had been made. Despite her mother's possible misgivings it was to be one of the happiest periods of Jane Grey's life.

Chapter IV

The Example of Catherine Parr

I t was only a short boat ride from Dorset House to Seymour Place, but Jane's new home opened a more independent world for her. At the best of times large aristocratic households were not very good at giving girls the kind of closely supervised lives their parents would have liked. Guardians were often at court or staying with friends, and the girls were left in the care of servants who had less reason than their parents to watch their manners and behaviour.[1] Even an experienced stepmother like Catherine Parr sometimes neglected her duties. The Protector's wife, Anne, Duchess of Somerset, was shocked to see Parr's ward, the young Princess Elizabeth, unaccompanied, out in a barge on the Thames one night that summer. There were no such complaints about Sudeley's care of Jane, but he was an indulgent guardian, with more pressing concerns than babysitting a ten-year-old girl. Jane, a confident child, must have enjoyed the novel sense of freedom this gave her, although she was never left entirely to her own devices.

When Jane wasn't at Seymour Place she was attending the Queen dowager's household with her guardian. In the last year of her life she would return to Catherine's former house at the royal manor of Chelsea. Here, in the summer the garden boasted orchards of cherry and peach, velvety damask roses and the warm scents of lavender and rosemary. Inside the noise and bustle was greater even than Jane was used to at Bradgate. In addition to the Queen's Privy Chamber and Maids of Honour, the household included upwards of 120 gentlemen and yeomen. At thirty-five Catherine Parr remained attractive; with a handsome husband she worked hard to stay beautiful, plucking her eyebrows with silver tweezers and dressing in the latest fashions. Children are always fascinated by the rituals of adult grooming and, to the later irritation of her tutor John Aylmer, Jane developed a similar fondness for carefully styled hair and fine clothes. She also grew to share the Queen dowager's love of music. Catherine and her brother, William Parr of Northampton, were the greatest patrons of musicians at court. The most famous, the five Bassano brothers, provided the only permanent recorder consort known in England before the twentieth century. One brother, Baptista, instructed the Princess Elizabeth in Italian, as well as in playing the lute.

Jane's visits to Chelsea, and the return visits to Seymour Place made by the Queen dowager, gave her the opportunity to get to know Elizabeth much better than she had hitherto, although she was acquainted already with some of the princess's personal staff. Elizabeth's governess Kate Astley and husband John were old friends of Jane's family; John Astley would later write a treatise on horsemanship and may have given them both riding lessons.[2] But the thirteen-year-old princess, who would one day govern the destinies of Katherine and Mary Grey, did not grow close to Jane. A fresh-skinned adolescent, with her father's red gold hair and her mother's famous black eyes, Elizabeth was too old to wish to play with Jane, and was, in any case, unusually self-contained. This gave her a reputation for arrogance in some quarters, but what it reflected principally was anxiety.[3] Elizabeth felt acutely the precariousness of her position.

In the first years of her life Elizabeth had gone from being her father's heir and the daughter of his most beloved wife, to the bastard child of a traitor-adulteress. This had changed again in 1544, when she was restored in line of succession, but she remained illegitimate in law and was now an orphan, dependent on the goodwill of others. Although she loved Catherine Parr for the kindness she showed,

Elizabeth was disgusted at her stepmother's hasty remarriage and, as she observed to her half-sister, Mary, based in St James's, she felt there was nothing they could say about it, without putting themselves in danger. Sudeley was the brother of the Protector, whom they had little reason to trust, and who had kept the lands and income Elizabeth's father had left her, largely in his own control. Elizabeth, utterly powerless, was obliged to make the best of what was to her an uncomfortable situation at Chelsea – and Jane was not a particularly welcome presence in Elizabeth's bleak and uncertain world. Under the terms of Henry's will, Jane Grey was Elizabeth's heir, and Elizabeth had seen already how one heir could leapfrog another, from one parliamentary statute to the next. As Elizabeth was notoriously vain, it also can't have helped that Jane was proving more adept at her studies than either she or the King, both of whom were considered exceptionally intelligent.*

Jane's quick mind was absorbing a curriculum of studies that shared similarities with those of Edward, who was now reading Justin the Martyr's summary of Greek history and copying phrases from Cicero's *Offices* and the *Tusculan Disputations*. This progress in Latin and Greek was matched by her religious education. Evangelicals were enthusiastic for women to be involved in the study of theology and Catherine Parr set Jane an impressive example. For years she had applied her knowledge of Scripture to the promotion of Church reform, and much of the autumn in Catherine's household was taken up with her religious projects. The translation of Erasmus's *Paraphrases of the New Testament*, which she had overseen (and to which the Princess Mary had contributed), was prepared for publication (and would prove a bestseller).[4] But she was also completing an original work of her own, written when Henry was alive, and which she had not then dared make public. Entitled *The Lamentation of a Sinner*, it described her search for salvation. It was

---

* John Foxe, who knew Aylmer, claimed that Jane was a better student than Edward, and Elizabeth's later tutor, Roger Ascham, recorded her superiority to Elizabeth. Neither had reason to exaggerate.

distinctly Lutheran in tone, and Henry had considered Luther a heretic, but Jane's step-grandmother, Katherine Suffolk, helped persuade the Queen dowager the time was ripe for its publication.[5]

For the first time Jane had a sense of what it was like to be a member of a network of clever women, working together and propagating new and exciting religious ideas.[6] The evangelical reformation, meanwhile, was proceeding apace all around her. The ambassador to the Hapsburg Emperor, Charles V, complained that the preachers giving the public sermons at court seemed 'to vie with each other as to who can abuse most strongly the old religion'.[7] By July they had asserted the evangelical belief that salvation was not attainable by man through his own efforts, such as charitable works, but was the gift of God for an elect few. By August the use of the rosary was abolished and the Mass was under attack, with 'much speaking against the sacrament of the altar, that some called it Jack in the box, with divers other shameful names'.[8] Stained-glass windows in churches were smashed and the carved figures of Christ torn down. The iconography of God was now idolatry, but that of the King and the nobility remained everywhere. Indeed the arms of the King were now being painted on church walls. Bishop Gardiner questioned the logic of this to the Privy Council. He also warned it was surely illegal to break Henry VIII's religious settlement during Edward's minority, but such pleas and arguments fell on deaf ears.

The Bible did not raise any objections to heraldic symbols, but to objects worshipped as God. Praying before a statue or image might not be to worship it, but it could appear close to it. As for the illegality of changing the national religious culture, Somerset and his allies believed that Edward would learn to applaud their actions before he came to his majority. Images of saints, with which Edward had been surrounded, were removed from his rooms, and his mind was being as cleansed of the past as his environment. Edward's reformist tutor, the gaunt John Cheke, was 'always at his elbow' whispering to him in his chapel, 'and wherever else he went, to inform and teach him'. Edward responded eagerly, but the evangelicals needed to project Edward as the font of reform, not merely as an obedient pupil. It was claimed, therefore, that his ability to absorb what he was taught was such that, 'it should seem he were already a [spiritual] father' rather than a boy, 'not yet ten years old'.[9] The radical Dorset would have liked to see still faster progress in religion than was being made, but he also had more earthly matters to consider. In particular he had concerns that Sudeley was proving unable to develop Jane's friendship with the King.

Somerset had barred Catherine Parr and Sudeley from access to Edward. This was miserable for the boy. Catherine was the only mother Edward had ever known, his *Mater Carissima*, who, he had once said, held 'the chiefest place in my heart'. In getting Edward to write a letter giving them permission to marry, however, Sudeley had proven how dangerous their access to the King could be. The ability to shape the King's mind, to fill it with carefully coloured opinions and edited information that favoured one's own interests and condemned one's enemies, was central to the operation of politics in an autocratic monarchy. While the King's mind was young and impressionable, as Edward's was, it was all the more important to control access to him. Sudeley was therefore kept well away from him. But he assured Dorset that he nevertheless remained the King's favourite uncle. Edward had complained, he said, 'divers times' that 'his uncle of Somerset kept him very straight' and would not let him have money when he asked for it.[10] Sudeley explained he was thus able to earn Edward's gratitude with gifts of £10, £20, even £40, slipped to him through John Fowler, one of the Grooms of the Privy Chamber. While Edward was fond of him, however, Sudeley knew that the truth was he had to place new and higher stakes if he was to achieve the power he wanted.

Katherine and Mary Grey were used to their sister leaving them to spend periods at court. But Jane's leaving for Seymour Place was of a different order and surely more deeply felt. The ordinary memories of everyday life, such as the dancing horse, taken from Bradgate by one of the servants to entertain the townsfolk of Leicester, were less often shared.[11] For Frances also, it must have been hard. Jane was still very young and, no matter how commonplace it was to send a child away, she had to overcome her natural instincts to do what was considered best for her eldest daughter. Even when Frances was away at court, or staying with friends, she knew her children, whether at Bradgate or Dorset House, were being cared for in an environment she had some control over. Giving that up to a known womaniser like Sudeley was a cause for anxiety. But things were far worse at Seymour Place than she ever suspected.

If there was one thing that would have advanced Sudeley's ambitions more effectively than marrying a King's widow, it would be to have married a King's daughter. Jane's enquiring mind and sharp eyes could not fail to have noticed how especially friendly Sudeley was with the Princess Elizabeth. Whenever the Queen dowager and her stepdaughter visited them at Seymour Place he was always up first and, still in his nightshirt and slippers, he would breeze down the corridors to the door of Elizabeth's chamber, look round and wish her good morning. Elizabeth's governess Kate Astley warned Sudeley that it was 'an unseemly sight to go to a maiden's bedchamber barelegged' and was causing gossip amongst the servants. But Sudeley retorted that he was doing nothing wrong. Soon he was going into Elizabeth's room. Sometimes she was still in bed and he would 'put open the curtains, and bid her good morrow, and make as though he would come at her'.[12] Elizabeth did not dare reprove him. She had not forgotten Sudeley was the brother of the Protector: as he made his advances she simply shrank under her covers.

Increasingly Elizabeth's feelings towards her stepfather became confused. Having a powerful figure show her so much attention was exciting and, at just fourteen, it was not easy to distinguish predator from protector. There may have been an element too, of wanting to revenge herself on her stepmother for her betrayal of her father in marrying so quickly after his death. There is only one time, however, that Elizabeth's emotions are recorded as having come to the surface, during this period. This was when, to her great distress, her young tutor, William Grindal, died of plague at the end of January. Sudeley and Catherine were anxious to choose his replacement, but here, outside the complex parameters of the adult, sexual arena, Elizabeth's natural self-assurance could show through, and she insisted on making her own choice: a man she could trust. She picked the thirty-three-year-old Roger Ascham, who had taught Edward alongside John Cheke and been Grindal's tutor at Cambridge.

Jane also liked Ascham. He was easy-going with a taste for good wine and gambling at cards. He got on particularly well with the Astleys, with whom he recalled enjoying 'free talk, always mingled with honest mirth', and Jane would later write a letter commending him to a future employer.* Outside the schoolroom, however, Sudeley's reckless familiarity with Elizabeth was beginning to cause tensions in his marriage. Sudeley and Catherine enjoyed a passionate, but volatile relationship. He was a jealous lover and Catherine was sometimes frightened of his rages. But she was now pregnant and had her own anxieties. At thirty-six she was old for a first-time mother and feared Sudeley saw Elizabeth as a potential replacement, were she to die in childbirth. There were even rumours, which she may have heard, that Sudeley had expressed an interest in marrying the princess before he had begun to woo her.[13]

Kate Astley's complaints about Sudeley's behaviour with Elizabeth had resulted in the Queen dowager deciding to accompany Sudeley on his early morning perambulations. But she couldn't be with him all the time. The final straw for Catherine came in May when she was six months pregnant. Elizabeth and Sudeley had disappeared and Catherine went looking for them. When she found them Elizabeth was in her husband's arms.[14] Catherine and Sudeley had a furious row. The embrace does not seem to have been overtly sexual, but Catherine later explained to a shocked Elizabeth the grave risk she had taken with her reputation. As the daughter of an infamous adulteress, Elizabeth had more reason than most to be careful with her good name. To prevent any further opportunity for scandal or for

---

* The Dorsets also later employed his wife, Alice, and a cousin at Bradgate.

some misdeed on Sudeley's part, Catherine suggested Elizabeth stay for a while with Astley's sister, Joan Denny. The chastened Elizabeth left a week after Pentecost, ashamed and shaken by what had occurred.

It was Jane alone who accompanied Catherine Parr to her guardian's Gloucestershire estate at Sudeley for the summer. The orphaned Elizabeth must have reflected bitterly that Jane would now replace her in Catherine's attentions. If she had felt any malice towards Catherine, it had vanished and she felt remorseful that she had allowed herself to hurt a woman who had shown her nothing but warmth and generosity. For Jane, on the other hand, there was a danger Elizabeth's leaving would encourage a sense of entitlement. While the illegitimate Elizabeth was banished, she, who was the apple of her father's eye, took her place as the princess of the households. Sudeley, meanwhile, still didn't acknowledge that he had behaved irresponsibly with Elizabeth. 'Suspicion,' as he wrote in one of his poems, 'I do banish thee.' He was a 'master of noble blood ... of manner good, And spotless in life.' His behaviour was simply, 'sporting'.[15] He was now only looking forward to fatherhood. He liked to hear Catherine describe how his child was stirring in her womb and shared with her his hopes of a son who would grow up to avenge all the humiliations they endured at his brother's hands. He had prepared a nursery at his house furnished for a prince. There were scarlet curtains of silk taffeta, a chair upholstered in cloth of gold, carved stools, rich hangings, carpets and a gilded salt. All the signs of the baby's expected arrival were there, from the cradle where he would sleep, to the three feather beds and goblets for his nurse and servants.[16]

Jane had to get used to the noise of further extensive building works while she was at Sudeley House. Her guardian was spending a fortune on his Gloucestershire seat (although nothing like the £10,000 his brother spent that year alone on Somerset House). But it was a happy time for Jane, studying under the Queen dowager's guidance and with a fine library of books to read. There were upwards of twenty-two volumes in Catherine's personal collection, some in English, others in French or Italian. Only seven, however, were religious works: Catherine was losing her passion for theology.

Sudeley even seemed bored by the twice-daily prayers given by the chaplains. Hugh Latimer, who was the spiritual adviser of Jane's step-grandmother, complained later he avoided them 'like a mole digging in the dirt'.[17] If Jane reflected on this she would have worried that he was tempting fate: God punished such behaviour, she was taught.

In August, when the baby was almost due, Jane's father came to visit and she was able to catch up with family news. Her sister, Katherine, who had just turned eight, was now studying Greek with the new chaplain, Thomas Harding, a former Regius Professor of Hebrew at Oxford. She did not show the same aptitude for her studies as Jane, but she made up in charm what she lacked in intellectual drive. Everyone liked Katherine. Little Mary Grey was also doing well. Jane could imagine her dashing about, the long tippets sewn at her shoulders known as the 'ribbons of childhood' streaming behind her as she ran and played: a small, determined figure, as yet ignorant that she was not the beauty her sisters were said to be. There was news too, for Jane, of the extended family, and especially the sisters' uncle, Lord John Grey, who was commanding cavalry in the war with Scotland. Somerset hoped to achieve what King Henry had failed to do and unite the two kingdoms, by marriage or force. The family was fearful for Lord John after the almost fatal injuries he had received at the battle of Pinkie in September 1547, but they thought his troops had cut a fine spectacle when they had left London in July, dressed in blue coats guarded in yellow, and he had, thus far, survived this campaign unhurt.[18]

Sudeley was anxious, however, to discuss other matters with Jane's father and, when the adults were alone, Dorset found him full of plans. To Sudeley's delight, his brother, the Protector, had begun to make enemies. There were those who felt the evangelical reformation was losing impetus. The radical preacher, John Knox, later complained that Somerset spent more time with his masons than he did with his chaplains. And the regal style of his Italianate palace irritated on a further account: it reflected the lofty attitude he held towards his colleagues. There were profound concerns about the expense of the war with Scotland and the high inflation the country was suffering, but Somerset was dismissive of the anxieties of his fellow Councillors and sometimes even appeared contemptuous of them. He had brutally expelled Sudeley's brother-in-law, William Parr of Northampton, from the Privy Council for taking the novel step of divorcing his wife and marrying his mistress, the court beauty Elizabeth Brooke – an action that reflected, in turn, Somerset's fears that parts of the country were restive over the religious changes already introduced.[19]

Sudeley outlined to Dorset, as he had already to Northampton, a future in which Edward had come of age and rejected the unpopular Protector in favour of his younger uncle. There was a danger, Sudeley explained, that his brother would not give up power without a fight. It was necessary, therefore, to prepare for the struggle ahead. Northampton had been advised to 'set up house in the North Country' where, on his core estates, surrounded by tenants and friends, he would be a powerful figure.[20] Dorset was also now given detailed instructions on how to build up an effective military follow-ing. Gentlemen had too much to lose to be trustworthy, Sudeley told him. It was better to gain the loyalty of yeomen for they were 'best able to persuade the multitude'. Dorset was advised to 'go to their houses, now to one, now to another, carrying with you a flagon or two of wine and a pasty of venison and to use a familiarity with them, for so shall you cause them to love you'.[21] The talk of war seemed unreal to Dorset, but it was also fascinating. The aims were presented as altruistic: to protect the King from the overweening Somerset. But they coincided also with his personal interests. Dorset's honour had been slighted by the Protector's failure to recog-nise better his place within the royal family. As he returned to Bradgate he had to consider whether he should fight to protect it and whether the horrors of battle were justified by his duties to the King.

The Queen dowager's confinement, meanwhile, was coming to an end and on 30th August 1548 she went into labour. Catherine had suffered a difficult and uncomfortable pregnancy, but she eventually delivered a healthy baby girl. Sudeley, despite his hopes for a son, was overwhelmed by the thrill of first-time fatherhood. His daughter was to be called Mary, after Edward's elder half-sister, and he wrote to his brother, the father of many daughters, declaring his a most spectacular beauty. For a few days all seemed well and Jane Grey rejoiced with her surrogate family. Gradually, however, Catherine grew delirious: the fatal sign of puerperal fever. In her delirium she was tormented by her old fears about her husband's desire to marry Elizabeth. 'Those that be about me careth not for me,' she confided to her servant Lady Elizabeth Tyrwhitt as Sudeley stood over her. 'Why sweet heart, I would you no hurt,' he reassured her. 'No, my Lord, I think so,' she replied, and whispered, 'but my Lord you have given me many shrewd taunts.' Sudeley lay down beside her on the bed and tried to comfort her. But she soon burst out with another accusation: she had not dared spend as much time with her doctor as she would like for fear of making him jealous.

Sudeley persisted in his efforts to reassure and soothe Catherine and, as it became clear she was dying, Jane and the other women read the Scriptures with her. They would have prayed also, as the chaplain arrived to perform the service for the Visitation of the Sick. The priest was expected to exhort Catherine to ask forgiveness for her sins and to forgive all those who had offended her, and before she died on 5th September, Catherine and Sudeley were reconciled. Her will left her husband everything she had, 'wishing them to be a thousand times more in value than they were'.[22] For his part, Sudeley was left stunned by his wife's death. The happiness at the birth of his daughter had tapped into a deep well of feeling and now he was plunged into desperate grief. 'I was so amazed I had small regard either to myself or to my doings,' he later recalled. Politics were forgotten. He went with his baby daughter to his brother the Protector's house, to recuperate, and ordered that his own household be broken up. Jane Grey was to be sent back to Bradgate. But he asked first that she fulfil the role of chief mourner at Catherine's funeral.

The eleven-year-old Jane performed her first public role with great dignity. She walked behind the Queen's coffin in the procession from the house to the chapel at Sudeley, her small figure erect in a black gown, the long train 'borne up by a young Lady'. She was, perhaps, the fifteen-year-old Elizabeth Tilney, the younger sister of the favourite lady-in-waiting of Henry's fifth wife Katherine Howard, and a friend who would accompany Jane on the last procession of her life.[23] The funeral ceremony in the chapel was modest and took only a morning, but it was of disproportionate historical significance. This was the first Protestant royal funeral in English history. The biblical translator Miles Coverdale conducted the service in English and gave the sermon. In it he stressed that the alms given for the poor at the funeral and the candles burned were not to profit Catherine's soul but to honour her memory. In reformed teaching there was no purgatory, where in Catholic belief sinners may, after death, do penance for their sins while the living pray for their release: the elect went straight to heaven, while the rest went to hell. Jane did not pray for Catherine, therefore, although she surely remembered her distraught guardian and his motherless baby.

When the service was over, and Catherine buried, Jane returned home. The records of the towns she travelled through on the road to Bradgate record the expenses laid out to entertain their royal visitor. When she was a little girl, Jane often saw her parents going off to Leicester and other local towns before returning with gifts from the mayor and the aldermen's wives. There would be strawberries, walnuts, pears and home-made treats such as the spiced wine, ippocras.[24] Now she was treated with similar deference. Jane's mother was not getting back the child she had said goodbye to a year before, but a questioning, maturing girl with a strong sense of her own dignity.

Chapter V

The Execution of Sudeley

Jane's younger sisters had endured their share of mourning at Bradgate. Their mother Frances, who had been fond of Catherine Parr and kept her portrait all her life, had lost her younger sister, Eleanor, Countess of Cumberland, the previous November. Eleanor was still only in her twenties and left a husband stricken with shock, as well as an only daughter.[1] Then, on 3rd January 1548, when the family were celebrating the Christmas season at Bradgate, Dorset had received news that his younger sister, Anne Willoughby, was also dying. This branch of the Willoughbys, kin of Katherine Suffolk, were based in Nottinghamshire, not far from Bradgate, and the two families were very close.

Katherine and Mary understood something of Jane's grief, then, as they prepared to welcome her home after the Queen dowager's funeral. The excitement of having their sister with them again and the hopes of exchanging confidences, soon gave way, however, to the awkwardness of readjustment. The three-year gap between Jane and Katherine seemed suddenly very wide. While Katherine and Mary Grey were both still of an age when they wanted to please their parents, Jane was more questioning. At eleven she was showing the same rebellious streak her father had had at her age. Dorset used to infuriate his Latin teacher, Richard Croke, by laughing at rude jokes about the clergy, and then, when Croke complained, by stirring up the other pupils against him.[2] Jane felt equally irritated by the restrictions and demands imposed on her at Bradgate. She had got used to a long rein at Seymour Place and resented her mother's efforts to reassert her authority. Frances, in turn, was angered and worried by Jane's defiance.

In Tudor thinking, to rule and to obey were the essential characteristics of an ordered society. Frances believed that, with discipline, Jane's youthful wilfulness could be transformed into willpower and become a force for good. Without it, however, she would pursue only her own selfish appetites. That, Frances feared, was dangerous for Jane and for society. As the heiress of a noble house, and perhaps even a future Queen, Jane could do great things for her country, or great harm. Frances was furious that Sudeley had not done a better job of guiding her child, and to her horror, less than a fortnight after Jane's return home, Sudeley asked for her to be sent back to him.

Sudeley's grief over his wife's death had passed rapidly through the early stages of numbness and denial that follows bereavement. He now grasped it as fact, with all its implications. Her wealth was being returned to the crown. This dealt a severe blow to his finances and status. That could not be helped, but returning Jane to her parents was an act of political self-mutilation that he could yet rectify. Sudeley had written on 17th September pleading with Jane's father for her return. He anticipated that Frances, in particular, would be unenthusiastic and assured Dorset that he would be keeping on Catherine Parr's gentlewomen, the unmarried Maids of Honour, 'and other women being about her Grace in her lifetime'. Everyone, Sudeley swore, would be, 'as diligent about [Jane], as yourself would wish'. His own mother would take charge of the house, and would treat Jane 'as though she were her own daughter. And for my own part, I shall continue her half father and more.'[3] Sudeley then wrote to Jane in a suitably strict, fatherly manner. Jane, picking up her cue, thanked him reverently. 'Like as you have become towards me a loving and kind father, so I shall be always most ready to obey your godly monitions and good instructions,' she replied.[4]

Frances was unimpressed, however, by Sudeley's assurances and Dorset, aware that Sudeley's status had fallen with the death of Catherine Parr, agreed with his wife that it would be better if Jane now stayed at home. Dorset wrote thanking him for his care of Jane thus far, and then reminded his friend that Jane was very young, and while he regarded him as an excellent father figure, he could not also be a mother to her. With Catherine Parr dead, Sudeley could surely see that 'the eye and oversight of my wife shall in this respect be most necessary'. Jane was on the cusp of adolescence, a crucial age for 'the addressing of the mind to humility, sobriety and obedience'.[5] Dorset concluded hopefully that he still intended to take Sudeley's advice about Jane's marriage.

Frances then wrote her own letter to Sudeley. As Jane's guardian and the Queen dowager's widower, Sudeley was a member of the family and Frances referred to him in her letter as her 'good brother' and to Jane as his 'niece'. She also accepted that when it came to Jane's marriage they would ask for his advice, as her husband wished. But she made it clear that she did not expect any marriage to take place for a good while yet. Having been married herself at sixteen, Frances did not want her daughter hurried into a husband's bed. Frances concluded her letter expressing the hope that she could keep her daughter with his 'goodwill'.[6] It was not to be. Within days Sudeley was on the road to Leicestershire determined to change their minds. When the sisters and their parents greeted him at Bradgate he also had a friend at his side, Sir William Sharington, the Under Treasurer of the Royal Mint.

Jane had seen Sharington often at Seymour Place, and Katherine and Mary may have remembered him from the previous autumn, when he had accompanied Sudeley to Bradgate on another visit. A handsome, charming man, he had an elegant, aquiline nose, though his eyes were dark-ringed and prematurely lined. Sharington had used his position at the Mint to perpetrate extensive frauds.[7] Sudeley knew what he had done and in exchange for his secrecy Sharington was providing him with money. This included the ready cash Sudeley needed to buy Jane's wardship. But Sharington also had talents that

Sudeley would make good use of at Bradgate. He could be extremely plausible. The previous autumn he helped persuade Dorset to vote with Sudeley against a bill in Parliament confirming Somerset's letters patent as Lord Protector – Dorset had been the only peer to do so. Now Sharington had the task of persuading Frances to return her daughter to Seymour Place, while Sudeley worked on Dorset.

Sudeley knew his most effective leverage with Dorset remained the promise that he could deliver the King's hand in marriage to Jane. And he had a piece of good fortune in this respect. Jane's principal rival, the infant Mary Queen of Scots, had been sent to live in France so that she could be betrothed to the Dauphin, Francis. Sudeley assured Dorset that 'if he might once get the King at liberty' then he could immediately have Edward married to Jane. Dorset hummed and hawed, but, as he later recalled, Sudeley 'would have no nay'. Sharington, meanwhile, was doing an excellent job at weakening Frances's resolve, reassuring her that all her fears were misplaced. Eventually, 'after long debating and much sticking', she agreed that Jane should be returned to Sudeley's care and her husband followed suit.[8] It was a decision they would soon regret, as would Jane.

Life at Seymour Place that autumn of 1548 was not as Jane remembered it, despite the comforting presence of her old friends from Catherine's Privy Chamber. The Queen dowager's stabilising influence on Sudeley was gone and a part of him had not quite accepted she was dead.

Sudeley spoke often of promoting a parliamentary bill that would prevent people slandering Catherine Parr's name over her decision to marry him so quickly after Henry VIII's death. But there were also rumours circulating that he wanted to remarry. Some claimed Sudeley had his eye on the Princess Mary, others that he hoped to marry Lady Jane Grey. He laughed at that suggestion, but admitted to his former brother-in-law, Parr of Northampton, that there would be 'much ado' for Jane's hand. His ward would be twelve in May and able to make a binding marriage contract under canon law. He believed the Somersets, in particular, 'would do what they could to obtain her for [their son] Lord Hertford'.

Northampton asked Sudeley if his real intention might be to marry the Princess Elizabeth rather than Jane. Sudeley replied that 'he had heard that the Protector would clap him in the Tower if he went to Elizabeth',[9] though he could see no other reason why he shouldn't marry her, if she were willing. As he told other friends, it was far better that Elizabeth should marry within the kingdom than outside it. Elizabeth, however, had learned the lessons of the previous spring when Sudeley had embarrassed her with Catherine Parr. She was acutely aware that she could not marry without the permission of the King and the Privy Council, and refused even to see Sudeley without a warrant. But some of her servants were prepared to help him, believing, rightly or wrongly, that this was what Elizabeth truly wanted. Two or three weeks before Christmas, Jane noticed the familiar full face of Elizabeth's cofferer, Thomas Parry, at Seymour Place. Parry, who as cofferer managed Elizabeth's money, appeared several times, walking alone with her guardian in the gallery where, out of her earshot, they discussed the financial details of a possible marriage to Elizabeth.[10]

Such dabbling in a matter of high state caused considerable alarm with other servants in Elizabeth's household. The princess's tutor, Roger Ascham, was so appalled by Parry's actions that he asked for permission to return to Cambridge for the entire Christmas season. Kate Astley's husband John, equally concerned, argued furiously with his wife over the arrangements. One of these arguments was so heated that afterwards Elizabeth noticed bruising on her governess's arms (Astley claimed that a doctor had been bleeding her to cure some ailment). The atmosphere at Seymour Place, meanwhile, was equally charged. Sudeley's friends and servants desperately tried to dissuade him from his course. It was against all sense of decency and right order that a man without royal blood should align himself with an heir to the throne. 'Beware,' one warned Sudeley: 'It were better for you if you had never been born, nay, that you were burnt to the quick alive, than that you should attempt it.' Men had died already for attempting royal alliances during King Henry's time and it would put Elizabeth's life at risk.[11] They begged him instead to improve his relations with his brother. But Sudeley only blustered about how he would use Parliament to get the Governorship of the King's Person in spite of the Protector, and seize his rightful share of power.

Sudeley judged that Somerset's political position was continuing to weaken as he persisted in his arrogant treatment of his colleagues. In this he was correct. Somerset often ignored advice and once slapped down a Privy Councillor in such a humiliating manner that the man was reduced to tears. Somerset's most faithful ally on the Council, William Paget, was moved to write to him in the middle of Christmas night, to warn him of disaster ahead.[12] But not everything was going Sudeley's way. Within the Privy Council it was Sudeley who was judged the immediate threat to national stability. Dorset, aware there was an impending crisis, demonstrated his usual poor political judgement by throwing in his lot with his friend. Whatever happened, Dorset promised Sudeley, he would 'defend him against all men, save the King'. Night after night during the Christmas season, Katherine and Mary Grey saw their father leave Dorset House for Seymour Place, where Jane saw him arrive along with their great Leicestershire neighbour, Francis Hastings, Earl of Huntingdon. Sometimes Sudeley would leave them to go on forays to court. There were accusations later that Sudeley was planning to kidnap Edward and Elizabeth. Dorset may have hoped he would, believing Sudeley planned a double wedding, with Edward marrying Lady Jane Grey and he marrying Princess Elizabeth. If so it was an ominous portent for Jane of the danger in which her father was prepared to place her in pursuit of his ambitions.

The evidence suggests, however, that for the moment at least, Sudeley was merely picking up gossip from the King's Groom, John Fowler. Sudeley would moan over a drink in the Privy Buttery to Fowler how he wished Edward were old enough to be independent of Somerset, a time too far off to do him any good. On 6th January, the feast of the Epiphany and the last day of Christmas, Sir William

Sharington's house, Lacock Abbey in Wiltshire, was searched on the orders of the Council and incriminating evidence of his fraud at the Royal Mint discovered. Sharington understood what was expected of him and to save his skin gave up all he knew about Sudeley's ambitions, including his hopes of marrying Elizabeth. Others were then rounded up. The young Earl of Rutland, whom Sudeley had attempted to recruit as an ally, was called in for questioning at Somerset House in the middle of the night. Terrified, the twenty-one-year-old repeated what Sudeley had said about the need for those who loved the King to build up a following amongst 'honest and wealthy yeomen who were ringleaders in good towns'. One of Sudeley's servants had a brother in Rutland's household and Sudeley learned what the earl had said before morning. He hoped, nonetheless, to brazen it out. The next day he went to Parliament as usual and left at dinnertime with Dorset, to whom he confided what Rutland had said. They ate at Huntingdon's house and returned to Seymour Place with a group of friends. These included Jane's youngest uncle, Lord Thomas Grey. In contrast to the brothers Sudeley and Somerset, her father and his brothers were close.

Jane must have known something was wrong from the nervous conversation of the servants. Behind closed doors, Sudeley was boasting that he had been called to see the Privy Council, but had refused to go. Lord Thomas was unimpressed, pointing out that the Council could simply arrest him. He advised Sudeley to trust his brother as 'a man of much mercy'.[13] Sudeley refused to contemplate it. In the palace next door, meanwhile, Somerset was proving more amenable to advice – the worse for Sudeley. His enemies were insisting to Somerset that his life would only be safe when his brother was dead. That night, the Clerk of the Privy Council, Sir Thomas Smith, and the Privy Councillor and lawyer, Sir John Baker, came to arrest Sudeley. Jane would have recognised the sickly Smith, even behind his long beard and heavy coat. He was a friend of her tutor John Aylmer. Baker, a man in his fifties, was distinguishable by his grey hair; he was old by the standards of the day, but 'Butcher Baker', as he came to be called, would send many young men to their graves before his time was up.* Sudeley accepted his arrest quietly, hoping that all would be well. Others, however, proved less sanguine.

When the Council's men came for Elizabeth's cofferer Parry, he ran up to his chamber, tearing off his chain of office and crying, 'I would I had never been born, for I am undone.' In the Tower the Astleys both gave full confessions, telling all they knew about Sudeley's plans to marry Elizabeth and his visits to her bedchamber. Only the fifteen-year-old Elizabeth remained composed in her interviews. Faced with the danger she had long feared she defended her servants as well as herself, at times proving forgetful, at times angry over slurs that she was pregnant by Sudeley, but always consistent in her denials that she ever intended to marry anyone without the Council's permission. It is possible that Parry's kinsman, William Cecil, was giving Elizabeth vital advice – it would help explain the trust she later developed in him – but Elizabeth was never prone to losing her nerve.

Jane was returned to Dorset Place, while her father, like the other witnesses, was called to the Council for interview. Despite their testimony on Sudeley's plans, there was no real evidence that Sudeley had ever intended to seize the King, as was claimed, or commit any treason. Ways, therefore, had to be found around the difficulties of a trial. Sudeley had hoped to use Parliament to bring an end to the autocracy of the Protectorate: instead Parliament was used to bring an end to his life. A bill was introduced condemning him for high treason. It was passed without dissension in the Lords. In the Commons there was fierce argument, but in March 1549 a packed House eventually passed the Act of Attainder. Edward was obliged to assent to his uncle's death in words set down for him, and he did so with visible reluctance. Lady Jane Grey was then left to make sense of the fate of the family of which she had become part. By the end of the year they would all be dead – the baby Mary

---

* Under Queen Mary, Baker would forget his evangelical past and burn his former co-religionists, earning his nickname, 'Butcher Baker'.

Seymour dying after illness in the house of Katherine Suffolk to whose care she had been bequeathed, and who resented the expense and inconvenience.

Jane was taught that misfortune came from God as a punishment for sins, but also as a warning to repent. In that sense it could be a blessing, for it gave the sinner the chance to clean the slate. This was how Sudeley saw events, as he explained in a poem composed in the Tower:

> ... *God did call me in my pride*
> *Lest I should fall and from him slide*
> *For whom he loves he must correct*
> *That they may be of his elect.*

It was not in Sudeley's nature, however, to accept his end with passivity. He intended one final throw of the dice, last messages for Elizabeth and her half-sister, Mary, which he wrote in orange juice using a hook 'plucked from his hose'. The letters were said by someone who saw them to tend 'to this end, that they should conspire against my Lord Protector'. Sudeley hid his message in the soles of his velvet shoes.[14] They were still with him on the morning of 20th March 1549 when he was taken to Tower Hill to die.[15]

Public executions were carefully choreographed and the rituals of a beheading followed a strict code. Prisoners gave a last speech in which they would pronounce themselves judged guilty by the laws of the land, and content to die, as prescribed by the law. It was a final act of obedience, one that acknowledged the supreme importance to society of the rule of law. They would then hold themselves up as examples of the fate of all those who sinned against God and King. If they were innocent of the crime for which they were convicted, they knew that God was punishing them for something, and also that, on some level, they had failed the society into which they had been born. They did not doubt that they deserved to die. Their speeches concluded with a request for forgiveness and the hope their sovereign would reign long and happily.[16]

We only have hints at how Sudeley behaved, but assuredly his execution did not follow this usual script. According to one account, as Sudeley laid his head on the block he was overheard asking a servant to 'speed the thing that he wot [knew] of'. The messages to the princesses were then discovered and there appears to have been a struggle. A Swiss witness wrote to a friend saying that Sudeley had died most unwillingly.

What is also apparent is that the Council was extremely disturbed by whatever had occurred, and not surprisingly so. The regime was about to impose an evangelical Prayer Book on a largely unwilling population. Princess Mary, who remained stubbornly conservative in religion, was going even further than Bishop Gardiner in arguing that this was illegal, and that Henry's religious settlement could not be overturned while Edward was still a minor. Hugh Latimer, Katherine Suffolk's spiritual adviser, had articulated the government's response in a sermon at court that Lent, arguing that Edward's precocious Godliness meant that he wasn't a 'minor' in the usual sense. But Sudeley's messages had undermined this claim, suggesting that Edward, far from being a spiritual father, was the puppet of malign forces from which he needed protection. They had also hit another raw nerve: they reminded everybody that Mary was Edward's heir under their father's will. The obvious means to attack Mary's claim was the 1536 Act of Succession, which had declared Mary illegitimate. It had, however, also declared Elizabeth illegitimate, making it nigh impossible to use the act against one sister without excluding the other. That risked proving divisive amongst evangelicals, since Elizabeth conformed to her brother's religious decrees. If she had been executed along with Sudeley for arranging her marriage without the King's permission, the problem would have been solved. But inconveniently, she remained alive.

The Council now needed to discredit Sudeley's actions as forcefully as it could. Latimer was employed to give the sermon, and it proved excoriating. Sudeley was damned from his pulpit as 'a man the farthest from the fear of God that ever I knew or heard of in England', and one who had died, 'irksomely, strangely, horribly'.[17] It is not Latimer's words, however, but the epitaph Elizabeth is said to have given Sudeley that is remembered. On hearing of his beheading she is reported to have said that he had died, 'a man with much wit and very little judgement'. The same assessment could have been made of Jane's father, who, despite his intelligence, had allowed himself to become so closely involved in Sudeley's reckless plans. But he had survived Sudeley's folly and the wheel of fortune was turning. His days in the political wilderness would soon be over, and those of his three daughters with him.

Chapter VI

Northumberland's 'Crew'

The ten-year-old Edward Seymour, Earl of Hertford, rode his horse hard. The skinny, long-limbed boy was the son that Somerset hoped to see married to Jane Grey. On this day, 5th October 1549, he knew, however, that his father's status as Lord Protector, and perhaps his life, depended on the message he carried. There were two men with whom Somerset formed the 'Mighty Tres Viri' (triumvirate) of the Protectorate: one was John Dudley, Earl of Warwick. The previous day, however, he had marched through the city with members of the nobility and Privy Council, the early moves in an attempted coup against Somerset. The second, Sir William Herbert, commanded the royal army in Wiltshire along with Lord Russell. It was to them Hertford now rode for help. The forest of turrets and gilded weathervanes of Hampton Court soon disappeared from view as his horse raced west.

It was autumn, and the roads were quiet, but the tumultuous events of the summer had taken their toll on the standing of the Lord Protector. That June the country had been rocked by rebellions. The risings were triggered on Whit Sunday, 10th June, by the forced introduction of the new Prayer Book, which was written in English for the first time. In parts of Cornwall where little English was spoken, congregations could not understand what their priests were reading to them. In Devon, where they could, they declared the government's service a 'Christmas game'. Something that looked very like the Mass and could be called the Mass remained. But the new Communion service reflected the evangelical view that Christ was not present, body and blood, in consecrated bread and wine. To the Devon parishioners it seemed a parody. The following day, in the Devonshire village of Stamford Courtney, the congregation forced their priest to say the Mass once more. This defiance lit a tinderbox of anger against the ruling elite that spread rapidly, even in areas where the new religion had taken root.

Just as the great men were stripping the churches of gifts made by parishioners, but which they had condemned as idolatrous, so they were also expanding their estates at the expense of the rest. They had bought up farms, and enclosed the common land that saved the new landless peasants from starvation when paid work dried up. By the end of May huge crowds had been plundering the houses of unpopular gentry near Bradgate (where the Grey sisters were based), killing deer in parks and tearing down enclosures. Henry VIII would not have hesitated to crush these rebels without mercy, but when Harry Dorset, as the local nobleman, received his orders from the Council on 11th June, he was warned only to prevent the gentlemen under his command behaving in a manner that might be considered confrontational.[1] To Somerset it was self-evident that the big landowners were greedy and he believed that enclosures were contributing to inflation. In anticipation of a government investigation that would lay the issues to rest, and against the pleas of colleagues on the Council, he had negotiated with the rebels and granted pardons wherever he could. This, however, had been interpreted as weakness.

By 2nd July, the riots had spread across the Midlands, the Home Counties, Essex, Norfolk, Yorkshire, and Exeter was under siege. Within ten days Norwich was also threatened with an army of 16,000 at its gates. William Parr, the Marquess of Northampton, was sent to negotiate with them, but the rebels had attacked the government forces as they slept in the city. They fought the rebels through the darkened streets, outnumbered ten to one, before retreating with heavy losses. England was left on the brink of civil war.

Jane, Katherine and Mary had sat through sermons that summer explaining the terrible wickedness the rebellions represented, although only the elder two could understand anything of what was being said to them. The rebels, they were told, were sinning against God and King. The social order reflected the divine Chain of Being and if the demands of the King or the nobleman were unjust, the yeomen and peasants had, nevertheless, to endure their suffering, peaceably, accepting it as a punishment for their sins. To do otherwise was to overturn good order, and where 'there is any lack of order', observed one Tudor writer, 'needs must be perpetual conflict'. Lucifer had brought disorder into the cosmos when he rebelled against God, and fear of chaos fed into horror stories of lawlessness during the Wars of the Roses. If the rebellions continued the gates would open 'to all abuse, carnal liberty, enormity, sin and babylonical confusion'. The Grey sisters were warned: 'No Man shall sleep in his house or bed unkilled.'[2]

From Bradgate on 17th August, Dorset had written to the Privy Council asking that they send his brother, Lord Thomas Grey, to help him keep order in the county. But more bad news had come by return of post. Lord Thomas could not be spared: the King of France, Henri II, had seized the opportunity offered by the crises to declare war. Lord Thomas was in command of 200 men sent to aid Lord John Grey in the defence of Ambleteuse in the Pale of Calais. The enemy was already advancing, Dorset was told. The town would, in fact, be lost before Lord Thomas had even arrived.[3] With the seriousness of the situation by then apparent even to Somerset, the policy of pardoning rebels was abandoned. The government used foreign mercenaries to crush the rebel armies, and it had been a bloody business. Dorset's kinsman, Lord Grey of Wilton, claimed he had never seen men fall so stoutly as the rebels he faced in Devon on 28th July. But fall, they had. Two and a half thousand were killed in the west. Then came the turn of the east.

John Dudley, Earl of Warwick, commanded an army of 12,000 professional soldiers and German mercenaries against Norfolk farm boys with hopes of 'an equal share of things'. Three thousand men died outside Norwich at Dussindale on 27th August. But there were casualties on both sides.

Fighting under Warwick, Dorset's brother-in-law, Sir Henry Willoughby, whose wife had died eighteen months earlier, was mortally wounded. His children, playmates of Katherine and Mary Grey, were now orphaned. Of all the deaths it was his that touched the Greys most, and the family took in his children. Thomas, the eldest, who was the same age as Katherine, had come to live at Bradgate as Dorset's ward. The younger two Willoughby siblings, bossy Margaret, who was Mary Grey's playmate, and the baby Francis, their mother's godchild, were placed with Dorset's half-brother, George Medley (his mother's son by a first marriage). The dreadful slaughter in Norfolk marked the end of England's last great popular revolt.[4] But it had marked also a loss of faith in Somerset. The duke had ignored, and even insulted, his colleagues as he grew into his role as alter rex. He had involved the country in ruinous wars with Scotland and now France. His decisions had opened the gates to disorder and brought England to the brink of civil war. For that he would not be easily forgiven.

The night after Hertford had left carrying his father's message to the army in Wiltshire, Somerset took King Edward from Hampton Court to the more secure location of Windsor Castle. It was dark and Edward, who had been told Somerset's enemies could kill him, carried a little sword to defend himself. It was the night's chill, however, that presented the most immediate danger, and by the time the eleven-year-old had arrived at Windsor he had caught a cold. As he shivered in the gloom of the castle, with few provisions and no galleries or gardens to walk in, his cousin young Hertford had reached the armies in the west. Sir William Herbert, the third member of Somerset and Warwick's 'Tres Viri', was immediately recognisable by his red hair, and the high style of a great man at court.

Herbert had a reputation for violence. It was said that, in his youth, he had murdered a man in Bristol and that when the peasants had invaded his park at Wilton in the summer he had 'attacked the rioters in person, and cut some of them in pieces'.[5] True or not it says something of the man that such tales were easily believed of him. But Herbert was much more than a mere thug. His first language was

Welsh, and ambassadors sneered that he could barely read English, let alone speak any European tongue; but he was clever, and sufficiently sophisticated to have married the elegant Anne Parr, sister of the late Queen dowager.[6] It made him a member of the extended royal family. Unfortunately for Hertford this would not, however, help his father. It was Herbert's brother-in-law, William Parr of Northampton, whom Somerset had kicked off the Privy Council for divorcing his wife.

As young Hertford soon discovered, Sir William Herbert had no intention of bringing the royal army to aid Somerset. The message the boy carried to Windsor on 9th October instead marked the end of the Protectorate. Herbert and his co-commander, Lord Russell, urged Somerset to step aside, 'rather than any blood be shed'. Somerset had no option but to comply and he threw himself on the mercy of the Council. Soon afterwards Edward was obliged to order his uncle's arrest. The former Lord Protector was lodged in the Tower on 14th October 1549. It was only two days past Edward's twelfth birthday and not yet seven months since the execution of his younger uncle, Thomas Sudeley.

It was a novelty for the three sisters to have a nine-year-old boy living amongst them at Bradgate. Katherine, in particular, must have enjoyed having a playmate her own age; one who shared the pleasures of the park, as well as the books that Jane always had her nose in. But Thomas Willoughby wasn't with them for long. He left the family to join Katherine Suffolk's two sons at Cambridge on 16th November. The sisters ended up seeing more of the younger siblings, Margaret and Francis. The Grey and Willoughby cousins were regularly in and out of each other's houses that winter, sometimes at Bradgate, sometimes at the Willoughby seat, Wotton, in Nottinghamshire, and often they were all at George Medley's house, Tilty in Essex. It was there the sisters headed, as they set off from Bradgate towards the end of November 1549 – Mary and Katherine Grey still riding their horses with a servant sitting behind them, holding them tight so they didn't fall when they tired; Jane treated as an adult, sitting side-saddle with a foot rest to keep her secure. Nurses, grooms and gentlemen servants also rode in the train, while other servants were carried in carts along with the baggage and mail. It was a spectacular sight on the quiet roads and bells rang in the villages and towns ahead to warn people of their arrival. Crowds came out to stare at the passing celebrities, or to offer fresh horses, food and places to rest.

The sisters enjoyed several days playing with their cousins at Tilty. Little Mary Grey, although much smaller than her friend Margaret, was equally strong-willed, and there must have been some impressive battling for dominance in their games. Then, after breakfast on 26th November, the sisters were mounted again on their horses, and travelled with their mother to the Princess Mary's house Beaulieu, also in Essex.[7] They recognised the turreted palace as it came in view, with its great gateway carved with King Henry's arms in stone. The sisters had visited the princess many times before. Their grandmother, the French Queen, and Catherine of Aragon had been friends as well as sisters-in-law, while their mother had served in Mary's household when Jane was a baby.

The princess – small and of 'spare and delicate frame' – was now thirty-three. She had suffered with menstrual problems and depression for years, and was regularly bled for them. But her fragile appearance belied a strong voice, 'almost like a man's', and 'piercing eyes'. She struck a formidable figure, and an unusually independent one. It was very unusual for a woman of her age and wealth to remain unmarried. But she was simply too good a catch to be free to take a husband. Her father had executed men he feared were plotting to marry their sons to his daughter. He didn't want Edward to have any dangerous rivals. Now, Edward's Privy Council would have regarded anyone seeking her hand with similar suspicion, and they had the legal veto on any choice she might have made. So she had to remain alone, watching her youth pass, resting her love only in God.

Mary Tudor must have seemed like a spinster aunt to the Grey sisters: intimidating, but also kindly. She enjoyed giving them presents of necklaces, beads and dresses. She gambled at cards with their mother, and played her lute for them all. It was said that Mary 'surprised even the best performers, both by the rapidity of her hand and by the style of her playing'.[8] Jane, who had learned so much about music from Catherine Parr, would have been impressed. But the Mass that the sisters had been taught to despise remained at the heart of Mary's daily routine: she maintained no fewer than six Catholic chaplains in her household, in the face of government objections. Life had not been easy for Mary since Whit Sunday 1549, when the new Prayer Book came into force. But she had not expected it to be so. She had demonstrated her contempt for the government's decree by having a high Catholic Mass said that day at her chapel at Kenninghall in Norfolk. The Council had tried subsequently to link her to the Devonshire rebels. When that had failed they demanded she cease having Mass said publicly in her chapels. She refused, arguing she had broken no laws, unless they were new laws of their own making: and she did not recognise these since the King, her brother, was not yet of an age to make them. For the time being her Hapsburg cousin, the Holy Roman Emperor Charles V (the nephew of Catherine of Aragon), protected her from retribution. But Mary was pessimistic about the future. Warwick had used conservative support to overthrow Somerset, and had looked to Mary for backing for his coup; but she had not, and did not, trust him. 'The conspiracy against the Protector has envy and ambition as its only motives,' she warned the imperial ambassador, François Van der Delft; 'You will see that no good will come of this move.'[9] Indeed, Dorset was at court, hoping that Northumberland would, in the end, prefer to side with evangelicals such as himself, who shared the developing religious beliefs of the King.

It may seem surprising that Frances maintained her closeness to Mary despite their religious differences. It was usual, however, for court women to keep open channels of communication between warring parties and sustain friendships across political and religious divisions. William Cecil's fiercely evangelical sister-in-law, Anne Cooke, would serve in Mary's household a few years later. Frances was simply performing a family duty in maintaining a good relationship with the heir to the throne. The cordial visits Frances and her daughters made to Beaulieu were, however, about to become more difficult. Three days after the Greys' arrival at Beaulieu, the question of whether Warwick was going to base his regime with the religious conservatives was answered resolutely in the negative with Dorset's appointment to the Privy Council. As the imperial ambassador observed, Dorset was 'entirely won over to the new sect'. The most 'forward' of the evangelicals rejoiced at his success.[10] But for Mary his appointment spelled real danger. Dorset's ambitions for his daughter, Jane, were matched, or even exceeded, by his enthusiasm for religious reform. The rediscovery of the New Testament through Greek seemed to the evangelicals to mark the beginning of the breaking of a code through which Satan's puppets in the Vatican had kept religious Truth hidden. Nothing could be more important to Dorset than overthrowing 'the vain traditions of men' expressed through the Church's teaching, in favour of what God willed, as revealed through his Word – and Mary presented an obstacle.

Within weeks of Dorset's promotion, remaining conservatives on the Council were expelled and the imperial ambassador was expressing fears for Mary. Dorset, Northampton and Herbert were the dominant figures in Warwick's 'crew', he said, and all were men who would 'never permit the Lady Mary to live in peace ... in order to exterminate [the Catholic] religion'.[11] Mary would eventually be driven out of England, he believed, forced to change her faith, or even killed. While the political situation remained unsettled the Grey sisters continued to come and go from their father's houses in London and Leicestershire to his half-brother's house in Essex. On 2nd December, Katherine and Mary returned to Tilty, arriving with their attendants and 'a great many gentlemen'. Katherine, in particular, was a light-hearted girl who enjoyed such parties, and little Mary Grey took her cue from her older sister in this regard. But the more serious Jane also joined them at Tilty, on 16th December, with her parents and uncle, Lord John Grey.

The family enjoyed a huge party at Tilty on Christmas Day and further celebrations on the 26th and 27th. The plays and festivities continued until almost the end of January 1550, broken only by a visit Katherine made to the sisters' sole surviving aunt, Elizabeth, the widow of Lord Audley, at nearby Walden Abbey. Lady Audley's only child, Margaret Audley, was a playmate, and also being raised as an evangelical.[12] There were no further journeys recorded to see the Princess Mary at Beaulieu that month. But it is probable the princess continued occasionally to welcome Frances and her daughters in the troubled years ahead. The cousins knew how quickly things could change in politics, and that the time could come when they might need the help of the other.

By February 1550, as the immediate political situation stabilised, the Grey sisters were settled at Dorset House on the Strand with their Willoughby cousins. For their father the rewards of office were already proving plentiful. Over the previous month he had been made Steward of the King's Honours and Constable of Leicester Castle, as well as being granted lands, lordships and manors in Leicestershire, Rutland, Warwickshire, Nottinghamshire, and the Duchy of Lancaster.[13] This vast increase in wealth ensured his wife and children could afford the finest new gowns for court functions where he was in daily attendance on the King.

Edward's day was a busy one. He rose early and was dressed by his four Gentlemen of the Privy Chamber, who remained on their knees throughout. He then enjoyed some exercise: ball games, dancing, riding, shooting the bow or other sports. Breakfast was followed by a morning prayer, and then two hours' tuition in Greek or Latin. Before and after lunch there could be meetings with Councillors. He would then have a lute lesson, an hour of French and then further Latin or Greek, before taking some more physical exercise and entertainments, dinner and bed, with all its attendant rituals. But around the routines of this isolated royal schoolboy, the court had the feeling of an armed camp.

Warwick was extremely security-conscious. A new contingent of guardsmen and armed yeomen had been attached to the King's Privy Chamber, as well as twelve bands of cavalry, of which Dorset commanded a hundred horse.* Access to Edward was also severely restricted. Nothing could be presented to him that had not been approved by the Council and his tutors first. For the Grey sisters, however, conversation with Edward was easier to achieve than for most. Not only was their father constantly at Edward's side, nearly all the King's personal servants were either family friends or relations, or the clients of those who were. Catherine Parr's brother, the Marquess of Northampton, was close at hand as Lord Chamberlain, and his brother-in-law, Sir William Herbert, as Edward's Master of the Horse. Northampton's cousin, Nicholas Throckmorton (who had shouted in support of Anne Askew as she was burned), was Edward's favourite Gentleman of the Privy Chamber, one of the four men who dressed Edward each morning, and played games and sports with him. But the figure who dominated the court was the new Lord President, John Dudley, the Earl of Warwick.

The Lord President, who would play a key role in Lady Jane Grey's future, was a towering figure, albeit one who had emerged from the shadow of the scaffold. His father, Edmund Dudley, had been a faithful servant to Henry VII and a brilliant lawyer. On his master's behalf he had squeezed the rich of their wealth until the pips squeaked. But when the first Tudor king died, the new monarch, the eighteen-year-old Henry VIII, had disassociated himself from his father's unpopular policies. The young John Dudley saw his father set up on charges of treason and executed as a royal public relations exercise. It had made him a cautious man, as well as a ruthless one. People found Warwick physically intimidating, the sense of the soldier's brute power all the more terrifying because he was so unusually controlled. He watched and waited before he made his moves and it was said that he 'had such a head that he seldom went about anything, but he conceived first three or four purposes beforehand'.[14]

It wasn't long before Jane discovered that Warwick had plans for her. He was keen to avoid the mistakes of the Protectorship. That meant treating Edward as a maturing monarch, training him for a gradual introduction into matters of state, while also involving fellow

---

* For this he received £2,000 a year: as much as he had agreed for Jane's wardship.

Privy Councillors in important decision-making. Warwick even hoped to work again with Somerset, who was released from the Tower that month, in February, and invited to rejoin the Privy Council in May. It seemed to Warwick, however, that the best way to bind the new allies was the traditional means of inter-family marriages. Somerset agreed, and the marriages he most wanted for his children were with members of the Grey family. Just as Thomas Sudeley had suspected, Somerset wanted Jane for his son, the young Earl of Hertford. Through his mother Hertford was descended from Edward III. This did not give him any noteworthy claim to the throne, but his smidgen of royal blood raised his rank and made him a suitable match for Jane. Somerset asked also that his elder daughter Anne be married to Jane's fourteen-year-old uncle, Henry Brandon, the Duke of Suffolk, who was being educated alongside the King.

Jane's step-grandmother, Katherine Suffolk, turned Somerset down flat. As she explained to Somerset's secretary – her friend William Cecil, a kinsman of the Greys – she disapproved of child marriages. 'I cannot tell what unkindness one of us might show the other than to bring our children into so miserable a state as not to chose by their own liking,' she told him.[15] Warwick was obliged to step into the breach and marry Anne Seymour to his eldest son, Lord Lisle. But if Somerset was still hoping to capture Lady Jane Grey he hoped in vain. Dorset was prepared to make vague promises about Jane's future, but he declined to write anything down. If there had been any betrothal it would have emerged during government investigations into Hertford's actual marriage in 1560. Dorset believed that he was in a stronger position than he had ever been to achieve the ultimate prize for his favourite daughter. A German client of Dorset called John of Ulm, who was writing to the chief pastor of the Zurich Church, Heinrich Bullinger, and outlining Dorset's role in driving forward religious change, noted how carefully educated Jane was. Dorset was the 'thunderbolt and terror of the papists', he observed, while Jane was 'pious and accomplished beyond what can be expressed'. She was to be the pious Queen of a Godly King, the rulers of a new Jerusalem that Dorset intended to help build.[16]

Chapter VII

Bridling Jane

It was late in the summer of 1550 when the Princess Elizabeth's former tutor, Roger Ascham, arrived at Bradgate. He was en route to take up a post to the English ambassador at the court of Charles V. Ascham had come principally to say goodbye to his wife Alice, and the Astleys, Elizabeth's former governess and her husband: all based at Bradgate since the break-up of Elizabeth's household following Sudeley's arrest. But Ascham also hoped to see Jane, to thank her for a letter of reference she had sent to his new employer. A prime purpose of Jane's education was to coach her to perform on the public stage and the letter demonstrates she was already playing the role of a great patron. As Ascham would discover, however, the thirteen-year-old was finding the pressure intense.

Jane was expected to excel in all fields, including dance and Greek, manners and philosophy, but the duty of obedience was the lesson she was finding hardest to absorb. 'Unless you frame yourself to obey, yea and feel in yourself what obedience is, you shall never be able to teach others how to obey you,' her future nephew, Philip Sidney, would explain to his son.[1] The harder this lesson was taught, however, the more Jane struggled against it, and she had begun to avoid her parents' company. When Ascham reached the house he was told that the entire household was hunting in the park, save for Jane who had chosen to stay behind. He found her alone in her chamber looking 'young and lovely'. She had just broken off from reading Plato's *Phaedo*, which describes the courage Socrates displayed in the face of death. 'When I come to the end of my journey,' Socrates says as he prepares to take hemlock from the executioner, 'I shall obtain that which has been the pursuit of my life.'[2] Many lesser students struggled with the Greek and, perhaps, with its arguments for the immortality of the soul. But to Ascham's amazement it was apparent that Jane read it 'with as much delight as gentlemen read a merry tale in Boccacio'.*

Ascham chatted with Jane for a while, before summoning up the courage to ask why she was reading Plato instead of being in the park with everyone else? Jane smiled and replied that 'all their sport in the park is but a shadow to that pleasure that I find in Plato! Alas! Good folk, they never felt what true pleasure meant.' Ascham, oblivious to the authentic voice of the teenage know-it-all, was delighted to find a young woman with such a love of philosophy, and he wondered what might have drawn her to it 'seeing not many women [and] very few men, have attained thereunto'. At that, however, Jane seized the opportunity to launch an attack on the wrongs she believed she was being dealt at the hands of her parents.

I will tell you, and tell you a truth which perchance ye will marvel at. One of the greatest benefits that ever God gave me is that he sent me so sharp and severe parents and so gentle a schoolmaster. For when I am in presence of either father or mother, whether I speak, keep silence, sit, stand or go, eat, drink, be merry or sad, be sewing, playing, dancing or doing anything else, I must do it, as it were, in such weight, measure and number, even so perfectly as God made the world, or else I am so sharply taunted, so cruelly threatened, yea, presently sometimes with pinches, nips and bobs, and other ways, (which I shall not name, for the honour I bear them), so without measure misordered, that I think myself in hell, till time come that I must go to Mr Aylmer,

---

* The famous collected tales of love by the Italian author who had inspired Chaucer.

who teaches me so gently, so pleasantly, with such fair allurements to learning, that I think all the time nothing whilst I am with him. And when I am called from him, I fall on weeping, because whatever I do else but learning is full of grief, trouble, fear and wholly misliking unto me. And thus my book hath been so much my pleasure, and brings daily to me more pleasure and more that in respect of it, all other pleasures, in very deed, be but trifles and troubles unto me.[3]

Years later, Ascham recorded this conversation in his memoir *The Schoolmaster*, and used it to support his thesis that pupils did better if their tutors treated them kindly. The passage has been misused since, however, as 'proof' of the cruelty of Jane's parents – and especially of Frances – in contrast to the kindliness of Aylmer. Jane, like many girls her age, may well have preferred the world of books to that in which she was forced to engage with demanding adults, but Ascham's image of a kindly Aylmer and bullying parents was never an accurate one, and has been used in a way that would surely have appalled him. The reason for the later slandering of Frances's reputation, in particular, is shameful. Since the eighteenth century she has been used as the shadow that casts into brilliant light the eroticised figure of female helplessness that Jane came to represent. While Jane is the abused child-woman of these myths, Frances has been turned into an archetype of female wickedness: powerful, domineering and cruel. The mere fact that Frances was with the rest of the household in the park, while Jane read her book, became the basis for a legend that she was a bloodthirsty huntress. The scene in Trevor Nunn's 1985 film, *Lady Jane*, in which Frances slaughters a deer on white snow, is inspired by it and establishes her early on in the film as a ruthless destroyer of innocents: a wicked Queen to Jane's Snow White.

A letter Ascham wrote to Jane only a few months after his visit gives a more accurate idea of his feelings at the time than later recollections, which were coloured by subsequent events and the desire to promote his arguments on teaching. That Ascham thought Jane remarkable is evident in this letter. He told her that in all his travels he had not yet met anyone he admired more: he only hoped that

Katherine, who at ten remained a beginner at Greek, would one day follow in her footsteps. He had nothing but good words, however, for both her parents, who, he noted, delighted in her achievements. Dorset had invested in Jane all the hopes a nobleman normally placed in a son, and in the sixteenth century that inevitably meant a rigorous, even harsh, educational regime.

Jane's favourite writer, Plato, was well heeded when he said that children were born for their country, not for themselves – especially if they were destined for high position. Jane was suffering, certainly, but she endured no more than the standard lot of the elite of children and young adults destined to be England's future leaders. The Brandon brothers, much loved by their mother, could not even eat lunch without also being obliged to feed their minds. Before they sat for their meals, the boys were expected to read passages of Greek, then, while 'at meat' they disputed philosophy and divinity in Latin. When the meal concluded, they had to translate the Greek passages they had read at the beginning. Jane chafed at such demands, but the supposedly 'gentle' Aylmer was in complete agreement with Jane's parents that she needed discipline to flourish. As he observed, Jane was 'at that age, [when] as the comic poet tells us, all people are inclined to follow their own ways'. And he asked the advice of leading divines on how best to 'provide bridles for restive horses' such as this spirited girl.[4]

A still more revealing insight into the household at Bradgate is given in the contemporary letters of exiled German divine, John of Ulm, to the Zurich pastor Heinrich Bullinger. Although Ulm admired Dorset, and was supported financially by him, Jane's father emerges from this correspondence as a man of immense vanity. Dorset was forever showing off his 'eloquent' Latin, to learned men, 'with whom he mutually compares his studies'. These included the family's Cambridge-educated chaplain, James Haddon, and the preacher John Wullocke, who would later play a leading role in the Scottish Reformation. While Jane's modern biographers frequently describe Frances as the dominant partner in the marriage, it is Dorset's obsession with his royal connections that is also striking. 'He told me he had the rank of Prince,' Ulm confided in Bullinger, adding that, although Dorset didn't wish to be so styled in public, he was content to be referred to as such in private. Ulm urged Bullinger to flatter Dorset with a dedication to a forthcoming theological work, the fifth part of his *Decades*, on Christian perfection. Ignoring Frances, despite her importance as Henry VII's granddaughter, he added that Bullinger should also cultivate Jane, as the heir of the great 'Prince'.

That autumn, as Ulm waited for Bullinger's promised fifth *Decade*, he translated a portion of the pastor's treatise on Christian marriage from German into Latin for Jane. She responded enthusiastically, retranslating it into Greek and presenting it to her father for the New Year of 1551. 'I do not think there ever lived anyone more deserving of respect than this young lady, if you consider her family,' mused Ulm, '[or] more learned if you consider her age; or more happy if you consider both.'[5]

It was in late April or early May of 1551 that the copies of Bullinger's fifth *Decade* on Christian perfection at last arrived in England. As promised the dedication read: '[To] the most illustrious Prince and Lord, Henry Grey, Marques of Dorset ... a vigorous maintainer of real Godliness'.[6] Dorset had recently left for Berwick, on the volatile border with Scotland, where he served briefly as Warden of the Three Marches responsible for keeping order in the region. But Ulm followed. He reported back to Bullinger that Dorset had arrived in the north with numerous preachers, as well as 300 cavalry. Ulm had delivered the treatise to him and then headed for Bradgate, where 'a most weighty and eloquent epistle' had arrived for Jane, along with another copy of the *Decades*.

Ulm arrived in Leicestershire on 29th May, and spent the following two days, 'very agreeably with Jane, my Lord's daughter, and those excellent and holy persons Aylmer and Haddon [the chaplain]'. Katherine and Mary Grey were, it seems, elsewhere, as was their mother. The family owned properties from Cumberland in the north to Devon in the south-west and Essex in the east. They could have been visiting any of them, staying with friends or acting as the guests of local towns. Even the six-year-old Mary was now being given gifts from burghers seeking her goodwill. The Chamberlain's accounts in Leicester that year record payment of '4sh and 4d' for a 'gallon and a half of wine, peasecod and apples' for Mary, though the wine was surely destined for others.[7]

At Bradgate Ulm found Jane, who had just turned fourteen, anxious to show off her language abilities, and was shown a letter she had written in Greek to Bullinger. It fulfilled all the requirements of the formal style drawn from Greek oration and Ulm was impressed by its maturity. Jane was encouraged to write several further letters to Bullinger over the next two years. They resemble the correspondence of the famous Marguerite of Valois, the late Queen of Navarre, with her spiritual mentor, Bishop Briçonnet of Meaux. The Queen, who died in 1549, had been greatly admired for her brilliance and her piety, and she was the perfect model for a Tudor princess such as Jane. But while Jane's letters are academically impressive, the self-abasement and expansive vocabulary of the high style are unsettling for the modern reader. 'I entertain the hope that you will excuse the more than feminine boldness in me, who, girlish and unlearned as I am, presume to write to a man who is the father of all learning', runs one letter from Jane to Bullinger: 'pardon this rudeness which has made me not hesitate to interrupt your more important vocations with my vain trifles and puerile correspondence.'[8] Happily, however, the young girl can, sometimes, be spotted through the thick verbiage.

In Jane's first letter she expressed amazement that Bullinger could find the time, 'to write from so distant a country, and in your declining age, to me'. Bullinger, at not quite forty-seven, seemed impossibly old to Jane. She was grateful for his 'instruction, admonition and counsel, on such points especially, as are suited to my age and sex and the dignity of my family'. Jane complained she missed the advice she used to receive from the Strasbourg reformer Martin Bucer, who had died in February. Such religious exiles were the principal source of radical ideas in England, and Jane's father, along with his friend Parr of Northampton, their leading patrons on the Privy Council. Jane assured Bullinger, she was now reading the *Decades* every day, gathering 'as out of a most beautiful garden, the sweetest flowers'.[9]

Amongst these were Bullinger's comments, in the dedication to her father, on the importance of reading the Old Testament in Hebrew, as well as reading the New Testament in Greek. She was now learning Hebrew, she said, and asked 'if you will point out some way and method of pursuing this study to the greatest advantage'.[10]

Ulm was certain that Bullinger would be impressed with Jane's 'very learned letter', but he had also heard some interesting gossip at Bradgate, which he passed on. 'A report has prevailed and has begun to be talked of by persons of consequence, that this most noble virgin is to be betrothed and given in marriage to the King's Majesty.'[11] This claim was an extraordinary one. At that very moment, William Parr, Marquess of Northampton, was in France at the head of a diplomatic mission, with instructions to arrange the formal betrothal of Edward to Henri II's daughter Elizabeth. Ulm, however, repeated what he had learned at Bradgate to other friends in Europe.

Uncertain that Bullinger would have time for the task of overseeing Jane's Hebrew, and anxious that Jane's language skills be developed by someone steeped in the theology of Switzerland, Ulm wrote to a professor in Zurich called Conrad Pellican, asking him to help teach Jane her Hebrew. By way of incentive he told Pellican that he had heard she was one day to be married to King Edward, and raved about Jane's 'incredible' achievements thus far. These included, he noted, the 'practice of speaking and arguing with propriety, both in Greek and Latin'.[12]

Jane, it seems, was being trained in the art of rhetoric: the mastery of language as a means to persuade, edify and instruct. It was an area in which a dynamic mind such as hers was likely to excel. But it was also considered suitable only for a woman being prepared for a significant role, such as that of a King's wife. 'Oh! If that event should take place, how happy would be the union and how beneficial to the Church!' Ulm sighed.[13] He admitted, however, that he nursed a fear that the brilliant religious leader being honed at Bradgate might yet be blasted by a 'calamity of the times'. People were suffering the economic fallout of Warwick's deflationary policies and there were major riots again in Leicestershire that summer. It was not revolt, however, but a natural disaster in July that provided the bitterest reminder of just how cruel fate could be. A mysterious disease known as the 'sweating sickness' was sweeping England. The epidemics, which vanished altogether after the sixteenth century, would arrive suddenly and disappear quickly. But, while they lasted, they brought illness and death with frightening speed.

Edward recorded in his journal that the sweat arrived in London on 9th July and immediately proved even more vehement than any epidemic he remembered. If a man felt cold 'he died within three hours and if he escaped it held him for nine hours, or ten at most'. Seventy people died in London the next day, and on the 11th, the King reported, '120 and also one of my gentlemen, another of my grooms fell sick and died'.[14] In Leicestershire, a Bradgate neighbour, Lord Cromwell, succumbed and, on the early morning of the 14th, it struck within the Grey family. In their rooms at Buckden, the former palace of the Bishop of Lincoln, Katherine Suffolk's sons, Henry and Charles, awoke that morning with a sense of apprehension. It was the first symptom of the illness. The brothers were soon seized with violent, icy shivers, a headache and pains in the shoulders, neck and limbs. Within three hours the cold left them and their temperatures rose dramatically. It was then that the characteristic sweating began.

The boys' mother rushed to her children's bedside from her estate at Grimsthorpe in Lincolnshire as their pulses began to race and an incredible thirst took hold. But finally exhaustion brought an irresistible desire to sleep. The elder brother, Henry, Duke of Suffolk, was already dead when their mother arrived. The younger, Charles, followed before seven o'clock on the morning of 15th July. Katherine Suffolk was devastated by their loss. Henry, at fifteen, 'stout of stomach without all pride'; Charles 'being not so ripe in years was not so grave in look, rather cheerful than sad, rather quick than ancient'.[15] She sat alone in the dark, refusing food. The boys' tutor Thomas Wilson worried as he saw his mistress lose weight, 'your mind so troubled and your heart so heavy ... detesting all joy and delighting in sorrow, wishing with [your] heart, if it were God's will, to make your last end'. He begged her to be 'strong in adversity'.[16]

Katherine of Suffolk's friend and Lincolnshire neighbour, William Cecil, also wrote to her with words of comfort. Her letter to him replied miserably that nothing thus far in her life had made her so aware of God's power. That she was being punished for her sins she was certain. The preacher Hugh Latimer had even told her which ones: it was her greed in enclosing land and depriving the poor of food. She could not bear to see anyone, she told Cecil. Although she was certain her children were with God and she knew she should rejoice, she found she could not. At Grimsthorpe she kept their clothes and possessions: black velvet gowns furred with sable, fashionable crimson hose, tennis rackets and the rings they practised catching with lances at the tilt. Her shock and dismay, if not her pain, was felt across the evangelical elite. Her sons were amongst the brightest hopes of their generation. The great Latinist, Walter Haddon, the brother of the Bradgate chaplain James Haddon, wrote a eulogy in their memory; the King's tutor, John Cheke, composed an epitaph, while Wilson wrote a prose biography and several Latin poems, a volume of which was dedicated to Dorset.[17] Jane's place as a Godly leader, by example, for her generation was now more important than ever.

Chapter VIII

❖

Jane and Mary

The chapel at the Princess Mary's palace of Beaulieu lay across the courtyard, opposite the great hall. Inside it had a distinctive layout, with a large ante chapel at right angles to the body of the main chapel. As Jane crossed by this ante chapel she noticed, to her irritation, a consecrated Host was placed on the altar in a golden receptacle known as a 'monstrance'. In Catholic belief the Host was the transformed body of Christ, but to Jane its veneration was the idolatrous worship of a piece of unleavened bread. When Mary's servant, Lady Anne Wharton, walking beside her, dropped to one knee and made the sign of the cross, Jane asked sarcastically whether 'the Lady Mary were there or not?' Lady Wharton replied tartly that she had made her curtsey 'to Him that made us all'. 'Why,' Jane retorted, 'how can He be there that made us all, [when] the baker made him?'[1]

Lady Wharton reported her exchange with Jane to Mary, who is said by the martyrologist John Foxe, to have 'never loved her after'. There is no evidence of that, and Mary later showed fondness for the younger Grey sisters, particularly the affectionate and easy-going Katherine. But the princess had good reason to be both angry and concerned that Jane had insulted her religious beliefs in her own house. At the time of the Grey sisters' last recorded visit to Beaulieu, in November 1549, Mary had guessed already that the fall of the

76

Protectorship had marked only the beginning of her misfortune. After the peace treaty with France six months later, in March 1550, the regime had less to fear from Mary's protector, the Emperor Charles V, and was becoming increasingly radical. The religious changes Jane's father, Dorset, was promoting were the most extreme England would witness before the Puritan Commonwealth a century later. Music was being expunged from churches; art was similarly attacked and tombs destroyed along with their exhortations to pray for the dead. A horrified visitor from Europe described the newly stark appearance of England's churches, with 'no images in relief, nor pictures, no crosses, no sepulchres raised above the ground ... in place of the altar is a table set with a cloth but without candles', on the white surfaces of the church walls were written passages from the Bible, 'in the middle of which one sees the arms of the King'. In Oxford, bonfires were consuming nearly every book in the university library.[2] At the same time Mary found her right to have Mass said publicly in her own chapels was under attack.

Dorset's closest political ally, Parr of Northampton, had led the case against Mary within the Council, arguing that it had been agreed that 'she alone might be privileged with but two or three of her women'. Northampton, described by Roger Ascham as 'beautiful, broad, stern and manly', was cut from similar cloth to Dorset. A sophisticated courtier, educated alongside Dorset in the household of the late Duke of Richmond, he shared Dorset's passion for hunting, learning and, above all, religious reform. The two marquesses are linked in the sources from this period like Tweedle Dum with Tweedle Dee. Together they were always at the King's side and Mary knew that Edward, like Jane, was already showing himself a fervent evangelical. Edward's public note-taking during sermons and his recent striking out of the mention of saints in the oath of a new bishop, had all advertised his enthusiasm for the new religion. She must have feared that, like Jane, he too would attack the practice of her beliefs in her own house, in due course.

By Christmas of 1550 the Council had ordered the arrest of Mary's chaplains for saying Mass in her absence. But worse followed when

Mary visited Edward for the seasonal celebrations. Her warm greeting for her thirteen-year-old brother was met with exactly the confrontation she had surely feared would soon come. With the two marquesses, Dorset and Northampton, standing by to witness her humiliation, Edward cross-questioned his older sister on whether she was having the Mass said publicly in her chapel. She burst into tears under his assault and, to the embarrassment of the two marquesses, the shocked boy then also began to cry. They wrapped up the meeting as quickly as they could, affirming 'that enough had been said and ... that the King had no other thought except to inquire and know all things'.[3] But it was not to be the end of the matter.

Mary's household was a magnet for Catholic dissenters. The Masses she held attracted an important following at court and in the areas in which she lived, while even 'the greatest lords in the kingdom were suitors to her to receive their daughters into her service': amongst them the family of Edward's old playmate, Jane Dormer.[4] It was a problem that needed to be addressed, and Edward followed up what he had said to Mary with a letter demanding she obey his laws on religion.[5] Despite his tears he had not relented. Mary, arguing he was still not of an age to overthrow his father's religious settlement, continued to have Mass said, even laying on extra services 'and with greater show'.[6] But in March 1551 the young King informed Mary that he had suffered her stubbornness long enough and that henceforth she could only hear Mass in her private apartments.[7] When she persisted in having her Mass said in the chapels there were consequences.

At Easter 1551 several of Mary's friends were arrested after attending Mass in her house. By July she feared she was on the point of being imprisoned or even murdered and considered fleeing abroad. In the end she decided that it was her duty to stay. It was August 1551, the month following the death of the Brandon brothers, with the Grey sisters all at Bradgate, when matters came to a head. Three of Mary's servants were ordered to go to Beaulieu and prevent other members of the household from hearing Mass. They refused and were imprisoned for contempt. The King's Council then sent their own men to carry out his orders. They arrived during the rising heat of the morning carrying Edward's letters. Mary received them on her knees, in symbolic submission to the will of the King. As the papers were handed to her, she kissed them, 'but not the matter contained in them,' she said, for that, 'I take to proceed not from his Majesty but from you, his Council.' The silence while she read the letters was broken only by her exclaiming: 'Ah! Good Mr Cecil took much pains here.' Cecil, Katherine Suffolk's friend, had survived the fall of his master Somerset to become Secretary of State. Only as the men left did Mary lose her composure, shouting through a window about the risk to their souls they were taking by their actions. But she knew that this was a battle she had lost. As she admitted, if the Council arrested her chaplains they could not say Mass and she could not hear it. She warned her brother, however, that she 'would lay her head on a block and suffer death' before she heard the Prayer Book service.[8]

The imperial ambassador Jehan Scheyfve complained about Mary's treatment, but to no effect. Warwick insisted it was the King's will and that Edward's orders had as much weight as if he were aged forty. It was Parr of Northampton, however, who articulated once again the most aggressive comment against Mary. He challenged the right of the ambassador to refer to her by the title 'Princess of England', insisting she be referred to only as the King's sister. This had obvious implications for Mary's right to the throne as Edward's heir: a matter of particular concern that autumn. Edward was looking pale and thin after contracting a mysterious illness in the summer, from which he was still recovering. Suddenly, however, the aggressive attacks on Mary began to recede. She was still not allowed to hear Mass outside her private apartments, but Warwick, ever cautious, had reason to be reluctant to risk provoking her continental cousins, the Hapsburgs, further. The Emperor's sister, Mary of Hungary, was threatening to invade England to rescue Edward from his 'pernicious governors', and Mary's humiliating treatment was galvanising support for her in England too. Warwick had discovered, furthermore, that Somerset was hoping to take advantage of this and was plotting with the conservatives to bring him down, together with his radical evangelical 'crew'.

Warwick considered carefully how to manoeuvre Somerset to his destruction. He learned from one of the King's teenage friends, Lord Strange, that Somerset had asked him to promote his daughter, Lady Jane Seymour, in the King's affections by telling Edward how suitable a bride she would be. Only nine years old, but highly educated, Lady Jane Seymour, the niece of Henry VIII's third wife, was already demonstrating a precocious intelligence. With two of her sisters she had celebrated the French peace treaty with the publication in Paris of 130 couplets of Latin verse composed for the tomb of the Queen of Navarre, who had died in 1549. She would one day become Katherine Grey's closest friend. But in 1551 Somerset's ambitions for his daughter threatened Dorset's hopes for his own. None of this constituted treason, however, so Warwick needed to catch Somerset in some other, capital, offence. The answer, shortly arrived at, was to accuse him of planning to invite Warwick and Northampton to a feast and there 'cut off their heads'.[9]

Edward was told about the alleged murder plot during the second week of October. Simultaneously Warwick and his allies were empowered with promotions: Dorset became the Duke of Suffolk, the title having fallen into abeyance with the tragic deaths of the Brandon brothers; Warwick was made Duke of Northumberland.[10] Northampton's brother-in-law, Sir William Herbert, became Earl of Pembroke, while William Cecil was knighted. Five days later, Edward saw his uncle, Somerset, arrive at court at Whitehall 'later than he was wont and by himself'. His journal recorded baldly that: 'After dinner he was apprehended.' Quickly and without fuss Somerset's allies were rounded up: 'Sir Thomas Palmer was taken on the Terrace, walking there. Hammond passing the Vice-Chamberlain's door was called in by John Piers to make a match at shooting and so taken. Likewise John Seymour and Davey Seymour were taken too.' Their ruin had arrived during the banal routines of an ordinary day: with an invitation to a shooting match, a hand on their shoulder as they passed a door, or an encounter during an evening stroll.

It was Harry Suffolk – as the King now called Dorset – who signed the order for Somerset to be sent to the Tower: a neat revenge for the Protector's rival ambitions for the marriage of his daughter. The

Duchess of Somerset joined her husband in the Tower the next day. She was blamed widely for all his troubles. Proud and beautiful, Anne Somerset had never been popular, and damning her served a useful purpose. It helped explain how the man who had helped introduce evangelical religion to England had fallen into wickedness: even the first man, Adam, was brought to sin by Eve, it would have been remembered. The first sign of Mary's rehabilitation at court since she was deprived of her Mass was an invitation in November for the reception of Mary of Guise, the dowager Queen of Scots. She turned it down. It was, instead, Frances who sat on the Queen's left on 4th November 1551, while Edward sat to her right under a shared cloth of state. Jane was also there, as Edward noted in his journal. Beside the funeral of Catherine Parr, it is the first time we know of Jane being present at a public reception.

Jane had ridden with over a hundred other ladies and gentlemen, to escort the dowager Queen of Scots through London to Westminster. In the great banquet that followed she sat with the other court ladies in the Queen dowager's great chamber, enjoying three courses of delicacies. The court women were all dressed 'like peacocks' in jewels and rich clothes, their hair loose as a compliment to the Scots style. There was no sign of the Princess Elizabeth, any more than of her half-sister Mary, but Elizabeth had met the Queen dowager earlier in the week and had left a memorable impression. While most guests had their long hair 'flounced and curled and double curled' on to silk-clad shoulders, Elizabeth had 'altered nothing, but to the shame of them all kept her old maidenly shamefastness'.[11] Elizabeth had a natural gift for visual messages, and this one was designed to appeal to her brother.

The King's tutor in political affairs, William Thomas, had presented his master recently with a work promoting modest and Godly dress in women. Elizabeth, whose reputation had been so tainted by her association with Sudeley, had cleverly stolen a march on Jane as the leading evangelical princess. But Jane's father, together with her tutor Aylmer, were equally determined that the younger girl learn quickly from Elizabeth's example. Just before Christmas a series of letters went out from the Grey family's magnificent new home at Suffolk Place in Southwark, which Frances had inherited from the Brandon brothers. They were directed to the pastor of the Zurich Church, Bullinger. Jane's father begged Bullinger to continue guiding his daughter in modesty and decorum, writing to her 'as frequently as possible'.[12] Aylmer then wrote asking specifically that Bullinger should 'instruct my pupil, in your next letter, as to what embellishment and adornment of person is becoming in a young woman professing Godliness'. He noted that despite Elizabeth's example, and preachers declaring against fashionable finery, at court 'no one is induced ... to lay aside, much less look down upon, gold, jewels and the braiding of hair'. If Bullinger addressed the subject to Jane directly, however, he believed 'there will probably, through your influence, be some accession to the ranks of virtue'.*

Aylmer need not have been so anxious about Jane. The enormous effort that had gone into her education had shaped by now a most determined evangelical, and she was not short of reminders of the futility of vanity. On every barge trip to Whitehall, Jane passed Seymour Place where Catherine Parr had lain with her ambitious husband. Next to it was Somerset House, the Renaissance palace that the former Protector had been building, and would never live to see completed. In December, Somerset was tried and condemned to death on the basis of the trumped-up murder plot, with the new Dukes of Suffolk and Northumberland – Grey and Dudley – his judges. Many evangelicals were horrified that the man who had introduced 'true religion' into England should die convicted of attempted murder. Harry Suffolk assured the German John of Ulm that the King was keen to spare his uncle's life, and claimed Northumberland hoped this would be possible. But although the Archbishop of Canterbury, Thomas Cranmer, begged Northumberland to show Somerset mercy, the Lord President's principal concern was that the sentence be carried out with minimum disruption.

---

* It is likely that, like the Queen of Navarre, Jane would have used her mentor's letters in her spiritual meditations.

Edward, the kindly child who had comforted his friends when they lost at cards, was to play the role of executioner of a second uncle. But first, a spectacular Christmas season was planned at Greenwich, providing a distraction from the grim task ahead. The great public spaces of the royal palaces were like bare stages when the King was not in residence and for weeks carpenters and painters, masons and joiners had been put to work. Furniture and tapestries were added to the public rooms and silver plate brought, along with any other props necessary, 'to glorify the house and feast'.[13] When Christmas arrived there were plays, masques, tournaments, and a Lord of Misrule. This pagan survival was vested on a courtier who presided over a world turned upside down. Even an execution could be parodied – and was. Misrule attended the decapitation of a hogshead of wine on the scaffold at Cheapside in January, and the red juice flowed to cries of laughter instead of dismay.[14] At Suffolk Place, however, the twelve-day festivities enjoyed by the young Grey sisters were more determinedly decorous.

The family chaplain, James Haddon, complained to Bullinger that the common people of England insisted on amusing themselves 'in mummeries and wickedness of every kind'. But, he reported smugly, this was not the case with 'the family in which I reside'.[15] The austerity we associate with seventeenth-century Puritanism was already evident in the household. John Aylmer disapproved of music at home as well as at church, and the three Grey sisters were expected to limit the amount of time they spent playing or listening to it. Thus deprived, Katherine and Mary later showed no great interest in music that we know of. There was some friction, however, between the pious expectations of Aylmer and Haddon on the one side, and the great living expected of the nobility as a reflection of their status. The servants at Suffolk Place were banned from playing cards at Haddon's insistence, but Frances and her husband continued to do so in their private apartments, and for money.

Haddon put his employers' bad behaviour down to 'force of habit' and 'a desire not to appear stupid, and not good fellows, as they call it'. He had hoped to shame them into change by addressing their failings in a sermon to the household on the wickedness of cards, but was given short shrift for it. Even the Godly King Edward liked to gamble and Haddon confessed that the duke and duchess had told him he was 'too strict'. It was hard, Haddon moaned to Bullinger, to persuade courtiers to 'conquer and crucify themselves'.[16] The eleven-year-old Katherine, who showed no signs of wanting to mimic Elizabeth in anything, must have been a particular concern. But Haddon's frustration was alleviated somewhat by Jane. She had responded enthusiastically to Aylmer's suggestion that she imitate Elizabeth's plain style of dress, and in the process made a point of snubbing the Princess Mary. Aylmer later recalled that Mary had sent one of her ladies to Jane with a set of fine clothes of 'tinsel cloth of gold and velvet, laid over with parchment lace of gold'. New Year was the traditional time for such gifts. But Jane, looking at the magnificent gown, asked the gentlewoman brusquely: 'What shall I do with it?' 'Marry,' the woman replied, 'wear it.' 'Nay,' snapped Jane, 'that would be a shame to follow my lady Mary against God's word, and leave my Lady Elizabeth who followeth God's word.'[17] Aylmer felt no small satisfaction over this incident, which he recorded after Elizabeth became Queen.

With the Christmas season over, Londoners awoke early on the morning of 22nd January to find a curfew in place. The streets were full of soldiers. Somerset's execution was about to take place on Tower Hill. As was so often the case with state killings, efforts to veneer the crude business of taking a man's life were disrupted by moments of farce. Somerset was making a dignified final speech from the scaffold when it was interrupted by the arrival of two horsemen clattering on the cobbles. A cry went up: 'A pardon, a pardon, God save the duke!' and hats were cast into the air. But Somerset realised before most in the crowd that the horsemen had come to witness the execution. He begged them to be quiet so that he could prepare to die. It was not yet 8 a.m. when he tied his handkerchief around his eyes. He admitted he was afraid and as he laid his head on the block there was a sudden flush in his cheeks. But he was ready for the end. Unfortunately the executioner was not. The collar of

Somerset's shirt covered part of his neck. The headsman asked Somerset to stand up again and move it. He did so and when the axe fell at last it struck cleanly, cutting off his head with one blow. The duke's corpse was then thrown into a cart and returned to the Tower for burial.[18]

Somerset's ten children – some no more than infants – were left parentless. Their mother remained in the Tower; their father's property was attainted and returned to the crown. The twelve-year-old Hertford, who had tried to save his father in 1549 by galloping to Wiltshire to beg for help in defence of the Protectorship, lost his title along with much of his inheritance. It was as plain Edward Seymour that he was placed as the ward of Northumberland's elder son, the Earl of Warwick. The earl was married to Hertford's sister, Anne, but she could not easily console him. She suffered a physical collapse after the execution. His younger sister, the nine-year-old Lady Jane Seymour, whom Somerset had wished to marry to the King, was left in a kind of limbo until May. She was then placed in the care of the widowed Lady Cromwell in Leicestershire, not far from Bradgate, from where Harry Suffolk could keep an eye on her. For Somerset's royal nephew, meanwhile, the belief that his uncle's fate was God's work, and he was only God's instrument, may have assuaged the agony and guilt of signing the death warrant. But some later remembered that he used to cry in his rooms, and another contemporary story survives that hints at emotional turmoil.

An Italian, visiting England shortly after Somerset's execution in 1552, witnessed a grim incident that took place during a boating trip in the presence of the court. Edward asked to see a falcon, which he had been told was the best he had. He then demanded it be skinned alive. The falconer did as the King ordered. As Edward then looked on the bird's gruesome remains, he commented: 'This falcon, so much more excellent than the others, has been stripped, just as I, the first among all the others of the realm, am skinned.'[19] Brutally deprived of his mother's family, his loneliness must have felt raw indeed. Several of Somerset's allies were also executed, although Somerset's old friend, Sir William Paget, who had written desperately in the middle of Christmas night 1548, warning him of the folly of his arrogance, was more fortunate. He was merely accused of fraud and humiliated by having the Garter taken from him as one who had no gentle blood on his mother or his father's side. All that now remained was for Northumberland's 'crew' to turn on each other, as their children were pushed ever further into the already blood-soaked political arena.

PART TWO

❖

Queen and Martyr

❖

'. . . you would not be a queen?'

'No, not for all the riches under heaven.'

Henry VIII, Act II scene iii
William Shakespeare

Chapter IX

No Poor Child

In May 1552 Jane turned fifteen, the same age at which her mother had been betrothed, and she had no serious rivals left as Edward's future bride. Lady Jane Seymour was now the daughter of an executed criminal. Plans for Edward to marry the daughter of the French King, Henri II, had also fallen through in March, when Edward had formally declined to ally against the Emperor, Charles V. Increasingly, furthermore, Jane was being treated as the leading evangelical woman in England. She was being sought out as a patron by such figures as Michel Angelo Florio, the first pastor of the Stranger's Church for religious exiles in London, and was looked up to and admired by pious, female intellectuals, as Catherine Parr had once been.[1]

An anonymous letter in Greek written to Jane at about this time, and believed to be from Sir William Cecil's wife, Mildred Cooke, enclosed with it a gift. It was a work by Basil the Great, the fourth-century Bishop of Caesarea, whom Lady Cecil had translated and with whose greatness Jane was now compared. 'My most dear and noble Lady,' the letter began. Basil the Great had excelled 'all the bishops of his time both in the greatness of his birth, the extent of his erudition, and the glowing zeal of his holiness'; yet Jane was his match, 'worthy both in consideration of your noble birth, and on account of your learning and holiness'. The gift of this book was only 'ink and paper', but it was expected that the profit Jane would gain from it would be more 'valuable than gold and precious stones'.[2] The phrase would stick in Jane's mind. It referred to the Old Testament axiom that wisdom was worth more than rubies, and this was something she passionately believed to be true.[3] Jane remained in regular correspondence with the theologian and pastor Heinrich Bullinger, and sent his wife gifts, including gloves and a ring. But she was also widening her circle of contacts in Europe. Jane was keen particularly for Bullinger to introduce her to Theodore Biblander, who had translated the Koran, as well as being a famous scholar of Hebrew. It was said later that she had even begun to learn Arabic.[4]

Jane hoped her pretty sister Katherine would follow in her footsteps, not just in the study of Greek, but also in piety. Katherine was still not yet showing many signs of having a serious nature, and little Mary had not yet begun to study classical languages, but both were very young, and much could be expected of them in the future.

Watching, meanwhile, as Jane continued to step confidently forward on the public stage, her father surely hoped that it would now not be long before his ambitions for her to be a Queen consort were fulfilled. Edward, like Jane, was maturing fast. The King had been attending Council meetings since August 1551 and much was being made of the fact that he had passed his fourteenth birthday. It was at this age that his late cousin, James V of Scotland, had come into his majority and Edward had insisted his orders no longer needed to be co-signed by the full Council. Such self-assurance gave the regime confidence in facing down the charge that it was illegal to make changes to the national religion during his minority. Edward was 'no poor child, but a manifest Solomon in Princely wisdom', trumpeted the polemicist John Bale, as a radically revised Prayer Book was prepared for publication.[5] This book was everything Harry Suffolk hoped for.

Strongly influenced by Bullinger and other Swiss reformers, the new Prayer Book was to sweep away all the half measures of 1549, damning the 'fables' of the Mass and offering a reshaped funeral service that removed all prayers for the 'faithful departed'. The sense of a connection between the living and the dead, central to medieval religion, was finished. One of the Grey sisters' family chaplains, a man called Robert Skinner, was also working with their friend Cecil on a new statement of doctrine, forty-two articles of faith that would take the English Church closer to the Swiss model.[6] But while the revolution continued at brisk pace, there were growing divisions within its ranks. Archbishop Cranmer would never forgive Northumberland for the execution of the 'Godly Duke' of Somerset and was concerned by the increasing radicalism on the Privy Council, led by Harry Suffolk, Parr of Northampton and Northumberland. Cranmer refused to abolish kneeling for communion in the new Prayer Book and was furious when the Council allowed a final coda, a 'black rubric', inspired by the radical John Knox, that explained kneeling was permitted only to add dignity to the service.

Meanwhile, others within the elite had more secular concerns. The King's coffers were empty, and there were many who were envious and afraid of the influence Northumberland wielded over Edward. Having engaged the King's trust with his enthusiastic support for religious reform, Northumberland had sealed it by maintaining a close relationship with the boy. He had become a father figure: according to a servant of the French ambassador, the Sieur de Bois-dauphin, Edward revered Northumberland almost as if he were the older man's subject, rather than the other way round. Periodically, there were even accusations that Northumberland wished to be King himself. Only one man stood out as a potential rival to Northumberland's position, his fellow soldier-politician, William Herbert, Earl of Pembroke, and the Welshman's position at court was looking increasingly shaky.

Pembroke had benefited hugely from his marriage to Anne Parr, sister of the late Queen dowager, Catherine. It had made him a member of Edward's extended family, while Northumberland remained an outsider. But when Anne Parr died in February 1552, Northumberland moved quickly to take advantage of Pembroke's weakened position. Within two months Pembroke had been sacked from his role as Master of the Horse, which had given him close access to Edward, and replaced with Northumberland's elder son, the young Earl of Warwick. There is some evidence that Pembroke intended to retrieve his position by marrying his son Henry, Lord Herbert to Katherine Grey. His wife had been an old friend of Frances, dating back to their days in Catherine Parr's Privy Chamber, and a betrothal may have been discussed, or even arranged, before she died.[7] In any event, the next logical move for Northumberland was to secure a royal relative of his own.

Northumberland's elder three children (all sons) were married. But his fourth son, Lord Guildford Dudley, was not. A later story that he was his mother's favourite is a myth,[8] but Guildford was a handsome youth of seventeen, tall and fair-haired – personal attributes that were all by the way. In great families it was the eldest son who was important, followed by his sisters, who were given dowries and expected to form great alliances. Younger sons were worth no more than 'what the cat left on the malt heap'. Guildford Dudley's elder brother, Lord Robert Dudley, the future Earl of Leicester, had married the daughter of a Norfolk squire because, as a third son, only a respectable union was expected of him. Guildford was even further down the pecking order; but nevertheless, Northumberland had a very ambitious marriage in mind for him.

Jane's father would never have agreed to her marrying Guildford. But there was another royal, who like Jane was an heiress of marriageable and childbearing age. The bride Northumberland had in mind was the fifteen-year-old Margaret Clifford, daughter of Frances's late sister, Eleanor. She was, like the Grey sisters, a descendant of Henry VII through their mutual grandmother, Mary Brandon, Duchess of Suffolk. She was also the heir to vast estates in the north, where Northumberland hoped to become a great magnate. Unsurprisingly, Margaret's father, the Earl of Cumberland, had no wish to marry his daughter to a fourth son and made a series of excuses as to why it was not possible. But Northumberland then asked the King to intervenc. It was a mark of just how much influence he had with Edward that while he was with the army attending to disorders in the Northern Marches, the King was busy acting as his marriage broker.

On 4th July, Edward sent an extraordinary letter to Cumberland 'desiring him to grow to some good end forthwith in the matter of marriage between the Lord Guildford and his daughter; with licence to the said earl and all others that shall travail therein to do their best for conducement of it'.[9] Cumberland was left to digest this royal command as Edward's first summer progress began. It was to take him to the towns and palaces of the south, offering the first opportunity for people outside London to see their King. On 7th July they removed to the royal palace of Oatlands, then to Guildford and Petworth; then to the house of Sir Anthony Brown in Sussex, where the King thought they were over-feasted. Harry Suffolk, always at the King's side, attended the monarch with twenty-five personal cavalrymen, riding under the Grey standard of a silver unicorn in a sunbeam of gold. We don't know where the sisters were that summer, but their mother had been taken ill and they may have remained with her at Sheen, in Richmond, a former Carthusian monastery, granted to Harry Suffolk after Somerset's trial and conviction. Come August, the citizens of Portsmouth, Southampton and Salisbury were out in force to greet Edward's arrival.

The delighted crowds, cheering their King, saw a boy of almost fifteen in scarlet silks and jewelled caps who, despite being small for his age and slightly built, bore himself with all the gravitas of a Tudor monarch. It was a relief to all that Edward appeared happy and well. There had been a scare in April when Edward had fallen ill with measles and smallpox, but he seemed to have recovered, as he had from his bout of illness the previous summer. For Harry Suffolk, anxiety focused instead on Frances. Her condition became so serious that around 25th August he was called home urgently. He wrote a note to Cecil on the 26th making his excuses for his sudden departure from court. 'She has a constant burning ague and stopping of the spleen,' he told Cecil; 'it is to be feared death must follow.'[10]

Happily, his prayers, and those of their children, were answered. Frances survived whatever it was that had ailed her. The King, however, despite appearances – enjoying himself, as he wrote to a friend, 'in pleasant journeys, in good fare' – was already in Death's grasp and the world of the Grey sisters was about to come crashing down.[11]

The New Year of 1553 was heralded at Greenwich Palace with 'sports and pastimes for the King's diversion; which were in as great variety and pomp, as scarcely ever had been seen before'.[12] At the traditional exchange of gifts Frances presented Edward with a purse of knit silver and gold containing £40 in half sovereigns. He in turn gave her three covered gilt bowls, a mark of his continued affection for the family. A more substantial gift followed a little later that month when Edward granted her husband yet another great property, the Minories, a former abbey near the Tower. Royal regard always carried with it significant material benefit and their friend, the 'broad, stern and manly' Marquess of Northampton, was also living in style in a new London residence. The fact that it was formerly Winchester House, the residence of the conservative bishop, Stephen Gardiner, who was now in the Tower, must have made that success all the sweeter. ''Tis merry with the lambs, now the wolf is shut up' was Katherine Suffolk's comment.[13]

Jane, while enjoying the festivities of the season, knew, however, that all was not well with her cousin the King. He seemed unable to shake off a nasty cough and had not had the strength to write his journal since the end of November. As increasingly he struggled to clear his lungs, the imperial ambassador Scheyfve began to wonder if his cough was 'a visitation and a sign from God'. Evidence from medical historians suggests that Edward had tuberculosis, contracted in the summer of 1551 and reactivated when he caught measles the previous April. According to a Spanish source, Mary had begun to pick up hints of plans to exclude her from the succession that summer, 1552.[14] But while it was inevitable that Edward's possible death and the issue of the succession would be considered when the King had been gravely ill, Northumberland and his allies would not have disbanded their private bands of cavalry, as they had done in November 1552, if they had appreciated then the severity of the King's condition. The famous Italian astrologer, Girolamo Cardano, who was much admired by Edward's tutor, Sir John Cheke, had, at the end of the summer, cast the King's horoscope and declared he would live for forty years. It was only now becoming apparent to them that the man could prove wrong.

By the beginning of February the King's cough was causing him considerable pain and the Princess Elizabeth sensed a cooling in her relationship with her brother. She wrote a letter expressing concern about his health and querying gossip that she had lost his goodwill.[15] Her sister, Mary, meanwhile, took a more aggressive stance and put on a demonstration of strength. She arrived in London on 6th February to see Edward, attended by a retinue of over two hundred. The regime responded with a great display of respect. Everyone was very aware that she was Edward's heir under the terms of her father's will and the last Act of Succession of 1544, which had been confirmed in Edward's own Treasons Act of 1547.[16] Northumberland's eldest son, Warwick, was sent to greet her, while Frances joined the Duchess of Northumberland to ride in Mary's train through the capital. This show of togetherness could not, however, disguise the threat that Mary's possible succession posed to the regime and to the evangelical religion.

Northumberland was unpopular in the country, which was impoverished and, in many areas, angry over the religious changes, while Mary had good reason to resent him, along with Suffolk and Northampton. There had been no let up in the ban on her Mass. The imperial ambassador believed that the coming Parliament would give the King his majority, and so enable him to write a legal will that would exclude Mary from the throne.[17] Northumberland was concerned, however, that the Commons would be difficult to manage in the poor economic climate. A controversial subject like the succession risked unlocking debate on many sources of discontent, and the regime couldn't afford to lose control of events with Edward now so obviously ill.[18] Beside, it had been argued with success since 1551 that Edward's orders had as much weight as if he were forty.

The pale and sickly King made a brief appearance in the ceremonies at the opening of Parliament on 1st March. Afterwards,
however, when the velvet and ermine robes were packed away again,
he lay in his rooms, exhausted, and remained there for over a fortnight. The Venetian ambassador, who saw him, thought it clear he
was dying. When Parliament was dismissed at the end of the month
nothing had been discussed concerning Edward's majority or the
succession. But the evidence suggests that, as the weather grew
warmer and the King enjoyed a brief revival in his health, it was put
to Edward that he write a will. He proved able to do so in his own
hand.[19]

Headed boldly 'My Device for the Succession', Edward's subsequent testament covered barely more than one side of a sheet of
paper. The fifteen-year-old was certain he was on the mend and his
will explored the succession in the manner of an academic exercise
rather than an urgent legal document. The first and most important
decision Edward made was to exclude his half-sisters, Mary and Elizabeth, from any right to the crown. According to an anonymous
French source, Edward's pious tutor, Sir John Cheke (knighted in
1552), and his confessor, Thomas Goodrich, Bishop of Ely, urged him
on in this.[20] But it is unlikely they needed to. Cheke's tutorage had
shaped Edward's mind, and although Edward later justified his
actions on the grounds of his sisters' illegitimacy, it was the need to
protect the religion in which he had been raised that dominated his
thinking.[21] Edward feared, he admitted, that Mary would undo his
religious programme. He had not forgotten, furthermore, that Elizabeth's mother had died a traitor to his father and an adulteress,
hardly the ideal beginning for a Godly dynasty.[22] Having excluded his
sisters, Edward then bypassed the Stuart line, as his father had done.
The explanation he outlined was a nationalist one. The leading
representative of the Stuart line, Mary Queen of Scots, was foreign
born (and, it was later argued, therefore excluded under a law dating
back to the reign of Edward III). The next in importance, her cousin,
Lady Margaret Douglas, had three strikes against her: she was of
questionable legitimacy, married to a Scot (Matthew Stuart, Earl of

Lennox) and her sons were being raised as Catholics. That left Frances, the senior representative of the Brandon line, next in line to the throne. Edward, however, still more than his father, believed that only a man should wield the full authority of the crown. Henry VIII's objections to female rule had been pragmatic ones, and reasons of personal and dynastic vanity; but for Edward antipathy to female rule had a religious basis.

The campaigns against idolatry had expunged all that was sacred and feminine from churches: Catholic devotion to the mother of God was considered by reformers to be a diversion from the proper worship of Christ and the crowned figures of the Virgin had been destroyed along with those of ordinary female saints and mystics. There was no longer a Queen of Heaven and according to the evangelicals' reading of Scripture, rule by women on earth was also ungodly, being against the divine order. Edward left his throne, therefore, not to a woman, but to the sons Frances might have, followed by the sons her daughters might have and after them those of her niece, Margaret Clifford. He then considered the implications of another male minority. Though Edward had not had a mother to watch over his interests during his minority, he was aware of historical cases of women ruling as regents on behalf of their underage sons. He declared therefore that Frances – or whoever proved to be the mother of the heir – could be 'governor' until her son reached the age of eighteen.[23] To ensure this didn't break any biblical injunctions against female rule, he added a proviso that the regent could do nothing without the sanction of an inner core of the Privy Council, and when the boy reached fourteen, his agreement would also be required (an indication that Edward believed he personally had passed a significant birthday). As yet, of course, there were no male children in the Brandon line, but Edward decreed that if this remained the case on his death, then Frances was to be appointed governor until such time as one was born. He clearly did not think this a likely event, however, since he made no further mention of the Council's sanction for her rule.

By 11th April, Edward was still well enough to leave the gloom of Westminster and travel by barge to the airy rooms of Greenwich

Palace. The guns on the Tower and the ships on the Thames fired their salutes in farewell, the great booms sounding a sombre note to those travelling with the dying King.[24] His will had left the throne, on his death, an empty chair. He had named only those female vessels through which heirs might be born. Of these Frances alone was married, and her husband was not considered an impressive politician or soldier. He had lasted only a few months in his post of Warden of the Northern Marches in 1551. If he could not cope with a few Scottish raiders and criminal families, how could he be trusted to keep England from civil war during a regency? Furthermore, although at thirty-five Frances was still of childbearing age, no child of hers had survived since Mary Grey had been born nine years earlier and she had been so ill the previous summer that she had nearly died. As the implications of this dawned on those who had most to lose from Mary Tudor's possible accession, it seemed clear that the only answer was to marry off the next generation of royal princesses. The Grey sisters, and their cousin Margaret Clifford, had to be lined up for a race to the birthing stool, and married in a manner that would bind the most effective and ruthless members of the regime against Mary Tudor's cause.

According to William Cecil, it was Northampton's second wife, Elizabeth Brooke, who came up with the idea that Jane Grey be married to Northumberland's fourth son, Lord Guildford Dudley.[25] Five years earlier the Protector Somerset had thrown Northampton off the Council for living with Brooke as his wife. Since he had become a leading member of Northumberland's 'crew', however, a private bill had been passed through Parliament that declared his childhood marriage to Lady Anne Bourchier void and that to Elizabeth Brooke valid, 'as if the said lady Anne had been naturally dead'. It meant Northampton could keep control of the vast Bourchier estates, as if he were a widower, as well as allowing his marriage to Brooke to be recognised. If Mary became Queen, however, all this would be reversed: there was no question of her allowing divorce, for she regarded marriage as a sacrament that could not be broken. Brooke had good reason, therefore, to want to prevent Mary becoming Queen, just as her husband did. Parr of Northampton has been despised by generations of historians for his weaknesses of intellect and character. But incompetence does not equate to a lack of ambition, and he knew that a marriage between Guildford Dudley and Jane Grey would ensure that John Dudley, Duke of Northumberland did not switch sides.

Northumberland's evangelical beliefs had shallower roots than those of Northampton and Harry Suffolk. When he was plotting the fall of the Protectorate he had demonstrated a willingness to consider working with religious conservatives. There was a danger he would do so again. Brooke, or her husband, appears to have broached the marriage plans first to her former brother-in-law, Pembroke, who hoped to marry Katherine Grey to his son. Pembroke in turn then approached Northumberland.[26] The duke proved enthusiastic. The Greys, however, would take more convincing. Frances claimed later she had vigorously opposed the match between Guildford and Jane, and it is possible that she did so. She had previously indicated that she did not want Jane to marry while very young.[27] Her husband may also have had political concerns about the proposal. If Jane married Guildford and had a son, control of the crown would slip from the Greys to the Dudleys, and in particular to the intimidating figure of Northumberland.[28]

This would explain why Northumberland was driven reportedly to use threats and promises to get Harry Suffolk's consent. The marriage was the King's wish, Suffolk was told, and would gain him a 'scarcely imaginable haul of immense wealth and great honour to his house'.[29] Jane was then obliged to accept the decision, although it was later claimed she also did so only reluctantly.[30] She must have known there had been hopes that she would marry the king. The junior grandson of the executed traitor, Edmund Dudley, was surely a disappointing replacement, and the speed with which the marriage was arranged gave Jane little time to be reconciled to it.

A few days later, on 28th April 1553, the imperial ambassador recorded news of Jane's betrothal and of the King's deteriorating condition. Every day he grew thinner and his agonising cough, worse. 'The matter he ejects from his mouth is sometimes coloured a greenish yellow and black, sometimes pink, like the colour of blood,' the ambassador noted. 'His doctors and physicians are perplexed and do not know what to make of it. They feel sure the King has no chance of recovery unless his health improves in the next month.'

As the King's health failed, Northumberland remained assiduous in his treatment of Mary, hoping not to raise her suspicions of the plans being laid against her. In stark contrast to 1551, when Parr of Northampton had insisted that Mary not be referred to as a princess, Northumberland now emphasised her right to her full arms as a 'Princess of England'. 'This all seems to point to his desire to conciliate the said Lady and earn her favour, and to show that he does not aspire to the crown,' the imperial ambassador observed. He added, however, that the news of Jane's betrothal to Guildford looked suspicious, and he was not alone in this assessment.[31] Rumours that the King was dying had reached the public, and in the taverns and markets the marriage was 'much murmured at'. Those who were wise kept their views to themselves, the antiquarian William Harrison recalled later in the century; but the foolish openly expressed concerns for the King's well-being and several men and women had their ears cut off for spreading such stories.[32]

Mary's allies at court were, however, keeping her informed of the developing situation, while her household built up support for her in the areas where she held her estates. Unaware how powerful she was growing, the regime was, meanwhile, making a belated effort to prevent her gathering recruits at court by seeking to address quarrels within its ranks. Strenuous efforts were made to heal the rift with Archbishop Cranmer that had opened after Somerset's execution, and plans were laid to release the Protector's widow, Anne Somerset, from the Tower.

It soon emerged that William Herbert, the Earl of Pembroke, was also back in Northumberland's embrace. His son, Henry, Lord Herbert and Lord Guildford Dudley, were to become brothers-in-law, with the twelve-year-old Katherine Grey marrying Pembroke's son on the same day that Jane Grey was to marry Guildford. At twelve Katherine was only just old enough under canon law to be legally wed, but she, at least, was not unhappy at the news. She knew and liked the fifteen-year-old Lord Herbert. Poor little Mary Grey, aged eight, was to be betrothed to a middle-aged kinsman, Lord Grey of Wilton. His face had been disfigured by a Scottish pike, thrust through the roof of his mouth at the battle of Pinkie in 1547, and the battle-scarred warrior must have looked terrifying to the undersized Mary. He was regarded, however, as 'the best soldier in the kingdom': a man to have on your side if there was to be fighting ahead.[33]

Three further marriages designed to unite and shore up the regime were also planned. Though the number of names may seem confusing only one detail is really significant: these marriages all bound Northumberland's family closer to the Greys and to other significant royals. Northumberland's youngest son, Henry Dudley, was to marry Suffolk's only evangelical niece of marriageable age, Margaret Audley. His daughter, Catherine Dudley – also aged only twelve – was to marry Henry Hastings, the teenage son of the Greys' neighbour, the Earl of Huntingdon. Huntingdon had never been close to Northumberland, but his wife was of Yorkist royal descent, making his son an evangelical male with a claim to the throne, albeit a distant one. The third marriage was announced a few weeks later. The Earl of Cumberland who had rejected Guildford Dudley for his royal daughter, Margaret Clifford, despite the pleading of the King, now mysteriously agreed to marry her instead to Northumberland's ageing older brother, Sir Henry Dudley. Since he was conservative in religion, and had nothing to fear from Mary's accession, he appears to have bowed to pressure of a different kind: fear, not of Mary Tudor, but of Northumberland. The duke's modern apologists claim that these six arranged marriages were just normal aristocratic unions. But nobody at the time thought so, or even pretended that this was the case. It would be truer to say that he was not the only one to benefit from them: if the evangelical elite was to stay in power they needed Northumberland on their side. And this was the price.

Chapter X

A Married Woman

On 25th May 1553,[1] Northumberland's London residence, Durham House, witnessed a triple wedding. The young couples wore silver and gold, fabrics forfeited to the King from the Duke of Somerset in 1551 and, figuratively at least, marked with his blood. Guildford towered over Jane, but the fifteen-year-old Henry, Lord Herbert, standing alongside the twelve-year-old Katherine, just looked ill. He had been brought from his sick bed, where he had been lying for weeks. The young Lord Hastings was the third groom, matched with another child bride, Guildford's sister, the twelve-year-old Lady Catherine Dudley. The King, too unwell to attend, sent 'presents of rich ornaments and jewels' and the English nobility turned out in force. There were games and jousts, a great feast and two masques, one performed by the men of the court, the other by the women.

Observing this extravagant spectacle of blood pacts and power politics was the French ambassador, Boisdauphin. The French were as opposed to Mary becoming Queen as any English evangelical. They remained at war with her cousin, the Emperor Charles V, and feared that Mary, who had long looked to him for protection, might one day wish to wield her kingdom in his defence.[2] It was now widely accepted at court that Edward was dying and a decision over the succession was, therefore, imminent. Northumberland hoped

The French Queen, Mary Tudor, younger sister of Henry VIII and her husband, Charles Brandon, Duke of Suffolk. Henry nominated their granddaughters, the Grey sisters, heirs to the Princess Elizabeth.

The tomb at Westminster Abbey of Frances Grey (née Brandon), Duchess of Suffolk, the mother of the Grey sisters.

The ruins of Bradgate Manor, Leicestershire, one of the most romantic places in England.

Thomas Seymour of Sudeley, Lord Admiral of England, womaniser and guardian of Lady Jane Grey.

Above Catherine Parr, the sensual widow of Henry VIII and the first queen in English history to publish her own original work.

Edward Seymour, the 'Godly' Duke of Somerset and Lord Protector of England.

The step-grandmother of the Grey sisters, Katherine Brandon (née Willoughby), Duchess of Suffolk, 'the greatest heretic in the kingdom'.

Henry Brandon, Duke of Suffolk, 'stout of stomach without all pride', who was educated in a similar manner to Jane Grey but who died aged fifteen after succumbing to the fatal 'sweating sickness'.

Charles Brandon, who died aged fourteen on the same day and of the same illness as his brother, leaving their mother childless and grief-stricken.

William Parr, Marquess of Northampton and close ally of the Grey sisters' father, Harry Grey, Marquess of Dorset and Duke of Suffolk.

Above Edward VI, who was said to be 'no poor child, but a manifest Solomon in Princely wisdom'.

Left Jane Dormer, Countess (later Duchess) of Feria, playmate of Edward VI and favourite Maid of Honour to Mary I. She was involved in plans to smuggle Katherine Grey out of England.

My deuise for the Succession. ~~made~~   317

1 ~~For lakke~~ of 1554 ~~of~~ my body ᴀ. To the L Fran̄
~~ceses heires masles,~~ ~~If she haue any~~ before my death
L' Janes heires masles, To the L Katerins heires
masles, To the L Maries heires masles, To
the heires masles of the daughters which ~~she~~
she shal haue hereafter. Then to the L Mar
gets heires masles. For lakke of such issu,
To theires masles of the L Janes daughters
To theires masles of the L Katerins daughters
and so forth til you come to the L margets ^daughters heires masles.

2 If after my death theire masle be entred into
18 yere old, then he to haue the hole rule
and gouernance therof.

3 But if he be under 18, then his mother to
be gouernres til he entre 18 yere old ^and agremet
But to doe nothing ~~about~~ th'auise of 6 ~~6~~
parcel of a counsel to be pointed by my
last will to the nomore of 20.

4 If the mother die befor theire entre into 18
the realme to ~~the~~ be gouerned by the coūc
Prouided that after ~~he~~ he be 14 yere al
great matters of importaunce be ~~~~ ᵒꝑened
to him.

5 ~~If i died without issu, and ther were none~~
~~heire masle, then the L Frauncess to be~~ ^gouuernres
~~for lakke of her the her eldest daughters~~
~~and for lakke of them the L Margets to be~~

Edward's 'Devise for the Succession' altered his will to allow Lady Jane Grey to succeed him.

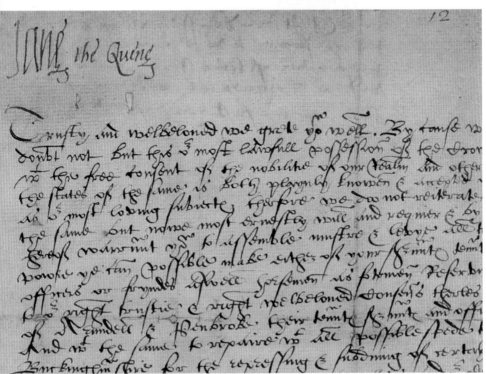

This controversial 'limning' or miniature, identified by David Starkey as Lady Jane Grey, may have been painted in the winter of 1561/2. If it is of Jane it is the closest we have to a likeness of her. The artist, Lavina Teerlinc, knew Jane personally and painted at least two limnings of Jane's sister Katherine. She habitually gave her subjects blue eyes, although Jane's are said to have been brown.

This document is signed in Jane's own hand 'Jane the Quene'. Although initially reluctant to leapfrog her mother's claim to the throne, Jane proved an active monarch during her brief reign and aggressive in defending her position as a ruling queen.

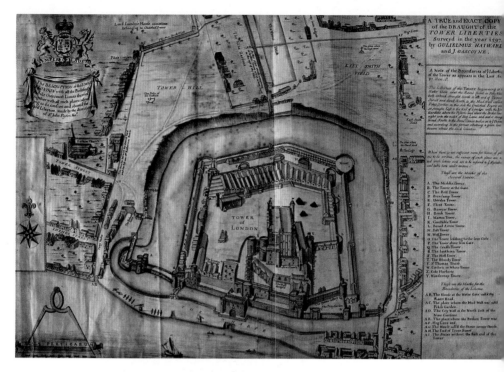

The Tower of London. Jane was resident at the Queen's House during her reign, and afterward in a small house towards the Beauchamp Tower where her husband Guildford Dudley and his brothers were incarcerated. The scaffold where she died was built alongside the White Tower.

The execution of Lady Jane Grey, as imagined by Paul Delaroche in 1834. The image reflects the eroticised cult of the 'Nine Days Queen' as a victimised child-woman.

Edward might live until September when a new Parliament could repeal the 1544 Act of Succession,[3] but most believed Edward had two months at the most. The imperial ambassador, Jehan Scheyfve, had learned that Edward's body was now covered in ulcers and horribly swollen. The tormented teenager could not sleep or rest without the aid of opiates. The government continued nevertheless to fight a rearguard action against the rumours concerning his health, cutting off the ears of any loudmouths discussing his possible demise, while now also disseminating counter rumours that his condition was actually improving. It was in this spirit of pretence that Mary Tudor composed a note of congratulations to her brother on the day of Jane and Katherine Grey's marriages.

With the wedding celebrations finished, Jane and Katherine retired into the houses of their respective fathers-in-law: Jane remaining at Durham House, and Katherine to the gloomy royal fortress of Baynard's Castle, nearby on the Thames. There was a portrait of Lord Herbert's late mother, Anne Parr, hanging on one wall. Katherine must have felt her absence but her sick husband brought out her protective instincts, and she was young enough to be able to shut out from her mind the roar of impending political crises. Jane had no such luxury. She was acutely aware of her place as her mother's heir, and the expectation that she could have a son who would one day be king. Scheyfve reported that it had been agreed that Lady Jane Grey's marriage to Guildford Dudley would not be consummated because of her tender age.[4] It is likely he confused Jane with Katherine. But it may be the Greys were reluctant, even at this stage, for Jane to fulfil her wedding vows, and conceive the son that would disinherit Frances from her prospective role as Governor of England on Edward's death. If so, it was an argument they lost. Jane's marriage was consummated; had it not been, this would have emerged later.

On 28th May, Edward's doctors confirmed to Northumberland privately that the King would not live beyond the autumn. Soon afterwards, the imperial ambassador heard 'from a good source' that the French had promised Northumberland their support in any plans that deprived Mary of the succession. Edward meanwhile was making small, but highly significant, changes to his will, ones that would confirm the Greys' suspicions of Northumberland. He drew a line through the provision that Frances would rule as governor if he died before any male heirs were born and inserted a short phrase above the line. The throne was to pass to Frances's male heirs, but in the absence of such issue 'before my death' the throne was to pass to Lady Jane Grey '*and her*' heirs male. Since Frances was not pregnant and had no sons, she was, effectively, excluded from becoming governor or claiming the throne, which would pass directly to Jane as Queen regnant. Edward could justify this because his father had – deliberately or otherwise – also excluded Frances.

According to information gathered later by the papal envoy Giovanni Francesco Commendone, it was Northumberland who gave Jane the shocking news that she was now the King's heir. It left her completely stunned and 'deeply upset'. The strength of her religious beliefs, and her refusal to accept even the gift of a dress from Mary, suggests she would have been content to see Mary excluded from the succession – but she had no desire to take her mother's place. Commendone learned that Jane asked permission to return home briefly to see her mother, but the Duchess of Northumberland refused, reminding Jane she needed to be on hand for the moment of the King's death. Jane, however, was not the kind of person to blandly accept an order she did not like, so she crept out of Durham House and took a boat down the Thames, home to Suffolk Place.

Jane's father was furious that her mother was being passed over in line of succession[5] and convinced that Northumberland's intention was to crown Guildford, nominally as Jane's co-ruler, but with the intention that he would be the dominant partner.[6] There was nothing the Greys could yet do to regain control of the situation: when the time came, however, and Jane was Queen she could deny Guildford the crown. As Frances comforted her daughter, the Duchess of Northumberland sent an angry message to Suffolk Place threatening to keep Guildford with her if Jane did not return. Such a breach would have risked a public scandal which neither family could afford, and so, it seems, an accommodation was reached.

The contemporary diplomatic traffic reveals that Guildford and Jane were soon together at Catherine Parr's old house in Chelsea. There the young couple entertained their friends in the house the Queen dowager had turned into a 'second court'. The roses were already in bloom, their heady scent redolent of happier times. But if any romance began to develop between Jane and Guildford it came to an abrupt end when the honeymooners and several of their guests fell victim to food poisoning. The source was believed to be a salad made by a cook 'who plucked one leaf for another'[7]. Jane came to suspect her mother-in-law, however, for, as she lay incapacitated at Chelsea, Edward's decision to name her his heir was being sealed at Greenwich.

Senior judges had been summoned by the King to ratify his will. With Parr of Northampton and Sir John Gates – Northumberland's eyes and ears in the private quarters of the King's Privy Chamber – standing by, Edward gave his reasons for disinheriting his sisters in favour of Jane. Then, gathering what strength remained, he instructed his judges to draw up a legal document that would declare his decisions concerning the succession and his reasons for them. As the judges retired, however, some expressed concern that Edward's will could not be enforced until the Act of Succession of 1544 was rescinded.[8] Nervously, they delivered their judgement before the Council. The physically powerful Northumberland promptly threatened to strip down to his shirt and fight with anyone who denied the King's wishes. The frightened judges were then called to see Edward, swollen and wretched on his bed. The King (who appears to have been given private legal advice) insisted that he, and not just his father, had the right to bequeath the crown by testament, and that his will could be ratified by Parliament. He also promised pardons under the Great Seal for any treason they might be committing by obeying his instructions. Fourteen of the judges agreed to do as he asked, but four, possibly five, refused. Frances was then summoned to see Edward.[9] He expected and, perhaps, demanded, her submission to his decision to pass her over in favour of her daughter.

Over the next week the last details of the legal document the judges had been instructed to draw up were concluded and on 21st June the nobility and leading officials were asked to sign it. Edward claimed that he had considered the question of the succession for a considerable period, 'as well since the time of our sickness as in the time of our health'.[10] He drew attention to the illegitimacy of his sisters, who, he noted, were only his 'half blood', and gave stark warnings of the dangers of their marrying foreigners. By contrast there was praise for his married and betrothed cousins, Lady Jane, Katherine and Mary Grey. He described them almost as if they were his true sisters. The Grey girls had been 'natural born here within the realm, and have also been very honourably brought up and exercised in good and Godly learning, and other noble virtues'. Their education was very similar to his; 'Trust and hope' could be placed in them.[11]

The Privy Council, Archbishop Cranmer, the Officers of the Household, the civic dignitaries, and twenty-two peers all signed the document and swore a solemn oath to uphold its provisions.[12] But some of the signatories remained uneasy. Not only did the statute of 1544, which had declared Edward's half-sisters his heirs, remain in place, so did the 1547 Treasons Act, which made it a capital offence to change its provisions. Was English law really no more than a way of advertising the royal will, as King Henry and his son Edward believed? Not everyone thought so. The radical bishop, John Hooper, insisted that they should put their trust in God's providence and accept Mary as Queen. She was middle aged already, and if she had no children, the evangelical Elizabeth would be her heir. Most of the doubters who signed, possibly including Sir William Cecil, who was Surveyor of Elizabeth's estates, were waiting upon events before deciding their next move. But a few, including a number of anonymous figures on the Council, had already gone so far as to inform the imperial ambassadors that they hoped Charles V would assist Mary, when the time came.

In a desperate effort to keep Edward alive until Parliament could be called in September, an old woman renowned as a healer was brought in to care for the King; but her potions could do nothing for him, and the efforts of his doctors – which included, apparently, dosing him with arsenic – only added to his agonies. Edward had been raised by councillors, tutors and divines, since he was orphaned at the age of nine. He had, as King, been utterly in their power. Many had idealistic motives. But this is where it was ending: in pain, tenderly inflicted, for their own ends.

Edward's subjects were increasingly restless. It was being said that Northumberland was 'a great tyrant', and that he was poisoning the King with the intention of handing the country over to the French.[13] These rumours grew after the events of 27th June. Edward made his last public appearance that day, showing himself at a window to prove to the gathering crowds that he was not yet dead. What they saw, however, of the thin and wasted boy, even from a distance, convinced them that, though still alive, his death would not be long coming. That night, Northumberland was seen entering the residence of the incoming French ambassador, the aristocrat Antoine de Noailles. The news of the clandestine visit spread rapidly and two members of the public were chained to a post and whipped 'for opprobrious and seditious words' about Northumberland and his allies.[14] In the Privy Chamber, Edward was now coughing up the stinking remains of his lifeblood. His favourite Gentleman of the Privy Chamber, Nicholas Throckmorton, had whiled away hours over the previous months playing board games with the royal invalid, but Edward was now too ill to play, and far beyond further medical help. There was nothing left for those at Edward's bedside but to pray and comfort him, as best they could.

On Sunday 2nd July, the contents of the King's will were signalled to the public for the first time in a church service that excluded the usual prayers for the Princesses Mary and Elizabeth. The following day, as Mary travelled to London to see her brother, she was warned of his imminent death and of possible plans to seize her. She changed course, and on 5th July, Mary was heading for Kenninghall at the heart of her estates in Norfolk. From there she could flee to Flanders and to the protection of her cousin the Emperor. But, to the amazement of Sir John Gates, when the news reached the Lord President he showed no obvious concern about it. 'Sir, will you suffer the Lady Mary escape, and not secure her person?' he asked incredulously. Northumberland may have hoped that Mary would escape abroad. She had proved an awkward subject to her brother, and they would be well rid of her. He did not believe the Emperor would want to attack England while he was at war with France, and if Mary stayed he doubted also that she would try any military enterprise. As one of her supporters observed, he was 'very ready to despise the plans of a mere woman'.[15] To pacify Gates, however, he later ordered his son, Lord Robert Dudley, to pursue Mary with a small contingent of horse and bring her to London.

Between eight and nine on the evening of 6th July, Edward sighed: 'I feel faint.' One of Northumberland's sons-in-law, Sir Henry Sidney, gathered the boy in his arms and Edward uttered his last words: 'Lord have mercy upon me and take my spirit.' The suffering of the boy had ended at last. Northumberland intended that the news be kept secret for three days, as the death of Henry VIII had been. He needed to prepare for possible unrest in London over the exclusion of Mary, or, perhaps, of Frances. The capital was the evangelical heartland of England, but the people still had a strong sense of 'right order'. Everyone lived according to their place in the social hierarchy, obedient to their superiors and expecting obedience from their inferiors. Mary was King Henry's daughter, and that of a much-loved Queen; Jane was not, and in any case, Frances preceded her in the line of succession. Why, the people would wonder, should Frances be superseded by Jane unless Northumberland wanted to rule through his son? There had been rumours for years that he sought the crown, based on nothing but fear and hatred of him. That his detractors now had something more made the rumours dangerously potent. Northumberland and his allies needed to plan carefully.

The next morning, 7th July, the Mayor of London and City magistrates were called to Greenwich and, along with the guard, they swore an oath of allegiance to Queen Jane.[16] The Tower was being reinforced, and Henry Sidney's wife, Mary Dudley, who was close to Jane in age, was dispatched to Chelsea to bring her by river to Sion, Northumberland's house at Richmond.

When they arrived the palace was empty and Jane was told only that she must wait there 'to receive that which had been ordered by the King'.[17] She must have guessed what was coming, if Mary Dudley had not already told her. In the capital divisions within the Privy Council ensured that news of Edward's death had even leaked to the public. The newly arrived imperial ambassador, the chilly, efficient Simon Renard, had heard the reports that morning and by the evening it was all over London. Mary first heard the news from her goldsmith who, riding hard from the capital, met her as she reached Euston Hall near Thetford on the Norfolk–Suffolk border. Mary responded cautiously. Had she proclaimed herself Queen before Edward was dead she would have been guilty of treason, so she waited for confirmation, as she continued moving ahead of Robert Dudley and his men.

At Greenwich, where Edward's body was being embalmed, the French ambassador arrived to reiterate to the Council Henri II's offer of support against any plots of the Emperor Charles V. The Councillors, however, not wanting to trigger a response from the Emperor, refused to confirm to the ambassador that Edward was dead.[18] Their fears about the Emperor were, in fact, misplaced. Mary's Hapsburg cousin was abandoning her cause. His ambassador, Renard, judged her position a hopeless one. Northumberland was master of the few armed forces of the realm and appeared to have the backing of the vast majority of the political elite. Renard believed they should offer their support to Queen Jane and make trouble for the French. That way they might, at least, save Mary's life.

The next day, 8th July, Jane was joined at Sion by Northumberland, Pembroke, Northampton, Huntingdon, and the Earl of Arundel – widower of her father's sister, Katherine Fitzalan. Arundel had been a conservative ally of Somerset in his plot to overthrow Northumberland in 1551 and had been lucky to escape with a term at the Tower and a large fine. It had been remitted only that month, in an effort to ensure that he did not join Mary's cause. As the noblemen knelt to her, Jane, still only sixteen, appeared overwhelmed by the enormity of what was happening, and seeing her confusion, they agreed to call for her mother to join them.[19] Frances arrived shortly afterwards, with Northampton's wife, Elizabeth Brooke, and the Duchess of Northumberland.[20] Once the adults had succeeded in convincing Jane that she was, indeed, Edward's rightful heir, she had the night to prepare for the events of the following day. On that Sunday morning Northumberland, as President of the Council, gave Jane the official news that Edward was dead before the assembled Council, nobles and their wives. Edward had shown great care for his country in his last hours, Northumberland said, and he outlined the contents of the document that confirmed that Jane had been named his heir, with her sisters after her if she had no children. When he had finished the assembled company, her parents and the Duke and Duchess of Northumberland, all knelt before her and swore to defend her with their blood. Jane's response was a dramatic one. She fell to the ground and wept.

It would be naïve to suppose that this display was spontaneous. In the sixteenth century, before the advent of newspapers, billboards, or television, political figures projected their messages theatrically. Jane's actions made the point very publicly that she had not sought the crown and that it had been imposed on her. But she had something else to add. Revisionist historians have argued forcibly that Edward, the maturing, evangelical monarch, was the driving force behind the decision that Jane be made his heir. At the same time it is blandly accepted, or even asserted, that Jane, who unlike Edward was not weakened by terminal illness, who was described by one of the King's own tutors as the more intelligent of the two, and who reputedly had already launched personal attacks on Mary and her religion, was nothing more than an innocent and manipulated girl. That Jane was very young there can be no argument. But she had been raised to be a leader of one side of an ideological struggle, in which her co-religionists were now facing the greatest confrontation of her lifetime.[21] Having been persuaded to accept the throne, and assured by the Council that she was Edward's legal rightful heir, she was now ready to embrace the role.

When Jane stopped weeping, she came to her feet and delivered a speech. In it she accepted her kingdom, with modest claims of inadequacy, but prayed that God would grant her 'such grace as to enable me to govern ... with his approbation and to his glory'.[22] And with that England's first Queen regnant made clear she intended to rule and not to be a mere cipher.

At the celebratory banquet that followed, Jane sat on a raised platform under a rich cloth known as a canopy of state, a symbol of her authority. When it ended the proclamation declaring Jane Queen and Mary and Elizabeth illegitimate was read. It highlighted too the danger that the Tudor sisters might reintroduce the 'Roman' religion or marry foreigners.[23] At Paul's Cross that morning, the Bishop of London, Nicholas Ridley, had already preached the rightness of Jane's cause, and declared Mary and Elizabeth 'bastards'. There had been an ominous reaction, however, amongst his congregation, who were 'sore annoyed with his words, so uncharitably spoken by him in so open an audience'.[24] King Henry's daughters, it seemed, still had the support of the people, if not the evangelical elite.

Chapter XI

Jane the Queen

Monday, 10th July, began early for Jane. The summer sun had only just begun to warm the cool air on the river as she arrived by barge at Westminster from Richmond. In her rooms a green velvet gown, printed with gold and with huge sleeves was laid out for her, along with a jewelled headdress in white. Jane was poised to take formal possession of the Tower, as all monarchs did before they were crowned. The colours of the clothes marked this ritual, chosen in accordance with the coronation order known as the *Liber Regalis*. Having dressed, Jane returned to her covered boat and was rowed on to Northumberland's palace at Durham House, where she dined at noon.

The Privy Council met afterwards. At the top of the agenda was the letter marked with the royal seal that had arrived from Mary in Norfolk. It informed the Council that she, and not Jane, was Edward's rightful heir and demanded their allegiance to her. As the letter was read out a frisson of fear ran through the Council. Northumberland had been certain that Mary would not dare mount a challenge without the support of Charles V, and had hoped that the Emperor would not wish to fight France and England. It now seemed, however, that they faced the possibility of civil war, and even foreign invasion.

When Jane's mother heard of the letter she and the Duchess of Northumberland burst into tears.[1] Jane, however, put on a brave face.

Like Joan of Arc, who defended France at the age of seventeen, she would protect her country and her faith against the threat she believed was posed by Mary. That afternoon, at two o'clock, the royal barges arrived at the Tower carrying Guildford and Jane, her father, Suffolk, the young couple's mothers and other ladies of the court, attended by a large following. Jane was greeted at the steps by Northumberland and the other Councillors, before being brought in procession to the Tower gates. She smiled broadly at the gathered crowds, her husband walking beside her under a canopy of state carried on poles. Guildford was dressed as a monarch's consort in silver and white, 'a very tall, strong boy with light hair who paid her much attention', the Genovese merchant Baptista Spinola commented. The merchant was close enough to the couple to note the freckles on Jane's face: 'She has small features and a well-made nose, the mouth flexible and the lips red. The eyebrows are arched and darker than her hair, which is nearly red.' He thought her thin and very small, despite her shoes, which had cork platforms to add height, but she struck, nevertheless, 'a gracious and lively figure'. Her eyes were 'sparkling and reddish-brown in colour', and 'when she smiled she showed her teeth, which are white and sharp'.

Jane's smiles were not reciprocated by the crowd. 'The hearts of the people are with Mary the Spanish Queen's daughter,' Spinola observed. As the procession continued he heard expressions of disgust that Frances was carrying her daughter's train, a striking visual reminder of how the correct order of things had been overthrown. Behind Frances were the nobility amongst whom, Spinola was assured, several important faces were missing. Jane was 'an extreme heretic', he was told, and the missing nobles 'did not come into the procession for that reason'. Northumberland's efforts to unite the political elite had clearly failed, but he could at least be reassured that the missing faces belonged to only a small minority.

At between four and five o'clock in the afternoon the procession reached the Tower. There was a great salute of guns and Jane and Guildford walked into its shadows with their attendants. As the huge gates closed firmly behind them, a blast of trumpets called the

crowd's attention. Two heralds read to the restive crowd the proclamation declaring Jane Queen and the daughters of Henry VIII
excluded from the throne as illegitimate. It was then taken to Cheapside and Fleet Street and read again. When the heralds had finished
their task at each place, however, few cried 'God save her' and, at
Cheapside, a boy called Gilbert Potter declared loudly that it was
Mary who had the right to the throne. His master, a gunner at the
Tower, promptly reported him and the boy was arrested and put in
the pillory. At eight the following morning, to another blast of trumpets, he had his ears cut off, while a herald, dressed in royal livery,
read out his offence. It was a savage beginning to Jane's reign and the
mutilated teenager was widely pitied.

As notices were pinned up across London outlining King Edward's
will, a messenger arrived at the Tower with news of Mary's continuing defiance. She had proclaimed herself Queen and in Norfolk and
parts of Suffolk noblemen, knights and gentlemen were coming to
her support with 'innumerable companies of the common people'.[2]
Mary's household officers had been preparing for up to a year for her
exclusion from the succession. Friends, neighbours and kinsman were
now being mobilised, while the common people were motivated by
loyalty to the Tudor name, and dislike of Northumberland together
with the regime that had killed so many of them in 1549. Mary had
been persuaded to say nothing of the divisive religious issue, but for
Jane it was central, and her notices continued to reiterate the proclamation's warnings of the dangers of popery. In East Anglia the major
towns followed London's lead in proclaiming her Queen, but she
needed to rally support across the provinces in the face of Mary's
attacks. Letters drafted by Northumberland in a hurried scrawl gave
notice to the Lord Lieutenants of the counties of her 'entry into our
Tower of London as rightful Queen of this realm' and required them
'not only to defend our just title, but also assist us ... to disturb,
repel, and resist the feigned and untrue claim of the Lady Mary,
bastard daughter to our great uncle Henry VIII, of famous memory'.[3]
Each notice was marked boldly in her own hand 'Jane the Quene'.
Some military preparations had begun already. In Leicestershire,

Jane's uncle, George Medley, had arrived at Bradgate with armour and weaponry. In London, meanwhile, carts and horses were being seized. Jane intended that her father be sent with an army to capture Mary, and on the morning of the 12th, Londoners woke to the sound of drums. Recruits were being offered 10 pence a day to fight in defence of the Godly Queen Jane. Behind the solid walls of the Tower, however, the hearts of Jane's Councillors beat to a less assured rhythm.

The people's reaction to Jane's accession was troubling, and while she was signing letters warning that Mary would hand the country over to strangers, others worried about it being handed to Northumberland. Ever since he had become Lord President there had been rumours that he had designs on the throne for himself and his family. The previous summer, when he had tried to ally Guildford with Jane's royal cousin Margaret Clifford, one of the late Duke of Somerset's former servants had claimed that such ambitions lay behind it. With Guildford married to Queen Jane all the rumours of the past looked troublingly prescient. Jane Grey's parents half believed them, and even some of Northumberland's most fervent friends suspected they were true. The French ambassador was despatching home optimistically about 'the new King' Guildford, while Guildford's Spanish godfather, Don Diego Mendoza, penned letters referring to Guildford as 'His Majesty'.[4] Since Jane was loyal to her father, and believed that as Queen she had a personal responsibility to God for how she ruled, there was a chance of a clash ahead with her husband, and there is some evidence that one of Mary's secret supporters on the Council now sought to engineer its early arrival.

The papal envoy, Giovanni Francesco Commendone, who arrived in England later that summer, records that Jane later described how the Lord Treasurer William Paulet, Marquess of Winchester, brought her the crown jewels, though, she claimed, she had not asked for them. That he did so, on 12th July, is confirmed in another later letter from Mary to the Marquess of Winchester.[5] It was also the case that Jane had declared that she would not be crowned for a fortnight or more, so there was no immediate need for her to see the jewels.[6] Jane described how the Lord Treasurer suggested she try on the crown 'to see if it did become me', and as she hesitated added 'that another would also be made to crown my husband as King'.

Jane's nineteenth-century hagiographers and their modern imitators have painted Winchester's actions as misplaced flattery. The Victorians produced innumerable prints depicting Jane modestly shrinking from the crown as he offers it to her. But as Jane was signing herself 'Jane the Quene' on a daily basis, she wasn't shrinking from the crown in any meaningful sense. The imperial ambassadors had, furthermore, already identified Winchester as being someone who was unhappy with Northumberland's seizure of power and Jane's rule.[7] What is most significant in this account is Winchester's comment that a crown would be made for Guildford. It confronted Jane with the expectation that she would be sharing her throne with her husband. The envoy's account goes on to describe how this succeeded in triggering a furious row between Jane and her husband which concluded with Jane agreeing with Guildford that he would be made King 'by me and by Act of Parliament' in September. As soon as he left the room, however, Jane changed her mind and called for the Earl of Arundel and for her sister's father-in-law, Pembroke. She then informed them that she was content to make her husband 'a duke, but not a King'.[8] Another later report claimed the title Jane had in mind for Guildford was 'Duke of Clarence'.[9] If the version of events recorded by Commendone is to be believed, Jane had asserted her role as Queen, independent of her duty of obedience to her husband, but hers was a house divided, and Mary had friends other than the Lord Treasurer ready to exploit this weakness.

While Winchester was showing Jane the crown jewels, two of her most loyal subjects, Parr of Northampton's father-in-law, Lord Cobham, and the Privy Councillor Sir John Mason, arrived at the residence of the imperial ambassadors, Scheyfve and Renard. They warned the ambassadors of dire consequences if they were to contact Mary and advised them to make arrangements to go home, adding that they considered their missions had terminated with the death of King Edward. Renard's reply was conciliatory. He offered assurances of the Emperor's goodwill towards Queen Jane, while expressing concern that the French King, Henri II, was stirring up trouble in England in order to place his ward Mary Queen of Scots on the throne.[10] Rumours that Northumberland had made a private deal with the French had been growing for days and, after hearing the ambassador's comments, Jane's delegates sat speechless, 'staring at one another'.[11] Renard was in a position, furthermore, to add fuel to suspicions about the duke. A kinsman of Northumberland, Henry Dudley, was poised to go to France to see Henri II, and Renard had intelligence that Northumberland was prepared to buy French support with 'Calais, Guisnes, and Hammes, the English possessions of the mainland, and Ireland'.[12] Henry Dudley was in fact more closely related to Harry Suffolk than to Northumberland (he was Suffolk's first cousin), and all those who supported Queen Jane needed to ensure that the French would ally against the Emperor if he took up arms in Mary's cause. But the imperial ambassadors had done a fine job in raising further doubts about Northumberland's motives, with the suggestion left hanging that, if Jane proved truculent, he might replace her with the eleven-year-old Mary Queen of Scots.

Cobham and Sir John went straight to Arundel and Pembroke with what they had heard.[13] Their choice of confidants is significant. Arundel had only been brought on to the Council in July and his loyalty was already in doubt: an open letter, written by an anonymous supporter of Mary to Gilbert Potter, the boy whose ears had been cut off, was being prepared that day, praising Potter's actions and naming Arundel as one of those unhappy with the new regime.[14] Pembroke, who had the previous year lost his post as Master of the Horse to Northumberland's eldest son, had no love for the duke. It was apparent now the exclusion of Mary was not going as smoothly as the regime had hoped. Hatred of Northumberland was playing a role in this, and Pembroke could see a way out for himself if he jumped ship. But the timing had to be right.

That night the munitions and men that were to be sent against Mary began to arrive at the Tower. Three cartloads of guns, small bows, arrows, spears, pikes, armour, gunpowder, tents and victuals all rumbled into the fortress as Londoners looked on.[15] Jane confirmed her father as her choice to lead the army and urged him to confront Mary, 'saying with great boldness that she could have no safer defence for her Majesty than her own loving father'.[16] Harry Suffolk had, however, begun to suffer fainting fits. Stress and anxiety may have contributed to this, but he would be ill with colic and 'the stone' for months to come. As soon as she realised her father was ailing, Jane asked the Council to let him stay and to choose someone else to lead her army.[17] The man they picked was their fellow Privy Councillor, Northumberland, who was told that his victory over the Norfolk rebels in 1549 made him uniquely qualified for the post.

The duke, whose political antennae were more acute than those of either his daughter-in-law or her father, was suspicious that the Council was so keen for him to leave the capital, but it was not a commission he could reject without inflaming suspicions that he was 'ruling' Queen Jane. He therefore accepted the role, despite his misgivings, telling the Privy Councillors: 'Well, since ye think it good, I and mine will go, not doubting of your fidelity to the Queen's Majesty, which I leave in your custody.' Northumberland then went from the Council Chamber to see Jane who 'beseeched him to use his diligence' in the coming battle against Mary. He replied that he would do all he could.[18]

The following day, as the final military preparations were made, Northumberland ordered his chief officers to meet with him at Durham House. They included Lady Mary Grey's betrothed, the pike-scarred Grey of Wilton, Parr of Northampton, who had fought alongside him in 1549, and Sir John Gates, men Northumberland would be able to trust in the confrontation ahead. What he feared most, however, was not the enemy but a stab in the back from those who remained behind.

As his fellow Councillors gathered that afternoon to wish him every success, he delivered a farewell speech, reminding them as forcibly as he could where their duties lay. 'My Lords, I and these other noble personages, and the whole army, that now go forth ... [do so] for the establishing of the Queen's highness.' He was sure, he declared, of the Council's loyalty, for they were all bound by 'the holy oath of allegiance made freely by you to this virtuous lady the Queens highness', who had accepted the crown only 'by your and our enticement'. But if the army was betrayed, he warned, they had safe-guards in place. 'Consider also,' he continued, 'that [this is] God's cause.' Their primary intention was always to keep out papistry. 'And think not the contrary, but if ye mean deceit ... God will revenge the same.' One of the Council reassured him: 'My Lord, if you distrust any of us in this matter you are much deceived; for which of us can wipe his hands clean thereof?'[19] And with that Northumberland and his fellow Councillors sat down for a last supper, the duke still wondering how many would play Judas when he and the army were gone.

Before Northumberland left he had a final audience with Jane at the Tower. She confirmed his commission as head of the army and 'he took his leave of her' with her full support. He must also have said a goodbye to his son, Guildford, whose brothers, including the youngest, sixteen-year-old Lord Henry Dudley, had all declared their willingness to fight on Jane's behalf. As Northumberland walked out through the Council Chamber, he saw Arundel who told him that he was sorry that he was not serving alongside him and that he would willingly 'spend his blood even at his foot'. It was a lie.

The following day, 14th July, Jane's army left for East Anglia, amidst the stony silence of the crowds gathered along the roadside. As they passed through Shoreditch, Northumberland was moved to comment: 'The people press to see us, but not one sayeth God speed us.'[20] With the threat of possible disturbances Jane ordered a guard for the gates of the city that night and a curfew was announced, to run between eight in the evening to five in the morning. To the west, in the Thames Valley, meanwhile, news of the sullen mood in London was helping raise support for a gentry-led rebellion with ordinary people flocking to support it. Jane learned that Mary had been proclaimed Queen in Buckinghamshire, while she, Jane, had been condemned as a 'Queen of a new and pretty invention'.[21] But it was in East Anglia, where the towns had been so quick to proclaim Jane Queen a few days earlier, that the rebel numbers were growing fastest; Mary's household and friends were successfully recruiting even the evangelical elite to her cause.

The next morning, as Northumberland and Northampton headed towards Bury St Edmunds to cut off Mary's support from the Midlands, people fled to Mary's standard at Framlingham Castle in Suffolk. A description is recorded of the army eventually arrayed for her inspection. Mary's father may have doubted a woman's ability to inspire men in arms, but she came from fighting stock. Her mother was the daughter of the warrior queen Isabella of Castile, who had fought the Muslim Moors. As she rode up to her troops, a slim, erect figure on a white horse, Mary's men went into battle order. 'The infantry made ready their pikes, the cavalry brandished lances, the archer bent his bow ... Each man kept rank and did not even move a finger's breadth from the position assigned him.'[22] Mary's horse shied at the glittering display of steel and fluttering banners, so she dismounted and walked along the line. As she did so each man knelt to the ground and from time to time she stopped to give words of encouragement. Mary was always good with the ordinary man, and it was her good fortune that the ordinary man hated Northumberland and those who had denied them social justice for so long.

In the Tower, Jane had learned that five royal ships off the Norfolk coast had mutinied and the sailors had forced the officers to go over to Mary's side. Some Councillors began to ask if the rebellion against Jane was God's punishment for their denying Mary her rights. As reports came in that the tenants of noblemen loyal to her were refusing to serve them against Mary, so 'each man then began to pluck in his horns', afraid of the popular anger they had stirred up. Jane, however, continued to send out letters to sheriffs and Justices of the Peace demanding their allegiance: 'Remain fast in your obeisance and duty to the Crown Imperial of this Realm, whereof We have justly the possession,' she ordered. Her father was surely at her side, sick as he was, but there was no Northumberland pressing Jane to remind the state's officials that each owed their duty, 'to us, your sovereign Lady, who means to preserve this Crown of England' from the hands 'of strangers and papists'.[23] She was determined to fight on.

Aware now of the discontent even within her Council, Jane ordered a strong guard to be mounted around the Tower, and at seven o'clock the gates were shut. The keys were carried up to the Queen in person. Outside Bishop Ridley, at least, remained loyal and he gave another devastating sermon at Paul's Cross that Sunday, once again condemning Mary and Elizabeth. It received no better response from the crowd than the first, but Jane did not despair. On 18th July she began raising new troops to be led into rebel Buckinghamshire by 'our right trusty and right well-beloved cousins, the Earls of Arundel and Pembroke'. There was real anger in Jane's letters against those who would betray her. She was sure the rebels in Buckinghamshire would, in the end, either 'lack heart to abide in their malicious purpose' or receive 'such punishment and execution as they deserve'.[24] But, as Jane cried out for blood, fresh men and weaponry, already her generals had betrayed or abandoned her. Northumberland and Northampton, had received 'letters of discomfort' from friends on the Privy Council warning that all was lost, and fled Bury St Edmunds at nightfall, 'when the lamps had been lit'. They headed for Cambridge, the intellectual heartland of the evangelical revolution.[25]

In the Tower there was an air of unreality as another day dawned. Ordinary life was carrying on even as disaster descended. Jane had agreed to be godmother to the infant son of a radical evangelical called Edward Underhill. That morning, the 19th, the ceremony went ahead in the church on Tower Hill. Jane remained busy at her duties as Queen and her mother's cousin, Lady Throckmorton, the wife of Sir Nicholas, stood proxy in her place.[26] At the same time in the town square in Northampton, Sir Nicholas was trying to prevent a Catholic knight, Sir Thomas Tresham, from proclaiming Mary Queen.[27] The crowd was against him and he only narrowly escaped being lynched thanks to a group of gentlemen who pushed him on to a horse and held back the infuriated mob as he rode away. In the peace of the chapel on Tower Hill, however, such drama seemed far away. By tradition, the godmother chose the child's baptismal name. Jane's feelings for Guildford, despite any differences, may be gauged by the fact the little boy was named after him. Jane's father was also represented as the child was blessed. Harry Suffolk was still hoping the tide would turn in his daughter's favour, and that of her young husband. He signed a letter that morning to the Councillor Lord Rich[28] in Essex, informing him of the treachery of the Earl of Oxford and requiring his continued loyalty to Jane. Pembroke, a co-godparent, had signed it alongside him.[29] But in truth, Pembroke, together with Arundel, was now ready to bring Jane down.

With his business in the Tower completed Pembroke returned to his London home, Baynard's Castle. It was to prove a bitter day for Lady Katherine Grey, as her father-in-law prepared to betray her sister and her parents. That afternoon the Lord Mayor arrived along with a number of Councillors. Suffolk had been told they were leaving the Tower for a conference with the French ambassadors (concerning plans to send foreign auxiliaries from the Netherlands to help Northumberland) and so had allowed them through the guard.[30] Over the next couple of hours there was considerable coming and going (perhaps witnessed by Katherine), with the Lord Mayor leaving briefly only to return with a large number of his aldermen. When they were all gathered Pembroke announced that they would be riding to Cheapside to proclaim Mary as Queen. Many of those present wept tears of relief that civil war could now be avoided.

As the procession formed outside Baynard's Castle and set off towards Cheapside, the news spread before them. By the time the dignitaries had ridden up the hillside to St Paul's churchyard the crowds were so great that they could hardly pass. But their horses were urged through the throng until at last they reached their destination. With Sir John Mason, Lord Cobham and the Earl of Arundel amongst those present, Mary was then proclaimed to the sound of trumpets and the shouts of the crowd. Pembroke threw a cap full of coins into the air in celebration and pennies rained down from the windows of the houses around. In stark contrast to Jane's proclamation in London nine days earlier, bonfires were promptly built and church bells rang while men ran through the streets shouting 'the Lady Mary is proclaimed Queen!' When the Council's soldiers arrived at the Tower, Suffolk knew his daughter's cause was lost and he ordered his men to put down their weapons. The soldiers informed him they would arrest him if he did not leave the Tower willingly and sign the new proclamation. He did as he was asked and on Tower Hill read the proclamation declaring Mary Queen. He then returned to tell his daughter, as gently as possible, that her reign was over.

Suffolk found Jane with her mother and her ladies-in-waiting. According to the papal envoy Commendone, Jane did not lose her composure as her father delivered the grim news. Instead, when he had finished, she reminded him that he had helped persuade her to accept the crown. Jane admitted that she had found his arguments convincing, but then 'many men would be deemed to be wise if their shrewdness could not be judged by the results'. Her father then took down her canopy of state, his ambitions dismantled in his hands as Jane retired to an inner chamber with her mother and ladies-in-waiting, 'with deep sorrow, but bearing the ill fate with great valour and endurance'.[31]

Not long afterwards, Lady Throckmorton, who had been enjoying dinner in her house after Guildford Underhill's christening, returned to the Tower and entered the silent throne room. She was astonished to find the cloth of state removed and all the symbols of Jane's reign defaced, 'a sudden change!' She discovered also that the Duke of Suffolk had left with Frances for Baynard's Castle. The Greys hoped Pembroke could be persuaded that Northumberland and his family alone should take the fall for their actions in excluding Mary from the succession. Lady Throckmorton tried to leave as well, but it was too late: the guards' orders had changed and she was held along with the other prisoners: Jane, Guildford and the Duchess of Northumberland.[32] The intended allocation of blame was already evident.

The details of the coup reached Northumberland in Cambridge that night. He was angry at those who had helped convince him he had been acting in God's interest in supporting the evangelical cause against Mary. His men were deserting and, like his father, he faced ruin for his loyalty to the wishes of a dead monarch. He had already sent the new Queen a message asking for her orders and begging a general pardon. The tears streamed down his face as he told the vice-chancellor of Cambridge University that 'Queen Mary was a merciful woman, and that he doubted not thereof'.[33] The following day Northumberland read the new proclamation and declared for Mary, with Northampton at his side. Thus 'Jane was Queen for only nine days and those most turbulent ones', a friend wrote to John of Ulm, the German academic who had had such high hopes for her.[34]* He referred to the days since she had been proclaimed Queen at the Tower. Her reign had, in fact, lasted just over a fortnight.

From her house at Hatfield, Elizabeth composed a prompt letter of congratulations to her half-sister, Mary. The young princess absorbed important lessons from Jane's brief reign. She would not forget that Protestant bishops had declared her a bastard, along with Mary, and that the Protestant elite had proclaimed her so in favour of one of the Grey sisters. The ordinary people, by contrast, had supported Mary's rights of succession, and by inference hers. Elizabeth would recall also how, in the end, the elite had turned against Jane, in part, because her husband was a Dudley and that his name was hated. Jane's Secretary of State, Sir William Cecil, filed away the documents marked 'Jane the Queen', scribbling on one simply: *'Jana non Regina'* ('Jane not the Queen'). It might have been her epitaph. But it was as a prisoner in the Tower that she would truly come into her own.

---

* It is said by some modern historians that the 'nine-day Queen' was a later invention, intended to imply Jane's reign was a nine days wonder. But this letter is contemporary and is the probable origin of the phrase.

Chapter XII

A Prisoner in the Tower

S tripped of her canopy of state, Jane was now mocked by the
Tower guards. The imperial ambassadors reported that both she
and Guildford received 'sour treatment, very different to that meted
out to them during their reign'.[1] Jane had been moved to rooms in a
small house next to the royal apartments within the Tower, and
Guildford to the Beauchamp Tower close by. There they were
divested of valuables down to their small change. Their friends and
relations were, meanwhile, being brought in as prisoners almost
daily.

On the morning of 25th July 1553, Londoners were out in force for
the arrival of Northumberland and two of Guildford's brothers,
Ambrose and Henry. The mood of the waiting crowd was ugly.
Arundel, in charge of the prisoners, feared that Northumberland
might be lynched and asked him to remove his distinctive red cloak
before he passed through the City gates. Northumberland did as he
was asked. The prisoners then rode up the hill towards the Tower,
with their escort of cavalry and men at arms, under a barrage of
rocks, pebbles and cries of 'Traitor!', Northumberland's cap in his
hand in a gesture of penitence.[2] His sixteen-year-old son, Henry
Dudley, began to cry, but then a boy, about the same age, burst
through the armed ranks that lined the route, and started running up
and down the road, shouting and flailing with his sword. It was

apparent he had no ears, that he was, in fact, the mutilated Gilbert Potter, the first victim of Jane's brief reign.

The next day Parr of Northampton arrived at the Tower under guard, together with Robert Dudley. Jane was doubtless sorry to see Northampton a prisoner, but it would have been her father's arrival at the Tower on the 27th that distressed her the most. The family had hoped that Northumberland alone would bear the responsibility for the proclamation that declared Jane Queen and condemned Mary. The imperial ambassadors had been told, as if it were fact, that Northumberland was preparing to give the French Calais in return for their support for his son being made King. They had also been informed that Guildford had tried to pressure Jane into giving him the title, but Suffolk's arrest indicates that their claims were regarded with scepticism. It was left to Frances to defend the family line and she rode immediately to Mary, now at Beaulieu in Essex, to do so.

Frances arrived at Beaulieu at two o'clock on the morning of the 29th. It was here in the chapel that Jane had once berated Mary's servant, Lady Wharton, for genuflecting before the Blessed Sacrament. There cannot have been much sleep for Frances as she waited for her morning audience with Mary, but the Queen had both a forgiving nature and a long memory. A quarter of a century earlier, Frances's mother had done her best to convince Henry VIII of the folly of abandoning Catherine of Aragon in favour of Anne Boleyn. Those bitter years seemed very close now. Despite all her father had done – the break with Rome, his annulment of her mother's marriage to him in order that he might be free to have a male heir – she was Queen. Later that morning, after her prayers, Mary listened as Frances pleaded that the Grey family were victims of Northumberland's ambitions, with Harry Suffolk's illness ascribed to Northumberland having poisoned him. Her contention was, it appears, that having poisoned Edward (as many believed), Northumberland was determined to kill Suffolk also for acting as Jane's protector.[3] Guildford would then have become co-ruler, or

Northumberland would have placed a malleable eleven-year-old Mary Queen of Scots on the throne.

Frances's story was a little overwrought, even by the high standard of contemporary conspiracy theories. The facts remained, furthermore, that Jane had raised an army against Mary, the rightful Queen, and had signed documents calling her a bastard, as the imperial ambassadors flagged vigorously. Scheyfve and Renard, who had arrived at Beaulieu only a few hours before Frances, had enormous influence with Mary, representing, as they did, her cousin the Emperor. They were appalled when they discovered that she wanted to pardon Suffolk and his daughter, arguing that Jane, at least, should remain in the Tower. To release her, as they would persistently remind Mary, risked 'scandal and danger'.[4] Reluctantly, Mary agreed to deny her a pardon at this stage, but Jane's father, Suffolk, was pardoned the very next day. The good news was carried to the city of Leicester where grateful officials gave the messenger a large tip.[5] But Suffolk remained in the Tower for almost another fortnight, too ill to be moved. His servants claimed he might die, but it was Jane the family really feared for. The day after Suffolk was pardoned, Jane was charged with treason and faced an almost certain death sentence. Treason trials were not then designed to establish guilt or innocence, but to advertise the wickedness of the offender, and the case against Jane was a straightforward one. The family needed to redouble their efforts to achieve a pardon for her.

On 3rd August, the new Queen made her formal entry into London in a procession of nobles and courtiers to claim the Tower. Mounted on a horse trapped in cloth of gold to the ground, Mary wore a gown of violet velvet, the skirts and sleeves of which were also embroidered with gold.[6] She shared marked physical similarities with Jane. Like her much younger cousin she was 'of low stature ... very thin; and her hair reddish'. A witness judged her to be also 'more than middling fair', but at thirty-seven the bloom of youth had faded and she had become lined by anxiety.[7] Jane was not permitted to plead her case with the Queen as she entered the Tower, but Mary met those prisoners who were due for immediate release. The most prominent of these was Edward Courtney, a great-grandson of Edward IV. He had been in the Tower since 1538, when his father had been condemned to death for plotting to marry him to Mary. He was then only twelve, but had remained imprisoned during Edward's reign as a continued source of possible danger. Now, however, all those who did not want to see the Queen marry a foreigner, placed their hopes in a marriage with Courtney – and soon, if Mary was to stand a chance of bearing children.

Lady Katherine Grey, meanwhile, was to be divorced. Katherine had a very different character to her elder sister. Where Jane was passionate about ideas, Katherine's passions were of the heart and she had grown very close to her young husband Henry, Lord Herbert, during their traumatic weeks together. Both claimed desperately that the marriage had been consummated, in order to prevent an annulment, but it was a naïve gesture. Katherine was about to turn thirteen and her father-in-law, Pembroke, who had yet to live down his early role in Mary's exclusion from the succession, could not afford to take any chance that she might become pregnant. Katherine was to be sent back home to live with her mother and sister, Lady Mary Grey, whose betrothal to the battle-scarred Lord Grey of Wilton was also dissolved, surely to the relief of them both.

After the Queen had spoken to Courtney and the other prisoners, she was taken to the royal apartments where she was shown the crown jewels, retrieved from Jane. They included a ducal coronet of precious stones that had, perhaps, been destined for Guildford. There was a picture of Jane's grandmother, 'the Lady of Suffolk', in a yellow box, 'a picture of Queen Catherine [Parr] that last died' and a small portrait of Edward – whose body still lay unburied at St Peter's Church, Westminster.[8]

Through all the events of the past weeks, Edward's coffin had stood on its trestle, watched over by twelve gentlemen, but without any candles to brighten the dark: they were considered papist. His funeral could now at last go ahead. It took place on 8th August, according to the reformed rituals. Mary had wanted her brother to be given a full Requiem Mass with prayers for his soul, but the imperial ambassadors feared it would appear confrontational, so she held a Mass for him in private and gave him the public service he would have wanted. Ten days later, Mary issued a conciliatory proclamation promising a settlement of religion 'by common consent', asking that in the meantime people live under the religion 'they thought best'.[9] And there was another crowd-pleaser: the trials of the traitors Northumberland and Parr of Northampton had begun.

Northumberland observed bitterly at his trial that several judges present had signed the oath backing Edward's will. He reminded them also that he had done nothing without their authority and by warrant of Queen Jane under the Great Seal. To this, however, his judges replied that the seal of a usurper had no validity, and that they had no attainder against them. Northumberland and Northampton were then found guilty of treason and condemned to die. The next day the same verdict and sentence was pronounced on Sir John Gates and Sir Thomas Palmer, who had been the key witness in the trial that had condemned the Duke of Somerset for attempted murder.[10] It was said Northampton might be saved if he gave up his second wife, Elizabeth Brooke, and returned to his first, Anne Bourchier. Northumberland, meanwhile, had begged Mary to grant him the privilege of a beheading (instead of the usual traitor's death of hanging, drawing and quartering), and for mercy for his children. But he had also indicated his continued hopes for a pardon with two additional requests. He asked for Councillors to visit him in order that he might pass on secrets of state, and that 'I may have appointed to me some learned man for the instruction and quieting of my conscience'.[11] It signalled a possible conversion of faith.

Northumberland's execution was set for 21st August and by eight that morning the axeman was in place and a crowd of up to 10,000 had gathered on Tower Hill. Suddenly, however, the guard left. At nine o'clock, Jane, looking through the window of her rooms in the Tower, saw the duke and the other condemned men going to the Tower's chapel. Inside, the ancient rituals of the formerly banned

Mass were again being performed. As the prisoners prepared to receive communion, Northumberland turned to the congregation. 'My masters,' he began, 'I let you all to understand that I do most faithfully believe this is the very right and true way, out of which true religion you and I have been seduced these sixteen years passed, by the false and erroneous preaching of the new preachers.' The words electrified the chapel. Had not Northumberland been, with Northampton and Suffolk, the leading promoter of the evangelical religion in England for the past three years? The imperial ambassador Renard declared that his religious conversion was worth more than a month of sermons. But if Northumberland hoped it would save his life he was wrong. Hours later the Lieutenant of the Tower warned him that he should prepare himself for death the following morning. Gates and Palmer were given the same message. Northumberland wrote a frantic letter to Arundel asking him to plead with the Queen to allow him his life, 'yea the life of a dog, that I might but live and kiss her feet'.[12] As night fell, however, no word came from Mary. Despite his efforts to marry into the royal family Northumberland remained an outsider. And so Northampton and Suffolk, who had been as loyal to Jane as he, were to live and he to die, along with the more minor figures of Gates and Palmer.

The next morning, at nine o'clock, Northumberland was again processed into Mass with the other condemned prisoners and then returned briefly to his lodging. About three-quarters of an hour later, Gates emerged from the house of the Lieutenant of the Tower and sat at the gate to the garden awaiting his appointment at the scaffold. The guards then fetched Northumberland, who appeared dressed in a cloak of 'crane coloured' grey damask; he was followed by Palmer.

Northumberland addressed Gates bitterly: 'God have mercy on us, for this day shall end both our lives. And I pray you forgive me whatsoever I have offended; and I forgive you with all my heart, although you and your counsel were a great occasion thereof.' Gates had encouraged Northumberland to send his son, Lord Robert, to arrest Mary. Perhaps he believed that agreeing to do so had been his fatal error. It was later suggested by the Grey camp, however, that there was more to it than that: it was Gates who had persuaded Edward to change his will in Jane's favour.[13] 'Well my Lord,' Gates retorted; 'I forgive you as I would be forgiven; and yet you and your authority was the only original cause of all together; but the Lord pardon you and I pray you forgive me.' The men bowed, and Northumberland proceeded to the scaffold.[14]

Standing by, watching, were the sons of the former Protector Somerset, the fifteen-year-old Hertford and his younger brothers. The previous day Northumberland had begged their forgiveness for his part in their father's death, and they were now to witness justice being carried out. The waiting crowd was, again, enormous. 'So many came on horseback and on foot that it was a sight to see,' a Spanish witness recorded. Having mounted the scaffold Northumberland leaned over the rails to deliver his last speech. He reiterated his offences against Queen Mary and begged forgiveness. But he insisted that he was not alone in planning to alter the succession, or even 'the original doer thereof . . . for there were some other which procureth the same, but I shall not name them, for I will hurt now no man'.[15]

Was Northumberland referring to Gates? He was a junior figure, as he had reminded the duke. There were, as Northumberland suggested, several people, from the apex of the evangelical elite, who had, over time, helped shape Edward's thinking and whom he now blamed for what had passed. Northumberland conceded that greed and personal ambition had played a part in his decisions and he understood that people would be cynical about his sudden conversion, but he was angry with the evangelicals who had brought him here. With his executioner standing only feet from him, he declared 'as ye see I am in no case to say aught but the truth'.[16] If he was lying and still hoping for a last-minute reprieve, he was taking an enormous risk. He knew that if the axe swung at that moment he would be facing eternal judgement. Northumberland stripped off his doublet and took the blindfold proffered by the executioner. As he knelt down on the straw he made a sign of the cross on the ground – a Catholic gesture – and said his last prayers. He then knelt up to adjust the bandage around his eyes and threw himself flat upon the beam on the ground, clapping his hands together in a sign to the executioner. 'Oh, my good lord, remember how sweet life is, and how bitter the contrary,' Northumberland had written to Arundel. With one blow his head fell. Sir John Gates was not so lucky. It took three blows to remove his head. Then, with the beam slippery with their blood, it was the turn of Sir Thomas Palmer.

An ageing man, now in his fifties, Palmer leapt like a youth on to the scaffold. He freely confessed himself guilty of the lies that had helped send the Protector to the scaffold for attempted murder. But he was optimistic about the next life. He had learned more of God's goodness, he said, 'in one little dark corner in yonder Tower, than ever I learned by any travels in so many places as I have been. For there I say I have seen God, what he is, and how unsearchable his wondrous works are, and how infinite his mercies be.' He believed God had forgiven him. 'And should I fear death, or be sad thereof? Have I not seen two die before my eyes and within the hearing of mine ears? No, neither the sprinkling of the blood or the shedding thereof, nor the bloody axe itself, shall not make me afraid.' He turned to the executioner whose white apron was splashed red. 'Come on good fellow,' he said; 'art thou he that must do the deed? I forgive thee with all my heart.'[17] His head was taken, like the duke's, with one blow. Jane then watched their remains return in a wooden cart to the church where they had attended Mass.

It was common knowledge that Queen Mary remained determined that Jane's life would be spared, and that she intended to grant Jane a pardon after her trial had run its course.[18] The Grey camp had been feeding her arguments to give the imperial ambassadors that this would be a safe decision as well as the merciful one. On the eve of Northumberland's trial Mary had assured Scheyfve and Renard that Jane had not been privy to the plans to usurp her throne until a late stage. They were told, for good measure, that Jane's marriage to Guildford wasn't valid because she had been betrothed already to a member of Bishop Gardiner's household – a man of sufficiently low rank for her to be excluded as a possible rival Queen were they to be reunited.[19] The ambassadors were unimpressed, however, and no more was heard of the groom. So Jane's situation remained precarious when, a week after Northumberland's execution, she prepared to meet a Mr Rowland Lee for dinner in the Tower.

An official at the Royal Mint, it wasn't every day Lee sat down to eat with a prominent and controversial royal figure. But their host was a friend of his, a Mr Partridge, whose rooms were above those where Jane usually dined. Partridge had seen her there one day and invited her to eat with his wife and friend. He was, perhaps, Hugh, brother of 'Sir Miles Partridge', an old gaming companion of Thomas Palmer, who had been executed in February the previous year as an ally of the Duke of Somerset. The family were radical evangelicals, naturally sympathetic to Jane, but also enemies of Northumberland, and Hugh may have been serving as a gentleman jailor to his brother's executioners and former friends.[20] When Lee arrived at Partridge's rooms, Jane was already seated at the head of the table: a young girl with a poise and confidence beyond her years. Looking up, she raised her glass and drank to Lee, bidding him 'heartily welcome'. He snatched at his hat, but Jane reassured him that she was happy for him to keep it on. Lee then acknowledged the Partridges at the table, Jane's manservant and her gentlewoman, who was introduced to him as Mrs Jacob. Jane had at least three gentlewomen serving her in the Tower. Two were relations: Elizabeth Tilney (whose elder sister had served Henry VIII's doomed fifth wife, Katherine Howard) and Mistress 'Ellyn' – or 'Allan' in modern spelling. Mrs Jacob is often described as Jane's nurse, but this was an invention of the late seventeenth century, designed to highlight the poignancy of a young girl being locked in the Tower. It is more likely she was the wife of one of the Jewish musicians at court, such as Queen Catherine Parr had employed.[21]

Jane boldly opened the meal with a toast to Mary: 'The Queen's Majesty is a merciful princess; I beseech God may she long continue, and send his bountiful grace upon her.' Jane still hoped for a pardon, a wish, reportedly, she had expressed more directly in the past few days in a letter she had sent to Mary exonerating herself of ever having wished to be Queen.[22] She then led the conversation. Jane wanted to hear what news they had on Mary's religious policy. Who had preached at Paul's Cross the Sunday before? Dr Thomas Watson, Jane was told, the former private chaplain of Bishop Gardiner.[23] There had been an incident the previous week when the preacher, Gilbert Bourne, had been stoned after talking in favour of the Mass, but Watson had taken no chances and preached surrounded by an armed guard of over 300 men. Jane wanted to hear more about the possible reintroduction of the Mass. 'I pray you,' she asked, 'have they the Mass in London?' 'Yea for sure,' Rowland Lee replied, 'in some places.'

Jane was appalled and, recalling that Mass was being said in the Tower chapel, expressed her astonishment at her father-in-law's sudden conversion. 'Who would have thought he would have so done?' she reflected. Her dinner companions told her that people were saying he had hoped for a pardon. 'Pardon?' Jane exploded. 'Woe worth him! He hath brought me and our stock in most miserable calamity and misery by his exceeding ambition.' How could he have dared hope for a pardon 'being in the field [of battle] against the Queen in person as General'? Did he not understand he was a man 'whose life was odious to all men? But what will ye more?' she continued, her fury unabated, 'like as his life was wicked and full of dissimulation, so was his end thereafter. I pray God, I, nor no friend of mine, die so.' Jane then announced she would die before compromising her beliefs. 'Should I who am young forsake my faith for the love of life? Nay, God forbid! Much more he should not. But life was sweet, it appeared; so he might have lived, you will say, he did [not] care how.' Quoting the Scriptures she concluded that he was damned: 'Who so denies Him before men, he will not know him in his Father's kingdom.'[24]

Jane's comments offer a telling commentary on the weeks since her fall, and her intentions for the future. She hoped for a pardon from the 'merciful princess' Mary, in common with her mother blaming Northumberland for her situation and that of her family. If the Mass were to be introduced, however, she would make a stand against it, and accept death if that was the price of so doing.

A fortnight later, on the 13th or 14th of September, Guildford's imprisoned brothers were given permission to see their wives. It is doubtful, however, that Jane would have been allowed to see Guildford. The later story that she became pregnant that winter originates in a piece of anti-Marian propaganda, written in an elegy ten years later. But she may have spotted Guildford from her window, exercising with his brothers on the roof of the Beauchamp Tower, as the restrictions on them began to be relaxed. Certainly she had seen Parr of Northampton make his regular visits to Mass in the chapel, along with the Bishop of London, Nicholas Ridley. Jane was tormented by the thought of the numbers of people being drawn back to what she judged Catholic idolatry. And matters were only getting worse in this respect. Early in November, Parliament repealed all the religious legislation passed during the Edwardian period, which her father had done so much to promote. To Jane's intense pride he was amongst the few who tried to prevent the repeal.[25] But she intended to play her own part in defending her religion on the public stage of her trial on 13th November.

On that morning she was led out of the Tower with Guildford, his brothers Ambrose and Henry, and the Archbishop of Canterbury Thomas Cranmer, to be brought on foot to the Guildhall. The procession made its way through the streets, led by a man carrying an axe: a reminder that the prisoners were being tried for a capital crime. The first prisoner in the line was Cranmer, then Guildford, dressed dashingly in a black velvet suit slashed with white satin. Jane was behind him, looking every inch the star prisoner. She had dressed in the deepest black as a symbol of penitence, her black cape trimmed and lined with black; even the detailing on her French hood was black. She held a prayer book open in her hands to broadcast her evangelical piety, while another, covered in black velvet, hung from her waist. Here was not so much penitence, as defiance. Behind Jane came her ladies, Mrs Jacob and her cousin Elizabeth Tilney, and behind them Guildford's brothers, Ambrose and Henry. Transcripts of the trial do not survive, but Michel Angelo Florio, who had dedicated to Jane his Tuscan dictionary earlier that year, recorded that she remained cool and composed, from the clash of arms as she reached the Guildhall until judgement was read. The Chief Justice Sir Richard Morgan, who had been one of those imprisoned under King Edward for attending Mass in Mary's chapel, condemned her to be burned alive, the automatic sentence for any woman convicted of treason. As the procession returned, the axe was turned inward as a sign the death sentence had been passed and many in the crowd wept in pity for Jane.

The possibility of a pardon still remained, however, and Mary let it be known once more that she did not want Jane to die. In yet another effort to appease the imperial ambassadors and convince them Jane was no longer a danger, it was said that the Grey sisters were illegitimate since their father had been betrothed to the Earl of Arundel's sister before he married Frances.[26] Suffolk, anxious to do what he could to help his daughter, also took the opportunity to profess undying loyalty to Mary, back-pedalled his attacks on the repeal of Protestant legislation, and said the Queen should marry whom she pleased, even if it was her rumoured choice, Prince Philip of Spain, the son of Charles V.[27] Suffolk hoped, perhaps, that in the event Mary would be diverted from a Spanish marriage by the Commons petition presented to her on 16th November. The signatories, who included religious conservatives as well as evangelicals, begged her to take a husband within the realm. Mary, however, had already accepted Prince Philip's proposal at a secret audience with the ambassador Renard.

The news, when it emerged later in the month, was deeply unpopular. Fears that England would be absorbed into the Hapsburg empires re-emerged and on the 26th a group of evangelical gentlemen close to the Greys met to plot a series of risings in the south, west and midlands. They included a kinsman of Frances, Sir Peter Carew, Northampton's cousin, Sir Nicholas Throckmorton (whose wife had stood proxy to Jane at the christening on the last day of her reign) and a first cousin of Elizabeth Brooke, Thomas Wyatt.[28] They were to be joined by two noblemen. The first was Courtney, who had hoped that his years in the Tower were to be rewarded with a crown, as the husband of Queen Mary, but who had merely been awarded the earldom of Devon. The second was Harry Suffolk. In his daughter's last days as Queen, Jane had called men to arms to defend the crown, 'out of the hands of strangers and papists'.[29] As Carew outlined to Suffolk, these were the rebels' intentions: to prevent Mary's marriage to Philip of Spain and reconciliation with Rome. The conspirators intended to replace Mary with Elizabeth, whom they hoped to marry to Courtney. Jane was regarded as a spent force. Suffolk was happy to agree to this. Jane had never wanted to be Queen, and he was motivated by religious principle above personal ambition.[30]

The Mass was set to be reintroduced by royal proclamation in December and Suffolk feared this would leave England at the mercy of priests. 'The duke holds to the true God,' despite the 'devil whose agents are striving with all their might to lead his lordship astray', the Bradgate chaplain James Haddon wrote to Bullinger in Zurich. Suffolk knew that if his plot failed his daughter could be executed. But if Jane's speech at Partridge's dinner table reflected her true feelings, she would have surely judged this a gamble worth taking.

Chapter XIII

A Fatal Revolt

It was bliss for Jane to walk in the crisp winter air after months spent in her dark rooms in the Tower. From 18th December she had the freedom to walk in the Queen's garden. Mary intended that the next step would be a pardon for Jane and her return home to Bradgate. Parr of Northampton was due to be released at the end of the month. Mary had not yet fully grasped, however, that Jane's beliefs were as strongly held and profound as her own. Jane had no intention of compromising her faith as Northampton had. On the contrary, she intended to take a lead in attacking the re-establishment of the Mass.[1] Jane had already composed a vociferous letter, damning all those who attended Catholic communion. It was to be widely circulated in England, and eventually in Europe as well.

The letter was addressed to one of the Grey sisters' former tutors, Dr Thomas Harding. A humanist scholar and former Regius Professor of Hebrew, he had been a chaplain at Bradgate in 1547. In November, however, the family had learned that he had 'wonderfully fallen away' from 'Protestantism' (as the evangelical religion had begun to be called) and had embraced the Catholic faith.[2] Jane's letter, which was clearly aimed at all those tempted to follow Harding, condemned him in language so strong her Victorian admirers refused to accept that their 'gentle Jane' could have been responsible for it. 'I cannot but marvel at thee, and lament thy case,' Jane wrote to Harding, acidly. A man who had once been a member of Christ's Church was 'now the deformed imp of the devil', his soul 'the stinking and filthy kennel of Satan'. She compared the Catholic taking of Holy Communion to an act of satanic cannibalism. How could he, she asked, 'refuse the true God, and worship the invention of man, the golden calf, the whore of Babylon, the Romish religion, the abominable idol, the most wicked Mass, wilt thou torment again, rent and tear the most precious body of our saviour Jesus Christ, with thy bodily and fleshly teeth?'

Jane took the opportunity to attack also the pragmatists who accepted the religion of the crown rather than encourage divisions that could lead to violence. What did unity matter, she asked, if it was the 'unity of Satan and his members . . . thieves, murderers, conspirators, have their unity'. 'Christ', she reminded, had come 'to set one against another', not to bring peace but a sword, and she exhorted them to 'Return, return again unto Christ's war.'[3]

The plans for the revolt in which her father was involved were finalised on 22nd December. The rebellion was to begin three months later on Palm Sunday, 18th March. Carew and Courtney were to lead a rising in Devon, while Jane's father, Sir James Croft and Thomas Wyatt were to lead others simultaneously in Leicestershire, Herefordshire and Kent. They would then converge on London. If Jane's letter to Harding was asking people to prepare for a purely spiritual battle, she was surely not so naïve as to believe that a different interpretation might not be put on her words. Jane may have never wished to be Queen, but it does not follow that she wanted the Catholic, Mary, to keep the throne. Her tutor John Aylmer recorded that she had said in the past it 'would be a shame to follow my Lady Mary against God's word, and leave my lady Elizabeth, who follows God's word'. It was Elizabeth the rebels now intended to place on the throne, and Carew told Suffolk that once Mary was overthrown, he would personally lead the fallen Queen to the Tower and release Jane.[4] Unfortunately for Jane, however, Carew then started boasting about the rebels' plans. Rumours began to spread that there would be armed resistance to oppose the Spanish marriage in Devon and

Carew was summoned to court to be questioned. He failed to appear.

On 21st January, Bishop Gardiner extracted the gist of the plot from Courtney, whom he had befriended during their years together in the Tower. Suffolk's brother, Lord Thomas Grey, then heard at court that the plot had been discovered and rode straight to Sheen to warn Suffolk that 'it was to be feared he should be put again in the Tower'. Lord Thomas advised Suffolk to bring the rising forward. In Leicestershire, 'amongst his friends and tenants, who durst fetch him?' Lord Thomas asked. It was difficult, however, for Suffolk to think clearly. He was still ill with 'the stone' and had spent several days in bed. Panicked and in pain he chose to trust his brother's judgement, just as he had trusted those who had suggested his daughters' marriages, and earlier, Jane's wardship.[5] On the 25th, Carew abandoned their plans and fled to France.

Wyatt, however, proved of sterner stuff, and raised his standard at Maidstone. The news of 'stirs' in Kent was promptly brought to the Queen at Whitehall. Suffolk, still at Sheen, was already preparing to leave for the Midlands when a messenger arrived summoning him to court.[6] The Queen wished to give him the opportunity to prove his loyalty by offering him the chance to lead troops against Wyatt. Suffolk dismissed the messenger as quickly as he could. 'Marry,' he told him, 'I was coming to her grace. Ye may see I am booted and spurred, ready to ride, and I will but break my fast and go.'[7] Having tipped the messenger and instructed his servants to give him plenty of beer to drink he then left for Bradgate. He had as yet made no preparations to raise an army. The only ready money he had was the 100 marks his secretary John Bowyer had collected at short notice from a debtor in London. But there was now no turning back. Suffolk and his brothers, Lord Thomas and Lord John, were declared traitors as soon as they failed to arrive at court.

The following morning at Whitehall, Suffolk's Leicestershire neighbour, the Earl of Huntingdon, offered to pursue and arrest them. Huntingdon had been a political ally of Suffolk's since the days of Thomas Sudeley's plots against the Protector. His son was Jane's brother-in-law, having married Northumberland's daughter, Catherine Dudley, in the triple wedding of May 1553. But he seized the opportunity to redeem himself in the eyes of the Marian regime. In destroying the Greys he would also achieve total dominance of Leicestershire, an ambition his family had held for generations. He promised Mary that he would do his duty and left immediately with her orders.

The weather was bad and the roads 'foul and deep' as Suffolk made his way north.[8] He had arranged, through Bowyer, to meet his brothers at St Albans, but they missed each other. Instead they eventually caught up at Lutterworth where Suffolk was waiting for his brothers in the house of one of his tenants. They stayed two nights and, anxious to avoid the divisive religious issue, tried to recruit men in the area with the rallying cry: 'Resistance to the Spaniard!' People's concerns about Mary's marriage had been answered largely, however, by the contents of the marriage treaty that had been published less than two weeks earlier on 14th January. It revealed that while Philip was to bear the title of 'King', his powers were to be very restricted. He could not take England into his father's war with France; if Mary predeceased him he was to hold no further authority in England, and he was granted no English patrimony. Even the lowliest member of a monarch's Council expected more from service to the crown. Not a blade of English grass, not a brick or a stone, was to be Philip's. Mary was Queen and he a mere consort. Suffolk's recruitment efforts also faced other difficulties. His former association with the unpopular Northumberland went against him, and he was naïve enough to admit to his lack of money.

When Suffolk reached Bradgate on the 28th he had only a small band of followers. Letters from court, meanwhile, were on their way to JPs in the counties informing them that Suffolk's claim that England was to be handed to the Spanish was a lie. His real intention, the letters claimed, was 'to advance Lady Jane his daughter, and Guildford Dudley her husband'.[9] Suffolk responded with his own letters, denying these claims. His actions were explained instead in a series of proclamations, which offered sixpence a day to those who would oppose the Spanish marriage. A neighbour, Dr Francis Cave, helped draft another letter to the Queen justifying the revolt. That afternoon Suffolk ordered his servants to put on their armour and asked one of his secretaries to help dress him in his. Tensions were running high and the nervous man was clumsy as he strapped the protective plate on the duke's leg. Suffolk, irritated, cuffed him. That evening, the 29th, Suffolk arrived with his men at Leicester. He was welcomed and the city gates shut on his orders. The bailiff of the local town of Kegworth had sent £500 in Suffolk's support.[10] It would help pay for a few men and Suffolk, convinced that the evangelical Huntingdon, sent in his pursuit, was planning to betray Mary and take his part, ordered that a message was sent to him outlining his next moves.

In the morning Suffolk's proclamation against the royal marriage was read. But the Mayor of Leicester was growing fearful. 'My Lord, I trust your Grace means no hurt to the Queen's majesty?' he asked the duke. 'No,' Suffolk assured him, and resting his hand on his sword he swore loudly: 'He that would her hurt, I would this sword were through his heart.' But when Suffolk left for Coventry that afternoon he still had only about 140 horsemen with him, and most of them were his own servants.[11] They included Jane's tutor John Aylmer, and John Wullocke, the chaplain who would one day play an important role in the Scottish reformation.

Another of Suffolk's secretaries[12] had gone ahead to raise support in advance of their arrival. Despite the duke's efforts not to draw attention to the religious issues, Protestants in the city had assured him that, 'My Lord's quarrel was well known as God's quarrel', and invited the duke to come 'without delay'. As Suffolk approached the city he learned that Huntingdon intended to arrest him, not help him, and that his troops were hard on their heels. The city ahead offered the hope of protection, but when they were within a quarter of a mile Suffolk was warned the gates were bolted. As he may have feared, his close association with Protestantism had not helped him and the majority of citizens were in armour, ready to resist his entry. Suffolk realised the only option now was to turn and run.

The company rode hard to Suffolk's nearby castle at Astley where they stripped off their armour. His brothers, Lord Thomas and Lord John, borrowed frieze coats of wool felt from the servants to disguise their rank, while Suffolk divided his remaining money amongst his followers and told them to escape as best they could. He hoped to flee to Lutheran Denmark, though he would have to evade Huntingdon's men first. His keeper, Nicholas Laurence, found a place for him to hide, in the hollow of an oak tree in Astley park. But he was not there for long: only the next day Huntingdon's men forced Laurence to confess his master's whereabouts and dogs were used to run Suffolk to ground. The hunter in the park had become the hunted. Suffolk's brother, Lord John, was also found, hiding under hay. Lord Thomas got as far as Wales before he too was caught.

The rebels in Kent, meanwhile, still appeared to have a good chance of success. The men Mary had raised in the City to fight the rebels had deserted and were now under Wyatt's flag. By 3rd February, when the news reached London and Jane that Suffolk had been captured, the rebels had advanced into the suburbs around Southwark, where they looted and burned Bishop Gardiner's palace. There was hope for her yet. Two nights later the rebels shot and killed a Tower waterman on the river. At Whitehall, meanwhile, there was panic. An armed guard had been assembled in the Presence Chamber, their pole axes ready in their hands, and Mary's ladies-in-waiting were crying, 'We shall all be destroyed this night.'[13] Cannon at the Tower were moved with great commotion to face the rebels on the other side of the water and at dawn the next day the people of Southwark woke to find the great guns trained on their homes. They urged Wyatt to move on. As he advanced further into London one of his spies was hanged in St Paul's churchyard, along with an under sheriff for Leicester caught carrying letters for Suffolk.[14] The approach of the rebel army was focusing minds. Although the intention of the rebels was to have Elizabeth as their Queen, this was not clear at court. Jane and Guildford were potentially dangerous figureheads, totemic to the rebel cause. As they had been already found guilty of treason and condemned to die, it would also be a simple matter to allow those sentences to be carried out.

The next day, therefore, as the rebel advance continued, Mary agreed to sign the warrant for Jane and Guildford's executions. The sentences, burning for Jane and hanging, drawing and quartering of Guildford, were to be commuted to beheading, but it was intended that the sentences be carried out within days.

Jane, although, a prisoner in the Tower refused to be also a prisoner of events. Her father had wanted her to be a queen and an evangelical leader. She had been the former, against her better judgement, but she remained determined to fulfil her destiny as the latter. She would be the 'innocent usurper', martyred for her stalwart Protestantism, and set an example to others to defy Queen Mary's idolatry. 'If my faults deserve punishment, my youth at least, and my imprudence were worthy of excuse,' she noted; 'God and posterity will show me favour.'[15]

Jane knew that her father would be brought to the Tower, but it was Guildford who seems to have first thought of leaving a message for him. He sent Jane an old prayer book that must have been used many times by prisoners in the Tower. He had inscribed it with a farewell to Suffolk that was full of warmth and affection, despite the earlier accusations from the Grey camp of his former ambition to be crowned a King: 'Your loving and obedient son wisheth unto your grace long life in this world, with as much joy and comfort as I wish to myself, and in the world to come life everlasting. Your humble son to his death, G. Dudley.' Underneath Jane wrote her own message in more overtly Protestant terms. Guildford still hoped for life but she assured her father she believed they were to die as martyrs: 'The Lord comfort your grace, and that in His Word wherein all creatures only are to be comforted. And though it has pleased God to take away two of your children, yet think not, I most humbly beseech your grace, that you have lost them, but . . . that we, by losing this mortal life, have won an immortal life.' As she had honoured him in this world, she promised she would pray for him in the next, 'Your grace's humble daughter, Jane Dudley'.[16]

As Jane prayed in her rooms, the Wyatt rebels continued to fight their way towards the heart of London. By dawn on 7th February they reached Knightsbridge. Jane and Guildford were due to be executed that morning, but this was abandoned as the Queen's scout brought news to court of the approaching rebels. As the drums called the muster to arms, and the City rang with the shouts of people fleeing the area, the Privy Council urged Mary to leave London immediately. She refused. Mary had given a rousing speech at the Guildhall a week earlier, declaring herself wedded to her realm and the mother of her subjects. The response to Mary's speech had been emotional, and she faced the rebels confident that the people were on her side, and God also. Her manner was such that some feared she intended to mount her horse and lead her army in person.[17] In fact she had made a still braver decision: she placed her army in the hands of Pembroke, who had betrayed her for Jane's cause the previous year.

The battle in London continued all day. At one point the royal troops at Charing Cross broke and at court there were shouts of 'Treason!' Pembroke had changed sides, it was said, and there was 'running and crying of ladies and gentlewomen, shutting of doors and such a shrieking and noise as it was wonderful to hear'.[18] From the roof of the White Tower, Parr of Northampton watched the fighting rage below. He had been released from the Tower at the end of December only to be rearrested in the house of Wyatt's mother. He kept his emotions in check as the battle ebbed and flowed, until late afternoon when it was clear that the rebels had been defeated. He then put on a great display of rejoicing.

Neither Jane's reaction, nor that of her husband, is recorded, but at 5 p.m. she and Guildford heard the cries and clanging of metal that heralded the arrival of new prisoners. They included Sir Thomas Wyatt, Northampton's brother-in-law Thomas Brooke, and several other rebels, still dressed in mail and spurs. They were pulled, shoved and abused as they were taken to their cells. Prisoners continued to arrive the next day until the Tower rooms were full. The warrant to execute Jane and Guildford had, however, not yet been signed, and now that Mary was safe she was reluctant to do so. The Privy Council, including those who had proclaimed Jane in the summer, joined together with the imperial ambassadors to press her into it, and the executions were set for Friday, 9th February.

To help Jane prepare for her death, and in the hope of cleansing her soul from the infection of heresy, Mary sent her personal chaplain, John Feckenham, to the Tower. A former Benedictine monk, Feckenham was a kindly, jovial man in his early forties. He had resisted the Edwardian reforms and had ended up in the Tower, so he knew well what it was like to be interred there. He was also extremely persuasive: Feckenham would later claim no less a figure than Edward VI's tutor, John Cheke, as one of his converts. When he arrived at Jane's rooms in the Tower, Jane took in briefly the priest's stocky figure, round face and high colouring. She told him she was expecting him, but that it was too late for them to debate theology. She had to prepare to die. Jane must have looked pathetically young to Feckenham, and when the priest returned to court he begged the Queen to grant Jane a few more days of life so that he could give her instruction. Mary agreed: the sentence of death was commuted for Jane and Guildford from Friday until Monday, 12th February. Two days later, on the Saturday Jane's father and her uncle, Lord John, arrived at the Tower, brought by Huntingdon with an escort of 300 horse.

The smell of mud and defeat was in the air once more, but Jane was well prepared for Feckenham's next visit. Amongst her writings in the Tower is a prayer she said for courage. 'Lord, thou God and father of my life, hear me poor and desolate woman,' she prayed; 'arm me, I beseech thee, with thy armour, that I may stand fast.'[19] She was now 'girded about with verity' and wearing 'the breast plates of righteousness'. It must have seemed that her whole life had led to this point.

Jane had not forgotten Anne Askew, burned for heresy by Henry VIII in 1546, and whose arguments with her persecutors had been recorded for posterity.[20] Jane intended to preserve the best of her exchanges also. Feckenham found Jane as cool and composed as she had been for her trial. He told her how sorry he was to see her in such a terrible situation, although he could see she bore her pain 'with a constant and patient mind'. Jane retorted dryly that far from regretting her situation, she regarded it as a 'manifest declaration of God's favour towards me'. It was an opportunity to repent her sins, just as the execution of Thomas Seymour of Sudeley had been for him. As such she welcomed it. Feckenham then asked: 'What is required of a Christian man?', and over the following hours the determined priest and the passionate sixteen-year-old debated the path to salvation: Jane for the Protestant view that faith alone was required, and Feckenham reiterating Catholic belief that people have a role to play in their fate and that acts of charity and other 'good works' are also necessary. They debated too the Real Presence of Christ in consecrated bread and wine, with Jane attacking the Catholic Church as 'the spouse of the devil' for its 'idolatrous' interpretations. But then it was over, and they were back where they had begun.

Feckenham observed sadly that they would never agree. 'True,' Jane replied; 'except God turn your heart.' She warned that unless he changed his opinions he would go to hell, 'and I pray God, in the bowels of his mercy, to send you his Holy Spirit; for he hath given you his great gift of utterance, if it pleased him also to open the eyes of your heart'.[21]* Feckenham asked Mary again for a pardon for Jane, but Bishop Gardiner was now prepared to join voices on the Council to undermine his efforts. That Sunday afternoon, Gardiner preached before the Queen in her private chapel. To the evangelicals he was a demonic figure, with 'frowning brows, eyes an inch within the head' and 'great paws like the devil'.[22] They certainly had good reason to fear him. The bishop was about to declare that Protestantism and treason were one.

Gardiner began by reminding the congregation of Catholic teaching. That God had given man free will, and that good works are

---

* It was not to happen: Feckenham died in the infamous Elizabethan prison at Wisbech, rather than give up his religion.

necessary for redemption. Certain divines, he continued, had betrayed the English Church after the death of King Henry by preaching heresy. Then he addressed Mary. Gardiner had a 'boon of the Queen's highness'. He recalled she had pardoned many traitors who had proclaimed Jane as Queen in July 1553. From this act of mercy, he argued, 'open rebellion was grown'. He asked, 'that she would now be merciful to the body of the commonwealth' and that 'the rotten and hurtful members thereof' be 'cut off and consumed'. It was a chilling phrase and afterwards, as the congregation milled together, they were in no doubt that 'there should shortly follow sharp and cruel execution'.[23]

That night was the last Jane had to compose her final letters. She knew her father was in great distress over her fate and his hand in it. She wanted to reassure him it was God who had brought her here, that he was only God's instrument. 'Father,' she began,

> *although it pleases God to hasten my death by one by whom my life should rather have been lengthened; yet can I so patiently take it, that I yield God more hearty thanks for shortening my woeful days, than if all the world had been given into my possession, with life lengthened at my own will. And albeit I am assured of your impatient dolours redoubled manifold ways, both in bewailing your own woe, and especially, as I hear, my unfortunate state; yet, my dear father (if I may without offence rejoice in my own mishaps), herein I may account myself blessed, that washing my hands with the innocence of my fact, my guiltless blood may cry before the Lord, 'Mercy to the innocent!'*

She reminded her father that he knew, better than most, how she had been pressed to accept the crown. Now she looked forward to escaping 'this vale of misery' to a heavenly throne. 'The Lord that hitherto has strengthened you, so continue you, that at last we may meet in heaven,' Jane concluded.[24]

No letters to Jane's mother survive, or to her youngest sister, Mary. Frances may have destroyed them. She knew that in order to protect her younger children she would have to conform – or at least appear to do so, as their friend William Cecil and many others were doing. It is possible Jane understood this, although her letter to Katherine suggests otherwise. Written on blank pages in a copy of the New Testament in Greek it asked Katherine to prepare for martyrdom. It did not seem to matter to her that Katherine was only thirteen years old. Jane's principal concerns were intellectual and religious. Jane wanted this letter to rouse anyone who read it to make a stand in defence of their beliefs. She wrote to Katherine as the sister who would inherit her mantle, and she did not, therefore, need to compose a similar letter to Mary Grey:

> *I have sent you, good sister Katherine, a book, which, though it be not outwardly trimmed with gold, yet inwardly it is of more worth than precious stones. It will teach you to live it will learn you to die ... Trust not that the tenderness of your age shall lengthen your life ... for as soon as God will, goeth the young as the old. Labour always and learn to die. Deny the world, defy the devil, and despise the flesh.*

If Katherine was tempted to save herself by accepting the Catholic faith then, 'God will deny you and shorten your days.' The damnation of the apostate would await her. 'As touching my death, rejoice as I do,' Jane continued, 'for I am assured that I shall for losing a mortal life find an immortal felicity.' She concluded her letter: 'Farewell dear sister; put your only trust in God, who only must uphold you, your loving sister, Jane Dudley.'[25]

The papal nuncio Commendone recorded that Guildford also had a last message which he sent to Jane.[26] It was that 'before dying, he wished to embrace and kiss her for the last time'. Jane, however, did not want any distractions from her prayers and 'she let him answer that if their meeting could have been a means of consolation to their souls, she would have been very glad to see him, but as their meeting would only tend to increase their misery and pain, it was better to put it off for the time being, as they would meet shortly elsewhere, and live bound by indissoluble ties'.[27] They were words of affection, but not of passion.

At light the next morning, the noise of hammering could be heard as the scaffold intended for Jane was erected by the White Tower. As a royal princess she would have the privilege of being executed in the privacy of the Tower grounds. The sound found its echoes throughout London as pairs of gallows were set up at every gate in anticipation of captured rebels, and also on Tower Hill, where Guildford was to die. Just before ten Jane saw her husband being led from the Beauchamp Tower.

Guildford stopped at the main gate where Sir Anthony Browne was standing and grasped him by the hand. Sir Anthony was a Catholic, but he was also Lord John Grey's brother-in-law: it made him family. Guildford asked Sir Anthony to pray for him before asking the same of the other gentlemen standing with him. Amongst them was Sir Nicholas Throckmorton's brother, John, who had drawn up Jane's proclamation as Queen. Guildford walked through the gates; on the other side the sheriff waited to escort him to Tower Hill. Parr of Northampton was again on the roof, this time of the Devlin Tower, to watch the tall, fair boy meet his end. There was no priest to attend on Guildford, which suggests he had refused one. He simply said his prayers and laid himself flat on the block. If Jane was a martyr, was not he also? She had thought so, which was why she had told her father he too would claim an 'immortal felicity'. It took one blow to take off his head. As Jane emerged from Partridge's lodgings for the last walk of her life, Guildford's body was carried into the Tower's chapel, his blond head wrapped in a bloody cloth. Jane, who seemed 'nothing at all abashed', then followed the Lieutenant of the Tower, Sir John Bridges, to the scaffold.

She was dressed in the same black gown that she had worn for her trial and, as then, she carried an open prayer book. Her ladies, Mistress Allan and Elizabeth Tilney, 'wonderfully wept', but Jane's eyes remained dry as she read her prayers. Having mounted the steps of the scaffold by the White Tower, she went to the rails and turned to the select audience. The traditional admission of guilt was to be a qualified one:

Good people, I am come hither to die, and by a law I am condemned to the same. The fact, indeed, against the Queen's Highness was unlawful, and the consenting thereunto by me: but touching the procurement and desire thereof by me or on my behalf, I do wash my hands thereof in innocence, before God, and the face of you, good Christian people, this day.

At this she wrung her hands, still holding her prayer book.

I pray you all, good Christian people, to bear me witness that I die a true Christian woman, and that I look to be saved by none other means, but only by the mercy of God in the merits of his only son, Jesus Christ: and I confess, when I did know the word of God I neglected the same, loved myself and the world, and therefore this plague or punishment is happily and worthily happened unto me for my sins; and yet I thank God of his goodness that he has thus given me time and respect to repent.

'While I am alive,' she continued, 'I pray you to assist me with your prayers.' She wanted no words said for the dead, as Catholics did.

As Jane knelt down she turned to Feckenham and, suddenly, he had a glimpse of the uncertain child behind the brave martyr: 'Shall I say this psalm?' she asked as if he had been one of her father's chaplains. 'Yea,' he replied. And so she recited the heartbreaking *Miserere mei Deus*, in English:

Have mercy on me O God, according to thy steadfast love; according to thy abundant mercy blot out my transgressions ... the sacrifice acceptable to God is a broken spirit; a broken and contrite heart, O God, thou wilt not despise.

Jane then stood up, gave Elizabeth Tilney her gloves and handkerchief, and Thomas Bridges, the brother of the Lieutenant of the Tower, her prayer book. She had inscribed it inside for his brother: 'Good master Lieutenant ... Live still to die, that by death you may purchase eternal life ... For, as the Preacher says, there is a time to be born, and a time to die; and the day of death is better than the day of our birth. Yours, as the Lord knows, as a friend, Jane Dudley.'[28]

As Jane began to untie her gown the executioner stepped forward to help her. Revolted, she ordered him to leave her alone and turned towards her two women. They took the gown and helped her remove her headdress and neckerchief. The executioner knelt and asked her forgiveness, which she gave 'most willingly'. He asked her then to stand on the straw. It was at that moment that she saw the rough beam of wood that served for the block. 'I pray you dispatch me quickly,' she asked. As she knelt, however, she was suddenly anxious that her request meant the blow could come at any time. 'Will you take [my head] before I lay me down?' 'No, madam,' the executioner replied.

Jane tied her handkerchief around her eyes. Blinded she had to feel for the block and in a rush of panic she realised she couldn't find it. 'What shall I do? Where is it?' she asked. Everyone standing there now saw the child that Feckenham had heard, looking for reassurance and help. Appalled, one of them guided her to the block. She laid her head upon the beam, stretched out her body and said: 'Lord, into thy hands I commend my spirit!' There was a fountain of blood, 'and so' a witness recorded, 'she ended'.[29]

PART THREE

Heirs to Elizabeth

'I swear, 'tis better to be lowly born,
And range with humble livers in content,
Than to be perk'd up in a glist'ring grief
And wear a golden sorrow.'

Henry VIII, Act II scene iii
William Shakespeare

Chapter XIV

Aftermath

O n the green, within the walls of the Tower, the scene on the scaffold resembled that of the butchery of an animal in a farm-yard. It was still possible, however, to recognise the remains on the straw as those of a slightly built girl. Surveying the gore, a French diplomat was amazed that something so small could produce so much blood. Jane's head had been cast into the same pit in the Tower chapel as that of Guildford.[1] Whether her body was later buried with it, we cannot be sure. The graves were re-dug and moved in the nine-teenth century. Her bones, along with those of Anne Boleyn and other executed traitors, now lie jumbled together in a grave behind the north wall, to the left of the altar, although some anonymous bones are still found beneath the chapel floor.

But while the dead show no weakness, know no temptation to compromise, for Jane's younger sisters, the messy business of living continued. Katherine and Mary were aged thirteen and nine respectively and their immediate situation was a terrifying one. Jane and Guildford's deaths marked only the beginning of Bishop Gardiner's 'cruel and sharp' executions. On the same day the Princess Elizabeth received a troubling request for her presence at court, and the pairs of gallows being built at every London gate were completed. On the Wednesday the hangings of the traitors began. At Cheapside there were six; at Aldgate one (hung, drawn and quartered, his intestines removed and genitals cut off while he was still alive). At Leadenhall there were three; at Bishopsgate one (also drawn and quartered) and at Charing Cross four. Three were hanged in chains at Hyde Park Corner, and so the carnage across London continued. The dozens of screaming, dying rebels included a royal footman and members of the guard.[2] But the Grey family also had blood left to spill.

Jane's sisters had little time to mourn her before their father faced his trial. On Saturday 17th February 1554, just five days after Jane had died, Harry Suffolk was escorted from the Tower to Westminster Hall under heavy guard. The great scaffold where Guildford had died had been made ready for his execution, though he faced the coming ordeal before his judges 'very stoutly and cheerfully enough'. The charge was high treason 'for levying war in the county of Leicester'; for posting proclamations opposing the entry to England of the Queen's betrothed, Prince Philip of Spain; 'for compassing the death and final destruction of the Queen'; and finally, for unsettling the crown.[3] Suffolk pleaded innocent to all charges, arguing that it was not treasonable for a peer to defend his country from strangers.[4] But Suffolk's own supporters had said: 'My Lord's quarrel was well known as God's quarrel,' and his judges took the view that Protestantism, rather than patriotism, lay behind his actions[5] and found him guilty on all counts. His former brother-in-law, Arundel, delivered the sentence of death. Suffolk was then returned by barge to the Watergate at the Tower. The river ran black in the shadow of the fortress and as he got out of the boat his expression was described as 'very heavy and pensive'.[6] He asked the men standing about to pray for him, and five days later his daughters were given a ray of hope that he might yet live.

A large number of rebels brought to Whitehall, their hands bound and nooses around their necks, had been pardoned as they knelt before the Queen. There was support at court for Suffolk and his brothers to be shown similar mercy. Lord Grey of Wilton, betrothed to little Mary Grey in the rash of royal marriages the previous year, remained a vocal friend. But, whatever Katherine and Mary hoped, their mother, Frances, knew their father would not be pardoned of treason twice. With her husband as good as dead, she focused her efforts instead on salvaging a future for her surviving children. Bradgate was forfeited to the crown along with the rest of her husband's wealth and estates. She had to rescue what she could and pleaded successfully with the Queen that, if she could not pardon Suffolk, she would forgive him. This, at least, opened the possibility of rehabilitation at court and the restoration of some of the attainted lands.

The night of 22nd February 1554, was to be Suffolk's last. Mary sent two of her own priests to the Tower, doubling the efforts she had made to save Jane's soul, but 'they were in no wise able to move him'.[7] He spent his last hours reading the theological works of Heinrich Bullinger, whom he had encouraged to guide Jane's spiritual development.

At nine o'clock the following morning, Suffolk left the Tower under guard to Tower Hill. He was accompanied by one of the Queen's chaplains, Hugh Weston, a fellow Leicestershire man. Perhaps that was why he was chosen. More likely, however, it was because he had spoken recently in a public debate on Eucharist doctrine against the Bradgate chaplain, James Haddon. As the crowd waited for the rituals of the execution to begin, Weston gave a sermon attacking Suffolk's religious beliefs.[8] The time when the Queen had invited people to follow their own religion was over. The doomed duke was so angry that when Weston began to climb the stairs of the scaffold behind him to minister to him in his last moments, he turned around and pushed the priest back. Weston grabbed on to him, and both fell to the bottom of the scaffold. There was an undignified struggle until Weston shouted out that it was the Queen's wish that he follow. Suffolk then gave way. When the duke reached the top of the scaffold he regathered his dignity and addressed the crowd: 'Masters, I have offended the Queen, and her laws, and am justly condemned to die.' He asked for the Queen's forgiveness. Weston, standing by, then confirmed: 'My Lord, her grace has already forgiven you and prays for you.' Suffolk defiantly now reiterated his Protestantism and, on his knees, said the Psalm of the persecuted, '*In te Domine, speravi*': the prayer of the just man under affliction.

> ... *I have heard the blame of many that dwell round about. While they assembled together against me, they consulted to take away my life ... Deliver me out of the hands of my enemies; and from them that persecute me ... Let me not be confounded, O Lord, for I have called upon thee ...*

At last, Suffolk stood up and gave his cap and scarf to the executioner, who knelt to ask forgiveness. 'God forgive thee and I do,' Suffolk told him, 'and when thou dost thine office, I pray thee do it well, and bring me out of this world quickly, and God have mercy to thee.' At this desperate juncture, a man to whom the duke owed money, and who had managed to get a place on the scaffold, stepped forward. 'My Lord,' he asked, 'how shall I do for the money that you do owe me?' Aghast, Suffolk replied: 'Alas good fellow, trouble me not now, but go thy way to my officers.' The man was bundled away while Suffolk took off his gown and doublet, tied a handkerchief around his face to cover his eyes, knelt down and recited the Our Father. Then he laid his head on the block and said: 'Christ have mercy on me.' The axe swung and his head fell with one stroke.[9]

On 9th March, Suffolk's brother, Lord Thomas Grey, was also tried and 'cast [to lose] his head'.[10] It was rumoured he had carried messages from Suffolk to the Princess Elizabeth, and on Palm Sunday, 18th March, the fearful princess walked the drawbridge from Tower wharf into the fortress where it was now her turn to be imprisoned. In common with Jane she had generous accommodation: four rooms within the royal palace, and she too had servants to attend on her. But this was the palace (in the inner ward of the Tower to the south-east) that her mother Anne Boleyn had left for her execution, and Elizabeth had seen, on the green, the scaffold where Jane had died. She was interrogated closely, but was careful to give nothing away, and, in contrast to the period of Sudeley's arrest in 1549, this time, her servants also held fast. Elizabeth could not be sure, however, what others might reveal in exchange for their lives.[11]

The Grey sisters, meanwhile, cleaved to their mother, Frances, who encouraged them to play the Catholic. This does not mean that she had forgotten Jane, or her Protestant beliefs, as was claimed after the eighteenth century. The Bradgate chaplain, James Haddon, describing Jane's death to the Italian divine Michel Angelo Florio, told him that Jane had inherited her piety from both her parents and had been close to her mother. Frances, however, had seen that the evangelical cause had been tarred with corruption and treason. It was best to stay silent and allow Jane's example of Protestant piety and steadfastness to now rescue it from the mire into which it had fallen. An associate of James Haddon had already translated into Latin Jane's angry missive to the former tutor, Harding, and the letter to her sister Katherine, so that they could be understood by an international audience; and they were on their way to her old mentor Heinrich Bullinger in Zurich.[12] Haddon was terrified what the consequences might be if they were published and begged Bullinger to keep Jane's letters secret. But he was wasting his ink. Someone had delivered the handwritten originals, and a description of Jane's conversation in the Tower with Feckenham, to an evangelical printer in Lincolnshire called John Day.[13] It is likely that Frances was the source of the material. She would have had access to the original letters and Day's press was hidden on the estate of their old family friend and kinsman, Sir William Cecil. The subsequent pamphlet had the appearance of a martyrology, and a second edition, published later in the year, also included a detailed account of her execution, along with a prayer inspired by her death, written by John Knox.[14] Taken together, Jane's writings and her speech on the scaffold have been described as the most powerful contemporary attack on the reign of Queen Mary.[15] But if Frances was involved with Day, she had to be very careful to cover her tracks. Her friend and stepmother, Katherine Suffolk, had already received threats from the Lord Chancellor, Bishop Gardiner.

When Katherine Suffolk had remarried, during the terrible period of grief after she had lost her sons, the husband she chose was a man who would not threaten her independence: her Gentleman Usher, Sir Richard Bertie. It was highly unusual to marry a servant, and frowned upon, but it was a love match, and a very happy one. They had just had a daughter and she was recovering from the birth, when Gardiner had Bertie summoned to London. Katherine Suffolk had once been Gardiner's favourite godchild, and he her 'gossip', but this friendship and mutual affection had turned to bitter contempt as their beliefs had diverged. Gardiner recalled her quip when he was in the Tower, that it was 'merry with the lambs now the wolf was shut up', and, as he questioned Bertie on whether his wife intended to conform to the Queen's religion, he asked chillingly: 'doth she think her lambs now safe enough?'[16]

As soon as Bertie returned home to Lincolnshire, plans were laid for the family to flee abroad – as many friends were doing already, including the chaplain James Haddon. That suited Gardiner: from his perspective the more potential trouble-makers who left the country, the better. Exile was not an option for Frances and her children, however. The French, who were at war with the Queen's cousin, Charles V, would have given anything to have such useful pawns, but for that very reason any move they made to flee the country would be interpreted as treason. So they stayed, and Frances waited for the storm of blood to pass.

Wyatt was beheaded on 11th April and on 24th April the sisters' uncle, Lord Thomas Grey, who had been sentenced to death in early March, was also executed. His body was buried at All Hallows, Barking, without its head, which was left on public display. People were growing tired of the killings, however, and, three days later, Sir Nicholas Throckmorton was found not guilty of treason at his trial – an almost unheard of verdict. The public had decided that vengeance and justice had run its course and there was little chance that any jury would convict Elizabeth, whom Wyatt and Grey had refused to implicate. The princess was released into house arrest on 14th May. Pardons followed for Suffolk's half-brother, George Medley, and several of the Grey family servants. Lord John Grey's wife, the sister of the Catholic Viscount Montague, began also to make headway in her eventually successful petitions on her husband's behalf.

Frances, meanwhile, completed the rehabilitation of her family in stunning fashion. In April she had been re-granted numerous former Grey manors in Leicestershire, including the lease of Beaumanor, near Bradgate, the old and new park, with 'free warren and chase of deer and wild beast'.[17] She hung it with portraits of Catherine Parr and her Tudor mother, the French Queen, Mary Brandon.[18] Then in July 1554, Frances was invited to join the Queen's Privy Chamber. Only six months after Jane's death, Katherine and Mary were back at court with their mother, and without their father's ambition and religious fervour driving the family, their future looked safe, for the time being. And if they could not show their continuing grief there was satisfaction, at least, in the news that the Chief Justice Richard Morgan, who had condemned Jane, had gone insane. Foxe recorded that he later went to his grave screaming for 'the Lady Jane' to be 'taken away from him' – but this may be wishful thinking.

Katherine and Mary Grey soon grew used to the routines of court life. Queen Mary was an early riser and her ladies were all dressed and ready for their duties by nine. A livery was provided in russet or black cloth, with richer clothes for high days and holidays borrowed from the royal wardrobe. Opportunities for exercise were limited, but there was always the possibility of early morning 'aerobics' for those who wanted to keep fit: 'walk twenty paces', one sixteenth-century manual advised; 'jump of your tiptoes down backwards . . . stretch . . . your body'. Meals were at noon and at six. Much of the rest of the day might be spent whiling away the hours in sewing, making jellies and hot sweet drinks, gossiping, reading, playing music and gaming.

The high social point of the week came on Sundays when the public presented their petitions to the Queen as she processed into the royal chapel with her ladies following behind her. Katherine, in particular, could not easily forget Jane's last letter to her with its dire warnings that she 'defy the devil', or be denied by God. There would soon be martyrs enough, however, and Katherine's immediate objective was not for paradise in the next world, but an ordinary life in this one. Katherine had expected and wanted nothing more than to be a nobleman's wife and this was the role that she still intended to make hers. So she learned the rosary and observed the Catholic fish days on Friday and holidays, when the tables at court were spread with seal, pike and trout, porpoise, lobster and shrimp.

Mary Grey's friend, the orphaned eleven-year-old Margaret Willoughby, who had grown up alongside the sisters since her father had been killed fighting the Norfolk rebels in 1549, often sat with her cousins at the long table where they dined in the Great Chamber of the royal palaces. Margaret had been in their uncle George Medley's house in the Minories when Gardiner's men had searched it during the recent revolt and later saw him taken to the Tower. When he had returned, in May, he was no longer in a state to care for Margaret or her younger brother. Frances had therefore arranged for Margaret's little brother, her godson Francis, to go to school, and took Margaret in. Her husband's former ward, Thomas Willoughby, who was Katherine's age, had been made the ward of a Councillor of notoriously low birth, in due course to be married to his daughter. But Frances told friends that 'bossy Margaret' was already making an excellent impression at court, and hoped for better things for her.

Frances attended the Queen as she ate in a neighbouring room, under her canopy of state. Queen Mary had a particular taste for spicy food and her Ladies of the Privy Chamber were responsible for keeping the pepper she sprinkled on her food, as well as taking delivery of expensive imported items such as oranges and olives.[19] The Queen had never seemed so happy to them, and her vibrant mood was reflected in her wardrobe. She had new gowns made of velvet, damask and taffeta, in brilliant crimsons and rich mulberry reds.[20] All her adult life her Catholic faith had been her comfort and her cousin, Charles V, her protector. Now she was poised to marry the Emperor's son, Philip, and she was certain she would soon have children to secure the future for her religion and the souls of her subjects.

Mary's confidence buoyed up the public mood. The people wanted desperately the stability an heir would provide, even if it was a Spaniard's child. Her betrothed, Prince Philip, arrived in England on 20th July. He had been disappointed by the marriage treaty, which had given him no authority in England, and marrying a woman a decade older than he was promised to be more of a duty than a pleasure. But Philip was determined to make the best of the situation with which his father had presented him. He met Mary at Bishop Gardiner's palace in Winchester, three days after his ship anchored at Southampton. The Queen was waiting in a private room, standing on a platform surrounded by her ladies, with music playing 'very melodiously'. As Philip entered, Mary stepped down to greet him. It was ten o'clock at night, but Philip's Spanish entourage saw, in the fading light, a dignified woman who looked older than they had expected, and was so fair that it appeared she had no eyebrows. She was wearing a black velvet gown, richly embroidered with pearls, and a girdle of diamonds in a style more French in taste than Spanish, and they felt it did not flatter her.

To the English the twenty-eight-year-old Philip, by contrast, projected youth and confidence. Mary was delighted with the young man walking towards her, his muscular legs in white hose and his black cloak splashed with silver embroidery. He was handsome, 'with a broad forehead and grey eyes, straight-nosed and manly countenance', as well as a figure that was perfectly proportioned.[21] They kissed at the door, and walked hand in hand to their chairs where they took seats under the canopy that framed them as Queen and King of England.

The royal marriage was celebrated at Winchester Cathedral on 25th July 1554.[22] The cathedral was draped in cloth of gold, and Mary was also in gold, the great sleeves of her gown embroidered with diamonds. Another huge diamond that Philip had given her, glittered on her chest and, as she stepped into the church, followed by her ladies, her white satin kirtle sparkled with silver embroidery and gold thread. Philip, walking at a 'princely pace', was dressed to complement his bride in white leather embossed with silver and a mantle of fluted gold.[23] Around his neck he wore the collar of the Garter he had been awarded as he arrived in England, along with priceless jewels belonging to the crown of Castile. The couple exchanged their marriage vows on a platform erected in front of the main altar. The wedding ring, a plain band of gold, was then laid on the Bible and the prince added coins as a mark of faith. The Queen was expected to follow suit and her Catholic Stuart cousin, the Lady Margaret, Countess of Lennox, opened the Queen's purse – it was indicative of the diminished status of the Greys that she should have been chosen for this task, rather than Frances. The Queen, smiling, took her coins from the countess and added them to Philip's.[24]

The wedding party that followed the marriage had at least one gate-crasher: the Greys' friend Edward Underhill, whose son was christened 'Guildford' on the last day of Jane's reign. He had sneaked into the banqueting hall, despite the best efforts of the chief usher to keep him out, and blended in by helping take food to the tables of wedding guests: golden and silver platters of beef, lamb and game wafting scents of cinnamon, thyme and rosemary. He noted an enormous tapestry hung on one side of the hall, and on the other a cupboard displaying over 120 large vessels in silver or gold. King Philip and Queen Mary were seated on a dais at the end of the room, the Queen in the place of precedence on the right. Below them, the guests were seated at long tables, the men and women divided on either side of the room, laughing and signalling at each other.[25] They included Katherine Grey's former husband, Lord Herbert, who had been made a Gentleman of Philip's Privy Chamber. Katherine often still spoke of him to her friends, and of the future that had been blighted the previous year.

After the feast the men and women were united for the dancing in a neighbouring room. Underhill thought the Spaniards looked greatly put out because the English were clearly the better dancers, but as each were doing their own national dances his prejudice was probably the judge. After the party broke up Underhill displayed a last show of cheek, making off with a gigantic venison pie which he sent to his wife and friends to enjoy in London. The royal couple, meanwhile, retired to bed. If Queen Mary was nervous about what was to be her first sexual experience she never showed it, and a Spaniard observed simply that 'the rest of the night may be easily imagined by those who have gone through it'. The next day the Queen refused to be seen by anyone – an English tradition on the first day of honeymoon it was said – but when she did emerge she looked joyful.

Come mid-September the court was abuzz with news that she was pregnant. This wonderful news for Mary was spoilt only by the vicious rivalry between the English and the Spanish at court. Fights broke out frequently that autumn and even the court ladies quarrelled. The Spanish noblewomen found they had no one to talk to, complaining angrily that 'the English Ladies are of evil conversation'.[26] How Frances, Katherine and Mary behaved can only be imagined: their husband and father, respectively, having died to keep the Spanish out.

Philip, however, was soon winning some personal support with his tact and generosity, and to everyone's relief he encouraged the Queen to break the tedium of court life with lavish entertainments. There were several masques that winter, with the women taking centre stage at Christmas as 'amorous ladies' and cupids.[27] Beyond the glamorous life of the winners at court, Philip was also careful, however, to listen to those cut off from his wife's favour. He achieved pardons even for the four Dudley brothers who had been left in the Beauchamp Tower. Behind them, they left the name 'Jane' carved in the stonework.[28] Their freedom was a relief for Katherine and Mary Grey. The youngest brother, Henry, was still married to their cousin Margaret Audley, whom Katherine used to visit when her sisters were at Tilty in Essex with the Willoughby children. The reason Philip was showing the brothers kindness, however, was a troubling one for England. He wanted to build bridges with England's young men so that they would later be prepared to fight in his father's wars, and it was with this in mind that he invested in several sporting combats that winter, as well as the more innocent feasts and masques.

The first combat display Philip put on was a traditional Spanish *jeu de cannes*, in which participants carried targets and hurled rods at each other. Katherine and her friends thought the spectacle pretty enough, with Philip in red and everyone else in multicolour, but they were used to watching the more thrilling and violent entertainments of the joust, and many of the ladies seemed bored. Philip tried next a fight on foot, in which he won a prize for swordsmanship; but again, the English seemed to find it dull, so from January he organised the combats on horse that they preferred. Some of the most dramatic jousts were held to celebrate the wedding of Frances's seventeen-year-old niece, Margaret Clifford, the daughter of her late sister, Eleanor. Margaret had been the young princess to whom Northumberland had hoped to marry his son, Lord Guildford Dudley, in 1552, and then to his brother, Sir Andrew Dudley, in 1553. She had escaped both, but had kept the rich and fine fabrics Sir Andrew had sent for her bridal dress and she wore them for her wedding to Lord Strange, the heir of the Earl of Derby.[29]

The King and Queen had laid on a full day of celebration. There was a midday feast followed with jousting and a tourney on horse with swords, in which three of the Dudley brothers performed.[30] Supper was then followed with a *jeu de cannes*, which the King played with such enthusiasm that the Queen sent word begging him not to expose himself to danger.[31] She wanted to take no chances with their future. She had healed the breach with Rome and, to protect her faith and her country from the further malice of her Protestant opponents, had, against the advice of almost everyone around her, revived her father's old heresy laws.

Margaret Clifford's glittering wedding took place in the aftermath of the first of the notorious burnings of Mary's reign. John Rogers, a prebendary, or canon, of St Paul's, had been executed at the stake three days earlier. The deaths by burning that followed were truly terrible ones. If the fires were poorly built the prisoners died by inches, conscious and screaming, and many friends of the Grey family would burn in the months ahead, Archbishop Cranmer, Hugh Latimer, and Bishop Ridley amongst them. Some of them had overseen burnings in the past: Latimer had cracked jokes about the burnings of Catholic priests, which he had attended in King Henry's time. But it was not what people expected from a merciful princess. As this new terror took hold, the Spanish diplomats learned that another court wedding was in the offing. Some on the Privy Council were proposing that Frances Grey be married to Edward Courtney, who had been sent back to the Tower after the Wyatt revolt, but re-released after his second stint in prison in April.[32] Perhaps the Councillors in question hoped that Mary might consider Frances a possible heir if Elizabeth was excluded. While the law proclaiming Mary illegitimate was rescinded, the stain was left on her sister. The recent efforts to overthrow Mary in favour of Elizabeth had soured the relationship between the Tudor sisters irreversibly and Queen Mary made clear she did not regard Elizabeth as her father's daughter. She liked to tell her maids of honour that Elizabeth bore a strong resemblance to Mark Smeton, the attractive young musician whom Anne Boleyn was said to have kept in a 'sweetmeat cupboard', calling for marmalade when she wanted his sexual services. Queen Mary had indicated that her preferred choice as her heir was her Catholic cousin, Margaret Douglas, Countess of Lennox, to whom she had given a prominent role at her wedding. There were doubts too, however, over the countess's legitimacy. That left Frances – but Frances did not want to do anything to put her children in further danger or to weaken Elizabeth's position.

Indication of the Grey family's support for Elizabeth comes from Katherine Grey. Frances's former lady-in-waiting, Bess Hardwick, and her husband Sir William Cavendish, had picked Katherine as godmother to their newborn daughter in March. She had chosen the name Elizabeth for the child. In any event, the last thing Frances wanted was a royal marriage with the unstable Courtney, and the feeling was mutual. Courtney had told the Queen that he would rather leave the country than marry Frances. By the time Courtney left in May, Frances had, in any case, married another man. The sisters' new stepfather was one whose station was such that she would be precluded from any future calculations concerning the succession: it also meant, however, that Frances would most likely withdraw from court, leaving Katherine behind. Frances had seen how happy and successful Katherine Suffolk's marriage to her Gentleman Usher had been, and had decided on a similar match. Her choice was her Master of the Horse, Adrian Stokes, of 'Hogesdon Middlesex' – what is now Hoxton in Islington, a fashionable area at this time.[33]

There are various unpleasant, but apocryphal, stories about Frances's marriage. One is that Frances married Stokes within three weeks of her husband's execution, in early 1554. This tale may have arisen because of later confusion over the dating of the Tudor year: it ran from 25th March rather than 1st January, so any date up to 25th March 1555 would have been written as 1554. But the mistake looks deliberate. There is no reason to suppose Frances was married before May 1555, and the story is recognisably part of the process through which Frances was later transformed into the counterpoint to her 'perfect' daughter Jane.[34] Where Jane was described as gentle, Frances was therefore depicted as brutal, and where Jane was chaste, Frances was necessarily lustful. A portrait by Hans Eworth of the hard-faced Lady Dacre and her beardless twenty-one-year-old son, has, since 1727, often been described as being of Frances and Stokes. Popular historians have enjoyed making much of the resemblance of the female sitter to Henry VIII in his latter years, observing how it reflected on Frances's supposedly cruel nature and sexual incontinence. The figure of the boy, described as Stokes, was depicted by these writers as a vulgar youth, for whom Frances was transported by desire. Stokes was, in fact, a mature man of thirty-six (to Frances's thirty-seven), a former soldier and a highly-educated Protestant.[35] That he was of a lower rank than Frances is without doubt, but the popular story describing the Princess Elizabeth sneering about Frances marrying her 'horse keeper' is a reverse of the truth. Elizabeth is known to have expressed only envy at the happiness Frances found with Stokes.[36]

With her marriage, however, Frances did retire largely from court, with worsening health, and reportedly enduring a series of failed pregnancies. Her younger daughter, Mary, now ten years old, remained in her care. There is little about her in the sources until she was almost twenty years old, but Katherine, rising fifteen, was often at court, where she began to make her own life, against the current of Queen Mary's stormy last years.

Chapter XV

Growing Up

Katherine, as the daughter of the Queen's first cousin, had her own room at court, as well as personal servants. She could even keep pets. Katherine loved toy dogs and, more exotically, small monkeys. But she was in no way isolated with her animals. There was something of a boarding-school atmosphere at court for the Queen's young attendants and Katherine would sneak to the maids' dormitory in her nightgown to gossip and play.[1] There were complaints, years later, about maids keeping elderly neighbours up at night as they played noisy games, danced and laughed, and there were many such carefree times for Katherine, even amidst the intrigues and the unhappiness that overtook Mary's court after the summer of 1555.

The sense of optimism that had followed the news of the Queen's pregnancy in September had leached away as the period of the lying-in drew to a close at Hampton Court. When the expected birth date, 9th May, passed, the Queen expressed the opinion that the baby had been due in June all along. But when no baby appeared in June, rumours began to circulate that she was not pregnant at all, but ill. It was only in August, however, when even the optimistic Venetian ambassador was saying that 'the pregnancy will end in wind', that Queen Mary accepted she was not pregnant.[2] No official announcement was made to explain the non-arrival of the expected heir: there was just an embarrassed, horrified, silence. Philip left England shortly afterwards.

Bishop Gardiner died that November knowing it was only a matter of time before Elizabeth would be Queen. He also knew that he was, in part, responsible for this. He had been one of the principal ideologues of the royal supremacy in King Henry's time, believing that England could be Catholic without the Pope. This had been rudely disproved when the Edwardian Council used the royal supremacy to bring 'heresy' into England. According to one Elizabethan Catholic account, Gardiner spent his last hours listening to the gospel narrative of Peter's betrayal of Christ, weeping bitterly. All was now lost. Only Queen Mary still believed it was possible she could yet have a child. The ladies and gentlewomen of the Privy Chamber watched her writing desperate letters to her husband, pleading for his return so they could try again for an heir. When eventually he replied, however, he demanded an impossible price. He wanted a coronation, believing that if he was anointed King of England it would give him the power that the marriage treaty had denied him. Mary knew Parliament would never agree to it, and had to refuse him. Philip then demanded something that was personally repugnant to her: that Elizabeth, as her heir, be married to an, as yet to be chosen, imperial ally as soon as possible. After reading one such letter Mary angrily threw her mirror across the room.

The Queen had grown pale, almost shrivelled, from being bled constantly to ease her depression. By contrast, the twenty-three-year-old Elizabeth, brought to Hampton Court during the confinement, was a vision of youth and health: 'Short, slender, straight and amiably composed', her hair 'inclined to pale yellow, her forehead large and fair', 'her nose somewhat rising in the midst; the whole compass of her countenance somewhat long, but yet of admirable beauty'.[3] Mary could not bear to plan for the daughter of Anne Boleyn to be Queen, not even for her beloved husband and for her God.

Katherine's cousin, Lady Margaret Strange – the girl whom Northumberland had wanted to marry to Guildford in 1552 – hoped the Queen might nominate her as heir. It would be difficult to exclude Elizabeth as illegitimate without also excluding Lady Margaret Douglas, the Countess of Lennox, whose father had a wife living at the time her mother was 'married' to him. Since Mary Queen of Scots was acceptable to no one as the likely bride of the French dauphin, that left the heirs of Mary Brandon, Duchess of Suffolk. Of these, the Greys, Lady Margaret argued, were excluded by Jane's treason and that of Suffolk, leaving her, as the daughter of Frances's late younger sister Eleanor, the Queen's heir.[4] It was an argument that would come back to haunt her years later, but for the moment she was just regarded as a spoilt and silly girl, whom no one took seriously. The gentry were learning to use Parliament to prevent what they did not want – such as Philip's coronation and the Queen's wish to exclude Elizabeth by statute. Elizabeth would therefore be Queen; everyone knew it, and in Europe, the Protestant exiles were hoping to hurry Mary to her end.

It had always been considered a deadly sin to revolt against lawful authority. Katherine Grey remembered the sermons given during the rebellions of 1549. Hugh Latimer, burned the previous October, had preached that men should endure tyrants and leave their punishment to God: to rebel was to attack the divine Chain of Being. But some Protestant exiles were now developing new theories of resistance, arguing that the Queen's 'idolatry' made her authority unlawful and that it was therefore not only allowable to overthrow her, but a moral duty.

In March 1556 a plot to invade England from France was exposed when a conspirator from inside the Exchequer informed on his friends.[5] The intention of the plotters, it emerged, was to use Mary 'as she used Queen Jane', and to replace her with Elizabeth, who was to be married to Edward Courtney.[6] Although the plot is now an obscure one, it was better financed than the revolts of 1554, and several senior members of the gentry were involved. Ten were executed. Courtney escaped by remaining in Europe, only to die later in the year, poisoned by Philip's agents it was said. But Mary was left shattered by the revelations. The Venetian ambassador reported she aged ten years under the strain, and the atmosphere at court was left rank with paranoia. Once again the heretics had tried to overthrow and kill her. The corridors of the royal palaces were filled with the clatter of armed men, and in the towns men and women were burned in increasing numbers. Mary had intended to target only the clerics who spread heresy, but the fires were sweeping now over ordinary Protestants. An Italian Catholic described watching a man of seventy hobbling to the stake that year, 'willingly, angrily and pertinaciously', while behind him followed a young blind boy, also put to death.[7]

Katherine Grey, like her mother and sister, maintained her old friendships with Protestant friends, but these friends, like the Greys, disguised their true beliefs. As Jane's writings were republished in Geneva that summer, Frances rented a house from the Earl of Rutland, who had been one of the most stalwart supporters of Jane's brief reign. Her charge Margaret Willoughby had, meanwhile, been sent to join Elizabeth's household at Hatfield.[8] Katherine kept company with Elizabeth Brooke, the abandoned second wife of Parr of Northampton.[9] But she was enjoying particularly the friendship of Lady Jane Seymour, the clever daughter of the Protector Somerset, who had been her sister's rival for King Edward's hand. The two girls were close in age, at fourteen and sixteen respectively. They had known each other for most of their lives and shared the burden of having seen their fathers executed. Sometimes Katherine would clamber into Jane's bed at night to keep warm and the teenagers could then talk about their dreams. Katherine still hoped desperately that she might one day remarry Lord Herbert, if only the Queen would allow it.

There was a flutter of anticipation that the glamorous days of masques and feasts would return when Philip came back to England in March 1557. Instead of opportunities for romance, however, there was talk of war. A second plot involving the Protestant exiles and the French was uncovered only shortly after Philip's arrival. A group of between thirty and a hundred exiles had 'invaded' Scarborough from a French ship. Their leader was an incompetent fantasist called Thomas Stafford, whom Katherine and Mary Grey knew well. He had supported their father's rising in the Midlands in 1554 and his sister, Dorothy, would remain a lifelong friend of Mary Grey's.[10] Stafford and his followers were promptly rounded up and twenty-five of them, including Stafford, executed. It has been suggested that the invasion was prompted by an agent provocateur as their action succeeded in breaking the back of the peace party – those on the Queen's Council who wished to stay out of the Emperor's wars – freeing her to declare war with France in June.[11] Despite all the care taken with the marriage treaty, England was now aligned with the imperial cause.

Katherine saw many of her friends leave to fight in Europe that summer, among them her former husband Lord Herbert. Some, such as Henry Dudley, the youngest of the Dudley brothers, would never return, and, despite their sacrifices, in January 1558 Calais fell to the French. It was to prove a bleak beginning to one of the most terrible years in English history – one that saw the arrival of a mass killer: influenza. A population weakened by successive harvest failures began to die in their thousands and then tens of thousands.[12] Against this holocaust Queen Mary cut a desperate figure. The red damask gowns of her early years had given way to gloomy black velvets, cut loosely in the Spanish style, over her swollen belly. Mary had imagined she was pregnant again during the winter, but it had proved another sad illusion. Elizabeth and William Cecil, the Surveyor of her estates, and former Edwardian Secretary of State, were already meeting to plan their moves were she to die.[13] Philip had gone again, and the sickness ravaging the country soon reached the court. Several of the maids and gentlewomen of the Privy Chamber fell ill and had to be sent home. They included Katherine's friend, Lady Jane Seymour, who was escorted to her mother's house, Hanworth, in Middlesex, in a horse-drawn litter. Katherine was allowed to accompany her with the Mother of the Maids and stayed with the Seymour family for the summer, while her friend slowly regained her strength.

Despite the horror of the mass deaths, the weeks Katherine spent in the former royal palace of Hanworth were to prove some of the happiest she would ever know. Katherine was almost eighteen and in the full bloom of youthful beauty: slim, blue-eyed, golden-haired, with a ripple in her nose like a Botticelli Venus. She attracted the attention immediately of Jane Seymour's brother, the nineteen-year-old Edward Seymour, Earl of Hertford. It was Hertford who, aged ten, had galloped with a message for Lord Herbert's father, asking him for help against the coup gathering against his own father, the Protector Somerset. Herbert's father had refused that help, and it must have given Hertford no small amount of pleasure to try and steal his girl. The teenage Hertford was attractive in an imperious way. His thin, high-bridged nose gave his face a similar aspect to his mother, who was known for her arrogance and good looks. Katherine, like many young women before her, was extremely taken with Hertford and appears to have soon forgotten about her former husband, Lord Herbert. But if the attraction between Katherine and 'Ned' – as she called Hertford – was powerful, it was also dangerous to them both. Hertford's mother was a junior descendant of Edward III, a genealogical detail that gave him no serious claim to the throne, but which raised him above the ranks of non-royal aristocrats. It made him a highly suitable match for Katherine – as he had once been for her sister Jane, to whom his father had hoped to marry him. In this suitability lay the danger: for if Katherine were to marry Hertford, she could rival Elizabeth's claim to the throne; and if she had a son, the threat to Elizabeth would be multiplied.

It was unthinkable to anyone that a Queen should not marry, and whom she married was of crucial importance. Elizabeth's half-brother, Edward VI, had justified his leaving his throne to Lady Jane Grey in part by arguing that she had taken a suitable groom, while his sisters could yet marry a foreigner. The dangers of this had been reinforced by Queen Mary taking England into a war that was, essentially, her husband's fight. The revolts against Mary had all been carried out with the intention of marrying Elizabeth to Edward Courtney – they did not intend simply that Elizabeth should rule alone. Courtney was now dead, and it was therefore uncertain whom Elizabeth would choose. If Katherine married the heir of the Protector who had brought 'true religion' to England, it would make her a desirable alternative to the risky option of the unmarried Elizabeth. If they had a son, it was conceivable that there need be no female ruler at all – something particularly attractive to Protestants whose belief that female rule was against Scripture was hardening.

Thomas Becon, a radical divine who had visited Bradgate in the 1540s, had asserted as early as 1554 that in the Bible 'such as ruled and were queens were for the most part wicked'. But the polemicist Christopher Goodman had since gone further, insisting that divine law excluded all women from rule. The same view would be restated more forcibly early the following year in John Knox's infamous *First Blast of the Trumpet Against the Monstrous Regiment [Rule] of Women*, in which he argued that female rule was an insult to God. It seemed very possible that many Protestant supporters would prefer a male heir from parents of such impeccable Protestantism as that of Katherine Grey and Ned Hertford than an unmarried Elizabeth, if the option were presented to them. The romance that summer was, furthermore, proving no mere flirtation. Lady Jane Seymour, who was helping pass messages between the lovers, was asked by her brother 'to break with the Lady Katherine touching marriage'.[14] Did ambition play a role in his proposal? Perhaps, but that there was more to it than that, would become evident. Meanwhile, before Katherine was able to give any formal reply to his proposal, his mother discovered what was going on.

Anne Somerset had lived through enough mortal danger not to wish to see any more visited on her family. She had only recently remarried and in doing so had followed in the footsteps of the two Duchesses of Suffolk. Her new husband was her Steward, Francis Newdigate. The last thing she wanted was for her son to take the opposite course and destroy himself through a royal marriage. She pleaded with Hertford to forget about Katherine, but the nineteen-year-old earl informed his mother crossly that there was no reason why 'young folk, meaning well' could not be in each other's company, and that he intended to be in Katherine's, 'both in that house and also in the Court ... being not forbidden by the Queen's highness express commandment'.[15]

It was fortunate, perhaps, that the summer had come to an end. With the worst of the influenza over, Katherine and the other maids and ladies of the Privy Chamber were due back at court, at Whitehall, where there was to be little opportunity for Katherine and Hertford to see each other in the months ahead. The Queen's Maid of Honour, Jane Dormer – who had earlier been a playmate of King Edward – recalled an ominous conversation with Mary when the Queen greeted her at the riverside, on the young woman's return to court. Mary asked her how she was. Jane Dormer, who like Jane Seymour had been ill, replied she was 'reasonably well'. 'So am not I,' the Queen returned sadly.

Mary's health had been poor for some time, but in August it had worsened markedly as she too, apparently, fell victim to the influenza. By October, despite the care of the ladies and gentlewomen of the Privy Chamber, it was accepted that the forty-two-year-old Queen was dying.

Philip, caught up in the funeral arrangements for his father, Charles V, dispatched his anglophile Captain of the Guard, the Count of Feria, to London in his place. Feria arrived on 9th November. The Queen had by then retired to her house at St James's where Feria found her still able to recognise him but little else. She had been pressed to name her half-sister her successor before a parliamentary delegation two days earlier, and it was evident she had no more than days to live. What Feria needed to discover was whom Elizabeth was likely to appoint to her government, and whom she trusted. Fortunately the count had excellent contacts. He was a charming individual who had made many friends in England during previous visits and, significantly, was betrothed to Queen Mary's young favourite, Jane Dormer.

Feria learned 'for certain' that Katherine Grey's kinsman Sir William Cecil 'who was Secretary to King Edward, will be her Secretary'. An extremely cunning politician, 'a sly and subtle shifter', Cecil had survived the fall of his master, the Duke of Somerset, and his role on Queen Jane's Council, to make friends like Cardinal Pole at Queen Mary's court. Judged efficient and hard-working, he also was a man who liked, and got on well with, clever women. His wife, Mildred Cooke, was one of the most impressively educated women of her generation, he was a friend of the formidable Duchess of Somerset, and still more so of Katherine Suffolk. But that Elizabeth respected and trusted him was unfortunate from Feria's perspective. The thirty-eight-year-old Cecil was a Protestant ideologue who believed he was engaged in a war on evil in which Catholics represented the forces of darkness, and he was viscerally anti-Spanish. Just how dangerous he was to be to Spanish interests was not yet clear, however, and a more hopeful name was also mentioned to the count: that of Guildford Dudley's married elder brother, Robert Dudley. Lord Robert was one of those for whom Philip had earned a royal pardon – and Elizabeth was reputed to be very attached to him. They had known each other since childhood and had become closer after they found themselves imprisoned at the same time in the Tower. Lord Robert was tall and handsome, like Guildford, but as dark as Guildford had been fair. What other attributes in him Elizabeth favoured, time would tell.

In St James's Palace, meanwhile, for the first time in a long while, Queen Mary appeared happy. She told her attendants that she could see 'little children like angels playing before her' and there was sweet music playing.[16] She died during a final Mass on the morning of 17th November. Unlike Lady Jane Grey, England's first, but brief, Queen regnant, Mary had the opportunity to develop a model of Queen-ship. In common with her predecessor, Mary had relegated her husband to the role of consort, but following Philip into a war in which England had no clear national interest had negated the possible benefits to Elizabeth. Any husband Elizabeth married would be regarded as more than a mere spouse, as someone likely to have a direct influence in matters of state and therefore potentially dangerous to religious or national interests. Mary's speech at the Guildhall, as Wyatt's rebels threatened London, was more useful. She had claimed a role as the bride of her kingdom, responsive to its needs, and as the matriarch who ruled her subjects. These were ideas Elizabeth could build on. Katherine and the other gentlewomen laid out Mary's body, and the apothecaries, wax chandlers and carpenters were called. The Queen's remains were cleaned and embalmed before her body was placed in a wooden coffin lined with lead, and brought into the chapel at St James's. There it remained for almost a month on its trestle, under a rich cloth, while the funeral arrangements were made.

Many assumed Elizabeth would act vengefully towards Mary after the treatment she had received at her hands. But the twenty-five-year-old ordered that their father, King Henry's, funeral book be followed to the letter. She did not trust those who had been disloyal to Mary. The more forward Protestants were closely associated with treason and Protestant though she was, Elizabeth believed that those who had rebelled against Mary might yet turn against her, as so many of them had in 1553, when they put Jane Grey on the throne. Elizabeth was not going to set any precedents in disrespect to a Tudor monarch. In the royal chapel Katherine Grey and the other ladies and gentlewomen of the Privy Chamber therefore took it in turns to keep watch, and Mass was said around the clock. The brilliantly painted walls and carved images in the chapel were shrouded in black, as they had been for Henry VIII, only the golden thread on the rich cloth covering her coffin flickered in the candlelight.

The final ceremonies of the funeral began on 13th December when Queen Mary's body was processed from St James's to Westminster Abbey. The coffin was placed on a chariot surmounted by a carved image of the dead Queen dressed in crimson velvet, a crown on her head and sceptre in hand.[17] Elizabeth had threatened to force the attendance of those who hinted they did not wish to pay any last respects and the ladies of the court all took part in the procession. Katherine was dressed in her funeral garb like the others, the black cloth trailing to the ground.[18] At the church door the abbot, John Feckenham (who had attended Jane Grey on the scaffold), greeted Queen Mary's body, and four bishops sanctified the coffin with incense. That night watch was kept for the last time, the chant of the rosary echoing in the abbey along with the ancient prayers for the dead: 'Grant them eternal rest, O Lord, and let perpetual light shine upon them . . .' The next day the requiem was said not just for Mary, but also for Catholic England. When the funeral veils came down, the painted walls would be white-washed once more, and the old prayers silenced.

As the rituals drew to a close the Yeomen of the Guard in their scarlet coats lowered the Queen's body into her tomb in the chapel Henry VII had built. Earth was scattered and Mary's chief officers broke their wands of office on their heads, casting them into the pit to mark the end of her reign. The trumpets then blew and the Garter King of Arms proclaimed that the Queen lived, as Elizabeth I. England was now a 'kingdom in the hands of young folks', the Spanish ambassador reported, and governed 'by a young lass'.[19]

All were anxious to see what would happen next, not least Katherine Grey who anticipated the honour that would be paid to her as Elizabeth's English, Protestant heir.

Chapter XVI

The Spanish Plot

Katherine sat in one of the great barges following Elizabeth up the Thames. The livery of scarlet velvet that the Queen had provided helped to keep out the bitter January cold. It was the first day of the four-day-long coronation ceremonies and the colour and sound of the spectacle was overwhelming. The silvery notes of the flutes and the brass blast of trumpets competed with the bang and sparkle of fireworks. It reminded an Italian onlooker of the Venetian celebrations on Ascension Day in which an elaborately dressed figure of the Blessed Virgin was married to the sea: a prescient vision of a Queen older and sadder than the young Elizabeth who sat amidst the tapestries of the royal barge, as it was towed forward by a galley of forty men, pulling on their oars in shirtsleeves.[1]

Queen Jane never enjoyed a coronation ceremony such as this, and her sister Katherine had never attended one. Their father had, however, not only attended that of King Edward, he had also followed the barge of Elizabeth's mother, Anne Boleyn, in one of the 220 craft on the day of her coronation in May 1533. Thousands had lined the banks to watch the spectacle on the river. Mechanical dragons belched smoke, and musicians played as the great barges were rowed down the river. The following night at the Tower, where his life was to end, he had served the King Henry VIII at dinner, along with others to be appointed Knights of the Bath. They were then bathed and shriven in ceremonies that lasted until the Saturday morning. The ceremony of the Bath took place only on the eve of a coronation, but no Greys were to be elected by Elizabeth at the Tower, and neither Katherine, her mother nor her thirteen-year-old sister Lady Mary Grey attended on the Queen the following day. Frances's health was poor, which may explain why she is not listed for livery for the coronation; Mary Grey appears not to have been invited, and Katherine, who was, had been demoted from the Privy Chamber to the Presence Chamber: a public room to which all the upper gentry had access. Elizabeth had not forgotten that Katherine came from treasonous stock, and that her sister had been a usurper.

Katherine did assemble with the rest of the court at the Tower on Saturday for Elizabeth's state entry into London, but in the knowledge that she enjoyed no special mark of her royal status. It was three in the afternoon, as Katherine sought out her reduced place, only a couple of hours before dark. There were flurries of snow, but a witness recorded that through the gloom it seemed 'the whole court so sparkled with jewels and gold collars that they clear the air'.[2] At the front of the procession the assembled City aldermen, knights, lords, chaplains, archbishops, ambassadors and their servants, led the way towards Westminster, with the 'trumpeters in their scarlet gowns, and heralds in their coat armour'.[3] Then, carried on a litter of white cloth of gold lined with pink satin, came the Queen. Her long hair hung loose in a symbol of chastity, over Queen Mary's coronation mantle of cloth of silver and gold, and she wore a gold crown studded with jewels. Elizabeth understood, as her ancestors had, how the power of the monarchy was rooted, in part, in awe-inspiring displays of majesty.

'Ceremony, though it is nothing in itself, yet it does everything,' a nobleman reminded the restored King Charles II after the civil war and Commonwealth over a century later; 'ceremony and order, with force, governs all . . . and keeps everyman and everything within the circle of their own conditions.'[4] Walking alongside the Queen was an impressive 'multitude of footmen in crimson velvet jerkins, all studded with massive silver gilt', and Gentlemen Pensioners 'with hammer in hand and clad in scarlet damask'.[5] Elizabeth smiled to acknowledge the people as they pressed to see her. It was they, she believed, who had saved her, along with her sister Mary, from the pretensions of Queen Jane in 1553 – despite the betrayals of the nobility and of their brother's Privy Councillors. The people in turn were happy and grateful for her peaceful accession, but also wary of what the future held, since Elizabeth had brought on to her Council men like Cecil from the unpopular Edwardian regime.

Directly behind the Queen rode her Master of the Horse, Robert Dudley, who had, perhaps, the most hated name of the Edwardian period. Mounted on a magnificent charger he cut a tall, muscular figure: his dark hair curling on a suit of deep red, woven with gold thread, as he led Elizabeth's white hackney. It was easy to see what the Queen found attractive in him, but difficult to forget that his grandfather, father and brother had all been executed as traitors. Following Dudley came the ladies of the court, forty-five of them mounted on horses harnessed with red velvet saddles made for the occasion.

Katherine Grey, however, was seated on one of the line of richly decorated chariots. Each was upholstered in striped satin of scarlet and gold and studded with gold nails. They had no springs to compensate for the rutted roads, but Katherine sat comfortably on a fat hassock of crimson damask, as she admired the adorned streets. The railings from Blackfriars to St Paul's had been draped with silk, behind which stood the men of the Trade Companies, 'well apparelled with many rich furs, and their livery hoods upon their shoulders in comly and seemly manner'; their guards to the front 'in silks and chains of gold'.[6] Katherine could see the windows and balconies above were also festooned with needlework, cloth of gold, embroidered silks, and other brilliantly coloured hangings.

At several points the procession stopped for the Queen to comment on a series of pageants or 'dumb shows' that the new Secretary of State, William Cecil, had helped organise. Commissioned from Richard Grafton, the printer who had published Lady Jane Grey's proclamation as Queen, each signalled a political message. At the first, on Gracechurch Street, the figure of Anne Boleyn sat at the side of Henry VIII, as if there had been no divorce, accusations of adultery, or execution. That past was to be forgotten and the fact of Elizabeth's illegitimacy under canon and temporal law, overlooked. Highlighted instead in heraldic detail was Elizabeth's Tudor and Plantagenet genealogy. It laid out the basis of her right to the throne. The second pageant at Cornhill advertised, controversially, that under Queen Mary religion had been misdirected and would now proceed on a 'better' footing. The third, at Soper's Lane, alluded to Elizabeth's suffering in the Tower under Mary, and ranged the princess alongside the Marian martyrs: the mantle of the Godly Jane Grey was being passed to Elizabeth.

The fourth pageant, on Cheapside, drew attention to the recent suffering of the country from famine and disease: a boy sat on a stony mount 'dressed in black velvet, melancholy, pale and wan, under a dry and arid tree'. Alongside, promising a better future, stood a handsome youth dressed in rich clothes, smiling on a lush, green mount.[7] The great fountain that had for centuries graced Cheapside was supposed to have been painted in a similarly educative way, but the workmen had refused to carry it out. For some, the attacks on Mary grated. Not all the pageants were even to Elizabeth's liking. The last pageant, on Fleet Street, she would find particularly unsettling.

The loyalty of Cecil, and Elizabeth's other senior Protestant supporters, was rooted in her status as the divinely ordained ruler. God had chosen Elizabeth to be Queen. But they still believed that government by women was a deviation from the proper order. God's decision was accepted as a punishment for sin, one the theologian John Calvin equated to slavery in a letter to Cecil that year.[8] The pageant at Fleet Street was designed as a riposte to John Knox's blanket attack on female rule, something Lady Jane Grey's former tutor, John Aylmer, had been commissioned to do in print. Like Aylmer's later thesis, however, the argument it used infuriated Elizabeth, based as it was on the belief that rule by women was to be endured rather than embraced, and mitigated as best they could. In the pageant she was depicted as the biblical prophetess, Deborah, who rescued Israel from the pagan King of Canaan. So far, so expected: the Protestant Elizabeth was rescuing her people from the 'idolatress' Mary. But Deborah was also dressed in parliamentary robes, as if Elizabeth's monarchical authority was mixed with that of parliament, rather than superior to it, and at her feet were figures representing the three estates: the nobility, the clergy and the commons.

Elizabeth had told Feria she was determined 'to be governed by no one'; but the message of the pageant was that her rule was allowable because, in reality, male government would continue in her name. John Aylmer later spelt it out: a good Queen accepted the advice of her Godly councillors and 'it is not she that ruleth but the laws', and 'she maketh no statutes or laws, but the honourable court of parliament'.[9] If the message of the final pageant was lost on its audience, Richard Mulcaster, who was commissioned to describe the procession to the whole country, helpfully explained that it was designed so that Elizabeth 'might be put in remembrance to consult for the worthy government of her people'.[10] There was a distinct echo here of Edward's will and his plan that a female governor should rule in conjunction with the Council.

Elizabeth was left with much to think about that night, on the eve of her crowning at Westminster Abbey. Her father had made himself more powerful than any of his medieval predecessors. At the break with Rome in 1533, he had argued that he was the supreme legislator in England, above the law because he gave the law, wielding his absolute *imperium* (literally, 'command') over Church and state. But the break had led to what he had called a 'diversity of opinion' in religion. Powerful subjects were now driven not just by personal ambition but competing ideologies. And Elizabeth could also see what her father had not. By bringing Parliament into the divine process of the succession he had introduced the mechanism of consent. Elizabeth owed her position as Queen to two acts of Parliament, and she feared that if she did not prove Protestant enough for the taste of her Protestant supporters, or simply if she failed to produce a son, a further act of Parliament would be used to legitimise her deposition. Katherine, with her impeccable English, Protestant heritage, was Elizabeth's likely replacement.[11] It was in that knowledge that Elizabeth had demoted Katherine to the Presence Chamber, hoping to deny her political friends. It was fortunate for Elizabeth's peace of mind that she did not as yet know about Katherine's love affair with the Earl of Hertford, whose titles, lost when his father was executed, she had restored just the previous day.

The following morning the final day of the coronation began at Westminster Hall, from where Elizabeth was brought in procession to the abbey on a purple carpet a third of a mile long. She was dressed in crimson velvet and flanked by the Earls of Pembroke and Shrewsbury, with the rest of the court ranked in order of precedence. The status of the nobility and gentry was drawn from the same legends as the monarchy and these myths were constantly retold through royal ceremonies such as this, its symbols associating them with the spiritual qualities of the crown.[12] Carrying Elizabeth's train was the new Duchess of Norfolk, Katherine's cousin and friend, Margaret Audley. Although, like Katherine, still in her teens, she was already a widow. Her first husband, Henry Dudley, the youngest of the Dudley brothers, had been killed in the imperial cause in France, and she had married the young and popular Norfolk that Christmas. Katherine followed her cousin with the other ladies of the court, 'dragging their trains after them, going two by two, and being exquisitely dressed, with their coronets on their heads, and so handsome and beautiful that it was marvellous to behold'.

The church bells were ringing and by the time they arrived at the abbey the noise was deafening. But as Elizabeth mounted the steps of the dais in front of the altar to be presented to the congregation, a cacophony of 'organs, fifes, trumpets, and drums' were added, and it seemed to one onlooker 'as if the world were coming to an end'.[13]

The ceremony that followed owed much to the Edwardian inheritance: the Epistle and Gospel were read in English and there was no elevation of the Host after the Consecration. One of the most striking moments however came just before the bishop administered the coronation oath to the Queen: Cecil came to the octagonal stage where Elizabeth sat enthroned to hand over the text – the Secretary of State's quiet presence a strange and intrusive reminder of the importance of his counsel.[14] When the ceremonies concluded Elizabeth and her court returned to Westminster Palace for the banquet. The new Queen was carrying the sceptre and orb in one hand, the imperial crown in the other, and had 'a most smiling countenance for everyone, giving them all a thousand greetings'.[15] The dinner and celebrations at Westminster continued until nine that night, and afterwards the exhausted celebrants all returned home by water.

There would not be another coronation in England for over forty years, but in January 1559 it seemed very possible that it would come much sooner than that. Behind her smiles Elizabeth knew she faced very real dangers and that she could not trust completely even those around her upon whom she relied most.

The vital issue of the Queen's marriage was raised on the first day of her first Parliament. Only an heir could ensure political stability and there was shock when Elizabeth responded to Parliament's request that she marry by hinting she would not do so in the immediate future. Elizabeth understood very well why it was important to her country that she marry, but she was also acutely sensitive to the potential dangers to herself. The husbands of both previous Queens regnant had been widely mistrusted: Guildford Dudley, because of who his father was, and King Philip as a foreigner. Besides, Elizabeth did not yet wish to marry. She was in love with a man who was not free – Guildford's brother, Lord Robert. She had tried to reassure her MPs that if she did not marry she would pick a worthy successor, but this had only triggered rumours that she was unable to have children. And that, inevitably, had focused further attention on Katherine Grey as the next in line under King Henry's will.

Elizabeth continued to do her best to dampen interest in Katherine with petty snubs. The Queen was the font of all patronage and courtiers could not afford easily to irritate her by being friendly to those she had no affection for. Katherine complained bitterly, however, to the Spanish ambassador Feria. The Queen, she said, did 'not wish her to succeed', and she left him in no doubt that she was 'dissatisfied and offended at this'.[16] He learned later that Katherine had even lost her temper one day in the Presence Chamber, using 'very arrogant and unseemly words in the hearing of the Queen'.[17] These family rows could, he hoped, prove useful to his master, King Philip. Elizabeth had lost little time in ending England's involvement in the imperial war with France. Philip was concerned that if Elizabeth were to go further and form an alliance with Henri II, England could threaten Spain's empire in the Netherlands. It was essential to Spain, therefore, that the two nations remain on good terms. The ideal answer was a marriage alliance with the Queen, but Elizabeth had already turned Philip down and although, ostensibly, she was considering a marriage with his cousin, the Hapsburg Charles of Austria, her passion for her Master of the Horse was common knowledge. 'Lord Robert has come so much into favour that he does whatever he likes with affairs,' Feria dispatched to King Philip in April 1559. 'It is even said,' he continued, 'that her Majesty visits him in his chamber day and night. People talk of this so freely that they go so far to say that his wife has a malady in one of her breasts, and that the Queen is only waiting for her to die to marry Lord Robert.'

Feria was advising King Philip to prepare for this eventuality by coming to an accommodation with Dudley. But he also warned that such a marriage risked triggering a rebellion. The Dudley name remained hated and Lord Robert had the open enmity of the Duke of Norfolk. Although just twenty-one, Norfolk was England's leading nobleman: a cousin of the Queen, a prince with the common touch and a large following. If there was some form of civil disorder led by such a man, Henri II was likely to seize the opportunity to invade England on behalf of his daughter-in-law, Mary Queen of Scots. Philip needed therefore to have his candidate in place. From Feria's perspective, Katherine Grey seemed to fit the bill ideally.

The Count of Feria disliked Queen Elizabeth intensely. His residence at Durham House on the Thames was filled with those Elizabeth had expelled from convents and monasteries refounded under Queen Mary, and he feared for Catholic families like his wife's, the Dormers. Katherine seemed to him a sweet girl, in contrast to the 'vain and clever' Elizabeth. She had served in Queen Mary's Privy Chamber with his wife, and he considered her a friend. Importantly, she had also assured him that she was a Catholic. The fact that Katherine's mother had accepted from Elizabeth the Charterhouse at Sheen, whose prior was now a refugee at Durham House, and her uncle, Lord John Grey was pressing for a religious settlement that was far more Protestant than that Elizabeth wanted, might have stretched her credibility, but Katherine assured the gullible Spaniard that she was hated by her family.

Katherine lacked her mother's common sense and her elder sister's acute intellect, but she knew how to charm and if she was curious to discover where Feria's questions were leading, she soon had the answer. Feria had learned – probably from his wife – that Katherine no longer spoke of remarrying Lord Herbert as she used to, and, assuming she was now free of any romantic entanglements, he asked if he could guide her on a future marriage – perhaps to a Hapsburg? Katherine promised Feria that she would never marry without his consent.[18] Hertford had behaved indifferently to her for months, encouraged by his mother, Anne Somerset: Feria had now provided her with an excellent opportunity to make him jealous.

While Katherine was enjoying herself at Hertford's expense, and Feria's also, in Spain the ambassador's information was being taken very seriously. Plans began to be laid to smuggle Katherine out of England. They became more problematic when Feria was recalled home in May, but Jane Dormer, the Countess of Feria, remained in England and the Spanish hoped her sister, Lady Hungerford, could be used as a secret go-between with Katherine. It was intended that a small number of ships would be sent to England where they would drop anchor in the Thames. The incoming ambassador, Don Juan de Ayala, could then arrange to have Katherine smuggled on board one of them. Fate, however, brought these schemes to a temporary halt.

On 30th June 1559, the English ambassador to France, Sir Nicholas Throckmorton, saw Philip's great adversary, Henri II, injured in a jousting accident. The incident was reminiscent of the near fatal combat between Henry VIII and Katherine Grey's grandfather,

Charles Brandon Duke of Suffolk, in 1524. Henri was riding against his young Scots Captain of the Guard, the Comte de Montgomery, when, at the moment of impact, his opponent's lance pierced his headgear and shattered into fragments. Henri II was less fortunate than the English King, however: he was struck through the right eye by a piece of wood that penetrated to the temple. He was seen to sway, but managed to stay in his saddle until he dismounted. As the spectators rushed forward to help him he fell briefly unconscious, but then staggered to his feet and walked to his chamber. There he lay for the next eleven days as physicians fought for his life and Europe's princes held their breath. Henri's wife, Catherine de Medici, had prisoners executed and splinters thrust into the eyeballs of their decapitated heads to see what might be done to save him. But in the end there was nothing. The King of France died, the young Captain of the Guard was executed in a pointless act of vengeance, and in Spain, King Philip reappraised his options concerning England.

If Katherine were smuggled to Spain, Philip risked earning the implacable enmity of Queen Elizabeth. With Henri dead that no longer seemed a risk worth taking. His heir, the weakling Francis II, was unlikely to invade England, and even if he did, the cost to France would be so high that Spain could take advantage of it.

Katherine, oblivious to the kidnap plans, was, meanwhile, busy looking forward to the Queen's first summer progress and the hope of a revival of her affair with Hertford. The 'grass season' – which ran from July to October – was to become the annual period during which Elizabeth set off on an extended itinerary of visits to palaces and private houses, giving the Queen the opportunity to show herself to the people and enjoy herself on the way. On 17th July the cavalcade left Greenwich Palace for Dartford, Kent. The Queen was in buoyant mood and flirting outrageously with Lord Robert Dudley, but Katherine was miserable. There was, as yet, no sign of 'Ned' Hertford. Nor did he join them the next day at Lord Cobham's house, where the court was welcomed with 'great cheer'.

Hertford had written to their friend the Duke of Norfolk claiming to be ill. He was very sorry not to be with them, he said, but although he was suffering from 'weakness rather than sickness' he felt he must follow the advice of his physician and – more tellingly – of his mother. The duchess clearly remained very concerned about her son's continued affection for Katherine.[19]

A few days later the progress circled and reached the ancient royal palace of Eltham, near Greenwich. The Countess of Feria was about to leave England to join her husband and arrived at the palace with a contingent of Spanish diplomats to pay her parting respects to the Queen. Elizabeth felt considerably less warmly towards the countess than her half-brother and half-sister had done. The countess's grandfather had sat on the jury that sent Anne Boleyn to the scaffold and her father, Sir William Dormer, had held Elizabeth under house arrest for Mary in 1554. As Katherine and the other ladies in the Presence Chamber watched amazed, the Queen left the countess, who was seven months pregnant, standing in the heat, waiting to be called for her audience. The Spanish, concerned for the countess's well-being, urged her to sit down. But she refused. It would have been disrespectful to the Queen and, although she was leaving England, most of her family were not. As her physical distress mounted, one of the diplomats demanded the Queen immediately be told the countess wished to see her, 'and if she might not do that speedily [the countess] should go'. Coolly, the Lord Chamberlain, Howard of Effingham, told the diplomat to be patient. At that the ambassador, Ayala, snapped back that the Queen ought to remember 'whose wife [the Countess] is, and that the Count de Feria is not her vassal'. A diplomatic incident was only averted when the Queen relented and called for the countess.[20] Cecil reported, however, that the two women behaved as if nothing had happened, engaging in 'very much familiar and loving talk'.[21] The Queen even ordered the Lord Chamberlain and the train of the court to escort the countess on the journey back to her house at Rochester.

Katherine must have been relieved to bid the countess and her Spanish husband's schemes farewell. To her delight Hertford had arrived at Eltham and, despite his mother's warnings, it was soon gossiped amongst their circle 'that there was great love between them'. Some of Katherine's friends, certain that nothing could come of this, feared that Hertford was exploiting her, 'and that no further good would come thereof'.[22] But the young couple remembered the summer as the period during which they both truly fell in love, passionately and deeply.[23]

Especially happy were the hot August days spent at the turreted royal palace of Nonsuch in Surrey. It was an intimate palace that housed only the inner group of courtiers, and Katherine's uncle, Arundel (widower of her father's sister, Katherine), who was keeper of the palace, had arranged a series of parties. There was a huge banquet on the Sunday night they arrived with a masque and 'the warlike sounds of drums and flutes and all kinds of music, till midnight'.[24] The next day they enjoyed coursing in the park and a play given by the children of St Paul's. In the evening another banquet was served on gilded platters. The party that night went on until three in the morning. There were quiet times too, however, when Katherine and Hertford could walk through shady groves ornamented with trellis, and pathways cooled by marble fountains spraying pyramids of water.

Katherine and Hertford were not the only ones to lose their heads to their hearts that summer at Nonsuch. While Arundel had hoped to engage the Queen's interest in himself as a possible suitor, it became clear that Elizabeth's attention was fixed entirely on Lord Robert Dudley. In the well-built man who looked like a gypsy, Elizabeth saw a boyish sweetness she found irresistible. She knew what it was like to have a hated traitor for a parent, and perhaps the complexities of his family history made her feel still closer to him. Kate Astley, Elizabeth's governess since her days in the household of Catherine Parr, was so concerned by Elizabeth's evident infatuation that she fell on her knees, begging the Queen to take a husband quickly and quash the growing rumours that her relationship with Dudley was dishonourable. To this Elizabeth retorted sharply that since her Ladies of the Bedchamber were always with her there was no opportunity for her to behave badly. Should she ever wish for a dishonourable life, she added defiantly, she knew of no one who could forbid her. A shocked

Kate Astley warned Elizabeth that even rumours of such a thing could lead to civil war. Elizabeth, chastened, explained that she needed Dudley constantly at her side as she had 'so little joy'. He alone relieved the loneliness that had always been her lot. For Elizabeth the risks of being with Dudley were a price worth paying, just as for Katherine the dangers of an affair with Hertford seemed trivial compared to the emptiness of life without him.

On 10th August the party at Nonsuch came to an end, but Dudley remained at Elizabeth's side, at Hampton Court, and Hertford was on hand to comfort Katherine when her cousin Thomas Willoughby died after 'overheating' whilst out hunting. He was close too, almost two months later, when John Foxe published his Latin forerunner to his *Book of Martyrs*, the *Rerum in Ecclesia Gentarum*. It must have brought back many painful memories for Katherine, as it republished Jane's letter to her and gave a detailed description of Jane's death, as well as publishing several new verses written in praise of her courage and piety.[25]

Katherine hoped, however, that she was about to take a step towards a new life. It was at about this time, in early October, that Hertford rode from Hampton Court to Sheen to ask the 'Lady Frances to grant the goodwill that he might marry the Lady Katherine'.[26] How Elizabeth might react to news of Katherine's betrothal, he and Katherine would worry about later.

Chapter XVII

Betrothal

Frances's residence at Sheen House lay in Richmond Park, just across the river from Sion where Jane was first proclaimed Queen. It dated back to the early fifteenth century, when it was founded as a Carthusian monastery, and became the burial place of James IV of Scots, the husband of Henry VIII's elder sister, Margaret. He had been killed fighting the English at Flodden, reconfirming the centuries of enmity between the kingdoms that the marriage had been intended to end. It was this that lay, in part, behind Henry's later decision to exclude the entire Stuart line from the succession. Instead of God deciding who should succeed to the throne, Parliament had acknowledged Henry's power to make his illegitimate daughter Elizabeth, Queen, and to make the Grey sisters her heirs. But James's granddaughter, the seventeen-year-old Mary Queen of Scots, was now thumbing her nose at these decisions, and asserting the traditional rights of primogeniture.

To the fury of English Protestants and Catholics alike, and the horror of William Cecil, it had just emerged that the previous year, 1558, Mary Queen of Scots had had the dinnerware at her Paris wedding to the then Dauphin quartered with the arms of England. It had sent a message to the world that she judged Elizabeth a bastard usurper of her throne. That Elizabeth was illegitimate was not an argument she could easily refute. Her father's affair with her aunt,

Mary Boleyn, before he married her mother was well known. Under canon law his marriage to her mother was, therefore, invalid and incestuous. Unlike Mary I, Elizabeth never addressed the statement of illegitimacy against her, knowing it would raise too many awkward questions, and ugly stories. But it was insulting and threatening, to draw attention to it as the Queen of Scots had done. Someone at Sheen, however, showed the Stuarts equal contempt. The Elizabethan antiquary John Stowe later found the King of Scots' body had been dug up and thrown into a waste room, amongst all the old timber, stone, lead, and other rubble: a brutal advertisement of hatred for the Scottish claim.

Frances was delighted to see Hertford as he arrived at Sheen that October, 1559. He had been her father's godson and she was very fond of him. When he asked for her permission to marry Katherine she was both happy and relieved. Although still only forty-two, her health had been poor since at least the summer of 1552 when she had been described as having 'a constant burning ague and stopping of the spleen'.[1] She knew she did not have much time left and was keen for Katherine to be happily married before her death. She had called Hertford 'son' for some time, but while she confided in her husband, Adrian Stokes, that she thought Hertford 'very fit' for her daughter, she was concerned it would prove difficult to convince the Queen to give her permission for the marriage.

Stokes agreed the match was a good one and suggested to Hertford that he acquire as much support on the Privy Council for the marriage as he could muster before the Queen was approached. He did not think it would be difficult to find friends. Katherine's marriage would strengthen her position as Elizabeth's heir against the pretensions of Mary Stuart, who represented England's two traditional enemies: France and Scotland. Hertford thought this excellent advice and left for court assuring Stokes 'he would follow the same'.[2] Stokes then drew up a rough draft of a letter for Frances to Elizabeth, informing the Queen that Hertford bore 'good will to her daughter', and begging Elizabeth to assent to the marriage, which 'was the only thing that she desired before her death and should be an occasion to her to die the more quietly'.[3] The letter was then put aside for Hertford's return and to allow Frances to talk to Katherine.

Frances wanted to confirm with her daughter that the marriage was what she wanted. The answer Katherine gave when she arrived at her mother's house, was an emphatic yes – she was 'very willing' to marry Hertford.[4] There must have been many happy faces at Sheen that night as the family considered Katherine's future. But the earl returned soon after from court with gloomy news: his friends had warned him off a marriage at this stage. There was a suit being made to the Queen by the Protestant heir to the Swedish crown, Prince Erik. He had to wait to see how it would play out. Over the following weeks Hertford made it his business to befriend Prince Erik's brother, the Duke of Finland, who was in London promoting the suit, becoming the duke's regular tennis partner and companion. If Erik were to marry Elizabeth the duke would make a useful ally. Frances's health, however, was worsening rapidly.

On 3rd November the failing duchess petitioned the crown to sell off some of her jointure property which her daughters were to inherit, and on 9th November she drew up her will. Her first concern was her creditors. Debt was the chronic condition of the aristocracy and Frances did not wish to have any money owed left on her conscience. She remembered, perhaps, how a desperate creditor had assaulted her first husband on the scaffold. Everything else, not already passed on to her daughters, she left to Stokes, whom she made her executor.[5] He had proved a better husband to her than the father of her daughters.

Frances died on 20th or 21st November with her two daughters and a few close friends beside her. When Elizabeth was brought the news she promptly agreed to take on the expenses of the funeral for her 'beloved cousin'. Frances's second marriage had ensured that she had never threatened Elizabeth's position and the Queen was grateful for it. She awarded Frances in death an augmentation to her arms of a royal quartering as 'an apparent declaration of her consanguity unto us'.[6] Stokes and her daughters similarly gave careful thought to the other arrangements for Frances's funeral. In particular they had to consider what statement it would make about their attitude to Elizabeth's controversial religious settlement.

The Queen was a natural conservative. She had wanted to move to a moderate position nearer to that of the 1549 Prayer Book than that of 1552, which Katherine's father had helped introduce. She enjoyed religious ceremonial, candles and copes, disapproved of married priests and disliked the sermon-giving that was central to purer forms of Protestant worship. William Cecil, and allies such as Lord John Grey, had succeeded in pushing her religious settlement towards the 1552 position, but she had managed to insist on several concessions. The 1552 'black rubric' which denied that kneeling at communion implied adoration, was dropped; distinctive vestments were allowed for priests; and a couple of sentences on the administration of the bread and wine was added to imply that Christ was present, at least in some spiritual sense, in the elements.[7] The Grey sisters' step-grandmother, Katherine Suffolk, and Jane's former tutor, John Aylmer, complained vociferously about these changes. But tact had been a mark of Frances's relationship with Elizabeth in life, and her family ensured it remained so in death.

The funeral service was to be officiated by the new Bishop of Salisbury, John Jewel, who, like Frances, combined piety with prudence. He was a close friend of the family's spiritual mentor, Heinrich Bullinger. Earlier that year he had also delivered a stinging sermon attacking Thomas Harding, the sisters' former tutor at Bradgate, who had converted to Catholicism and was now living in exile.[8] But while Jewel referred to Elizabeth's religious settlement as a 'leaden mediocrity' in private, he had been careful not to embarrass her in public. The bishopric was his reward and he was regarded as a safe pair of hands to manage the funeral, which took place on 5th December.

Frances's body was brought in procession from Richmond to Westminster Abbey 'with a great banner of arms and eight dozen escutcheons, and two heralds of arms, Master Garter and Master Clarenceaux'.[9] Katherine, acting as chief mourner, followed the coffin dressed in black, her train carried by a gentlewoman assisted by an usher.[10] The diminutive Lady Mary Grey, who was now about fourteen, followed in line of procession. As Frances's body was brought inside the abbey it was set under a static structure known as a hearse, which was big enough to hold the coffin and allow the principal mourners to sit within it. Katherine sat at the head with the other mourners on each side. The herald, Clarenceux King of Arms (so called from the Duke of Clarence, brother of Edward IV), then opened the service asking loudly that: 'Laud and praise be given to Almighty God, that it has pleased him to call out of this transitory life unto his eternal glory, the most noble and excellent Prince the Lady Frances, late Duchess of Suffolk.'

The service was in English and distinctively Protestant, but Bishop Jewel's sermon 'was very much commended by them that heard it'. The sisters and the congregation all received communion in accordance with Elizabeth's Prayer Book and Frances was then buried in St Edmund's chapel on the south side of the choir.[11] Four years later her widower erected a monument that still remains. It is surmounted by her image, dressed in the ermine robes of a duchess, her royal crown on her head and in her hand a prayer book such as Jane carried to the scaffold, a reminder of their shared faith. Underneath Frances's epitaph is written in Latin:

> Nor grace, nor splendour, nor a royal name,
> Nor widespread fame can aught avail;
> All, all have vanished here. True worth alone
> Survives the funeral pyre and silent tomb.

Stokes could not have imagined how Frances's reputation would be traduced in centuries to come; and nor could her daughters. Mary Grey was comforted in her loss by the extended family with whom she would always remain close: friends such as Margaret Willoughby, whom Frances had taken under her wing in the terrible months after her husband and daughter were executed. Katherine, of course, had Hertford, but their hopes of marriage in the immediate future had been buried with Frances. Sometime that winter, while Katherine was still wearing mourning, Hertford wrote a verse describing his feelings about their situation. He compared his pain to that of the Greek classical hero Troilus, who was kept apart from his lover Cressida by political imperatives, as they were:

> *She stood in black said Troylus he,*
> *That with her look hath wounded me.*
> *She stood in black say I also*
> *That with her eye, hath bred my woe.*[12]

Underneath he recalled the story of the two lovers as told by Geoffrey Chaucer. The end of the story expressed his ultimate fear: Cressida marries one of her lover's enemies. Hertford was aware, perhaps, that the Spanish were again paying court to Katherine. Elizabeth's infatuation with Dudley was having an increasingly damaging effect on her reputation, and the Spanish ambassador was advising Philip that when the Archduke Charles came to England to woo Elizabeth he should also see Katherine, to whom, they judged, the crown would fall if the Queen were overthrown. Hertford's fears were misplaced, however: Katherine would not leave him. She loved him too much.

The new year of 1560 brought an incredible transformation in Elizabeth's treatment of Katherine. Suddenly she found herself promoted to attend on the Queen personally alongside the intimates of Elizabeth's Privy Chamber and old friends like Kate Astley. Spanish diplomats reported that the Queen was even talking of adopting Katherine. For Elizabeth it was a case, however, of keeping your friends close, and your enemies closer.[13] She had been informed of the Spanish plot to smuggle Katherine out of the country and she did not want to drive her into their hands. The suggestion that she would adopt Katherine implied she was poised to name her as her heir. In contrast, however, to the myth of Elizabeth as Gloriana, the great Protestant icon of English nationalism, in her heart she preferred – and would always prefer – the claim of Mary Queen of Scots to that of Katherine Grey. Catholic and foreign Mary might be, where

Katherine was Protestant and English, but Mary represented the dynastic principle and the absolute right of a monarch to rule. And for Elizabeth these took precedence over the religious and nationalist concerns of her Secretary of State, William Cecil.

The ideological differences between Elizabeth and Cecil were particularly acute at the moment Katherine found herself in the Queen's brittle embrace. John Knox, the divine who had so vociferously stated the case against the 'monstrous' rule of women, had arrived in Scotland the previous May and found a civil war in progress. He had promptly joined the Protestant-backed rebels fighting Mary's mother, the regent, Mary of Guise.[14] Cecil saw that if England were also to back the rebels they could together seize the opportunity to create a Protestant 'Britain'. Such a result would help secure England's northern border while uniting the whole island against Catholic Europe, and the Guise family, whom he saw as 'being professionally gathered to destroy the gospel of Christ'.[15] To his frustration, however, Elizabeth agreed only reluctantly on covert aid for the rebels and refused point blank to give any outright military support to those who took up arms against a rightful sovereign. Only when Cecil threatened to withdraw from any further involvement in Scottish policy did she give way – and Elizabeth resented having her hand forced.

When the French defeated the English army at Leith in May 1560, Elizabeth vented her anger on her Secretary. In an effort to rescue the situation Cecil left court to take charge of the campaign. But while he was soon turning defeat into victory in Scotland, back at court his influence over Elizabeth waned rapidly. From the close quarters of the Privy Chamber, Katherine saw Robert Dudley build on the Queen's disaffection with Cecil's Scottish policy and woo the Queen more passionately than ever. Elizabeth went out hunting with her 'sweet Robin' every day from morning till night. This did not trouble Katherine. As before, she and Hertford used Elizabeth's distraction to conduct their own affair. Hertford's brother, Henry, joined their sister, Lady Jane Seymour, and their servants, in delivering tokens and messages for the couple. The lovers also met in private, 'as time might serve and as folk of those years of that sort will do'.[16] Sometimes they used Jane Seymour's private chamber at court and, on at least two occasions Katherine visited Hertford at his London home on Cannon Row, Westminster. Several of their friends were aware what was happening, but it was the Queen who was the focus of scandal when Cecil returned from Scotland.

The rumours of a sexual affair, which Kate Astley had warned Elizabeth could end in civil war, were spreading. By mid-August they had reached even remote villages, with JPs in Essex questioning a woman from Brentwood who had claimed that the Queen was pregnant by Dudley. There was tremendous anger at court that Dudley was sullying the Queen's good name and standing in the way of her making a proper marriage. Norfolk warned the Spanish ambassador that Dudley 'would not die in his bed' if he did not change course, and a man called Drury was imprisoned for plotting his assassination. Nothing, however, would deter Elizabeth from Dudley's company, 'her only source of happiness'. Diplomats reported Cecil was in disgrace for his open hostility to Lord Robert and Spanish hopes that Katherine would make a Hapsburg marriage went back to the top of their agenda. Cecil tried to deflect their interest in her, assuring the latest Spanish ambassador, Bishop Alavarez de Quadra, that if anything happened to Elizabeth no woman would be acceptable to the Privy Council as a successor. Instead the likely choice, he told the Spaniard, was Dudley's brother-in-law, Henry Hastings, Earl of Huntingdon, who was of Plantagenet descent.[17]

Huntingdon was certainly a potential choice: Northumberland had married his daughter to him in May 1553 for exactly that reason. But Huntingdon was not a Tudor and had not been mentioned in any of the Acts of Succession. Like all convincing liars, Cecil had told the Spanish a half-truth. The Council didn't want any more queens – unless they were married already to a suitable husband. Several Councillors had expressed the desire to marry Katherine to the Earl of Arran, the leader of the Scottish Protestants and Mary Queen of Scots' cousin and heir. De Quadra had an informant who was prepared 'to lay a horse worth a hundred crowns that it shall so come to pass'.[18] For those few who knew about Katherine's romance, however, the Earl of Hertford had much to recommend him. It was his father who had introduced 'true religion' to England and, although young and inexperienced, he was a known quantity. Only circumstantial evidence remains to indicate who these people were, but Katherine's uncle (by marriage), the Earl of Arundel, appears to have been amongst them.

At the time of Elizabeth's accession Arundel had been one of her suitors. He carried a great name and as a young man he had been handsome; that he was no longer attractive he did not, perhaps, think important. He had spent a fortune on the entertainments at Nonsuch the previous summer, only to see Elizabeth lavish all her attention on Robert Dudley. Despite his conservative religious convictions, Arundel was now pursuing the teenage Lady Jane Seymour. If Elizabeth wouldn't make him King (and was riding for a fall with Dudley), Arundel hoped he could yet become a king's brother-in-law, through a marriage with Hertford's sister.[19]

By September 1560 Cecil was at the end of his tether with Elizabeth over her relationship with Dudley. At a meeting with de Quadra at Hampton Court on the 6th, he told the Spaniard that he wished to retire from public life. He 'clearly foresaw the ruin of the realm through Robert's intimacy with the Queen'. Elizabeth wanted to secure Dudley a divorce, he claimed, while Dudley kept saying his wife was ill because he intended to poison her and pass it off as a death by natural causes. Twice Cecil repeated that he wished Lord Robert dead.[20] That evening, however, it was Dudley's twenty-eight-year-old wife, Amy Robsart, who was found dead at Cunmor Place, the house of one of her husband's friends, Sir Richard Verney. The Queen learned something of what had happened the next morning and when the news broke it electrified the court. There had been rumours that Amy was ill, but since she had travelled extensively over the previous year it was difficult to imagine she had been dying. Then it emerged where the body had been found – at the bottom of a flight of eight stairs. If this was an accident it was not a long way to fall. It sounded staged.

The coroner's jury, who later viewed the body, brought in a verdict of death by misadventure. This suggests they suspected suicide. According to Cecil, Amy Robsart's marriage to Dudley in 1550 had been a love match. If so it must have been painful to know her husband was romancing the Queen and to sometimes overhear his servants (as she did) wishing her dead so he would be free to become King. On the day she died she had asked her servants to leave her alone and to go to the local fair. Some of them were worried about her state of mind. Amy, they recalled, had been notably melancholic – but suicide was an act of self-murder for which you went to hell. They were loath to believe that she would have gone so far. There was no shortage of people, on the other hand, who were willing to believe that Dudley had killed her. No act of wickedness was considered unlikely in a Dudley.

A manuscript circulating that autumn suggests what many courtiers believed had happened to Amy. According to this account, Verney had ordered a manservant to stay behind when the others went to the fair, and to kill Amy. The infamous condemnation of Dudley, the anonymously composed 'Leicester's Commonwealth' written later in the reign, added that the servant was afterwards murdered to ensure his silence and that Verney went to his death crying and blaspheming that 'all the devils in hell did tear him to pieces', for what he had done. Whatever actually happened, it was Dudley's assumed guilt that mattered as far as the future was concerned, both for Dudley and the Queen, and for Katherine and Hertford. As such the scandal must have been a matter of great interest to the guests at the dinner Katherine and Hertford attended the following evening at Bisham Abbey in Berkshire.

Katherine's hosts were Cecil's sister-in-law, Elizabeth Hoby, and her husband Sir Thomas. They had only moved into the house the previous summer after the death of Sir Thomas's brother, Sir Philip. He had been a keen admirer of Katherine's father and had built the dining chamber where the company sat.[21] At the table, besides Katherine and Hertford, were a number of close friends and relations: Cecil's wife Mildred, Cecil's cousin Lord Cobham, Cobham's brother-in-law, Parr of Northampton, Hertford's younger brother, Lord Henry Seymour, his sister, Lady Jane Seymour, and Jane's new suitor, the Earl of Arundel.[22]

De Quadra, looking back twelve months later, believed that Cecil wished to encourage Hertford to marry Katherine, fearing that Elizabeth would now marry Dudley. It seems more likely, however, that such a discussion would have taken place before Amy's death. The mysterious manner of Amy's death had, on the contrary, given Cecil good reason to hope that Elizabeth was now persuadable that marrying Dudley would destroy her. As the royal favourite left court to arrange his wife's funeral, he also had the Queen to himself.

Elizabeth was aware that the prejudice against female rule, rarely far from the surface at court, was now being openly voiced. 'The cry is that they do not want any more women rulers, and [the Queen] and her favourite may find herself in prison any morning,' de Quadra reported.[23] Cecil hoped Elizabeth would see sense quickly, and she did so. She could remember how divisive it had been amongst Queen Jane's Protestant supporters that her husband, Lord Guildford, carried the hated Dudley name. By the time Dudley returned to Hampton Court the first week of October, Cecil had turned the tables on him. As Cecil gloated to de Quadra, he had the Queen's assurance that she would not marry Robert. Secure in that knowledge Cecil spoke to Hertford about the growing rumours of his love affair with Katherine. A marriage between them risked destabilising the government and, just as Hertford's friends had warned him off the previous year, so now Cecil advised him once again to cool his ardour for Katherine. He was not a man to be ignored. Everything about Cecil was quietly expressive of power: the glint of gold buckles on his black sword belts, the silky satins of his dark suits, his unobtrusive ease of access to Elizabeth.

It was clear in those weeks, however, that the Queen was tormented by her decision not to marry Dudley. Knowing she couldn't express her feelings for him as his wife she intended to shower him with what marks of her esteem she could, and intimated she was to give him an earldom. The gesture was interpreted as a move to make Dudley a more suitable groom. That she loved Dudley remained painfully obvious and de Quadra was not alone in his belief that she might marry him after all. With tensions running high there were several unpleasant incidents at court. Two of Cecil's servants were reported to the Queen for refusing to raise their caps as Lord Robert passed by; a servant of Arundel's was punished for uttering 'lewd and unfitting words' about the history of treason in Dudley's family, while Pembroke's retinue exchanged blows with Dudley's men. The Spanish even picked up rumours of a planned revolt led by Protestant noblemen on behalf of the Earl of Huntingdon. From the Catholic side, meanwhile, Elizabeth's Stuart cousin, Margaret Lennox, the aunt of Mary Queen of Scots, asked them for financial aid in support of her claim.[24] Under such pressure Elizabeth was forced to draw back from ennobling Dudley, and vented her frustration by slashing the patent for the earldom with a knife.

Katherine was equally distressed by the sudden withdrawal of Hertford's affections. She did not know that Cecil had spoken to him but had heard that he was flirting with a girl called Frances Mewtas.[25] She sent a furious letter to Hertford at Cannon Row. The earl, afraid that if he continued to ignore Katherine he risked losing her for good, wrote back immediately via his sister at Hampton Court. He swore his love and again proposed marriage, but this time he added 'that to avoid all such suspicions he would, if she would, marry her out of hand, even as soon as the Queen's majesty should come next to London'.[26] When the court arrived at Westminster the couple met in Jane Seymour's private closet within the chambers of the Maids of Honour. With Jane as witness they made a formal act of betrothal, in which they promised to marry at Hertford's London home as soon as the Queen left the palace. Their promise was sealed, Hertford recalled, with 'kissing, embracing and joining their hands together'.[27] He also gave Katherine a 'pointed diamond ring'.[28] Katherine would keep it until the day she died.

Chapter XVIII

A Knot of Secret Might

When Katherine and Hertford discovered the Queen was planning to leave Whitehall for a few days' hunting, they put their plans into place. Katherine claimed her face was swollen with toothache and was given permission to remain behind with Jane Seymour for companionship. Hertford left court that night, suggesting they meet at his house at Cannon Row as soon as they could get away the next day.

Hertford was up at seven the following morning, already anticipating Katherine's arrival. In an effort to keep calm he read and went for a walk. Meanwhile his Groom of the Great Chamber, Christopher Barnaby, made up his bed. About an hour later his second groom, John Jenkin, arrived from Whitehall carrying the news that Elizabeth had left for Eltham. Hertford asked Jenkin to tell the other servants to avoid the Great Chamber. As the minutes ticked by, however, Hertford decided it would be best to get most of the servants out of the house altogether. He called his Gentleman Usher, John Fortescue, and told him that the servants should have a free day and could leave the house to carry out whatever business they had.[1]

Katherine and Jane Seymour, meanwhile, left Whitehall 'by the stairs at the orchard in the palace', and walked along the sands on the riverbank to Cannon Row.[2] It was a winter's morning, between Halloween and Christmas, and the breeze from the Thames was bitter.[3] Jenkin saw them arrive at the house from the direction of the Watergate between nine and ten. He dashed into the kitchen to tell the cook, William Powell, who ogled at the women as they passed the kitchen door. Powell had noticed Katherine at the house a couple of times before. The senior groom, Barnaby, bumped into them as he came down the stairs from the earl's Great Chamber. Jane greeted him by name and asked him where he was going. 'The earl's business,' he replied hurriedly. Hertford had asked him to deliver a message to a goldsmith. He was, perhaps, the craftsman from whom Hertford had commissioned Katherine's wedding ring. Hertford had designed it with five gold links, each inscribed with the line of a verse he had composed:

> As circles five, by art compact, show but one ring in sight,
> So trust unites faithful minds, with knot of secret might,
> Whose force to break but greedy death, no wight* possesses power
> As time and sequels well shall prove, my ring can say no more.[4]

Hertford greeted his sister Jane and Katherine with warm embraces. Jane, however, 'not tarrying half of quarter of an hour', left quickly to get the priest.[5] It appears Hertford had arranged for him to wait nearby. Left alone Hertford and Katherine kissed and exchanged sweet nothings, 'such as passes between folk that intend as they did'.[6] But Jane Seymour soon returned with the priest – a short, middle-aged man with fair skin and an auburn beard. His long black gown and white collar suggested he was one of the Protestant exiles who had been trickling back from the continent since Queen Mary had died. He had brought with him the Book of Common Prayer to carry out the ceremony, which took place with the priest standing to the right of the bedroom window, Katherine and Hertford facing him and Jane Seymour standing a little behind. The priest asked for the banns and, having ascertained that they were both free to marry, the

---

* A person or creature that brings ill fortune.

service proceeded. Hertford gave Katherine the gold-linked wedding ring and when their vows were complete there were smiles and the small company chatted briefly. Hertford then thanked the priest and Jane gave him an enormous tip of £10 as he left. A few banqueting meats had been placed in the room, which Jane offered Katherine. It was apparent, however, that the new bride wasn't interested in food or drink and Jane, 'perceiving them ready to go to bed', left them alone.

In later depositions Katherine and Hertford described how, as soon as the door was shut, they undressed in the same room in which they had married. He threw himself on to the bed first where she joined him, naked, save for the covering on her head. He remembered it later as one of the fashionable cauls she often wore – a skull cap made of trellised silk thread or goldsmith work, sometimes lined with silk. In fact it was a kerchief or veil Katherine had especially brought in her pocket and put on as a symbol of her new status as a married woman.[7] For two blissful hours the twenty-year-old bride and her young groom made love, 'sometimes on the one side of the bed, sometimes on the other'. They got up from the bed once, but soon returned and stayed in bed until the time came when Katherine had to return to court. She and Jane had a dinner engagement with the Comptroller of the Queen's Household, Sir Edward Rogers. Hurrying now, they dressed in minutes, while downstairs the servants in the parlour were making ribald cracks about what had gone on above their heads. The grooms would have to make the bed up again that evening. As the couple emerged from their room, Jane joined them and Hertford accompanied Katherine and his sister to the steps at the Watergate, where he kissed his happy new wife goodbye.

It appears that Katherine and Hertford had sex whenever and wherever they could, while endeavouring to keep their marriage from the Queen. As soon as the earl appeared at Katherine's chamber and her maidservants saw them whisper together they would discreetly disappear. With such help the couple rendezvoused several times to make love in the Queen's palaces at Westminster and Greenwich. They also met at Cannon Row, aided by Jane Seymour and her manservant, Mr Glynne. The lovers never dared spend the night together but it was hard to keep their feelings secret from the court. Katherine was forced to deny hotly to her cousin Lady Clinton that she enjoyed any 'company and familiarity' with the earl.[8] But Cecil was also concerned that Hertford was ignoring his advice to keep away from Katherine. The political landscape was stormy enough without the Protestant heir being involved in a dangerous romance.

Cecil's bête noire, Mary Queen of Scots, had been widowed on 5th December with the unexpected death of Francis II. By the New Year there was talk of her marrying Philip II's son, Don Carlos. Cecil feared that if she were to do so, Protestant England would face the might of Catholic Spain and France in her cause. Robert Dudley's behaviour, meanwhile, was causing additional anxieties. Dudley had approached de Quadra asking for Philip's support, were he to marry Elizabeth. In exchange, he offered to arrange for England to send a contingent to the Council at Trent, called by the Pope in the hope of ending the religious divisions in Europe. Dudley claimed he had Elizabeth's support for his scheme. If so, Cecil soon brought the Queen down to earth, and in mid-March she put Cecil in charge of dealing with de Quadra. Dudley, furious, told Elizabeth that he would move to Spain if he was so little thought of. It was a threat Cecil took seriously. The Queen still could hardly bear to be deprived of Dudley's company and Cecil feared that her resolve not to marry him could yet weaken. It was therefore vital to protect Katherine, and to this end Hertford was persuaded to take an extended holiday in Europe.

A subsidised trip around all the great Renaissance courts was an effective lure for the twenty-two-year-old earl, and that spring Hertford applied for the necessary licence. It informed the Queen he hoped to travel abroad 'for the sight of other countries and commonwealths ... to come to knowledge of things [appropriate to] his estate', the better to serve her in future.[9] Katherine, as usual, was told nothing by either Hertford or Cecil, and only learned about her husband's plans from his sister Jane. Her distress was made worse by the fact that she suspected she might be pregnant. What should she do if she was, she asked her friend? Jane replied that if she were, 'there was no remedy', but to tell the Queen. Hertford agreed: they would just have to 'abide and trust to the Queen's mercy'.[10] Katherine did not much care for that idea. Then, just when she needed the advice and companionship of Jane Seymour the most, her friend fell seriously ill. Whatever had ailed Jane in the summer of 1558 – possibly tuberculosis – had returned with a vengeance. She died on 29th March, aged nineteen.[11]

A few days later Jane Seymour's body was brought the short distance from the Queen's Almonry to Westminster Abbey. A junior descendant of Edward III, she was treated with the deference due to one of royal blood: her coffin was borne on a chariot in procession with the entire choir of the abbey, two hundred courtiers, sixty official mourners, and great banners of arms and heralds.[12] She was buried alongside Katherine's mother in St Edmund's chapel. Hertford, 'her dear brother', erected an alabaster wall monument with gilded letters commemorating her short life.

Not only was the earl deeply saddened by his sister's death, however, he was worried about Katherine. He asked her repeatedly 'whether she were with child or no?' But Katherine only said that she wasn't sure. The pressure on Hertford to go to Europe was immense, and the promise of adventure enticing. He wanted to do the right thing, but he also wanted Katherine to reassure him that it was all right to leave her.

When Hertford's licence was ready he met Katherine alone in the courtyard at Westminster. He told her 'that if she would precisely say that she was with child that he would not depart the realm, otherwise he would'.[13] Katherine, overwhelmed by the immensity of what was happening, and unable to discuss it with her late mother or any other woman who had had children, told him she was still uncertain. Hertford, exasperated, then made his decision to go. Before he left he wrote a will bequeathing Katherine lands valued at £1,000 a year and gave her the signed parchment, along with a sum of money. She was always short of ready cash and he was in the habit of giving her sums of between 100 and 400 crowns for her expenses. His final promise was that if she were pregnant 'he would not long tarry from her'.[14] On Hertford's departure, Cecil sought Katherine out at Greenwich to reassure her that his departure was a necessary one. A portrait of Cecil from this period depicts the man she saw. A light brown beard streaked already with grey, three warts on his cheek, and dark, penetrating eyes. It was foolish to develop a friendship with the earl without the Queen's consent, he reminded her. Katherine kept her thoughts to herself, but wished silently that Cecil had made the point as forcibly before she had married.[15]

Hertford arrived in Paris on 13th May and became quickly immersed in the many distractions France had to offer. With the ambassador, Sir Nicholas Throckmorton, he left for Rheims and the coronation of the ten-year-old Charles IX. He wrote to Cecil on the 20th, describing all his news – how the boy King was anointed by the Cardinal of Lorraine, the Queen of Scots' uncle, and how he preferred the look of the King's younger brother, the Duke of Orléans, who was tall and 'about the stature of the writer's little brother'. It sounded like an excellent educational experience and Cecil promptly packed off his nineteen-year-old son, Thomas, to join the earl. The teenager arrived in Paris soon after, armed with a long 'Memorial' from his father. It instructed him what prayers he was to say daily, how to study the Bible and when to make a general confession of his sins (exhortations ignored from the minute he met up with Hertford). The earl and Master Thomas Cecil visited 'Orléans, Blois, Amboise, Tours, Angers, and sundry fair castles and houses situate upon the Loire'.[16] They hunted, partied, and spent money like water. When the pious Cecil found out, he was livid. He had 'known many young men of better degree [than his son] spend a full whole year beyond the seas with much less [money]', he complained.[17] Hertford, however, was making an excellent impression where it mattered.

The earl had been introduced to Catherine de Medici, the widow of Henri II, and 'courteously embraced'. Then he was presented to the King, who told him that while he remained in France he should 'be

bold' in asking of him whatever he wanted.[18] Ambassador Throckmorton was impressed, but Cecil remained more concerned about
the one figure in France who would not have cared for Hertford –
Mary Queen of Scots. She had refused to ratify the Treaty of Edinburgh, which had required her to recognise Elizabeth's right to be
Queen of England, and was intent on returning to Scotland. By July
there was a mood of near hysteria in the Privy Council. Cecil was
certain that if Elizabeth did not marry soon, great evil would befall
the state. He had discovered, he confided in Throckmorton, a secret
plan to guarantee Mary's place as Elizabeth's heir if she agreed to
recognise Elizabeth's claim to the throne. For Cecil it appeared that
England was threatened by a world turned upside down, one in
which women rulers passed the crown to women rulers. 'God send
our mistress a husband, and by him a son, that we may hope our
posterity shall have a masculine succession,' he prayed.[19] But it was
Katherine who was about to have a child.

Katherine's pregnancy was in its eighth month. She could feel the
baby moving inside her, and see the ripple of a spine, hands and feet
pushing out from the womb but, almost paralysed with fear, she
could not think what to do about it. Since Hertford had left, the
Queen was showing 'a great misliking with her'.[20] Perhaps Elizabeth
had been persuaded to give Hertford the licence to travel after being
told of her affair with him.[21] In any event, Katherine did not want to
face the Queen's wrath alone and her efforts to contact Hertford had
failed. Letters sent to France addressed 'To My Loving Husband' had
received no reply.[22] Had he been warned not to communicate with
her; had he abandoned her? She had no way of knowing and, as she
faced the shame of having a child unrecognised by the father, her old
fears and jealousies returned. What proof was there she was married
at all? The only witness, Lady Jane Seymour, was dead and how could
she hope to find the priest? The exiles who arrived in England
without a preferment to go to, commonly waited in the capital until
Bishop Grindal managed to find them one and then vanished into
the country. Katherine began to concoct a desperate plan. Her
former father-in-law, Pembroke, had approached her in June

suggesting a remarriage to his son, Henry, Lord Herbert. With Hertford out of the way, he was sure Herbert stood a good chance of regaining her affections and, as Elizabeth's heir under current statute, she was a catch once more. Katherine had brushed Pembroke off.[23] Now, however, she reconsidered her position.

While Hertford, in blissful ignorance, planned to spend the summer in Paris before travelling to Italy, Katherine wrote to Lord Herbert to tell him that, as far as she was concerned, their marriage remained valid.[24] Herbert, delighted, began the traditional courtship ritual of sending pictures of himself and items of personal jewellery as tokens of his love and devotion. Katherine still hoped, however, that Hertford would come for her. As she packed and prepared for the Queen's summer progress into Essex and Suffolk, she asked Jane Seymour's former manservant, Mr Glynne, to take Hertford the urgent message 'that for troth she was quick with child'. Perhaps Mr Glynne spoke of this a little too freely, for at this point Herbert became aware of the real reason for Katherine's renewed interest in him. Hurt and humiliated, Herbert sent Katherine a note demanding she return his tokens. She, however, did nothing. On 14th July, the Queen's summer progress began and Katherine, as a member of the Privy Chamber, left with it for Wanstead, clutching a devastating letter from Herbert: 'I perceive your mind to keep my tokens back,' he wrote;

> but if I can not have them at your hands, I will seek them at that companion's hands . . . by whose practise to cover your whoredom and his own knavery and adultery you went about to abuse me . . . Having hitherto led a virtuous life I will not now begin with loss of honour to lead the rest of my life with a whore that almost everyman talks of. You claim promise madam of me when I was young, and since confirmed as you say at lawful years, but you know I was lawfully divorced from you a good while ago. And if through the enticement of your whoredom and the practise and device of those you hold so dear, you sought to entrap me with some poisoned bait under the colour of sugared friendship; yet (I thank God) I am so clear that I am not to be

further touched than with a few tokens that were by cunning slight got
out of my hands both to cover your abomination and his likewise.[25]

Their so-called marriage was clearly over. Katherine had been up the previous night until after midnight at a dinner given for the Queen by Cecil at the Savoy Palace. She was tired and did not want to reply to the letter on progress. When the court arrived at Wanstead and Havering later that day, her hopes rose that Hertford had, at last, replied to her letters. There was a package from him brought by his brother, Henry Seymour. It contained, however, only a pair of bracelets for her, along with several like them for other ladies at court. Elizabeth had requested Hertford to commission a French goldsmith to make chains and bracelets for herself and the ladies, 'to be gay in this court, towards the progress'.[26] He had simply done as she asked.

On Monday 16th July the progress reached Pirgo, the seat of Katherine's uncle, Lord John Grey. Robert Dudley, her sister Jane's former brother-in-law, was there, his servants in a new green livery. But Katherine said nothing to her uncle or Lord Robert. Her uncle, she knew, had laid out a heavy investment to entertain the Queen and she did not want to ruin his efforts. (Arundel had set the bar high when he had lavished his wealth on entertaining the court at Nonsuch in 1559, to the resentment of all who followed him.) As for Robert Dudley, he had never shown Katherine much affection: doubtless he remembered how his younger brother Guildford had been accused of trying to bully Jane Grey into making him a King, a story that may have cost him his head. So the court's progress continued through Essex, with Katherine keeping her fears to herself. They stayed at Ingatestone for the weekend, before proceeding to the royal mansion of Beaulieu. There Katherine received another letter from Herbert, this one laced with threats:

Like as a good while ago I was your friend madam, so your deserts
now ... makes me right sorry for that which is past of my part ...
Wherefore, without delay I require you madam to send me, by this

bearer, those letters and tokens with my tablature and picture that I
sent you ... or else, to be plain with you, I will make you as well
known to all the world as your whoredom is now, I thank God, known
to me and spied by many scores more.[27]

The weather was hot and humid on 25th July as the court left
Beaulieu for Felix Hall and Colchester. It was the oppressive forerunner of a summer storm. On the night of the 30th, when the court was
at the private house of St Osythe, the storm broke. For three hours
there was violent thunder and lightning, followed 'by great rains till
midnight, insomuch that the people thought the world was at an
end, and the day of doom was come, it was so terrible'.[28] But the next
day the court was on the road again, with Katherine's growing baby
pushing up to her rib cage, the bump hidden under the pleats of her
dress, as the horses, carriages and carts rattled along the rough roads.
On 5th August the court reached Ipswich, a town that was a hot bed
of the kind of Protestantism with which the Greys were associated
and which Elizabeth disliked. The Queen was infuriated to see the
ministers there were not wearing surplices and that many were
married with children. On the 9th she issued an order. Women were
forbidden henceforth from living in cathedrals or colleges and those
divines who ignored her orders would lose their ecclesiastical
promotions. Cecil moaned to his friend Archbishop Parker, that if he
hadn't put his foot down, she would have banned priests from
marrying at all and made those who had them put away their wives
altogether. It was an inauspicious time for the ill-tempered Queen to
now learn about Katherine's pregnancy.

That night Katherine turned to her friend Mistress Sentlow[29] (the
sister-in law of Frances's former lady-in-waiting, Bess Hardwick) for
advice. Young Sentlow was considered at court to be as stable as 'a
rock within the sea'. But when Katherine told her that she had
married Hertford and was pregnant by him, the rock crumbled, and
Sentlow 'fell into great weeping saying she was very sorry she had
done so without the consent or knowledge of the Queen's Majesty or
any other of her friends'.[30] The next day Katherine attended a

communion service with all the members of the Privy Chamber and the Queen. Whispers hissed among the pews and she realised by 'the secret talk she saw amongst men and women that her being with child was known and spied out'.[31]

Katherine urgently needed someone to intercede on her behalf with the Queen. Robert Dudley seemed to her the best choice. Despite everything that had passed, he was family. She knew, further-more, he had been helpful to her sister Jane's former tutor, John Aylmer, in 1559 after he had angered the Queen with his demands for more preachers. Late that evening, Katherine went to Dudley's lodg-ings in Ipswich and begged him 'to be a means to the Queen's high-ness for her'.[32] He agreed to do so, hoping, perhaps, that the news would spur the Queen to reconsider marrying him: Elizabeth would now need a child more than ever. When he delivered the news to Eliz-abeth the next morning, however, her reaction was one of fury. Katherine was ordered to the Tower under armed guard and messen-gers were sent to France demanding Hertford's immediate return.[33] Elizabeth suspected a plot, but had little idea who was involved or what course it might take. She fired off a letter to the Lieutenant of the Tower, Sir Edward Warner, commanding him to 'examine the Lady Katherine very straightly, how many have been privy to the love betwixt the Earl of Hertford and her, from the beginning'. Katherine, she continued, was to 'understand that she shall have no manner of favour, except she will show the truth'.

Warner was ordered also to interview Mistress Sentlow over two or three nights in the Tower, more if 'ye shall think meet', and, Elizabeth suggested, Warner might put the fear of God into her by sending for her secretly and hinting at 'diverse matters confessed by the Lady Katherine'.[34]

As Katherine arrived at the Tower the diplomatic community was aflame with rumour. Like Elizabeth, the Spanish ambassador, de Quadra, suspected there had to be more to the story than a simple love affair between Katherine and Hertford, a 'young man of little enough substance, although very heretical'.[35] He had heard that the Earl of Arundel was somehow involved, and recalled his interest in

Jane Seymour. Other names would also soon crop up. Amongst them was that of John Jewel, the bishop who gave the sermon at Frances's funeral. The most significant, however, was that of William Cecil. He had begun his career as servant to Hertford's father, the Duke of Somerset, and was related to the Grey family (Lord John Grey's daughter Frances was married to Cecil's brother-in-law). De Quadra believed Cecil had arranged Katherine's marriage in the immediate aftermath of Amy Dudley's death, fearing Elizabeth would marry Dudley with the backing of Philip II. He had then dropped the matter when he was back in the Queen's good grace.

Cecil, for his part, was shocked by the discovery of the marriage and deeply worried by Katherine's imprisonment. Mary Queen of Scots had returned to Scotland, as she had said she would. Her advisers had since sent notice to Elizabeth of the proposal that Cecil had outlined to Throckmorton in July: that Mary would renounce her immediate claim to the throne in exchange for recognition as Elizabeth's heir. Cecil believed that Elizabeth might agree to it. 'Thus is God displeased with us,' Cecil wrote to one of his friends as he delivered the news of Katherine Grey's disgrace.

Katherine was interrogated in the Tower on the 22nd August 1561. She was now in her ninth month of pregnancy, tired, and uncomfortable. She would give up little, however, by way of information. Warner reported that 'as to the love practises between her and the Earl of Hertford[,] She will confess nothing.'[36] In her own way Katherine was as rebellious and determined as her sister Jane had been.

Chapter XIX

First Son

H ertford knew he was in trouble before the Queen's messenger
arrived. He had spoken to Mr Glynne, the manservant Katherine had sent with her letters. Hertford needed to devise a plan,
however, before he returned home. His first priority was to stay in the
Queen's good graces as much as he could. Having sent the Queen the
bracelets she had requested for her ladies, he found an excellent flute
player to replace a French musician who had died in her employ. He
wrote with the good news. He also needed to contact friends at
home. But on 15th August the Queen's messenger arrived in Paris.[1]

The ambassador, Sir Nicholas Throckmorton, went directly to
Hertford's lodging and 'declared her pleasure for his immediate
return'. Hertford, anxious to delay a while longer, whimpered that
'he was sick in bed of a fever, and was grieved that he could not with
all diligence perform her commandment, and trusted that she
would not interpret the worse if he delayed his setting forward for
two or three days'.[2] Throckmorton asked why the Queen wished to
see him so urgently? Hertford claimed he had no idea. In fact, not
only did he know from Glynne that Katherine was pregnant, two of
his own servants had arrived from court and described her arrest.
Official letters soon followed informing Throckmorton of all the
details. He was sorry to see Hertford in trouble. Throckmorton
saw that 'in him are many good parts', and although unconvinced by

Hertford's 'illness', he informed the Queen that it would be diplomatic for Hertford to stay long enough to say his farewell to the French King.

Hertford refused to discuss with Throckmorton his marriage to Katherine, save to say 'that he will declare to the Queen and none other the whole bruit thereof'. But when he finally said his goodbyes on 26th August, Throckmorton put in another good word for him with the Queen, assuring her that 'His good behaviour here has been greatly to her honour and service.'[3] In England, meanwhile, Hertford's mother, the Duchess of Somerset, had written to Cecil distancing herself from 'the wildness of mine unruly child'. It did not seem to concern the duchess that foreign observers were picking up reports that the lovers might be executed. But then, if the duchess were out of the Queen's good favour she would be in no position to help them. Her letter, insisting she was 'one that neither for child nor friend shall willingly neglect the duty of a faithful subject', was not, therefore, as heartless as it may first appear.[4] There were others willing to help the couple too.

When Hertford reached Dover he breakfasted in the house of the mayor of the town with his friend Thomas Sackville. A well-known court poet, Sackville was the son of one of the few grandees to take to the field in arms in support of Jane Grey in 1553. He also had links to Cecil.[5] When the captain of Dover Castle arrived to arrest Hertford, Sackville left with whatever information he had gathered.[6] Hertford was delivered to the Tower on the afternoon of 5th September, and was there confronted with the full horror of the situation in which he had left Katherine. It was here that her sister had been executed and their fathers had spent their last days. Remorseful, he sent her posies and asked his jailors to find out from her servants how she was.[7] Doubtless also, he sought to coordinate their testimonies in order to protect their friends and to ensure the validity of their marriage was recognised so that their child would be legitimate.

The interrogations the couple endured over the following days were rigorous. Even the most intimate details of their lives were addressed. Their accounts tallied closely, save, tellingly, in those areas where the facts would indicate who knew what and when. To protect Stokes, for example, Hertford claimed that Frances had no idea he wanted to marry Katherine, something Stokes admitted was untrue when he was interviewed. Katherine, equally, would not produce the will that Hertford had given her, claiming it was lost during the progress – which still continued through the eastern counties; Elizabeth was not going to be diverted from her plans by Katherine's actions. When, however, Mary Queen of Scots' adviser, William Maitland of Lethington, arrived at court on 8th September it was clear the stress of discovering Katherine's pregnancy had taken its toll on the Queen. Elizabeth was at the ancient moated royal castle of Hertford when Maitland caught up with her.[8] Like her late half-sister, Mary, Elizabeth suffered bouts of depression, and like Mary, when she did so her weight dropped. Maitland described Elizabeth as 'To all appearances ... falling away ... extremely thin and the colour of a corpse.'[9]

The messages Maitland had brought with him would only pile more pressure on the Queen. While the letters from Mary Queen of Scots to Elizabeth were full of warmth, 'tending all to express the love and affection she bare unto her', the rest, from the Scots nobility, warned her that the surest way to keep Scotland's friendship was for Elizabeth to name Mary her successor: something she knew she could never do. When Maitland urged this last point during his interview, the Queen became visibly irritated. She retorted that she had expected a different message from Scotland, one concerning Mary's willingness to ratify the Treaty of Edinburgh, in which Mary would recognise Elizabeth's right to be Queen despite her illegitimacy. As her speech continued, however, Elizabeth's preference for Mary's claim to that of Lady Katherine Grey emerged strongly. 'I have noted,' Elizabeth told Maitland, 'that you have said to me ... that your Queen is descended of the royal blood of England and that I am obliged to love her as being nearest to me in blood of any other, all which I must confess to be true.' She assured Maitland she 'never meant ill towards her'. Even when Mary had offended her 'by bearing my arms and acclaiming the title of my crown' she had imputed 'the fault to others than to herself'. The succession was not a matter she wished to meddle in, in part, Elizabeth hinted, because it risked provoking a debate in England that would not be in Mary's interest. She declared, however: 'I here protest to you, in the presence of God, I for my part know no better [claim than the Queen of Scots] nor that I myself would prefer to her, or yet, to be plain with you, that case that might debar her from it.'[10]

It was an extraordinary statement. Elizabeth had made it quite clear she believed Mary's right of succession, under the tradition of primogeniture, took precedence over those decided by English statute as it stood, in support of her father's will. She denied there was any case to exclude Mary as a foreigner, or for any other reason, and indicated that she would nominate Mary her successor if she felt free to do so. Of her English heirs Elizabeth expressed nothing but bitterness: 'It is true, that some of them have made declaration to the world that they are more worthy of [the crown] than either [Mary] or I, by demonstrating that they are not barren, but able to have children.' She claimed, however, that the pregnant Katherine and her sister, the Lady Mary Grey, were unable 'to succeed to the crown by reason of their father's forfeiture'. This was the same failed argument their cousin, Lady Margaret Strange, had made years before during Queen Mary's reign, when she had claimed that the Duke of Suffolk's conviction for treason had cost the Grey sisters their right to the succession.[11] It was a mark of her fear and loathing for the Greys that she made it. But if there had ever been any doubts that Elizabeth preferred the claim of the Catholic, foreign Mary over the Protestant, English Katherine, she had now put them to an end. Maitland hoped that if he pressed Elizabeth further she might change her mind and name Mary Queen of Scots her choice of heir. At his final audience, however, Elizabeth explained in detail why she could never do this. 'First,' she informed him, 'I know what a dangerous thing it is to touch this string.' Elizabeth believed the confusion and uncertainty caused by changing laws on the succession, and the annulment of and anxiety over royal marriages, were together responsible for a series of revolts, from the Pilgrimage of Grace in 1536 to those of her sister's reign. Elizabeth would not risk provoking further unrest. This, she claimed, was why she had not married, instead considering herself married to her kingdom.

'Secondly,' she told Maitland, 'you think that this devise of yours [to name Mary heir to the English throne] should make friendship between us? I fear it should produce the contrary effect.' How could she trust that a powerful monarch, from a neighbouring country with a long history of enmity to England, would not take advantage of her new position? A Prince could not even trust the children who were to succeed them, she said.

'But,' Elizabeth continued, 'the third consideration' was the 'most weighty' of all: 'I know the inconstancy of the people of England,' she recalled, 'how they ever mislike the present government and have their eyes fixed upon that person that is next to succeed, and naturally men be so disposed: *plures adorant solem orientem quam occidentem* [more men worship the rising than the setting sun].' Elizabeth reminded Maitland how men had looked to her during the previous reign, hoping to use her to replace her sister, Mary. One day such men might wish to overthrow her. In that light Maitland could judge for himself how dangerous it would be for her to name Mary as her heir. Elizabeth, however, reserved her parting comment for the subject of Katherine and the threat she posed. She thought there was 'more matter hid in [the marriage with Hertford] than was yet uttered to the world', Maitland recalled, and that 'some of her nobility were partners in the making of that match'.[12]

As Maitland left for Scotland, Elizabeth's progress began, at last, to make its way back to London. She had always trusted the people over the court, and she took heart and comfort in the displays of loyalty from those who lined the route. When she reached Islington on the night of 22nd September, thousands of her subjects came out to greet her.[13] But, two days later, between 2 and 2.30 p.m. on 24th September, what Elizabeth dreaded, happened: Katherine gave birth to a son: Edward Seymour, Viscount Beauchamp, heir to Elizabeth under the will of Henry VIII, following his mother in line of succession. There was no more need for Cecil to fear a world turned upside down in which Queen succeeded Queen: England had a Protestant male heir. Hertford wrote the date in a small Bible written in French, acquired, most probably, during his carefree days in Paris. On the title page it had the Seymour family motto: '*Foy pour devoir*' (to duty true) and at the bottom the name E. Hertford, next to which was the signature W. Wingfield, the name of a family friend.[14] Following the entry for the birth of Hertford's son, was written a prayer in French asking that God bless the child and that Queen Elizabeth's heart be moved to pity for the parents. The earl had also written in Greek: 'In human affairs, nothing is certain.'[15]

Lord Beauchamp was baptised two days later in the Tower chapel, only feet away from the buried remains of several executed members of his family: his paternal grandfather, the Protector Somerset, his great-uncle, Thomas Seymour of Sudeley, his maternal grandfather, Henry Grey, Duke of Suffolk; and of course his aunt, Lady Jane Grey. A Roman diplomat reported that the Queen did not allow them a priest.[16]

The rivalries and tensions that had riven the court the previous winter on the death of Amy Dudley now broke forth once more. The Spanish ambassador heard that Robert Dudley had such words with the Earl of Arundel that he had stormed off home, with the intention of looking into testimony concerning the death of Dudley's wife. Dudley was now trying to make peace with him. Meanwhile, a Vatican diplomat in Lower Germany picked up information that Cecil, whose name was everywhere being associated with Katherine's marriage, was trying equally hard to achieve a reconciliation with Dudley. His relationship to Dudley would always be a complex one. Cecil had served his father and they had many friends in common. Although he often mistrusted Dudley, he hoped that they could unite for the sake of their religion. This boy of Katherine's was infinitely precious to the Protestant cause, and the Vatican diplomat declared the Queen was 'bent on having the child declared a bastard by Parliament'. Anything seemed possible such was Elizabeth's anger. A son!

In the Tower, Katherine recovered from the birth of her son in her rooms within the mansion house of the Lieutenant, Sir Edward Warner. He had also been Lieutenant of the Tower during the brief period that Jane was Queen, and much of the furniture around Katherine was also familiar. Most were cast-offs from the state apartments used during her sister's time. There was a chair in cloth of gold, half a dozen 'very old and coarse' tapestries, 'an old cast' cushion in purple velvet, and three green velvet stools that Henry VIII used to rest his feet on.[17] But Katherine was not unhappy. She had a healthy son, and her little dogs and pet monkeys were with her. Her husband's rooms were also only 10 feet away from her own and Warner's deputy was sufficiently sympathetic to allow messages to pass between the couple. In the outside world, meanwhile, a renewed effort was being made to promote Katherine and her son as Elizabeth's *legal* heirs. If it succeeded, and Elizabeth agreed to nominate them as her successors, they would all soon be freed.[18]

Leading Protestants had been disturbed by Elizabeth's refusal to exclude Mary Queen of Scots from the succession. At the Inner Temple law school, Hertford's poet friend, Thomas Sackville, and fellow students had joined forces with Cecil in trying to engage Robert Dudley as an ally. The school named Lord Robert their 'Christmas Prince'. This would make him the central figure of their twelve-day Yuletide revels, of which a visitor to London left a description.[19] The tourist was in the City when he heard the shot of cannon 'in so great a number, and so terrible that it darkened the whole air'. He asked a man passing by what it was. 'It is a warning shot to the Constable-Marshal of the Inner Temple to prepare for dinner,' the man replied. Curious, the next day he went to have a look at the Temple. Entering the gates he found a modest building, bustling with handsome, well-dressed young men. One, offering to show him the revels, took him to the dining hall. There he saw a dozen tables laid with linen, silver and gilt plate, beer, ale and wine. At one table, marked out by a green checked cloth, sat the Master of the Game with his Chief Ranger, dressed in green satins and velvets.

At another he saw the four Masters of the Revels. But in pride of place at the high table was Lord Robert Dudley.

The Christmas Prince was 'a man of tall personage, a manly countenance, somewhat brown of visage, strongly featured, and thereto comely proportioned in all lineaments of body'. He was being waited on by a carver, a sewer and a cupbearer, as well as numerous gentlemen servers, each bringing 'tender meats, sweet fruits, and dainty delicates confectioned with curious cookery'.[20] Each course was delivered to the blast of trumpets and the roll of drums, while between the courses there were entertainments. We know from records left by the Inner Temple what many of these were. On the feast of St Stephen's, for example, a huntsman brought in after the first course ten couples of hounds and released a fox along with a cat, both of which were quickly killed beneath the fireplace, to the sound of the hunting horn. There were also, however, more decorous, politically inspired, entertainments. On Twelfth Night, Robert Dudley watched the masque 'Beauty and Desire', in which he was presented as a highly desirable consort for the Queen. This was followed by a play that suggested the same but hinted that Katherine Grey should be named her heir until such time as Elizabeth had children.

The play *Gorboduc*, given at the Middle Temple in 1560, has been described as the most boring tragedy in the English language, but it represented, at the time, a revolution in drama.[21] Related in blank verse – the first play to use Shakespeare's favourite medium – it tells the story of a mythical King of the Britons (Gorboduc), who fails to settle the succession securely. When he is brutally murdered, his nobles are left unable to agree to whom the crown should fall. As the play comes to an end, England is on the point of civil war and a foreign prince, bearing the Scots title 'Duke of Albany', prepares to take the kingdom by force. At the opening of each act was another novel feature: a dumb show that delivered a visual message explaining how the drama should be interpreted. They emphasised in turn the dangers of political uncertainty, the misery of war, the importance of a monarch marrying within their kingdom, and how, if childless, they should name an English heir, with the backing of Parliament. The speech at the play's conclusion has Gorboduc's Secretary – a figure who bore a close resemblance to William Cecil – lamenting that the imminent war could have been avoided. If the King had listened to his wisest councillors and settled the succession with the backing of statute, there need have been no bloodshed.

> *Then parliament should have been held*
> *And certain heirs appointed to the crown*
> *To stay the title of established right*
> *And in the people plant obedience.*[22]

The possible role parliamentary support – or lack of it – had played in the fate of 'Jane the Queen', had not been forgotten. The authors of the play both had close connections to Hertford and Cecil. The first, Thomas Norton, was a protégé of Cecil and the childhood tutor of Hertford, in whose employ he remained.[23] Norton's co-author, Thomas Sackville, meanwhile, was the same young man with whom Hertford had breakfasted in Dover when he was arrested – a detail overlooked until now.

The play and the masque were brought subsequently to court, where they were both shown on 18th January 1561, with performances before the Queen at Whitehall. An eyewitness employed by Cecil recorded that the play's message, that Parliament should be used to settle the succession, was clearly understood by the audience.[24] But the play does not seem to be the only means by which support was being drummed up for Katherine's claim. A miniature or 'limning' of Katherine holding the baby Lord Beauchamp dates from this period, and it may be that the limning of Lady Jane Grey, with its spray of oak leaves for Robert Dudley alongside the gillyflowers for Guildford, does also; the iconography certainly fits.[25] There were other reminders in print of Robert Dudley's link to Katherine through Guildford's marriage to Jane Grey, including a ballad, published in November 1560, republished a couple of years later, in which Jane laments her fate and that of Guildford, as co-victims of their ambitious fathers.

Queen Elizabeth had no intention of paying the slightest bit of attention to the play, however, or any other propaganda in favour of Katherine's claim. The Vatican diplomat, who predicted that she wished to have baby Beauchamp declared illegitimate, was about to be proved correct. On 10th February, Lieutenant Warner received a letter from the Queen announcing the setting up of a Church commission 'to examine, inquire, and judge of the infamous conversation and pretended marriage betwixt the Lady Katherine Grey and the Earl of Hertford'.[26] The intended verdict was indicated in the phrase 'pretended marriage'. But for several days Katherine and Hertford were rowed up and down the river from the Tower to the Archbishop of Canterbury's palace at Lambeth for further rounds of interviews on their wedding arrangements.

It was evident from the information Katherine and Hertford gave that theirs was not a 'model marriage'. According to the Book of Common Prayer banns should be read three Sundays in a row before a wedding. Theirs, of course, had not been. Nor did anyone give the bride away. Nor did the bride and groom take communion. But these were minor quibbles. According to canon law all that was required for a valid marriage was consent by the bride and groom in the presence of witnesses. It was the death of Jane Seymour and the disappearance of the priest who had married them that made the commissioners' task in deciding their marriage invalid a simple one.

Robert Dudley had expected, and surely hoped, for such a result. Any enthusiasm he showed for *Gorboduc* would have cost him nothing, while gaining him friends, and his star was now rising again. At the Garter ceremony in April the young Duke of Norfolk, who had been Dudley's most bitter opponent, invited the Knights of the Garter to give Dudley their support in his courtship of the Queen. They all agreed to do so, save for Arundel and Parr of Northampton, who walked out of the proceedings. It is surely no coincidence that they were the two Councillors present at the Hoby dinner party two days after Amy Dudley was found dead, and were close to the Greys.

Cecil, the other loyal supporter of Katherine's cause, was equally angry that Dudley had failed to protect the interests of her son. But he soon dealt him a punishing blow. Cecil had been bribing de Quadra's secretary to spy on the ambassador and, on 28th April, the secretary made a statement describing his master's dealings with Dudley and the ambassador's opinion of Elizabeth's behaviour with him. It painted a devastating portrait of a woman foolish in love, and when Cecil revealed the findings it brought home to Elizabeth just how compromised her reputation would be if she were to marry Dudley. Lord Robert's hopes were dashed once more and Elizabeth feared that she would now have to do something about the succession.

Elizabeth wanted desperately to be able to trust the Queen of Scots. She was the one person who shared with Elizabeth the dangers and difficulties of being a Queen regnant. Elizabeth was sure that if only they could meet they would become mutually supportive. To the outside world the meeting would be a symbolic expression of their friendship: a dynastic alliance, akin to a marriage between two queens and two kingdoms.

In May, Elizabeth delivered her message to Mary in a three-day masque which she attended at Nottingham Castle. It was here, in the fifteenth century, that the medieval King of Scots, James I, had been imprisoned. Elizabeth wanted to bury the old enmities. The first night opened with the figure of Pallas riding into the hall on a unicorn, carrying a standard of two female hands clasped together. Then two female figures followed, one on a red lion wearing the crown of Temperance, the second on a golden lion, with the crown of Prudence. The next day Peace was drawn in on a chariot pulled by an elephant on which sat Friendship. Then on the final day Malice, in the form of a serpent, was trodden underfoot. The masque concluded with a song, 'as full of harmony as may be devised', which proclaimed that peace in Britain was dependent on dynastic (and not parliamentary) monarchy.[27] Mary was enthusiastic about this vision and to the delight of both queens a meeting was set for September in Nottingham.

Katherine and Hertford, however, had no intention of allowing their son to remain illegitimate and excluded from the succession.

Hertford was determined to appeal and in the meantime he succeeded in bribing two Tower guards, 'one George and one Dalton', to allow him to visit his wife. On 25th May, at about eleven at night, Katherine welcomed her husband into her rooms. They only had about an hour and they didn't waste it. She had a fine bed hung with silk-shot damask, covered with a silken quilt of red striped with gold – not unlike the cushions of the carriages at the Queen's coronation – and there they lay and made love, 'with joyful heart'. On the 29th Hertford visited once more and they returned to the bed.[28] But on a third night, the guards got cold feet and Hertford found the door to Katherine's rooms locked. She could hear him but there was nothing she could do to get the door open, although, as she later recalled, she longed to be with her 'sweet bedfellow' again.[29] As the days passed she missed his company all the more. She suspected that her 'naughty Lord' had conceived a second child with her and communicated this to Hertford who proved to be delighted by the news. Elizabeth's commissioners had argued that their first child was illegitimate on the grounds there were no witnesses to their promise to each other. It would be very difficult to argue this of their second baby. The couple had declared their marriage before the Archbishop of Canterbury and half of England, under interrogation.

As Katherine and Hertford rejoiced, new clouds were gathering over the hopes of Mary Queen of Scots and Elizabeth. A bloody religious war had broken out in France. Cecil had always connected 'the affections and dispositions of the Queen of Scots and the house of Guise' to the overthrow of Protestantism in Europe, and he feared a coming apocalypse for his co-religionists.[30] He was confirmed in this view, as were many others, when news reached England of a massacre of Protestants in France by the followers of one of Mary's Guise uncles. Mary Queen of Scots wrote immediately to Elizabeth disassociating herself from what had happened. But as Malice triumphed in France so it destroyed hopes of friendship between the two queens of the British Isles. On 15th July, only nine days after Elizabeth had issued her formal invitation for the September meeting in Nottingham, she sent word to Mary that the meeting had to be postponed until the following year. Mary wept in disappointment; Elizabeth was equally miserable. Her hopes of a political marriage with Mary were no more likely to be realised than a marriage with Robert Dudley. She remained utterly alone, and a brush with death would soon renew pressure on her to name Katherine her heir.

Chapter XX

Parliament and Katherine's Claim

Queen Elizabeth was at Hampton Court on 10th October 1562, when she began to feel unwell. She felt inexplicably tired; her head hurt and her back ached. She decided to have a bath and take a short walk. When she returned to her chambers, however, she began to feel hot, then cold, as a fever set in. A physician was called and diagnosed the potentially deadly smallpox. Elizabeth refused to accept it. There were as yet no blisters and her half-brother's terrible death had left her with a contempt for physicians. But sickness and diarrhoea soon followed and she became delirious. Dudley's sister, Mary Sidney – who had been Jane Grey's closest sister-in-law – nursed Elizabeth tenderly. On the seventh day, however, the fever was so violent that she was given up for lost.

As Elizabeth became unconscious the Privy Council met in urgent session to discuss the succession. But like the nobles in Norton and Sackville's play, *Gorboduc*, the Council could not agree on a candidate. Some Councillors wanted King Henry's will followed and Katherine to be declared Elizabeth's heir. Others claimed the will was fraudulent. They pointed out that it had not been signed with the King's own hand but only endorsed with a dry stamp. Of this group a few favoured the candidature of Henry Hastings, Earl of Huntingdon. Pembroke, who remained bitter about Katherine's humiliation of his son, was one such. Robert Dudley, who was Huntingdon's brother-in-law, was another. But Huntingdon had only his gender and adulthood to recommend him, and a far larger group of Katherine's opponents backed the claim of Mary Queen of Scots, or her English-born aunt, Margaret Douglas, the Countess of Lennox. It was suggested that 'jurists of the greatest standing in the country examine the right of the claimants'.[1] But with the Queen's death possibly imminent there was no time for that.

As the arguments on the Council grew more intense Elizabeth woke up. Believing she was dying she asked for Robert Dudley to be made Lord Protector with an income of £20,000 a year. She swore that although 'she loved and had always loved Lord Robert dearly, as God was her witness nothing improper had passed between them'. Her Councillors promised her wishes would be fulfilled, but without any intention that they would be.

That night, as the frantic discussions on the succession continued, the pox blisters began to appear. The pustules broke first in Elizabeth's throat and mouth, then spread outwards to her face and body. But she began to feel better. The smallpox had done its worst. In a week the blisters began to heal and, to her great relief, the scars did not prove disfiguring. Dudley's sister Mary Sidney was less fortunate in this respect. She fell ill a fortnight later, only to survive, her husband recorded, 'as foul a lady as the smallpox could make her'.

As Elizabeth's strength returned, the Council remained determined to settle the controversy of the succession once and for all. The ideal platform for thrashing out the arguments was Parliament and Elizabeth was in a situation that obliged her to call one. She needed to raise money for England's intervention in the civil war in France.

When the writs went out early in November the Spanish ambassador, de Quadra, picked up reports of leading figures holding secret meetings. They were using the cover of dinner parties to discuss strategy in support of their favoured candidates.[2] Norfolk, who attended a dinner of the Earl of Arundel's until two in the morning, was once again strongly supportive of Katherine's claim. De Quadra believed Norfolk hoped Katherine's son could be married to one of his young daughters. But the fact John Foxe was overseeing the forth-coming publication of the first English edition of his *Book of Martyrs* from Norfolk's house, was also a daily reminder to the duke of the iconic status of the Grey name to Protestants. When Elizabeth learned about the dinner, she wept tears of rage, and had Arundel sent for. But the earl refused to be intimidated by her dressing down and told her sternly that if she intended to be governed by passion, he would ensure his fellow nobles prevented it. As it was commonly said women were ruled by emotion rather than reason, the insult carried a particular edge.

Arundel also complained angrily to the Queen about the support being given for Huntingdon's claim. It was believed that Dudley was pressing his brother-in-law's case in the hope it would make him a more attractive groom for the Queen. It would be possible to argue the match would solidify the succession, ensuring that Eliza-beth's consort (Dudley) had an investment in her heir, to whom he was personally related. Elizabeth assured Arundel that she did not approve of Huntingdon's claim either, but to weaken Huntingdon she needed to empower another male heir. Since she had no inten-tion of helping Katherine's cause, or that of her son, Elizabeth now turned to Margaret Tudor's daughter by her second marriage, the Catholic Countess of Lennox. She had two sons, the elder of whom was the spoilt but beautiful teenager, Henry, Lord Darnley. Since the death of Francis II, the countess had been pushing Darnley as a suitable husband for Mary Queen of Scots. Not only was he second in line to the Scots throne, he had the advantage of being English born. This would go some way to answering the argument against Mary's succession that those born outside the realm of England were precluded under a statute dating back to the reign of Edward III. The Lady Margaret's amateurish intrigues from her base in the heart of Catholic Yorkshire, had not escaped Cecil's attention, however. The previous winter her husband had been sent to the Tower, while she and her family were placed under house arrest.[3] Elizabeth now had them released and young Darnley was invited to court.

Elizabeth made a great fuss of the new arrival, and listened avidly to Darnley's lute playing. Come the New Year, however, Katherine Grey was eight months pregnant and Cecil was preparing to flex Parliament's muscles on her behalf. The Queen opened the session on 12th January, dressed in her scarlet robes. She looked magnificent, all golden hair, velvet, and ermine. But her new MPs were largely Protestant and had no intention of supporting her preference for any Stuart claimant. Thanks to the careful planning of Cecil and his allies, only twenty-seven Catholics had managed to get seats, despite large swathes of northern and western England, and Wales, being conservative in religion. The Commons began discussing the succession almost immediately and a petition to the Queen was planned. On 26th January, Thomas Norton, acting as Cecil's agent, read the text before assembled MPs. The petition recalled Elizabeth's recent illness and drew attention to the supposed dangers posed to religion by Mary Queen of Scots. With assurances of love and affection it humbly requested the Queen to marry. It made clear, however, that even if she did marry, this would no longer be enough to satisfy the requirements of national security.

The petition demanded the succession be settled on a named heir. The Commons promised to uphold the Act of Succession of 1544, that had nominated Mary and Elizabeth as Edward's heirs despite their illegitimate status and, in return, asked that a definitive statement be made on the validity of her father's will. Once that was done the rightful heir could be declared. The alternative was described to Elizabeth in the familiar hues of the play *Gorboduc*, of which Norton was co-author. It painted a harrowing picture of civil war and foreign invasion, the destruction of noble houses and the slaughter of innocent people. 'We fear a faction of heretics in your realm,' the petition declared; 'contentious and malicious papists.' The Protestant faith, as well as peace, was at stake.[4]

When the Commons petition was presented to Elizabeth she told the MPs only that their request required consideration. To the Lords, however, who were considered her 'natural councillors' by reason of their hereditary status, she expressed anger. Did they not know 'that the marks they saw on her face were not wrinkles but the pits of small-pox'? Although already twenty-nine, God could still grant her children, as he had the ageing St Elizabeth, she reminded them. They would also do well to 'consider what they were asking as, if she declared a successor, it would cost much blood in England'.[5] It was at this juncture, with Elizabeth struggling desperately not to be cornered into naming her own replacement, that she learned – along with everybody else – that the twenty-two-year-old Katherine Grey was about to have a second child. No need here for a miracle pregnancy, such as the ageing St Elizabeth required. Elizabeth promptly had the Lieutenant of the Tower, Sir Edward Warner, locked up in his own prison for the lapse of security that had allowed Katherine and Hertford to enjoy their conjugal rights. But the general mood in London was one of elation. The ageing Sir John Mason reported to Cecil that 'broad speeches' were being made in the couple's favour, 'both in the City and in other sundry places in the realm', with people demanding: 'Why should man and wife be [prevented] from coming together.'[6]

Ordinary people saw clearly the injustice of making a child a bastard when the parents had declared themselves married. It would not have happened if it were not for the political imperatives. But those in more elevated positions, such as Mason, condemned Hertford's defiance as 'presumptuous, contemptuous and outrageous'. Mason, who had been one of the first in Queen Jane's Privy Council to betray her in 1553, thoroughly disliked this rebellious young man. 'There is not a more outrageous youth, neither one that better likes himself, neither that promises himself greater things,' Mason raged to Cecil. He had, he said, to be taught a severe lesson: 'His imprisonment fattens him, and he has thereby commodity rather than hindrance.'[7]

Elizabeth demanded the couple underwent interrogation once more. The details of their late-night liaisons in May emerged. But no amount of huffing and puffing from Elizabeth, or the irate Mason, could prevent Katherine's new baby being born. In the Tower at 10.15 on the morning of 10th February 1563, Katherine delivered a second son, Thomas. His elder brother, Lord Beauchamp, was still less than eighteen months old. '*Dieu le donne sa gran Benediction paternelle*' (God gives his great paternal blessings) wrote Hertford in the family Bible. At the christening two of the warders played godfather, but there was no time for prolonged celebrations. Hertford was hauled before the Star Chamber later that same day to face his punishment.

A large number of noblemen arrived to watch the proceedings, but they were told to give up their usual places to the Council. Most of the noblemen stayed anyway, and listened at the bar. Hertford's visits to Katherine in the Tower were detailed and, at the conclusion, he was found guilty of three offences. The first was impregnating Katherine, a kinswoman of the Queen, with her first child; the second was conspiring with the Under Keeper of the Tower to have access to her and impregnating her again; and the third was breach of his imprisonment. He was fined the ruinous sum of £5,000 for each offence, and jailed during the Queen's pleasure.[8] Hertford was returned to the Tower under close watch, but he remained unrepentant. He believed he could yet prove his marriage to Katherine was valid and knew they had many powerful people on their side.

The intense revival of interest being shown in the story of Jane Grey's life and death may be linked to support for Katherine, as well as to the publication of Foxe's hugely popular *Book of Martyrs*. A ballad, written in 1560, in which Jane lamented how she and Guildford were dying because of the ambitions of their fathers, was republished.[9] Roger Ascham wrote *The Schoolmaster* with its description of his meeting Jane at Bradgate, and her complaints about her bullying parents. Sir Thomas Chaloner, a friend of Cecil and the *Gorboduc* author Thomas Sackville, also composed his elegy praising Jane's learning as superior to all others, and claiming that she was pregnant when she was executed. Although the two latter works were not published for many years, the themes of Jane's innocence of ambition – and the punishment of her unborn child with her – resonated with Katherine's situation. But Katherine and Hertford also had more direct support. While Katherine tried to care for her newborn son in the Tower, as well as her toddler, moves were being made in

Parliament against the claims of her principal rival, Mary Queen of Scots.

De Quadra heard reports of a proposition in the Lords to limit the succession to four English families: that of Katherine Grey, her cousin Lady Margaret Strange, the Earl of Huntingdon and the Countess of Lennox. Mary Queen of Scots' emissary, Maitland of Lethington, returned from Scotland to protect his mistress' interests from any further such moves and soon found Elizabeth his best ally. She argued to the Council that nothing should be done to drive Mary into the arms of a European ally. But no sooner was the idea of limiting the succession to four English families batted away than another emerged. Discussions were held on a future parliamentary bill that would propose the Privy Council rule England after Elizabeth's death, with the addition of appointees named in her will, until such time as Parliament was called and declared a successor. This neo-republican proposal goes beyond – but was, perhaps, inspired by – the proposal in King Edward's original will that Frances, Duchess of Suffolk rule as governor with a Council, until a King was born – and it has the fingerprints of Edward's former Secretary of State, Sir William Cecil all over it.[10] While he believed passionately in a Protestant monarchy, he also believed that its survival could not be left safely to the Queen. Such a bill would, however, have sent a piercing light into the dark mysteries of royal power, exposing it for what it was – not something supernatural, but mortal and functional, that could carry on without a monarch at all. To Elizabeth's relief the bill fell through at an early stage, reportedly spiked by Katherine's rivals.[11] But behind the scenes, other plans she knew nothing about were being laid in Katherine's favour.

An MP and friend of Cecil called John Hales intended to write a book clarifying Katherine's rights to the succession. He was a colourful and controversial figure who had known Cecil since the days of the Protectorship. Easily identified at the House of Commons by his limp (his nickname was 'Club-foot Hales'), he had advocated to Elizabeth in an oration on the occasion of her coronation the benefits of a 'mixed monarchy' in which royal authority was shared by the institutions of government. Hales's research began with him approaching Katherine's uncle, Lord John Grey, and asking if he could confirm that her mother, Frances, had been legitimate. Katherine's grandfather, the old Duke of Suffolk, had a somewhat chequered marital history. He was always dumping brides when a better offer came along and had, in fact, been betrothed to some unlucky heiress when he had married Katherine's grandmother. Lord John assured him that Frances's legitimacy had been proven both in the ancient Church court known as the Arches and the Star Chamber. Hertford's stepfather, Francis Newdigate, gave Hales further evidence to this effect. Hales then moved on to investigate Henry VIII's will. Thanks to an unnamed friend, he had access to a chancery enrolment of the will made under the Great Seal during the reign of Edward VI.[12] The will supported strongly Katherine's claim. Hales sealed the arguments against the Queen of Scots by drawing attention to the law, dating back to the reign of Edward III, that excluded all those born outside the realm of England.

When Hales's tract was ready Lord John Grey and Francis Newdigate were both shown it, along with at least two other MPs. It was, in effect, the basis for a secret parliamentary motion to name Katherine the heir to Elizabeth. Newdigate was concerned, however, that even with the tract MPs would be loath to name Katherine while her sons were illegitimate. What was needed, the men decided, were 'sentences and counsels of lawyers from beyond seas', who could confirm the legality of the marriage.[13] While this monumental task began with Hertford's financial support, Elizabeth was coming up with a plan of her own. The Queen still wanted desperately to find a basis of trust with Mary. Her solution was to marry her to a man in whom she had complete confidence: Robert Dudley. She floated the idea first to Maitland of Lethington, coyly informing him that if his mistress wished to marry safely and happily, then she recommended Dudley. There is no reason to doubt Elizabeth's sincerity. Her proposal was not dissimilar to later Protestant efforts to arrange a marriage between Mary and Norfolk: it would encourage Mary to become a Protestant and secure an English dynasty for an English throne. But

Elizabeth's love for Dudley had always blinded her to his unsuitability as a royal spouse.

Maitland knew very well that Mary would be appalled by Elizabeth's offer. Her mother-in-law, Catherine de Medici, had sneered about Elizabeth considering a marriage with her 'horse keeper'. Why would she marry a servant when she could marry any king in Europe? Maitland told Elizabeth that Mary would be very touched that 'she was willing to give a thing so dearly prized by herself', but that she could not possibly marry Dudley, 'and so deprive [Elizabeth] of all the joy and solace she received from his companionship'.[14] Elizabeth remained determined, however, to advance her proposal. For this to happen it was necessary first for her to bring the Parliament to a close and end its damaging attacks on the Stuart claim. To achieve this as quickly as possible she suspended rather than closed the session. But before dismissing them on 10th April 1563, she also gave her promised reply to the Commons on the subject of their petition. The matter of the succession was a very difficult one, she told them blandly, and required further thought. The MPs were bitterly disappointed by this non-answer. Elizabeth hoped, however, that by the time they reassembled she would be able to present them with the fait accompli of Mary's marriage to Dudley. In the meantime, Elizabeth would ensure Katherine felt just how painful the consequences could be if you angered a Queen.

Chapter XXI

Hales's Tempest

In the summer of 1563 there was an explosion of cases of the plague in London. Elizabeth removed the court to Windsor and had a gallows set up on the edge of the town: anyone suspected of bringing the disease from the capital would be hanged. Katherine, her husband and children remained trapped in the Tower, meanwhile, waiting for the disease to breach the fortress's walls. By August the fatalities in London were running at a thousand a week. The city was literally decimated, with one in ten succumbing to the outbreak. Katherine's friends begged the Queen to allow the family to be moved elsewhere to spare their lives. Eventually Elizabeth agreed, but the family were to be separated and kept under house arrest, with their relatives bearing much of the cost.

Katherine's elder son, Lord Beauchamp, was to be sent to her mother-in-law, the Duchess of Somerset at Hanworth, along with Hertford. Katherine and the baby Thomas, were, meanwhile, to be sent to her uncle, Lord John Grey, at Pirgo in Essex. Elizabeth insisted that he was to 'plainly understand', that he was now Katherine's jailor, and that she had 'meant no more by this liberty than to remove her from the danger of the plague'. Katherine was not to be allowed 'conference with any person not being of his lordships household'.[1] She could not contact even her husband or her sister Mary Grey, who remained at court. No letters between the sisters survive, although Mary Grey's later actions suggest the nineteen-year-old secretly admired Katherine's bold gamble on happiness and believed that in time the Queen's anger would pass. It was difficult for her to accept that she and her sister posed the very real threat to Elizabeth that they did, simply because of who they were.

Katherine arrived at Pirgo on 3rd September with her son Thomas, his nurse, three ladies-in-waiting and two manservants. The first thing she did was to write and thank Cecil for his help in saving her family from the plague. She was sure that he knew that Hertford, 'my own dear Lord', was equally grateful, and she asked Cecil to continue to seek the Queen's pardon, 'which with up-stretched hands and down bent knees, from the bottom of my heart, most humbly I crave'.[2]

In the Tower Katherine's empty rooms presented a sad spectacle: the bed of 'changeable damask' was 'all broken and not worth ten pence'; much of the other furniture was 'torn and tattered by her monkeys and dogs'.[3] But she had known happiness there and, although Lord John described Katherine to Cecil as having arrived at Pirgo a 'penitent and sorrowful woman for the Queen's displeasure', it took a short while for it to sink in that she was now a long way from her husband and her elder son. She played with Thomas, dressed him in little jackets of russet velvet and matching silk hats corded with silver; she had thick red petticoats made to keep him warm in the winter, and new furs for herself. But the days soon began to drag. She lost her appetite and sank into depression, the illness from which so many Tudor women suffered. Less than a month after her removal from the Tower, Lord John expressed his concern for Katherine's health:

I assure you cousin Cecil (as I have written unto my Lord Robert) the thought and care she takes for want of her Highness's favour, pines her away: before God I speak it, if it come not the sooner, she will not live long thus, she eats not above six morsels in the meal. If I say unto her 'good madam, eat somewhat to comfort yourself', she falls a weeping

and goes up to her chamber; if I ask her what the cause is ... she
answers me 'Alas uncle, what a life is this to me, thus to live in the
Queens displeasure; but for my Lord and my children, I would to God
I were buried.'

Katherine's torment grieved her uncle, 'even at the heart roots'.[4] But
her suffering increased when four days after his letter was sent, her
son Beauchamp enjoyed his second birthday without her.

Cecil gave what practical advice he could to his old friend Lord
John, to whose son he was godfather and whose daughter was his
wife's sister-in-law. He said that Katherine might petition the
Queen and suggested the kind of phrases she might use. He even
offered to read it in draft form first. The final version could then be
delivered by Robert Dudley, the one man who could do so without
risk of losing the Queen's favour. On 7th November, the draft petition was ready and Katherine's uncle forwarded it to Cecil for his
approval, enclosing letters from them both. Lord John assured him,
that 'if you will have any one thing amended there I pray you note
it, and my man shall bring it back to me again. For I would be loath
there should be any fault found with one word written therein.'[5]
Katherine's letter reiterated her gratitude, along with that of 'my
own good Lord', and expressed her regret that 'All we can do is to
bear you our assured good will, and to pray for you, and to wish
you health.'[6]

Just under a week later, the final version was ready and delivered
by Dudley to Elizabeth. Katherine's petition abased her before her
monarch. She did not dare 'to crave pardon for my most disobedient
and rash matching of myself, without your highness's consent'. She
could only beg for mercy, while acknowledging that she did not
deserve it. She concluded, on her knees, 'long continue and preserve
your Majesty's reign over us'.[7]

Katherine hoped, and believed, that the petition would be enough,
and she wrote to Hertford expressing the hope they would be
together soon. The more passionate passages in this moving love
letter have never been published before. The Victorian parson who

printed part of the letter was shocked by its intimacy and since then it has lain forgotten.*

> *It gives me no small joy, my dearest Lord, to hear of your good health. I ask God to give you strength, as I am sure he shall. In this lament-able time there is nothing that can better comfort us, in our pitiable separation, than to ask, to hear, and to know of each other's well being. Although recently I have been unwell, I am now pretty well, thank God. I long to be merry with you, as I know you do with me, as we were when our sweet little boys were gotten in the Tower, the 25th or 29th of May. I wish you to be as happy as I was sad when you came to my door for the third time, and it was locked. Do you think I can forget what passed between us? No, I cannot. I remember it more often than you know. I have good reason to, when I reflect what a husband I have in you. It is a hard fate to be deprived of so good a man. Well, I say good, although you have been naughty. Could you have found it in your heart not to give me a second child so hard on the heels of the first?*
>
> *No, but while I would have liked to rest my weary bones ... I know our children are God's blessing. I don't doubt, also that I would will-ingly bear the pain of further childbirth, such is my boundless love for my sweet bedfellow, that I once lay beside with joyful heart, and shall again ... Thus humbly thanking you, my sweet Lord, for your husbandly concern in inquiring how I am, and in sending me money. I most lovingly bid you farewell: not forgetting my especial thanks to you for your book, which is no small jewel. I can understand it very well, for as soon as I had it, I read it with my heart as well as my eyes; by which token I once again bid you farewell and good health, my good Ned,*
> *Your most loving and faithful wife during life, Katherine Hertford*[8]

Katherine's hopes of seeing Hertford were soon dashed, however. The message came that the Queen would not forgive them. Katherine

---

* I have put the text into modern English to make it easier to follow.

began to wonder if she would ever see Hertford, or her elder son, again. 'What the long want of the Queen's Majesty's accustomed favour towards me has bred is this miserable and wretched body of mine, God only knows,' she wrote to Cecil with desperation on 13th December; 'I rather wish of God shortly to be buried, in the faith and fear of Him, than in this continual agony to live.'

Her uncle, Lord John Grey, wrote a few days later, fearing that Katherine was in a state of irreversible despair. She spent days refusing to get out of bed, 'and I never came to her, but I found her either weeping or else saw by her face that she had wept', he informed Cecil. Her servants were fearful of leaving her for the night, uncertain 'how to find her in the morning, for she is so fraught with ... thought, weeping and sitting still'. If these women were not watching her closely, he warned, 'I tell you truly cousin Cecil, I would not sleep in quiet'.[9]

The disappointment in the failure of Katherine's petition now triggered arguments between the Grey and Seymour families. Hertford's stepfather, Francis Newdigate, blamed Lord John Grey for what had happened, telling Katherine's cousin Lady Clinton her uncle should not interfere in a husband's place. When Lord John heard this he expressed outrage to Cecil. He had to provide everything for Katherine and her baby, he complained, they did not have so much as a cup to drink out of that he had not provided. Indeed, Katherine was so short of money that Lady Clinton had been obliged to purchase on her behalf a New Year gift of silk stockings for the Queen's Boleyn cousin, Lady Knollys, who was a vital ally.[10] It was only after he wrote to Hertford at Hanworth to complain that Katherine had been sent a measly £20 and the promise of beds and sheets, which had not yet arrived, Lord John continued.[11] A full inventory of the costs of Katherine's personal servants, the laundress who washed her clothes, and the old woman who looked after the baby's things, was enclosed with the letter, along with a list of cloth being made up into clothing for Katherine and the baby. It included:

Two coats for Mr Thomas, whereof the one is russet damask, the other
of crimson velvet
Of white cloth to make him petticoats, two yards
Of red cloth to make him like petticoats, two yards
Velvet caps for him, two, a russet taffeta hat for him . . .
Black velvet to make a gown for my lady Katherine, bound with sables,
ten yards; russet velvet to make a gown and a kirtle; black and russet
lace to the gown and kirtle . . .
Damask to make a night gown for my lady; crimson satin to make a
petticoat
A petticoat of crimson velvet; a velvet hood for my lady; two pairs of
black silk hose; black cloth to make a cloak two yards.

Linen to make smocks was also listed and cambric (also a form of linen) for ruffs and handkerchiefs.[12] Cecil passed the account on to Hertford and it was paid promptly. He had no wish for further quarrels having found no better luck in seeking a pardon. He had been sending the Queen small gifts and pleaded for further help from Dudley. But Dudley reported back, bluntly, that although 'he had moved the Queen's majesty of his behalf he did not find her in the mood, at present, to grant his prayer'.[13] The bitterness of both families was now focused on what they perceived as Elizabeth's cruelty. Hertford's stepfather, Francis Newdigate, attributed it to Elizabeth's desire to come to an accommodation with Mary Queen of Scots.[14] Lord John, meanwhile, angrily observed that it was now Lent, a time 'of mercy and forgiveness'. He wished he was the Queen's confessor to exhort her to forgive and forget; 'or otherwise able to step into the pulpit, to tell her Highness, that God will not forgive her, unless she freely forgive all the world'.[15] Instead of forgiveness for his niece, however, Lord John shortly found himself in custody and returned to the Tower, whose cold walls he had last known during Queen Mary's reign after the revolt of 1554.

If Elizabeth had ever the slightest intention of releasing Katherine and Hertford, it had been botched by the discovery of the efforts being made to clarify Katherine's rights to the succession, and undermine the Church commission's decision on their 'pretended marriage'. The Queen had learned of Hales's book, with its promotion of Katherine as her rightful heir, and of the approaches made to divines in Europe to declare on the legality of the marriage: approaches that had proved very successful. The divines had concluded that since marriage was a matter of the consent between two people, and Katherine and Hertford had both advertised such consent and followed it with sexual intercourse, they were legally married and their children legitimate. Elizabeth was furious. Walter Haddon, the brother of the late Bradgate chaplain James Haddon, referred to her wrath as the *tempestas Halisiana*: the storm raised by Hales. That a subject should look abroad and seek the opinion of foreign divines on a matter settled by her Church in England was bad enough. But that it should touch on the succession was worse. She particularly resented Hales's 'writing the book so precisely against the Queen of Scotland's title'. It endangered her plan to marry Mary Stuart to Robert Dudley and threatened to further sour relations with her Scottish cousin.

Katherine and her infant son Thomas were bundled out of Pirgo and placed under close arrest at the house of an Essex neighbour, Sir William Petre, at Ingatestone. Her uncle, meanwhile, was interviewed, as was Hertford's stepfather, Francis Newdigate, and his servants. Several of the names that emerged from these interviews were familiar to Elizabeth, as either friends or clients of Cecil's.[16] They included Cecil's heavyweight brother-in-law, the Lord Keeper Nicholas Bacon, who appeared to have given Hales legal advice. According to the Spanish ambassador, de Quadra, Dudley believed that Cecil had actually written the book. But to Dudley's irritation Elizabeth merely let Cecil know that she had noted the names of those involved who 'had access to him in their suites'. She then allowed the Hales matter to drop. De Quadra reported she felt there were 'so many accomplices in the offence that they must overlook it'.

Cecil was allowed to take charge of the investigation and his enquiries proved to be not very probing. Elizabeth did not want to be embarrassed by the names that might have emerged. It would have highlighted her weakness. But her anger over the betrayals had to be satisfied one way or another. 'Club-foot' Hales would spend a year in the Tower and a further four under house arrest, while Nicholas Bacon was banished from court and the Privy Council for several months. His health never recovered from the shock of his disgrace. The terror of the Tower also had a devastating effect on Lord John Grey. He died on 19th November 1564, 'of thought', his friends said, although Cecil preferred to put it down to gout.[17]

The principal protagonists at the centre of the drama suffered also. While the now three-year-old Lord Beauchamp remained with the Duchess of Somerset, Hertford was removed from Hanworth and placed with the aged Sir John Mason, who detested him and had previously complained to Cecil that prison was too good for him. Katherine was left at Ingatestone, with the baby Thomas, lonely and broken hearted. And while she was left to ponder that she might never see her husband or elder son again, it was now her sister's turn to follow her along the well-trodden path towards tragedy.

PART FOUR

❖

Lost Love

❖

'... Think ye see
The very persons of our noble story
As they were living: think you see them great,
And followed with the general throng, and sweat
Of thousand friends; then, in a moment, see
How soon this mightiness meets misery:
And if you can be merry then, I'll say
A man may weep upon his wedding day.'

Henry VIII, Prologue
William Shakespeare

Chapter XXII

The Lady Mary and Mr Keyes

Watching at the sidelines of her sisters' lives, the nineteen-year-old Lady Mary Grey had grown up intelligent, determined and well read. Despite such qualities she was not, however, thought of seriously as an heir to the crown. It was expected that status be indicated, at least in part, in beauty of ornament and person. The social order reflected the divine order in which what was good was also beautiful, and ugliness and deformity was associated with sin and that which was base. The English thus placed a great deal of importance on appearance, and Mary Grey's was unprepossessing. She was the shortest person at court, and described by the Spanish ambassador as 'crook backed and very ugly'. Mary Grey, quite literally, did not have the stature of a future monarch – but she sought to turn this to her advantage.

Mary Grey had admired her sister Jane and kept a copy of Foxe's *Book of Martyrs*, with its description of her brave death. But she also envied the happiness Katherine had enjoyed with Hertford – albeit briefly – and she too was now in love. The object of her affection was a widower twice her age, and with several children, called Thomas Keyes. He held the post at court of Sergeant Porter. This placed him in charge of palace security, a position given only to a man of unimpeachable loyalty and imposing physique, and Keyes was well known for both. He was a former soldier and reputed to be the biggest man at court, capable of dealing with drunken spats or more serious disturbances. Mary Grey saw him nearly every day at the palace gate. He stood with the guard who served under his command, each carrying a black staff with which they ensured the entrances to the palaces were kept clear and peaceful. There he courted the spirited and diminutive Mary in the traditional manner, with tokens of affection. One day he gave her his ruby ring, on another a gold chain with a little hanging bottle of mother of pearl. The physical contrast troubled them no more, it seems, than the differences in their age, rank and the potential danger of their conducting their romance without the Queen's knowledge.

Mary Grey may have convinced herself that if she married Mr Keyes it would be seen in a similar light to her mother's marriage to the lower born Adrian Stokes, one that would ensure she did not represent any further threat to Elizabeth. She understood that the timing of any such marriage was crucial nevertheless, but to the lovers' frustration the right moment never seemed to come. In the aftermath of Hales's book on the succession, Elizabeth was in a vengeful mood and, while Katherine continued to endure the tedium and misery of her house arrest in Essex, life at court seemed to lurch from one crisis to the next.

In the autumn of 1564, Elizabeth raised Dudley to the title Earl of Leicester to make him a more suitable spouse for Mary Queen of Scots. Confronted, however, with the possibility of losing his company forever, she then hesitated, and while she dithered, the Queen of Scots announced her intention to marry her Catholic cousin, Henry, Lord Darnley. It was a disaster for Elizabeth's hopes and appalled the Council. A Darnley marriage posed a threat arguably even greater than if Mary Queen of Scots married a Hapsburg or a Valois. It would allow the whole of Catholic Europe to unite behind her claim. Having been brought up in England, Darnley could even raise an English army from the Catholic north where he was born. This was no time for Lady Mary Grey and Mr Keyes to announce their intentions to marry to the Queen, especially since Elizabeth had been irritated by a fresh request from the

Council that she look more favourably on Katherine's claim. But the couple were growing impatient with the length of their courtship and love makes a fool of even the wisest, so while political attention remained focused on the marital intentions of Mary Queen of Scots, they began to make a few plans of their own. The date the lovers picked for their secret marriage was 16th July 1565, the day of a big court wedding due to take place at Durham House on the Strand. The match was a grand one, between Henry Knollys, a grandson of Mary Boleyn, and Margaret Cave, the heir of a fabulously rich courtier, Sir Ambrose Cave.[1] Elizabeth was invited and Mary Grey and Keyes intended that, while the Queen and most of the court were at Durham House, they would stay at Whitehall with a few of their friends and enjoy a modest celebration of their own.

Things did not go as expected, however, when the day of the great Durham House wedding came. Mary Grey and the other court ladies were waiting for the Queen in Whitehall's Privy Gardens in order to attend on her as she left, when the Spanish ambassador, Don Diego Guzman de Silva, arrived. He was looking flustered and the gardens were soon abuzz with why this was. The ambassador said that he had been on the point of leaving his house for Whitehall, when the father of the bride, Ambrose Cave, appeared. He was immediately recognisable by the yellow garter he had worn on his arm since Elizabeth had dropped one while dancing. Cave asked the ambassador if he could come to the wedding later, rather than arriving with the Queen. He explained that he had invited the French ambassador to dine, expecting him to leave afterwards and so avoid any clashes over precedence. Each ambassador, as the representative of their King, would naturally demand to hold rank over their rival, so it was best not to have them both in the same room at the same time. The Frenchman was, however, now refusing to leave the party. De Silva replied to Cave angrily that he had no intention of giving way to a Frenchman. 'Well,' Cave huffed; 'If you do go I do not know how you will get rid of him unless you take him up in your arms and throw him out of the window.'[2]

It was possible that to avoid a diplomatic contretemps, the Queen would have to miss the party. But, as Mary Grey knew, Elizabeth was devoted to the mother of the groom, Lady Knollys, and would do everything she could to avoid that happening. As the Queen arrived in the garden Mary Grey saw her call the Spanish ambassador aside. She would be very sorry not to go to the party, Elizabeth explained. Lady Knollys was her first cousin, a daughter of her aunt, Mary Boleyn. De Silva would not be budged, so Elizabeth sent Cecil and Sir Nicholas Throckmorton ahead to persuade the French ambassador to leave the party. To Mary Grey's immense relief they soon succeeded and the Queen set off for Durham House, with de Silva and most of the leading ladies of the court. The great wedding at Durham House lasted until 1.30 in the morning, with a feast followed by a ball, a tourney and two masques. This left plenty of time for Mary Grey and Thomas Keyes to have their own wedding.

While the stragglers were still leaving for the big party, Mary had supper in her chamber at Whitehall with three of her cousins. One was the bossy Margaret Willoughby who, as a little girl, had been orphaned in the Norfolk rebellion of 1549 and had lived with the Grey sisters under their mother's wing in 1554. She was now married to another, more distant cousin, Sir Matthew Arundell.* The other two were daughters of Lady Stafford, whose brother had supported Mary's father's 1554 revolt in the Midlands, and was executed following his 'invasion' of Scarborough in 1557.³ After they had finished eating they chatted for about quarter of an hour. Mary Grey then sent for a servant employed by Lady Knollys's sister, Lady Howard of Effingham. She was a sweet country girl called Frances Goldwell, of whom Mary was fond. She intended her to be a witness to the wedding, a role that would have been much riskier for anyone of high rank. Goldwell was having supper with her friends when Mary's call arrived. It must have seemed very romantic and exciting to Goldwell as she walked quickly along the rush-covered passageways to the

---

* Not to be confused with the Earl of Arundel whose family name was Fitzalan.

room near the Council Chamber where she was to meet Mary. Knowing how much her mistress would have been angered by what she was about to do added to the thrill: one of her gentlewoman supper companions had recently been sacked by Lady Howard.

The room by the Council Chamber had no candles lit. But the summer light had not yet gone, and Goldwell spotted Mary, waiting, along with one of Keyes's men, Jones. He was to carry the message that they were ready for Keyes to collect them. Shortly after the messenger delivered his news, the huge figure of Keyes loomed into the little room. He escorted the women along the gallery by the Lord Chamberlain's chamber, down a winding stair to his private rooms over the Watergate. It was nine o'clock and about eleven friends and relations had gathered for the wedding, along with a short, silver-haired priest, wrapped in a black cloak. Mary acknowledged Keyes's brother, and one of his sons, a friend of his from Cambridge and a servant of the Bishop of Gloucester, Richard Cheyney.[4] On Mary's side there was Mrs Goldwell and, outside the door, Margaret Willoughby, Lady Arundell. Seeing no evil she could suffer no evil, Margaret hoped. The giant Sergeant Porter and the diminutive Maid of Honour took their vows by candlelight and he gave her a tiny gold wedding ring. In about quarter of an hour they were married. The friends then celebrated with wine and banqueting meats, and when the party broke up Mary Grey and Thomas Keyes went to bed.

Less than two weeks later, on 29th July, the other, more anticipated, royal wedding took place: Mary Queen of Scots married Darnley in her private chapel at Holyrood, Edinburgh. She assured Elizabeth that she and the King, her husband, would do nothing to enforce their dynastic claim, or to seek to overturn the laws, liberties or religion of England. In return they asked to have the English succession settled in their favour, by an act of Parliament. Elizabeth knew, however, that the Parliament she had prorogued would favour Katherine's claim. The last thing Elizabeth wanted at this stage was any trouble from the Greys, but on 21st August 1565, just as the Queen was absorbing the news from Scotland, gossip about Mary Grey's marriage leaked out. 'Here is an unhappy chance and monstrous,'

Cecil informed a friend. 'The Sergeant Porter, being the biggest gentleman of this court, has married secretly the Lady Mary Grey; the least of all the court . . . The offence is very great.'[5]

Elizabeth, incandescent, had ordered the couple be placed in separate prisons, in separate towns, with Mary in Windsor and Keyes in London. The imperious Lady Howard was meanwhile cross-examining her servant, Mrs Goldwell. The country girl lied through her teeth about what she remembered, claiming that she hadn't heard or understood what was going on. Fortunately Lady Howard had always thought her very stupid. Her only punishment was likely to be dismissal – and Mary Grey had many friends able to take care of her. It was she, and Mr Keyes, who were in deeper trouble. As soon as Elizabeth had the details of their courtship and marriage they were condemned to languish in confinement as Katherine and Hertford had been.

Mary's jailor was at least to be a kindly one. It was the High Sheriff of Buckinghamshire, Sir William Hawtrey. He had just completed the rebuilding of his comfortable house at Chequers and he had an emotional attachment to Mary's family. He had been a friend of Margaret Willoughby's explorer uncle, Hugh, who had died under tragic circumstances. Hugh Willoughby had left England on 10th May 1553 having been commissioned by a group of merchants to discover a northern sea route to the east. Mary remembered seeing the three ships under her uncle's command. The whole court (except King Edward, who was too ill) had come out from Greenwich Palace to wave and cheer as they sailed down the Thames. The adventure had ended, however, when the ships grounded off the Russian coast. Hugh Willoughby had survived for weeks before eventually freezing to death along with almost the entire crew, but one captain made it to Moscow, and the subsequent trade with Russia had helped make Hawtrey a very rich man.[6] Hawtrey was willing, therefore, to be as generous to Mary as he was able under the restrictions Elizabeth had imposed.

Like Katherine, Mary Grey was forbidden from seeing anyone and going anywhere. She could not go even into the garden more than was absolutely necessary for her health. Of her servants, she could keep only a groom and one waiting woman. Her basic expenses as prisoner were to be covered by the Queen, as Katherine's had been. That meant prison food enough 'for her sustenance and health without respect to her degree or place'.[7] Now it was Mary's turn to write to Cecil, as her sister had, asking for help in begging the Queen for a pardon. The first surviving letter is dated November 1565. It thanks Cecil for his endeavours thus far and begs him to continue. Another, written in December, expresses surprise that the Queen had not yet forgiven her. Could Cecil tell Her Majesty that if she got her favour back she would do nothing to lose it thereafter? 'I am so unhappy a creature,' Mary wrote, praying that God put it 'into her Majesty's heart to forgive and pardon me my great and heinous crime'.[8] Numerous others followed, each signed 'Mary Graye', as if she had never been married. She had heard that Cecil did not believe she was truly sorry for her offence – but she was, she promised. She would welcome death rather than the Queen's further displeasure. Elizabeth's anger showed no signs of abating, however.

Mary Queen of Scots was now pregnant, and her enemies in England were more desperate than ever to oppose her claim to Elizabeth's throne. A series of tracts concerning the succession were published. Like those written by the Protestant exiles during Queen Mary's time, many threatened to undermine the authority of the monarchy and Elizabeth's divine right to rule. They argued a monarch could be excluded on religious grounds; that England enjoyed a 'mixed monarchy' with sovereignty rooted not only in the crown but also in Parliament – all arguments the absolutist Elizabeth abhorred.[9] The Queen was a dynastic legitimist to her fingertips and the Grey sisters represented what she detested and feared: the encroaching power of Parliament. So the months passed, with Mary Grey confined in a 12-foot-square room at Chequers, known still as the 'prison room'. From its two windows, on the north-east corner of what is today the Prime Minister's country residence, she could admire the fine elms and the beauty of the gardens that stretched into wide skies and rolling countryside. The gardens had evocative names like 'Silver Spring' and 'Velvet Lawns', but only rarely could she venture into them. The faded remains of the inscriptions and the sketches carved on the walls of the prison room are testimony to the dreary misery she endured. They include a crude figure whose arms appear to be turning into wings. Thomas Keyes, however, suffered still more severely.

Keyes had held a position of trust on which the personal security of the monarch depended, and his betrayal was judged accordingly. Instead of a country house he was put in The Fleet, a notorious London prison built in 1197 on the eastern bank of the Fleet River in Farringdon. The warden was ordered to place him in solitary confinement, and his huge frame was crushed into one of its small, cramped cells, putting him in constant agony. Keyes offered to agree to an annulment of the marriage if he might only be sent into retirement in his home county of Kent. Mary Grey may have suggested he do so, given that, unlike Katherine, she was signing letters using her maiden name. But, unfortunately for the couple, the Bishop of London found no grounds to declare their marriage invalid. Too many witnesses were their undoing, just as too few had been Katherine and Hertford's. The bishop did feel sorry, however, for Keyes and asked 'that the wretched man might be permitted to leave the noisome and narrow prison room he had inhabited for twelve months and depart into the country for change of air'. When this was refused the bishop suggested that he might be allowed to walk in The Fleet garden, 'his bulk of body being such as I know it to be, his confinement in the Fleet puts him to great inconvenience'.[10] The Queen agreed, but the permission was revoked after only a few weeks, and his torment continued.

Chapter XXIII

The Clear Choice

Katherine and her three-year-old son Thomas were moved from Ingatestone in Essex in May 1566, when her jailor, Sir William Petre, grew ill. They did not have to travel far, only a few miles north-east, to Gosfield Hall, the seat of a very old knight called Sir John Wentworth. Watching the changing scenery on her brief ride was a reminder, for Katherine, of the freedom she had lost, and when she arrived at Gosfield there was also a fleeting reminder of home. Her new country house prison shared many similarities with Bradgate, with its courtyard and the wide windows that filled the house with light. The new west wing allowed plenty of room for Katherine's little household. But the Queen's instructions to Wentworth were to keep Katherine completely isolated.

Wentworth told the Privy Council that at seventy-six and seventy-one, he and his wife were too frail to act as warders, and that his house was insecure. It would be easy, he warned, for men to come to the windows of any chamber in the house and talk to Katherine, 'or deliver letters unto her, or if she were so disposed, she may either let them into her chamber, or go out to them at the loops of the windows they are so great and wide'. Fearful of the punishment that would be visited on his family if he failed in his duties, he said it would be better for him to 'come up to London and yield myself prisoner, than to take upon me the charge to keep the said lady in such straight order as is prescribed unto me'.[1] The old man's appeals fell on deaf ears.[2] Cecil may even have been pleased he could not be a very strict warder. And Wentworth began to relax as he found Katherine a quiet prisoner, save for her determination to maintain contact with her husband and elder son, which she could have managed through her servants without his knowledge.

Her letters to Hertford went to the London house of Sir John Mason's widow. Mason – the man who had suggested Hertford be taken before the Star Chamber for having sex with Katherine in the Tower – had died in April 1566 and a new jailor had not yet been found.[3] Hertford replied to Katherine's letters with gifts, showering her with gold necklaces and other trinkets. The four-year-old Lord Beauchamp remained, meanwhile, with Hertford's mother, the Duchess of Somerset, deprived of both his parents. He was a lively, affectionate child, very like Katherine in temperament, but his grandmother despaired of ever reuniting him with his parents. She had sent many letters to Cecil complaining 'how unmeet it is that this young couple should thus wax old in prison', but, as Cecil explained, he himself was 'somewhat in disgrace for the part he had already taken as their advocate with the Queen'.[4] Events, however, were about to place new pressures on Elizabeth to acknowledge the royal family that she had broken.

On 19th June 1566, Mary Queen of Scots gave birth to a son, James, at Edinburgh Castle. It should have been a triumphant moment for the Stuart Queen, and on a political level it was. But her twenty-one-year-old husband, Henry Darnley, had emerged already in all his venality: effete, vain, spoilt and vicious. The strain of playing second fiddle to his wife had evidently proved too much for him, and in his anger and frustration he had allied himself to her enemies at the Scottish court. They had played on his sense of impotence, using her trust in her Italian Secretary, David Riccio, to make him jealous. One night in March, three months earlier, while the Queen was having supper in her private rooms with Riccio and the Countess of Argyle, Darnley had appeared with a group of men, and demanded Riccio come with them. Mary had tried to prevent Riccio being taken away, but with a pistol pointed at her pregnant belly, Darnley prised Riccio's fingers from her skirt, and held her back while Riccio was thrust out of the room. Fifty-five stab wounds were found in Riccio's body, and Darnley's dagger was left sticking in it. But Mary had since reconciled with her husband, at least in public. He was, as she reminded him, the father of her son.

The news of James's birth was greeted amongst Katherine's supporters in England with dismay. But they knew Elizabeth was short of money and obliged to recall the prorogued Parliament of 1563 to raise financial subsidies. She had hoped that when this moment came, Mary Queen of Scots would be safely married to Leicester. But that hadn't happened and when her MPs reassembled it was probable they would seek to get what they had been cheated of in 1563: a settlement of the succession issue. Elizabeth did what she could to prevent the inevitable. She asked her most loyal peers, William Herbert, Earl of Pembroke, Parr of Northampton, Norfolk and Robert Dudley, Earl of Leicester, to use their powers of patronage to ensure that the MPs did not discuss the succession. She also ordered Cecil to prevent the grant of the subsidies from being linked to either the succession, or her marriage. But her nobles and Councillors all considered it vital that the succession was settled, one way or another.

Cecil recorded privately his assessment of what the Council should try and achieve and the difficulties they faced. To require the now thirty-three-year-old Queen to marry would be the most acceptable option open to her, he wrote. To require her to decide on the succession was, however, what most people wanted. It seemed best, therefore, to require her to marry and if she did not do so immediately, to insist she decide on the succession. Cecil was also prepared to argue that the three estates in Parliament – the Commons, Lords and bishops – had a duty to 'counsel' the Queen on whom she chose as her heir. The Spanish ambassador, de Silva, believed the most popular candidates amongst the Protestants remained Katherine and the Earl of Huntingdon. In fact Huntingdon's support had fallen away. This must have had something to do with the various succession tracts that had followed Hales's book. None had found any legal basis for Huntingdon's claim. But not all Huntingdon's supporters now backed Katherine.

Huntingdon's brother-in-law, Robert Dudley, Earl of Leicester, had shifted his allegiance to the Queen of Scots. Although a Catholic she had shown herself, thus far, capable of ruling a Protestant country and willing to accept subjects of different faiths. She had a son, she was no ideologue (in contrast to her bitter opponents) and Leicester was certain she could be brought into an alliance with Elizabeth. Mary Queen of Scots had some additional support in the Lords, but here, as in the Commons, Katherine's position was a strong one, especially amongst the bishops.

As soon as Parliament was assembled in October 1566, the capital became alive with activities aimed at urging MPs to decide on the succession. A whirlwind of pamphlets was published.[5] Ordinary people, as well as their leaders, wanted to secure a peaceable transfer of power if anything were to happen to Elizabeth. At Lincoln's Inn, the young lawyers held a debate which concluded that no one born outside England should inherit the throne, 'even if she were the nearest in birth and the ablest'.[6] In the Commons, meanwhile, Katherine's supporters were the most vociferous in favour of a succession debate. When the day of the debate came, some MPs attempted to leave the chamber rather than anger the Queen by addressing the issue, but they found the doors of the Commons were shut, and punches were thrown by Katherine's supporters, who were determined to prevent them leaving. Once the subsequent debate was finished the Commons did what Elizabeth had feared. They agreed to appoint a committee to draw up a petition on the succession, and persuaded the Lords to join them. 'These heretics neither fear God nor obey their betters,' the Spanish ambassador commented.[7] Elizabeth's hand was to be forced.

At Gosfield, Katherine wrote cheerfully to her husband's servant Anthony Penne, asking him to assure Mrs Penne that she would come and visit her as soon as she could.[8] Mary Grey, who had been rebuffed in her request to meet the Queen at Lord Windsor's during her summer progress, had particular reason, however, to hope the Queen would soon free them. That summer a sadistic new jailor at The Fleet had taken charge of Keyes and he was now forbidden from preparing his own food. The jailor had confiscated the slings Keyes had used to kill birds he saw from his window, and was giving him rotten meat to eat instead. 'If it were her Majesty's pleasure and your honour's ... to fetter me with iron girds, I would most willingly endure it,' Keyes had told Cecil; 'but to bear this warden's imprisonment without cause, is no small grief to my heart.'[9] On one occasion he discovered his food had been dropped, deliberately or accidentally, in the poison used to cure The Fleet's dogs of mange. Mary Grey could not be certain he could survive such treatment for long. Her husband was a big man, but no longer a young one.

On 22nd October a delegation arrived from the Lords to explain to Elizabeth what had been agreed with the Commons concerning the petition. But her retort, delivered from her throne under a canopy of state, was sharp. The Commons would not have dared act so during her father's day. It did not become subjects to compel their ruler. As for the Lords, 'do what you will' she told them, 'I shall do nothing but according to my pleasure. All the resolutions which you may make have no force without my consent and authority.' It was a reminder of the meaning of absolute royal power. Elizabeth shared her father's view that the King 'was under God, but not the law because the King makes the law'.[10] The succession issues were too important to be decided by 'a knot of hare-brains' Elizabeth informed them, disdainfully. She would take 'proper' counsel, and having taken such counsel she would then let them know her will.[11] Elizabeth would become infamous for her refusal to come to decisions; it was condemned later in her life as feminine irresolution. In reality it was a means of saying no, while avoiding confrontation. The Tudor Queen is an example of what the writer Sally Kempton meant when she wrote that women are 'natural guerrillas', scheming from behind enemy lines, 'avoiding open warfare, watching the options, playing the odds'.[12] Elizabeth was using the demands that she rule through good counsel to her own ends. Usually it worked, but not on this occasion.

Three days later Elizabeth learned that her peers and bishops had confirmed their intention to join the Commons in their petition. She turned on her nobles in her anger. Norfolk she accused of being a 'traitor or conspirator or other words of similar flavour'. When Pembroke tried to defend him, saying he was only doing his duty in offering his advice, Elizabeth replied witheringly that he talked like a 'swaggering soldier'. She then turned on Robert Dudley, the Earl of Leicester. If the world had been against her, she had thought she could rely on him. He swore that he would die at her feet, but she snapped back: 'What has that to do with the matter?'[13] The three men and Parr of Northampton were then banned from her presence. She hoped she had now frightened the Lords sufficiently for the succession petition to be dropped. But it wasn't. On 4th November 1566, the Commons and Lords completed their negotiations and resolved 'to petition the Queen by common consent to deal with the matter of the succession'.[14] At that Elizabeth summoned a deputation of thirty men from the Lords and Commons. The Speaker was barred. The deputation was to hear Elizabeth's views the following day, not to give their own.

First came the dressing down, with Commons and bishops singled out for particular abuse. Elizabeth hoped to divide the latter from her secular peers and recalled bitterly the period after her brother's death when the bishops had 'openly preached and set forth that my sister and I were bastards'. Then Elizabeth reminded them of her reasons against receiving a petition on the succession: how she had been used as the focus for plots against her sister, and how a nominated heir could also be used one day against her. She would name her heir, she promised, but in her own good time, 'for it is monstrous that the feet should direct the head'. Elizabeth swore also that she would marry: 'I will never break the word of a Prince spoken in public place, for my honour's sake. And therefore I say again, I will marry as soon as I can conveniently.'[15] It was a bravura performance. But news of Elizabeth's speech was delivered to the Commons on 6th November amidst stony silence. And on the 8th arguments for delivering the petition on the succession began again.[16]

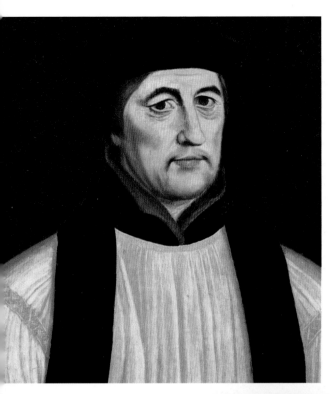

Stephen Gardiner, Bishop of Winchester, with 'hanging look, frowning brows…and great paws, like the devil's talons on his feet'. He linked Protestantism with treason, and called for Jane to be executed.

Mary I. She pardoned most of those involved in the usurping of her crown in 1553, but after the revolts of 1554 earned the obriquet 'Bloody Mary' for burning Protestants under her father's old heresy laws.

Lady Katherine Grey divorced Henry, Lord Herbert, at thirteen and at eighteen fell in love with another, in an affair that would prove her downfall.

This portrait of the hideous Lady Dacre and her son was, from the eighteenth century onwards, said to be of Frances, Duchess of Suffolk, and her second husband Adrian Stokes. It helped fuel Frances's false reputation as a female Henry VIII: lustful, domineering and cruel.

In this portrait of the young Queen Elizabeth, painted around 1560, she is still wearing the relatively simple clothing she adopted as the pious Protestant princess of the 1550s.

Mary Queen of Scots in her white weeds as the widow of Francis II. Elizabeth always preferred the claims of the foreign, Catholic Mary as her heir to those of the English, Protestant Katherine Grey.

Robert Dudley, Earl of Leicester, the elder brother of Jane Grey's husband, Guildford, and the love of Queen Elizabeth's life.

Katherine Grey as Countess of Hertford with her son Edward,
Lord Beauchamp, grandson of the Protector Somerset and
future heir to the throne under the will of Henry VIII.

Sir William Cecil, later Lord Burghley, consistently promoted Katherine Grey and her sons as Elizabeth's heirs, and pursued the rival Mary Queen of Scots to her death.

Lady Mary Grey as Mrs Keyes, showing off her wedding ring. This portrait hangs at Chequers, where she was imprisoned for two years, and is dated 1571, the year she was widowed.

Chequers, where Mary Grey was kept under house arrest from 1565 to 1567.

Effigies at Salisbury Cathedral of Lady Katherine Grey and her husband Edward Seymour, Earl of Hertford (*foreground*). The inscription celebrates the lovers re-united at last.

Following page London *c.*1572, showing Suffolk Place (1), Durham House (2), and Somerset House (3), west towards Whitehall and the Tower (4) to the east of London Bridge.

LONDINVM FERACISSIMI ANGLIAE REGNI METROPOLIS

Elizabeth responded to the assault on her royal will by issuing a decree forbidding any further discussion of the succession. According to the Spanish ambassador de Silva, Elizabeth was convinced this would put the matter to rest. He was not so sure, however, that 'it will be sufficient to bridle the insolence of these heretics'.[17] This sense of foreboding was fully justified. Debates began in Parliament on the rights of free speech, and new pamphlets were printed condemning the Queen's actions. Finally Elizabeth received a threat. On 11th November a paper was thrown down in the Presence Chamber: it declared that if she continued to forbid Parliament from debating the succession, 'she would see some things she would not like'.[18] Cecil, far from supporting Elizabeth during this crisis, was, meanwhile, working on the drafts of Parliament's petition. But with the world seemingly against her, Elizabeth now chose a tactical retreat. She withdrew her command that Parliament cease to discuss the succession and instead, politely requested they do so. She then remitted a third of the proposed financial subsidy. The reduction in the tax burden prompted a 'most hearty prayer and thanks' from the Commons and, thus bought off, the MPs did not bring up the issue of the succession again in this Parliament.

Elizabeth had beaten Cecil convincingly. He had only one more card to play. Elizabeth had specifically requested that he ensure that the subsidies were not linked in any way to the matter of the succession. But the preamble he wrote to the financial subsidy bill did exactly that. He linked the money to the Queen's promises to declare on the succession soon, and noted it was the duty of Parliament to press the Queen to do so.[19] Elizabeth, however, simply obliged him to write another. The Queen dissolved Parliament on 2nd January 1567, with a clear message for her MPs. The succession was a matter for 'a zealous Prince's consideration', not for 'lip-laboured orations out of ... subjects' mouths': she was Queen, and was not giving up such powers to them. Privately Elizabeth now had no intention of ever naming her heir. But she did remain determined that Mary Queen of Scots should emerge as the proper choice after her death. To achieve this, Elizabeth hoped she had simply to ensure the continued ruin of the Grey sisters and their immediate heirs. But in the face of all Elizabeth's efforts on her behalf, Mary Queen of Scots was about to self-destruct.

Hertford was not supposed to have visitors. The greedy, unpopular merchant, Sir Richard Spencer, who was his latest jailor, was expected to ensure that he did not. But the man who arrived at the door on a mid-February day in 1567 was the eldest brother of Robert Dudley, Earl of Leicester. This was not a figure Spencer's servants could easily turn away. Hertford was aware that the Dudleys backed the Stuart cause and not that of his wife. Something dramatic must have occurred. It had. News had reached England that Darnley had been murdered and that his wife, Mary Queen of Scots, was suspected of having ordered his assassination. Elsewhere Cecil's wife was informing a weeping Countess of Lennox of her son's brutal death.

According to the reports filtering down to London, the city of Edinburgh had been shaken by a violent explosion at two in the morning of 10th February. People ran towards the apparent origin of the blast at Kirk o' Field and found the Old Provost Lodging, where Darnley had been sleeping, a heap of rubble. Nearby, in the orchard, was his body, along with that of his valet. It was naked save for his nightgown and unmarked, although it seemed someone had carefully laid it out. The Dudleys, convinced the Queen of Scots was involved, had decided immediately to switch camp. The Spanish ambassador de Silva reported Leicester had sent his brother 'to the Earl of Hertford, Katherine's husband, to offer him his services in the matter of succession', while he 'went to see the Duchess of Somerset, the Earl's mother, with the same object'.[20] A shocked Elizabeth sent a personal message to the Queen of Scots urging her to seek justice for her murdered husband as soon as possible and to end the rumours of her involvement. But her dismay was matched in other quarters by delight. Cecil at last had an ideal opportunity to dispose of Mary Queen of Scots' candidature altogether.

By the end of April there were reports, emanating from amongst Katherine's supporters, directly accusing Mary Stuart of Darnley's murder. It was suggested she was acting in revenge for the murder of her Secretary, David Riccio. The Queen of Scots helped the slanderers' cause immeasurably, however, when in May 1567 she married the principal suspect in her husband's murder, the Earl of Bothwell. She may have believed he was the only man who could protect her from being the next victim of assassination, but her actions triggered a rebellion led by his erstwhile allies and fellow murderers amongst the other Protestant lords. He swiftly became a fugitive and Mary Stuart was imprisoned in a castle on a tiny island in Loch Leven. Her son, James, was crowned King of Scots in her place on 24th July. The fact the misogynist John Knox gave the sermon at the coronation was a reminder of Elizabeth's long-standing concern that she would be replaced by a male heir, if it ever became sufficiently easy to achieve. As Elizabeth had told Mary Stuart's messenger in 1561, a Prince could not even trust the children who were to succeed them.

Elizabeth feared her position was a dangerous one also. It was a relief to know that she had succeeded in having Katherine's sons declared bastards, but the Spanish ambassador had warned her that Katherine's camp were 'strong and might cause trouble'.[21] What Elizabeth wanted was for Mary Queen of Scots to have her throne back, as soon as possible. She called for Cecil and lectured him in 'a great offensive speech' for failing to do anything to save Mary Stuart, demanding that an English army restore her cousin at once.[22] Thinking on his feet, Cecil warned Elizabeth that a war might trigger the assassination of the deposed Queen. Elizabeth then backed down, but she admitted to de Silva that she remained afraid for her own safety. She ordered that the keys to all the doors leading to her chambers be hidden away, save for one. The terms of Hertford's imprisonment were also made stricter. 'They are possibly afraid of some movement in his interest as I am assured that certain negotiations are afoot respecting the succession to the crown,' de Silva reported.[23]

Elizabeth knew she had to contain any potential threat posed by the candidature to the throne of the Grey sisters, but she recognised that they were not personally dangerous. While poor Keyes remained in The Fleet, Mary Grey was moved in August from Chequers in

Buckinghamshire to the care of her step-grandmother, Katherine Suffolk. Her elder sister, meanwhile, was left to languish, almost forgotten, in Essex. When Katherine's ancient jailor, Sir John Wentworth, died in late September 1567, his widow and the executor of his will, a Mr Roke Green, were left with no orders about what they should do with her. For all the political drama, Katherine had been reduced to little more than a name, barely a person at all. The Wentworth household had grown very fond of Katherine and her young son. But at seventy-one, Lady Wentworth was shattered by her husband's death, and Mr Roke Green warned Cecil that she would not live long. He offered to take Katherine and Thomas into his own home, but warned Cecil it was 'nothing meet in many respects for such a personage'. He was a poor widower. Without a wife there was no one to run his house; he could afford almost no furniture and had several children of his own. But he promised he would do his best for Katherine if called on to do so:

> Sir, I do not deal thus plainly and truly with you for that I am loath to take charge of her ladyship (if I were meet for the same) for any misliking I have of her or hers, for I must for truths sake confess, as one that has had good experience of her Ladyship's behaviour here, that it has been very honourable and quiet, and her ladyship's servants very orderly.[24]

It was a touching letter from a decent, ordinary man, caught up in cruel and extraordinary events. But once Elizabeth understood the situation she instructed that Katherine and her child be placed under more careful guard. She was to be moved to a location further from the court, in Suffolk, at Cockfield Hall, the house of Sir Owen Hopton, a future Lieutenant of the Tower.[25] The Queen's latest letter of instruction reiterated that Katherine was to be kept totally isolated. She was not to be allowed to join her hosts for dinner if they had guests, or have any of her own. Hopton complained bitterly about the responsibility he had been given, but like the Wentworths before him, he would discover it was difficult not to like Katherine.

His prisoners rested overnight at Ipswich, the same town in which Katherine had stayed in 1561 when she had been forced to confess that she was married and pregnant.[26] The next day they arrived at the brick gatehouse of Cockfield, their fifth prison in seven years.

A wooden sixteenth-century travel chest, covered with leather and lined with linen, said to be Katherine's, remains at Cockfield. The sides are decorated with the biblical story of the prodigal son, who was welcomed home by his forgiving father. Katherine's chamber at Cockfield was described later, in the following century, as 'a very fair room'.[27] We even have some idea what was in it. The then owner of the house, Sir Robert Brooke, drew up a list of the furnishings. They included: 'the great barred chest', a 'high bedstead' and a 'pallet bedstead' for a servant.[28]

Sir Owen was shocked to see how pale and thin Katherine was. The slender shoulders of the woman at the centre of the great struggle for power between Queen and Parliament were bowed. She appeared lonely and deeply depressed. Her hopes of seeing her husband, or her now six-year-old elder son, had been dashed repeatedly and it was evident that Elizabeth had no intention of freeing her now. Katherine's position as Elizabeth's heir seemed fixed, but with this political success had come personal disaster. The prodigal daughter would never be welcomed home by the mother of the kingdom under such circumstances. Never again, Katherine believed, would she lie with her 'Ned' or play with their 'sweet little boys'.

Her stay at Cockfield would not be a long one, however. And the threat she posed to Elizabeth was about to conclude for good.

Chapter XXIV

While I Lived, Yours

S ir Owen Hopton sent to London for the Queen's physician, Dr Symondes, as soon as he realised Katherine was ill. The doctor came twice and Katherine seemed to rally, briefly. But on 11th January 1568, Sir Owen wrote to Cecil 'beseeching' for the doctor to return. Her condition had deteriorated since Dr Symondes's last visit. She had lain in bed for three days, eating little. 'And the worst is,' Hopton wrote, that she had given up hope of recovery. If Dr Symondes could only come again, Hopton hoped, 'he then shall show his cunning, and God shall do the cure'.[1]

Dr Symondes returned, as Hopton had requested. But on the night of 26th January Katherine told those around her what she had long suspected – and perhaps wanted. She was dying. Through the long dark hours that followed she said the Psalms, or had them read to her, repeating the words when she could. On five or six occasions she said what she believed was to be her last prayer before dying. Hopton, his household and her servants, were all horrified that someone of only twenty-seven could be so fatalistic. Lady Hopton and the women at Katherine's bedside tried to encourage her: 'Madam, be of good comfort . . .'; 'With God's help you shall live and do well many years.' Katherine, however, merely replied: 'No, no. No life in this world; but in the world to come I hope to live ever. For here is nothing but care and misery, and there is life everlasting.'[2] Her words echoed those of her sister Jane in her last letter to their father, just as some of her other prayers and comments would recall Jane's speech on the scaffold. 'Learn to die . . .' Jane had told her, and she remembered her sister now, as she awaited an end to her suffering.[3]

In the early hours Katherine felt herself become faint and cried out: 'Lord be merciful to me.' The women immediately started to rub and stroke her in an effort to keep her alive, and as Katherine prayed Lady Hopton again said: 'Good madam, be of good comfort, for with God's favour you shall live and escape this.' 'No, no, my Lady Hopton,' Katherine insisted. 'My time is come and it is not God's will that I shall live any longer. And his will be done and not mine.'

At about six or seven Katherine called for Sir Owen Hopton. 'Good madam, how [are] you?' he asked as he arrived. 'Even now going towards God, Sir Owen, as fast as I can,' she replied; 'and I pray you and all the rest that be about me to bear witness that I die a true Christian and that I believe to be saved by the death of Christ.' She had a favour to ask, she said, concerning her husband and children. There were messages she needed delivered, the first of which was to the Queen. 'I beseech you to promise me that you, yourself, with your own mouth will make my humble request unto the Queen's Majesty.' It was a dying plea to be forgiven for marrying without the Queen's consent. Katherine remembered how her mother had persuaded Queen Mary to forgive her father his treason, in his last hours, and how this had saved the family from ruin: if Elizabeth could only do the same for her family?[4] Katherine's message made clear how important this was to her. She begged Elizabeth to 'be good unto my children and not to impute my fault unto them'. They had few friends now and would have fewer when she was dead, she reflected, unless the Queen was a 'good and gracious lady unto them'. Finally she pleaded for the Queen to 'be good unto my Lord, for I know this my death will be heavy new[s] unto him'. Katherine hoped that he would now be freed, 'to glad his sorrowful heart withal'.[5]

Katherine's second request to Sir Owen Hopton was that he would deliver a few tokens to her husband. Calling for her lady-in-waiting she asked: 'Give me the box wherein my wedding ring is.' Katherine then opened it and took out the ring with the pointed diamond that Hertford had given her when they were betrothed in his sister's chamber at Whitehall. 'Here, Sir Owen. Deliver this to my husband. This is the ring that I received of him when I gave myself unto him and gave him my faith.' Hopton was startled. 'What say you madam,' he asked Katherine. 'Was this your wedding ring?' The existence of such a ring suggested that she and Hertford had, indeed, married, as they had always said. 'No, Sir Owen, this was the ring of my assurance [betrothal] unto my Lord. And here is my wedding ring,' she replied.

She then took the gold ring with its five engraved links and gave it to the stunned knight. 'I pray you deliver this also unto my Lord and pray him, even as I have been unto him ... a true and faithful wife, that he will be a loving and natural father unto my children.' She took out a third ring, mounted with a death's head. Such rings, known as a *memento mori,* were intended as a reminder to the wearer of their mortality. 'This shall be the last token unto my Lord that I shall ever send him. It is the picture of myself,' she said. The ring was engraved for her husband: 'While I Lived, Yours'.

As Katherine handed over the last ring she noticed that her finger-nails had turned purple. 'Look you, here he comes,' she said, 'Welcome Death!' She began to beat her breast with her fist and prayed: 'O Lord, for thy many mercies, blot out of thy book all my sins.' Sir Owen ordered her maid to dash to the church to ask for the bells to be tolled so that the villagers might pray for the dying princess. 'Yea good Sir Owen, let it be so,' Katherine told him grate-fully. But there was no time left for further prayers. 'Lord Jesus receive my spirit,' Katherine said abruptly, and closed her eyes with her own hands.[6] She died at nine o'clock that Tuesday morning.

There are a thousand doors to let out life and Katherine could have taken any one, but there is a suggestion that she had starved herself to death. Katherine's bewildered son, Thomas Seymour, left Cockfield Hall to join his brother in the care of her mother in law, the Duchess of Somerset, while someone remained behind to write down a description of his mother's last hours, and her pious Protestant end. Hopton could have delivered it to Hertford with the rings Katherine had asked him to take to her husband. He may also have visited Mary Grey. He and his wife would become close to the last of the Grey sisters following Katherine's death.[7]

One of Hertford's favourite poets, Thomas Churchyard, used the description of Katherine's death as the basis for a long poem published a few years later. But the poet altered the names of the star-crossed lovers to avoid royal anger. Despite Katherine's last requests, Elizabeth never truly forgave her for marrying Hertford and having children. The Queen ordered Sir Owen Hopton to 'take care of the interment and burial of our cousin the Lady Katherine, lately deceased, daughter of our entirely beloved cousin, the Lady Frances, Duchess of Suffolk'. But Katherine remained not 'beloved'. While Elizabeth put on a public show of grief, as was expected at the death of a relative, the Spanish ambassador reported that it was evident that she did not feel it. 'She was afraid of her,' he added, by way of explanation.[8]

Katherine was to be buried in the modest little local church at Yoxford, rather than at Westminster Abbey as her mother and royal relations had been. But protocol could not be ignored, and the funeral was to be carried out with the formality due to a Tudor princess. Katherine's body was carefully seared and embalmed by the surgeon, and watched over by her servants until 21st February, the day of her burial. Seventy-seven official mourners were sent from court, along with a herald, two pursuivants and four servants, all in specially made liveries. A hearse had been built in the church and was covered in precious cloth and a tomb prepared in the Cockfield chapel.

The turn-out for the funeral was large with 'a great number of comers to see the solemnity of that burial'.[9] Everywhere were representations of Katherine's arms: on six dozen finely drawn 'pencils'; a banner; four thin bannerolls; six great escutcheons painted on paste paper; two dozen more on the coarse linen known as buckram; a dozen small coats of arms for a valance; and two dozen more in paper framed in metal 'for garnishing of the house and the church', along with six dozen more in colours. These were visual symbols of who she was and what she had represented as Elizabeth's Protestant, English heir. But behind the staring crowds, and the procession of official mourners in their black cloth, was the real grief of her family. A local legend persists that even Katherine's little dog mourned her: so much so that he refused any meat and 'lay and died upon her grave'.[10]

For many decades after the funeral the evidence of the heralds' work remained in the chancel of the church at Yoxford. Even in 1594 pennants still hung displaying 'for the Lady Katherine a target [a small round shield] of England, and four standards of arms, 2 France and 2 England quarterly, a border . . . argent and azure'.[11] The colours had faded by then, although memories of her had not.

Chapter XXV

The Last Sister

M ary Grey was with her step-grandmother, Katherine Suffolk, when her sister died. She had arrived at her house in the Minories under the shadow of the Tower almost six months before, on 7th August 1567. She was accompanied by her previous jailor, Sir William Hawtrey. Mary knew the house well. It was part of an old abbey given by Edward VI to her father in January 1553, the year disaster overtook them all. Katherine Suffolk was about to set out for Greenwich Palace[1] and was surprised to see her granddaughter. Although she had received the Queen's orders concerning Mary's care she had not expected Hawtrey to bring her quite so promptly. Greeting Mary, she ordered her baggage to be unloaded: they would travel to Greenwich together the next day, she announced. In the meantime where was Mary's baggage, the duchess asked? Hawtrey explained that the princess had fallen on very hard times. Her possessions, he warned, were so few and worn he had furnished her rooms at Chequers at his own expense.

Katherine Suffolk was certain that Hawtrey was exaggerating. Mary Grey had been raised in the greatest luxury. She had to have a few good things, and the duchess asked Hawtrey to send whatever she possessed 'for the dressing up of her chamber'. Mary's belongings arrived at Greenwich in short order, but when they were opened her step-grandmother saw that Hawtrey had spoken the truth. Katherine

273

Suffolk wrote to Cecil, who was one of her oldest and closest friends, describing her shock as she unpacked the trunks: 'Would God you had seen what stuff it is! . . . She has nothing but an old livery feather bed, all torn and full of patches, without either bolster or counterpane, but two old pillows, the one longer than the other, an old quilt of silk so torn as the cotton of it comes out.' There was a canopy of a fine silk called sarsonet, in red, but it was 'scant good enough to hang over some secret stool'.* Otherwise there was just 'two little pieces of old, old hangings, both of them not seven yards broad'.[2] This posed a problem. The duchess herself had lost many of her own things during her years in exile under Queen Mary. 'The truth is,' she admitted to Cecil; 'I am so unprovided of stuff here myself, as at the Minories I borrow off my [friends].'

Katherine Suffolk hoped that Cecil could arrange for the Queen to lend Mary a few necessities. They needed enough to furnish a chamber, which Mary could share with her maid. Together they would then 'play the good housewives' and use Mary's old livery bed for her manservant. In addition she needed 'some old silver pots to fetch her drink in, and two little cups . . . one for beer another for wine'. Although she feared a bowl to wash in and a jug for the water might be too much to ask, 'all these things she lacks and were meet she had'. The duchess assured Cecil that anything the Queen lent to them would be returned in as good an order. As for Mary, 'I am sure she is now glad to be with me,' but she seemed sad even then, before her sister's death, and wasn't eating properly, 'not so much as a chicken's leg' in two days. The duchess admitted she even feared for Mary's health.[3] It was hoped, however, that surrounded by her loving step-family, Mary would rediscover her old spirit, and she needed that strength when the news reached her about Katherine.

Mary Grey was close to her step-relations, Katherine Suffolk's children, Peregrine and Susan Bertie. They still enjoyed much of the carefree innocence Mary had known at Bradgate with her sisters. But

---

* i.e. lavatory.

with Katherine's death Mary Grey's place in line of succession had become more significant. The Seymour boys, Katherine's sons, had been declared illegitimate, which left Mary Grey Elizabeth's heir under English law. Elizabeth therefore felt she had to take her claim seriously, even when it became plain that it was to be Mary Queen of Scots' rights of succession that would dominate the political scene in the years ahead. In May 1568, four months after Katherine Grey's death, Mary Queen of Scots escaped her island prison in Scotland and arrived in England in a fishing boat. Cecil persuaded Elizabeth to keep her Stuart cousin in prison, but had less success in encouraging her to release Mary Grey. She was not even allowed to remain at the house of Katherine Suffolk. Instead, in June 1569, she was obliged to move to yet another prison, this time to the London home of the rich merchant and former Lord Mayor, Sir Thomas Gresham. He was able to bear those costs the Queen was reluctant to take on.[4]

Gresham House, in Bishopsgate, was built on a large site between Crosby Palace and Winchester House. It had a substantial garden that Mary could walk in under supervision, as well as a chapel in which to pray for her freedom. But as Mary Grey soon discovered, the Gresham home was not a happy one. Sir Thomas had been a strikingly handsome young man, with a trim beard and penetrating dark eyes. But now, in late middle age, he was half blind and in constant physical pain from a badly set broken leg. His only son had died in 1564 and his marriage had turned sour. His wife, Anne, bitterly resented the charitable works he had taken on since their son's death and Mary Grey's presence in the house was a new source of conflict with her husband. She insisted that it was Mary's presence that prevented her from visiting her ninety-year-old mother in Norfolk, and she referred to their prisoner as the 'heart and sorrow of her life'. No opportunity was lost to nag her husband about their unwelcome charge and Gresham wrote regularly to Cecil begging for Mary's removal.

Mary spent most of the time locked in a room with her books. She had a Book of Common Prayer, a book of Psalms and at least three Bibles: the Geneva version, the officially approved Bishops' Bible, and one in French, such as that her brother-in-law Hertford had inscribed with the birth dates of his sons in the Tower. Several of her other books were also either in French or Italian: they included a grammar book in Italian – very probably the same one that Michel Angelo Florio had dedicated to Jane Grey in 1553, another in French by one of her father's old teachers, and three French translations of works by the Greek rhetorician Isocrates.[5] He was valued in the sixteenth century in particular for his practical advice on how a person should conduct themselves, 'in all times and tempests' – useful reading in the circumstances in which Mary found herself. Another favourite classical work was her English translation of the orations of Demosthenes. 'Nothing is easier than self-deceit,' he wrote; 'for what each man wishes, that he also believes to be true.' Mary Grey wished to be free. Was she foolish enough to believe it would ever happen?

Mary's widowed brother-in-law, Hertford, had been released from prison and was allowed to live at the modest Seymour seat of Wulfhall in Wiltshire. It was the original house the family had owned when they were mere gentry, before Hertford's aunt, the Queen Jane Seymour, had married Henry VIII. It was only a modest life, in exile from the court, but at least he was able to walk in his grounds when he wished and write to his children freely, as they did to him. The boys remained with his mother, the Duchess of Somerset, at Hanworth. Lord Beauchamp, aged eight, was already writing letters in Latin describing his daily studies, while Thomas, at six, was proficient in French. Mary Grey learned about their progress from time to time, along with news of political developments from which she could try to gauge how her circumstances might also change. Elizabeth's other royal captive, the Queen of Scots, was now in the care of the Earl of Shrewsbury and his wife. This was a curious twist of fate. Lady Shrewsbury had once been that favourite lady-in-waiting, at Bradgate, Bess of Hardwick.

Bess was now on her fourth marriage, but Mary Grey remembered the wedding at Bradgate at which she had married her second husband, Sir William Cavendish, by candlelight at two o'clock on an August morning. It was the same summer that Mary's sister Jane had left to be ward to Hertford's uncle, Thomas Sudeley. Mary's parents and sisters had subsequently played godparents to four Cavendish children.[6] Bess still treasured a portrait of Jane, and letters from Katherine. Strange that Bess, who had so admired and loved Mary Grey's mother and the family, should now act as jailor to the rival claimant. The Privy Council was divided on what to do next with the Queen of Scots. Cecil wanted Katherine's eldest son, Lord Beauchamp, named Elizabeth's successor, despite his 'illegitimacy'. But the two boys were still only young and might not survive into adulthood. Pembroke, Arundel and Leicester were therefore of the view that they should tie the Queen of Scots to the Protestant cause by marrying her to Norfolk, and name her as heir. Anxious to show her doctrinal flexibility, the Queen of Scots was already using the Protestant Book of Common Prayer for spiritual contemplation. But Elizabeth, no longer threatened by Katherine's claim, had no intention of turning her Stuart cousin into a more powerful rival and in this Cecil supported her to the hilt.

Elizabeth's opposition to the marriage with Norfolk quickly led to the collapse of the court campaign behind it. But it was also to lead to terrible bloodshed. When Norfolk's allies in the north, the powerful Catholic Earls of Westmoreland and Northumberland, were summoned to see the Queen, they were convinced there was a plan to place them in the Tower and execute them.[7] Their wives were not members of the Queen's Privy Chamber and, based far from the royal palaces, they had no means of knowing her mind. What they had come to believe, however, was that her Secretary of State made her decisions, and they knew very well how much Cecil hated Catholics. While, therefore, Mary Grey remained quietly in her room at Bishopsgate in the winter of 1569, the north saw a rebellion raised by the earls 'for the reformation of religion and preservation of the person of the Queen of Scots'. Their men marched under the banner of 'The Five Wounds of Christ', used by the Catholic Pilgrims of Grace in 1536. At Wulfhall, Hertford wrote to a friend, enclosing a book written by his old schoolmaster, Thomas Norton. It claimed that there was a long history of Catholics overthrowing their monarchs. Hertford recommended Norton's thesis, saying: 'I know you will like it, but the oftener you read it the better.'[8]

In November the rebels took Durham, where the Earl of Northumberland kicked the Protestant communion table out of the city's medieval cathedral rather than touch it with his hands. Once again the ancient rites of the Mass were said and Latin echoed under the great vaulting. But as the earls faced the risks of invading the south they lost their nerve. Within only six weeks the rebellion had fizzled out. If the rebels hoped for more mercy from a woman, in Elizabeth, than the Pilgrims of Grace had received at the hands of her father, Henry VIII, they were to be disappointed. Elizabeth's revenge, guided by Cecil, was to be on a similar scale. She ordered that at least one man should be hung in every village involved in the revolt. The orders were muted by those asked to carry them out, but the bloodletting was sufficiently memorable that there would be no more such rebellions against the Queen in England. Elizabeth had been badly frightened, but to Cecil's frustration she refused to blame Mary Queen of Scots for the Northern Rebellion. Mary Stuart thus remained imprisoned but alive, and Cecil wanted her dead. It was perhaps as a sop to Cecil and his allies that Hertford was now accepted back at court. There was good news also for Mary Grey. Her long-suffering husband, Thomas Keyes, had been released from The Fleet and given a post at Sandgate Castle, in his home county of Kent.

Mary could imagine her husband together with his children, enjoying the salty taste of the sea air, and Keyes certainly thought often of Mary. In May he even summoned up the courage to ask Archbishop Parker to be 'a means to the Queen for mercy, and that, according to the laws of God, he may be permitted to live with his wife'.[9] But the Queen was still not of a mind to be merciful to her last Grey cousin. Another summer passed, and another winter came to Gresham House in London with no hint of any forthcoming pardon from the Queen. As the new year of 1571 dawned Sir Thomas determined to ask the Queen directly that Mary Grey be removed from his home, even if she was not to be freed. Elizabeth had accepted an invitation to dine with him later that month, when she was due to visit the commerce centre he had created, known as the Exchange.

Built three year earlier, the Exchange was a spectacular square building of brick and stone, two floors high, adorned at each corner with a grasshopper – the Gresham family crest. Inside were covered walkways, supported with marble pillars. Its shops, however, remained largely empty. Perhaps the idea of a shopping centre was simply too novel for conservative Londoners; perhaps the grasshoppers put them off. Either way, a royal visit could change all that. In anticipation of the Queen's visit Sir Thomas went twice to the Exchange and asked the few shopkeepers to fill the stores with as many goods as they were able, and to decorate the stalls with little wax lights. In return he promised he would charge no rent that year. When the date of the Queen's visit came, 23rd January, the scene was impressive.

The day began with the Queen, attended by the nobility, riding on a litter in procession from Somerset House on the Strand, into the City at Temple Bar, through Fleet Street, along Cheapside, by the north side of the Exchange and, finally, to Sir Thomas Gresham's house in Bishopsgate. The socially ambitious Lady Gresham was beside herself with excitement and, with Lady Mary Grey safely locked away, a banquet was held for the Queen and a very dull play performed. Mary's servants, who were free to come and go, were able to tell her all the details. The principal character in the play, who bore a close resemblance to Sir Thomas, spouted a fountain of flattery for the Queen, and since Elizabeth enjoyed nothing more than compliments it was a great success. After dinner Elizabeth duly visited the Exchange. Elizabeth explored every inch of the arcades, admiring 'the finest wares in the City'. According to a poetic account written later in the century, Sir Thomas purchased a huge pearl at one store, crushed it to powder and drank it in a toast to the Queen. The day ended with Elizabeth calling for a herald and, to the blasts of a trumpeter, Sir Thomas Gresham's shopping centre was dubbed the Royal Exchange.

As Sir Thomas had hoped the Royal Exchange became an overnight success. The empty stores were soon filled with milliners and haberdashers, armourers and apothecaries, booksellers, gold-smiths and glass-sellers. Rents doubled, then tripled and quadrupled. But there also seemed to be good news concerning Sir Thomas's request that Mary Grey be placed elsewhere. In July 1571 he thanked Cecil (Baron Burghley since February) fulsomely for 'the removal of the Lady Mary'. Unfortunately he wrote too soon. Come August she was still with him and he was still pleading with 'the Lord of Bowrley' (as he pronounced it) to remember his suit for the removal of the Lady Mary.[10] Elizabeth had changed her mind. A possible reason may have been the exposure of the first of the so-called 'Catholic plots' that Burghley fomented in order to expose and destroy enemies. As early as April 1571, the Warden of the Cinque Ports and Constable of Dover Castle, Lord Cobham,[11] had secretly opened letters from a Florentine banker and double agent called Roberto di Ridolfi, before they passed out of the country. The letters described a plan to capture Elizabeth during her summer progress and, with the help of an invading army of 6,000 Spaniards, place Mary Queen of Scots on the throne. Cobham later claimed his brother, Thomas Brooke, had begged him to keep the letters secret from the Privy Council, 'for he said they would otherwise be the undoing of the Duke of Norfolk and himself'. Cobham did keep them quiet, but the evidence suggests that he did so with the approval of Burghley who wanted the corre-spondence to continue in order to gather evidence that would incriminate Norfolk and the Queen of Scots as well. Burghley's trap was sprung on 5th September with the public 'discovery' of the letters and Norfolk was put in the Tower on suspicion of treason. Mary Grey had known the duke since childhood. He had married two of her first cousins. John Foxe had produced his first English edition of the *Book of Martyrs* while living in Norfolk's house. But while the drama of Norfolk's coming trial was being played out on the public stage her thoughts were elsewhere.

Broken by ill health the effects of his long confinement in The Fleet – and despairing of ever seeing his wife again, Thomas Keyes had died. Lord Cobham heard the news on 5th September, the same day as Norfolk's arrest, and immediately wrote to Lord Burghley to ask if his brother could have Keyes's old post.[12] Mary, however, still knew nothing. Three days later her physician, Dr Smith, arrived at Gresham House and told Sir Thomas of Keyes's death. He had been sent so he could be on hand if Mary collapsed when she learned of her husband's death. As they had feared she took the news 'grievously'.[13] Mary begged Gresham to write to Burghley on her behalf, asking for the Queen's permission to raise her husband's orphaned children. She also wished to wear mourning, and Gresham asked Burghley if this might be permitted. He was not certain what the official status of her marriage was.

Shortly afterwards, Mary was moved out of London to take the air at one of Sir Thomas Gresham's country properties, Osterley in Middlesex. It was a beautiful house, 'a fair and stately building of brick', set in a lovely park. There were calm ponds where she could watch swans, kingfishers and a graceful heron that the family were especially proud of.[14] But it took a month before Mary Grey was well enough to write personally to Burghley. She asked once again for her freedom and for the Queen to pardon her. But there was a bitter and even defiant note in Mary's latest request that she be restored to royal favour: 'God having now removed the occasion of her Majesty's justly conceived displeasure towards her.'[15] For the first time she signed herself 'Mary Keyes'. It is notable that a portrait of Mary brandishing her wedding ring is dated 1571. Her anger made her an even more problematic prisoner and over the following months Sir Thomas's campaign to have Mary removed from his property became almost unhinged. He wrote to Burghley twice in one day in November 1571, and in January he begged for Mary's removal specifically for the 'quietness of his poor wife'.[16] It seems Mary quarrelled frequently with Lady Gresham. By March Sir Thomas was talking about 'my wife's suit for the removing of my Lady Mary Grey', and the 'bondage and heart sorrow she has had for these three years'.[17] But it wasn't until May 1572 that Elizabeth finally agreed to release Mary Grey.

Following the discovery of the Ridolfi plot the Queen was under tremendous pressure to execute the Queen of Scots and Norfolk for their supposed roles in it. Here, at least, was an act of mercy she could afford to make, and would please those who were baying loudest for the blood of her fellow Queen. But there were still a few practical details to be sorted out.

Elizabeth had not released Mary Grey's full inheritance to her and she did not have enough money to support herself. As the impoverished prisoner reminded Burghley: 'I have but forescore pounds a year of her majesty; of my own I have but twenty pounds; and as your lordship knows, there is nobody will board me for so little.'[18] Her cousin, Francis Willoughby, spent far more than her annual income every month just running his house in Nottinghamshire. Sir Thomas Gresham suggested that Mary be sent to her stepfather, Adrian Stokes. But he had just remarried, to Anne Carew, the widow of Sir Nicholas Throckmorton.[19] Mary told Burghley she feared it would be too much of a financial burden for Stokes to take her on as well as all his new stepchildren. Elizabeth agreed reluctantly, therefore, to pay her cousin a modest further allowance. Mary left the Greshams a few days later, with 'all her books and rubbish', Sir Thomas wrote dismissively.

On 2nd June 1572 Norfolk was executed. All his wealth, youth and popularity, could not save him from having to pay the price that others before him had met, those who had also involved themselves in royal marriages. But after seven years Mary Grey was free at last.

Chapter XXVI

❖

A Return to Elizabeth's Court

Mary Grey spent her first few months of freedom at Beaumanor in Leicestershire with Adrian Stokes and his new family. It was the house where she had lived with Katherine and her mother in the aftermath of the executions of her father and sister, Jane. Only a few miles from Bradgate, it was filled, as Bradgate had once been, with the sound of children's laughter. Stokes had a nine-year-old stepdaughter, Bess (the spirited future wife of Sir Walter Raleigh), and no fewer than six stepsons. His wife, the widowed Lady Throckmorton, was the cousin who had stood in for Jane as godparent to Guildford Underhill, on the last day of her reign. She had known Mary since infanthood and lavished affection on her. Mary noticed that her old bedchamber at Beaumanor still bore her name, as did her sister Katherine's. But at age twenty-seven and having just secured her liberty, she found it hard to be dependent on others. By February 1573 she had raised enough money, however, to run her own house in the London parish of St Botolph's-Without-Aldgate.

'Now that I have become a housekeeper,' Mary wrote proudly to her brother-in-law Hertford, 'I would willingly meet with some trusty servant.' She hoped he had such a man in his employ. 'I hear that Harry Parker, who was in my sister's service and is true and honest, is still in yours. Please let me have him for my sister's sake.'[1] Hertford had shown no signs of wanting to remarry. Although there had been rumours he had been interested in the widowed Lady Hoby when he was first accepted back at court in the aftermath of the Northern Rebellion, their intimate conversations were merely those of old friends who had much to reminisce about. She had been the hostess at a dinner party that he and Katherine had attended when Robert Dudley's wife had been found dead. We don't know if Katherine's servant, Parker, joined Mary's house, but we do know the names of several other servants she employed. The household included Katherine Duport,[2] a cousin from Shepshed in Leicestershire, and Henry and Anne Goldwell, relatives of the Frances Goldwell who had attended her wedding. There was also a gentleman groom, Robert Saville.

Mary's modest new home was a long way from the grand life she had enjoyed at Bradgate, but she furnished it comfortably. She had a good feathered bed and bolster, covered stools, little nests of silver bowls, silver spoons and silver trenchers, a fine silver gilt salt, a tankard and a silver gilt bowl with a cover.[3] It was barely enough to entertain with, but Mary often went out in her carriage to see her friends and relations. She still saw her step-grandmother Katherine Suffolk, and her children, Peregrine Bertie and Susan, Countess of Kent. She also remained close to her old playmate Lady Arundell – once the bossy little Margaret Willoughby – and Lady Stafford, whose daughters had dined with her before her wedding to Thomas Keyes. Although she had been denied permission to raise her husband's children, she grew very close to his daughter Jane Merrick and became godmother to Jane's child, Mary. As she stayed in contact with Hertford, and his younger sister, Lady Elizabeth Seymour, she was also kept informed about her nephews. Both were progressing well at Latin and arithmetic, but twelve-year-old Beauchamp could be lazy and was proving a disappointment to his music teacher. The man later complained that his brother Thomas 'would learn two lessons to my Lord's one, if I would teach him'.[4]

Outside the family, Mary's closest friend and 'gossip' was a woman called Mrs Morrison. She was careful also to cultivate her court contacts, however, especially her former friends amongst the

Ladies of the Queen's Bedchamber. Kate Astley had died in 1565 – two days after Mary had married Keyes – but Mary remained friends with Blanche Parry, who had served Elizabeth since she was a baby.[5] A few good words from Parry could facilitate a return for Mary to royal favour, and that this might be achieved was hinted at in the New Year of 1574 when the Queen accepted Mary's gift of 'a pair of bracelets of pomander and agate beads'. The following year her income from her mother's former lands was increased and she was able to invest in fashionable court dress. She had inherited only a few of the jewels that had belonged to her mother, such as a pretty pair of bracelets with reddish-orange jacinth stones. Now she could also afford a fine girdle of goldsmiths' work set with pearls and gold buttons, set off beautifully against a black velvet gown.

There were, however, some lapses of judgement in this regard. Mary owned a brilliant yellow kirtle which she wore (as they were intended) as an outer petticoat, but, teamed with her black gowns the diminutive princess must have been in danger of resembling a bumblebee. Perhaps wisely, she usually kept to black kirtles and restricted exuberant displays of colour to hidden red cotton petticoats guarded in black velvet and embroidered with gold lace which flashed as she raised her skirts and stepped into her carriage.[6]

If Mary's spirit was far from extinguished, so her mind remained as lively and curious as it had ever been. A war was being waged on England's stubborn Catholics. In the aftermath of the Northern Rebellion of 1569, Pope Pius V had excommunicated Elizabeth and released her subjects from their obedience to her. The consequences were disastrous for Catholics, who could now be treated as traitors by reason of their faith alone. Just as Protestantism had been associated with treason in 1553–58 so now Catholicism would be, and the active persecution of them had already begun. Mary's library included at least two books by William Fulke who propagated an apocalyptic interpretation of the Reformation as the final struggle between Christ and the anti-Christ. In this war on evil it seemed to men like Fulke fully justified that Catholic priests and their supporters should be castrated and disembowelled in public, as they would be before the decade was out. And Cecil saw to it that the latest two-volume edition of Foxe's *Book of Martyrs* (a copy of which Mary owned) was placed in every parish as a reminder of Protestant suffering under Catholic rule.

Mary's most intense concerns, however, lay in theological debates between the 'forward' Protestants, who came to be known derisively as Puritans, and the conservatives the Queen favoured. The debates had been triggered by the publication in 1572 of the so-called 'Admonition to Parliament' which attacked Elizabeth's religious settlement.[7] Mary acquired several works by the Presbyterian Thomas Cartwright, who endorsed and amplified the 'Admonition', as well as owning a defence of the status quo written by the future Archbishop of Canterbury, John Whitgift. Mary's own religious sympathies are suggested by her interest in some of the radical London preachers. She owned, for example, a collection of Edward Dering's celebrated 'Lectures Upon the Hebrews', delivered at St Paul's in 1572. Elizabeth loathed Dering, who had castigated her for allowing the corruption he saw in the English Church. Mary also owned a book of *Readings* by the Puritan John Knewstub who helped set forth the developing English version of Calvinist theology on God's 'Elect'.[8]

Several old family friends took the conservative side, however. Amongst them, and perhaps the most surprising, was Lady Jane Grey's former tutor John Aylmer. The man remembered as Jane's kindly guide had discovered secular ambition. He had turned his back on old colleagues from Bradgate days, such as the chaplain John Wullocke, in order to 'creep into favour' with the Queen and Church conservatives. Paraphrasing St Paul, he said of the views he had inculcated in Jane Grey: 'When I was a child, I spake as a child . . . but when I became a man, I put away childish things.' In 1576, Edmund Spenser's poetic work, 'The Shepheardes Calender', characterised him as a goatherd rather than a pastoral shepherd – a man whose chief motivation was to reach the top of the greasy pole. In 1577 he had his reward. He became *de jure* Bishop of London. It was a post in which he was to gain notoriety for greed, ill-temper and the vicious treatment he meted out to religious dissidents, Puritan as well as Catholic.

Mary Grey was careful, however, to avoid any personal involvement in controversial issues, either religious or concerning the succession, and in this respect she must have been amazed to see her mother's former lady-in-waiting Bess Hardwick, the Countess of Shrewsbury, take her own child down the path she had seen the Greys follow so disastrously.

In 1574 Bess had married her daughter Elizabeth Cavendish – Katherine Grey's godchild – to the Countess of Lennox's younger son Charles Stuart, brother to the murdered Henry, Lord Darnley. Lennox spent several months in the Tower for it. The mothers had ensured that their children's marriage had plenty of witnesses and although their gamble never paid out the prize of a male heir, a daughter, Arbella Stuart, was born in 1576. Her English birth gave her, in some minds, a superior claim to that of her cousin James VI of Scots. Bess was very proud of 'my jewell Arbell' as she called her. But Mary must have shuddered for her future.

By the end of the following year, 1577, Mary Grey was sufficiently rehabilitated at court to be appointed a Maid of Honour to Elizabeth. This was a very respectable position at court, but it was also a pointed comment on Elizabeth's disinclination to acknowledge the marriage for which Mary had served seven years under lock and key.[9] Mary spent that Christmas season at Hampton Court, the largest and grandest of Elizabeth's palaces. 'All the walls shine with gold and silver,' a foreign visitor reported, and 'many of the large rooms are embellished with masterly paintings, writing tables of mother of pearl, and musical instruments'. There had been a few alterations during the period of Mary's imprisonment. The ceiling in the Paradise Room at the end of the long gallery had been repainted and gilded, while in the Queen's bedchamber a new window had been built overlooking the gardens. But it was still much as Mary had always known it. The Christmas celebrations this year were marked with the usual plays and masques. Most of them were held in the great hall where elaborate scenery had been painted and daises constructed under its splendid hammer beam roof with staging for Mary and the other court ladies to perform on. It looked magical with little oil lamps strung across the room on wires.[10]

At the New Year, Mary gave Elizabeth two pairs of gloves decorated with four dozen gold buttons, each studded with a seed pearl. In return Elizabeth gave her a 'cup with a cover'. She was now in her forty-fifth year and beyond child-bearing age. When she became Queen in 1558 Elizabeth had been associated with the iconography of the biblical prophetess, Deborah, who had rescued Israel from the pagan King of Canaan. But Deborah had been a married woman, and while some still hoped Elizabeth would marry to serve England's diplomatic interests, others, such as Hertford, preferred the status quo, hoping that, since she could not have children of her own, eventually she would name his sons her heirs, and not complicate matters with a husband. A new iconography was called for and the phrase the Virgin Queen would be coined that August. It brilliantly co-opted England's traditional devotion to the Virgin Mary.[11]

But Elizabeth's sobriquet was bought at a high personal price. Elizabeth had once said that Robert Dudley's company was the only happiness she had ever known. In September, however, just weeks after her virgin 'title' was first deployed, he would marry her younger cousin, Lettice Knollys, whose resemblance to Elizabeth in her youth was a reminder of what might have been. Elizabeth had new favourites already and had honed a role as the unobtainable love object of her knights and nobles. The language of courtly love enabled them to pay their monarch homage in a way that reflected the traditional roles of men and women. But the plays and masques with their themes of love, youth and fecundity all mocked what the Queen was becoming: the once young, passionately-in-love princess in modest, Protestant attire tottering towards old age as decked-out as a plaster Madonna on feast days.

Mary Grey, who at thirty-three was over a decade younger than Elizabeth, was not, however, destined to witness the closing scenes of the Queen's reign. A familiar shadow fell over England in the New Year of 1578: plague. In London it brought death even in the cold weather of January when the epidemics were at their weakest. By the spring the rate of deaths from it was increasing. The rich usually fled whatever areas the plague appeared in, but Mary Grey was at her house in St Botolph's when she became ill in April. It is possible she thought she had special protection from a 'mystic ruby'. This magical treasure was said to be created by crystallisation of the blood in very old, wise unicorns and was found at the base of their horns, forming a distillation of their very essence. A piece of unicorn's horn was listed as being among Lady Jane Grey's possessions in the Tower and Mary also owned one. A good stone was so bright it could shine through clothing; but it could also serve a useful, even vital, purpose. According to the medieval alchemist, Albertus Magnus, mystic rubies would guard against plague.[12] And perhaps Mary Grey was not dying of plague – its symptoms were variable, and in its pneumatic form almost non-existent so there is no way of knowing – but by 17th April, Mary certainly knew she did not have long left and she drew up her will.

In it she described herself as 'Lady Mary Grey . . . Widow'. She was obliged to use her maiden name at court, but the reference to her widowhood makes it clear she was determined to maintain the memory of her marriage to Mr Keyes. Like her sisters, Mary also wished to advertise that she would be dying in the Protestant faith, trusting that her soul would be saved by Christ's 'death and passion only, without any other ways and means'. Her will then divided her modest possessions between her friends, relations and servants. Her mother's jewels she left to her step-grandmother Katherine Suffolk, along with the mystic ruby, asking the duchess to pass on something to the duchess's daughter, Susan Bertie, the Countess of Kent. To her cousin, Lady Arundell (her childhood friend Margaret Willoughby), she bequeathed her tankard of gold and silver. Adrian Stokes's wife, the former Lady Throckmorton, was left a silver gilt bowl with a cover. To her servants, Robert Saville and Henry Goldwell, she gave her 'black gelding and the bay', respectively; to her stepdaughter, Jane Merrick, she left her bed, whilst the bulk of her money went to Merrick's daughter, Mary – her godchild and her late husband's grandchild. There was something even for a servant boy, for whom she sought an apprenticeship 'to some good occupation'. Finally, Mary chose as her executors her kinsmen, Mr Edward Hall and Mr Thomas Duport: modest, trustworthy Leicestershire and Lincolnshire esquires.[13] 'As for my body,' Mary instructed, 'I commit the same to be buried where the Queen's Majesty shall think most meet.'[14] Three days later she died.

Elizabeth ordered that Mary Grey should be buried in Westminster Abbey.[15] The details of her funeral, lost for four centuries, were unearthed during research for this book at the College of Arms in London, where they had lain ignored as the funeral details of an insignificant daughter of the Earl of Kent.[16] The burial of the last of the Grey sisters took place on 14th May after Mary's body was brought in procession to the abbey. A dozen poor women, dressed in black, led it at the front – the traditional bedesmen who, before the Reformation, would have prayed for the soul of their benefactor. The heralds had prepared banners of her arms, the symbols of her great lineage, and there were four pallbearers for the tiny coffin on its chariot. Behind it the chief mourner, Katherine Suffolk's daughter, Susan, Countess of Kent, was attended by four gentlemen, four gentlewomen and four yeomen. The names of the other official mourners is a roll call of individuals whose lives and whose families had been intertwined with those of the Grey sisters: Mistress Tilney – from the family of Elizabeth Tilney, who attended Lady Jane Grey at the scaffold; Lady Elizabeth Seymour, the twenty-eight-year-old sister of Katherine Grey's husband, Hertford; Katherine Grey's last jailors, Sir Owen and Lady Hopton. There are also the names familiar from Mary's will, Goldwell, Duport, Hall, Saville – and Lady Arundell who had listened outside the door above Mr Keyes's rooms as he and Mary were married in 1565.[17]

Despite the antipathy of the male elite to rule by women, during most of Mary's life the English crown was dependent on women as heirs and the possible mothers of future Kings It was as the latter that the Tudor princesses were most valued. But Elizabeth understood well the dangers and possible cost of them marrying, and the fear of making a divisive or wrong choice ensured, eventually, that she never did so. The last sight of Lady Mary was of her small coffin disappearing into her mother's royal tomb. There she still lies in obscurity with no marker or monument, but, unlike her sisters, having achieved at the end of her life, freedom, and perhaps, peace.

With the three Grey sisters dead and Katherine's sons declared illegitimate, their cousin Margaret Clifford, now the Countess of Derby, the only surviving child of Eleanor Brandon, became Elizabeth's heir under the terms of Henry VIII's will. But it wasn't long before she too learned the price of such privilege. Within only weeks she was accused of employing a magician to cast spells to harm the Queen. The 'magician' in question, a well-known physician called Dr Randall, was tried and hanged. Margaret, who was suspected of having Catholic sympathies, was placed with a series of jailors, just as her cousins had been. She died eighteen years later in 1596, having never been freed.

Chapter XXVII

Katherine's Sons and the
Death of Elizabeth

Burghley continued to hope that one of Katherine Grey's sons would one day be King. Illegitimacy in law had not prevented Elizabeth's accession. And whether they were, in fact, illegitimate was, in any case, questionable. But when Katherine's eldest son, Lord Beauchamp, fell in love in the summer of 1581, it looked set to blight his chances of succeeding to the crown. He was nineteen, almost twenty, the same age his father, Hertford, had been when he fell in love with his mother. The setting was also the same: the Duchess of Somerset's house, Hanworth. The woman Beauchamp fell in love with, Miss Honora Rogers, was a respectable kinswoman from a Puritan family, but not nearly grand enough for the wife of a future King of England. For Hertford the affair was a betrayal of Katherine's memory and of his sons' royal heritage. He referred bitterly to Honora as *Onus Blowse* – which loosely translates as that 'tiresome tart' – and ordered Beauchamp to keep away from her.[1]

Beauchamp tried, at first, to reassure his father that his relationship with Honora was a mere flirtation. But at the same time as he was denying any serious interest in Honora he was writing to her, bemoaning their separation and hoping that 'the common saying "out of sight out of mind" shall not be applied to me'.[2] By the following year he had thrown off all pretence that he was not in love with her. His father's friends wrote letters to him, quoting from the Psalms and urging Beauchamp to follow his father's wishes. Even Elizabeth's spymaster, Sir Francis Walsingham, intervened to try and resolve the family breach, but without success. Hertford was so desperate that in August 1585 he had his errant son seized and brought to one of his houses. Beauchamp threatened to kill himself, rather than be parted from Honora, and pleaded with the Queen to support their intention to marry. Elizabeth, handed the opportunity to do further damage to Beauchamp's claim, willingly came to the rescue of the lovers – a most unusual move in a Queen who had gained a reputation for sexual jealousy. Hertford was then obliged to accept his son's marriage, with Elizabeth sweetening the pill by allowing the forty-six-year-old earl to marry his mistress of the past decade, Frances Howard, the daughter of Lord Howard of Effingham.[3]

Burghley, by now white-bearded, was deeply disappointed by Beauchamp's marriage, but there was always the younger brother to consider and his obsessive pursuit of the destruction of the Queen of Scots was, at last, making headway. Only the previous year, 1584, he and Walsingham had drafted a so-called 'Bond of Association', whose members agreed to have Mary murdered if Elizabeth's life was threatened. Burghley hoped to follow this with a neo-republican law similar to that he had sought in 1563 that would bring a 'Great Council' into effect on Elizabeth's death, with the power to choose her successor. Elizabeth put paid to that, but the following year, 1586, Mary Queen of Scots was found to be in correspondence with a young Catholic traitor called Anthony Babington. In essence Babington and his co-conspirators were accused of planning a Catholic uprising, backed by an invading army financed by Spain and the Pope. It was the Ridolfi plot – which had ended in the Duke of Norfolk's execution – all over again. This time, however, the Queen of Scots did not escape prosecution. She was tried and convicted for her involvement. Elizabeth, loath to allow the first regicide in England empowered by the state, tried to persuade her servants to murder her cousin under the Bond of Association. Burghley thwarted Elizabeth, however, and had the death warrant delivered. As he once said, paraphrasing Mary Grey's favourite author, Demosthenes, 'counsel without resolution and execution is pure wind'.[4]

Mary Queen of Scots was beheaded on 3rd February 1587, thirty-three years to the month after Lady Jane Grey. Like Jane she had cast herself in the role of martyr, but for the Catholic cause. Her death marked a watershed in Elizabeth's reign. Mary Queen of Scots' son, James VI of Scots, was a Protestant, and with Elizabeth no longer favouring a Catholic heir, but instead standing against a Spanish invasion attempt, her courtiers were able to cast her in the new role of Gloriana, the great icon of English, Protestant nationalism with which she remains associated. Burghley, however, aware that James VI blamed him for his mother's execution, continued to support the Seymour claim, his hopes vested in Katherine Grey's younger son, the twenty-four-year-old Lord Thomas Seymour. In 1589, Thomas appealed against the decision that had rendered him illegitimate, advertising the fact his parents had declared their marriage under interrogation before he was conceived in the Tower. His appeal was soon rejected, but it was clear as the new decade began that his generation, who had grown up during Elizabeth's reign, were impatient for change. Those who played out the rituals of court knew the lined face behind Gloriana's divine mask, and their prejudices against female rule were sharpened by the commonplace contempt the young have for the old – and especially for old women. Elizabeth's virginity began to be ascribed to a physical impediment rather than virtue, as her appearance increasingly inspired revulsion in her courtiers. And this was something Hertford intended to take advantage of when, in 1591, he was invited to host the Queen during her summer progress at one of his minor manor houses, Elvetham in Hampshire. As men were set to work on Hertford's estate in anticipation of the royal visit, a fantastic landscape was created. It included a huge artificial lake, built in the shape of a perfect half moon, on which model ships floated around an island large enough to hold a ruined fort 20 foot square. Dozens of temporary rooms were erected around it. There was a state room hung with tapestries and covered 'with boughs, and clusters of ripe hazel nuts', as well as dining rooms set with tables up to 23 yards long.[5] Elizabeth arrived at the edge of the estate on 20th September to be met by Hertford and an army of three hundred mounted retainers. Each wore chains of gold, and yellow and black feathers in their hats – a display of princely wealth and power dressed up as a mark of respect.[6] The themes of the planned entertainments, winter and spring, sexual desire and fecundity, were projected similarly as flattery while acting as a reminder, on a magnificent scale, that Elizabeth was a sterile old spinster. The shows, banquets, and fireworks that unfolded over the following three days were surpassed during Elizabeth's reign only by those organised by Robert Dudley, the Earl of Leicester, at Kenilworth Castle in July 1575. Hertford was careful, furthermore, to advertise the themes of the shows far beyond those who actually witnessed them. They were described in detail in a book he had printed and emblazoned with his arms, sending his message about the passing of the old and the coming of the new to a wide audience.

Within a few months of the famous Elvetham entertainments, Hertford's younger son Thomas Seymour had reinitiated his appeals on the validity of his parents' marriage. When these were no more successful than his earlier attempts, more direct measures began to be considered. It was expected that the old Queen could die at any time, and there were deepening divisions over the succession, with Burghley's own younger son, his political heir, the dwarfish Sir Robert Cecil, and Elizabeth's handsome last favourite, Robert Devereux, Earl of Essex, the leading figures of the opposing Seymour and Stuart factions. In 1594, the only son of Margaret Clifford, the thirty-five-year-old Ferdinando, Earl of Derby, grandson of Eleanor Brandon, died after a violent bout of vomiting. Some believed the Cecils had poisoned him as a rival to Lord Beauchamp and Thomas Seymour. Then in the autumn of 1595, Sir Michael Blount, the Lieutenant of the Tower, was caught secretly stockpiling weapons for Hertford and the earl found himself behind the Tower's walls once more. The Cecils worked hard for Hertford's release, which came after only a few weeks, but the will to take huge risks in pursuit of the crown for his heirs had begun to desert Hertford. In

1598 Lord Burghley, his father's former servant and the most lethal enemy of the Stuart cause, died. In 1600, his son, Lord Thomas Seymour, also predeceased him, aged only thirty-seven. The final blow to his ambitions came, however, in 1601 when Essex was executed following a failed revolt to force Elizabeth to name King James her heir. It left Robert Cecil free to achieve a secret rapprochement with James VI and by Christmas 1602, when Elizabeth's health was in sharp decline, Hertford and the large majority of the most powerful men at court, were all supportive of King James's future accession. There was, however, to be a final act in the drama of the Grey sisters and the hopes for a native dynasty.

On 30th December 1602, while the court enjoyed the seasonal entertainments at Whitehall, a servant to the Countess of Shrewsbury (the former Bess Hardwick) arrived at Hertford's house in Tottenham asking to see the earl alone. It was an unusual request from a servant, but Hertford suspected the reason behind it. Before Robert Cecil's reconciliation with James VI, Hertford had considered a plan that centred on his eldest grandchild, Beauchamp's teenage son, Edward Seymour. Hertford had hoped that while a poor marriage had damaged Beauchamp's claim to the throne, a brilliant marriage would revive it for his grandchild. The bride decided on as the most suitable choice was the Countess of Shrewsbury's granddaughter, Arbella Stuart. Arbella was a great-grandchild of Margaret Tudor, and since she, as well as both her parents, had been born in England, some judged her claim to be superior to that of the Scottish-born James. Her gender, however, counted against her.

While Elizabeth remained popular with the people, who had refused to rise in support of Essex in 1601, at court all the political and social ills of the decade were blamed on the fact England was ruled by a woman, with the weaknesses of character this supposedly entailed. Foreign ambassadors were regularly told that England would not tolerate another Queen. This ruled out Arbella's claim as Elizabeth's heir. But the accession of a foreigner also held little appeal, and Hertford hoped that a marriage between Arbella and the young Edward Seymour, which would unite the lines of Henry VIII's sisters, could create a joint candidacy capable of attracting wide-spread support. Hertford had dropped his plan only after Robert Cecil came to his accommodation with James VI, and, as he inter-viewed the servant who appeared at his house it became evident that Arbella knew about the proposed match.

Arbella Stuart had barely been seen for over a decade. Elizabeth had ensured she had spent her entire adult life, from the age of eighteen to twenty-eight, in the countryside, forbidden from coming to court. Hertford remembered a full-faced girl with dark blonde hair who was exceptionally well educated. Her parents had died when she was young and her grandmother had raised her as she had seen the Grey sisters raised. Living at Hardwick Hall in Derbyshire, however, Arbella was trapped in eternal childhood, with no prospect of a husband, and increasingly obsessed with the stories her grandmother had told of her parents' secret marriage and of the marriage of her mother's godparent, Katherine Grey. She was determined now to break free. Her message to Hertford – deliv-ered by her grandmother's servant – warned that her grandmother would do nothing without the Queen's permission. Arbella suggested, however, that his grandson, Edward Seymour, should come to Hardwick disguised as the son or nephew of 'some ancient grave man' who wished to sell land, or borrow money. As she had never met him she told the servant to ask Hertford that his grand-son bring by way of identification, either a picture of Lady Jane Grey or something in Jane's handwriting, both of which she was familiar with. Arbella suggested the Greek Testament that Jane had left Katherine Grey on her death. When the servant had finished relaying Arbella's message, however, Hertford sent him under guard to Cecil.

When Elizabeth learned what had happened the fears she had when Katherine Grey had married Hertford over forty years earlier, returned. Who was behind Arbella's actions, she wanted to know? There had been rumours for months that a small number of courtiers, keen to prevent a Scot inheriting the throne, were plotting a native Seymour/Stuart match. Sir Walter Raleigh, who had married

Adrian Stokes's stepdaughter Bess Throckmorton, was rumoured to be one such. When Arbella was interrogated, however, only a few servants and close family were named, and her distress was such she seemed half-mad. Arbella stopped eating and wrote a series of paranoid, rambling letters to the Queen concerning the wickedness of Hertford and Robert Cecil, who she clearly felt had betrayed her.

Elizabeth, meanwhile, was also showing signs of mental illness. She had been deeply depressed since the execution of her favourite the Earl of Essex following his revolt in 1601. Her health was deteriorating, and she was increasingly anxious that any sign of weakness could lead to her overthrow. Her teeth had long been in poor condition, but it seems an infection had developed into a fatal condition called Ludwig's angina.[7] Elizabeth had been generally unwell for months. By mid-March, however, abscesses under the tongue and in the throat were making it difficult for her to swallow, speak or breathe and she feared that even now she might not be allowed to die peacefully.

From the morning of 20th March until the night of the 22nd, the dying Queen sat on cushions in her Privy Chamber at Richmond Palace too afraid to go to bed. It was fully expected that civil war would break out on her death and many great houses, including that of Hertford, were reinforced with arms. Although Cecil and the Privy Council were united in support of the claim of James VI of Scots, the knowledge that Henry VIII's will, sanctioned by Parliament and excluding the Stuart line, remained extant, weighed heavily on everyone. As the end of Elizabeth's life approached, however, on Wednesday 23rd March, and she was at last in bed, the Council resolved to ask her one last time if she would nominate an heir. Elizabeth agreed to see them, but they found she could no longer speak. She attempted to sip some water to clear her throat, but seeing her in pain the Councillors suggested that she raise a finger when they named the heir 'whom she liked'. According to a sixteen-year-old Maid of Honour, the silence was broken only once – and it was not to name her heir. When the Councillors asked if Katherine Grey's son, Lord Beauchamp, should succeed her, Elizabeth croaked painfully: 'I will have no rascal's son in my seat but one worthy to be a King.'[8] They are the last words she ever spoke.

Elizabeth never named James as one 'worthy to be a King', but as she had always hoped, the way was now clear for a Stuart succession. The following morning, a few hours after the sixty-nine-year-old Queen died in her sleep, Sir Robert Cecil stood on the green outside Whitehall and proclaimed James VI of Scots, King of England. To the end Elizabeth was determined that dynastic legitimacy and a monarch's divine right to rule would prevail over the secular power of parliamentary statute. To King James it seemed this had been achieved – but the clock could not be put back to 1533 and the break with Rome, when Henry VIII had declared he ruled beneath God but not the law, because he gave the law. Ideas had been born that could not be unimagined and these ideas undermined the theoretical absolutism of the new King.

In 1558, when Elizabeth became Queen, her Protestant supporters had seen Henry VIII's imperial monarchy vested already in the weak vessels of a boy King and two Queens. As his '*imperium*' or 'command' over Church and state was seen as necessary to secure Protestantism, Elizabeth's supporters amongst the political elite sought to re-identify it with something other than the person of a mere woman. They did so in 1559, by defining monarchical authority as 'mixed', with a female ruler constrained or 'bridled' by the counsel of Godly men and by Parliament. Elizabeth's understanding, however, that even her closest supporters viewed her as a second-rate ruler (by reason of her gender), contributed to her subsequent failure to secure the future for Protestant England by marrying or nominating a Protestant heir whom they might elect to replace her. Elizabeth's willingness to see her crown inherited instead by a foreign Catholic encouraged in turn her most important subjects to develop a new, conservative form of republicanism. Burghley, his allies and political heirs, were not consciously anti-monarchical, but they had a sense of duty to the Protestant nation beyond the reign of a single monarch.

Despite appearances, when Elizabeth died James did not simply succeed under the traditional rules of primogeniture and according to the will of God. The Privy Council had assumed the power to offer the crown to the King they had chosen, as Burghley had often planned they should. Representative peers, gentry and Councillors, had all signed the proclamation that declared James King, on 24th March 1604. The procedure, which is followed to this day, has echoes of the signatures gathered in 1553, as Edward VI was dying, in support of Queen Jane. But James's accession was confirmed when laws were passed in 1604 that laid aside Henry VIII's will and the rules relating to foreigners inheriting the throne. The English political elite at last now had the adult male monarch they had wanted for so long, and with him sons and a male succession. James's rule would, however, quickly prove a disappointment. Even before he was crowned in July 1603 he had revealed many of the flaws for which he was to be remembered: his incontinence with money, his intemperate attraction to young men, his Scottish favourites and Scottish habits.

The political elite never learned to trust James and, in a few short years, the despised old Queen Elizabeth was forgotten and the ruffed, stuffed, figure of Gloriana was brought out of the trunk of national memory, in costumes heavy with meaning and parable. The glorification of Elizabeth became a popular means of criticising her Stuart successor, while the civic consciousness her reign as Queen had fostered set difficulties in the exercise of imperial kingship. James and his son Charles I would maintain rigorously Henry VIII's assertion that the King was 'under God, but not the law, because the King makes the law'. In the end, however, to disastrous effect.

Chapter XXVIII

❖

The Story's End

It may, perhaps, have been nothing more than a desire to right the wrongs of the past that led Hertford, in 1608, to seek out, and somehow find, the anonymous clergyman who had married him to Katherine Grey forty-eight years before. But King James agreed only reluctantly to give their heirs the right to inherit the title Earl of Hertford, and was careful not to remove the stain of illegitimacy. This proved a wise decision. Two years later Beauchamp's younger son, the twenty-two-year-old William Seymour, married Arbella Stuart without royal permission.[1]

Arbella had been invited back to court after the death of Elizabeth, but in the words of the Venetian ambassador, she was kept 'without mate and without estate'. The marriage to William Seymour was her riposte. Her husband's motives can only be guessed at, but, in any event, the fact that they had married was soon discovered. Predictably, James placed Arbella under house arrest and William Seymour was put in the Tower. Less predictably, he escaped and fled to France, but Arbella was caught on her way to join him. She died in the Tower in 1615. It is believed she starved herself to death, as Katherine is said to have done in 1568.[2]

William Seymour remained in exile, supported financially by his grandfather until the following year, 1616, when he returned to England. Gradually he was rehabilitated at court, but he had not received any significant degree of royal favour from King James before the old Earl of Hertford died in 1621 at the then remarkable age of eighty-two.[3] William, as his only surviving male heir, inherited the title and promptly had his grandmother, Katherine Grey, disinterred from her grave in Yoxford, Suffolk, and brought to Salisbury Cathedral to be buried with her husband.[4] Their magnificent tomb still stands in the easterly corner of the south choir aisle. The long-legged and refined figure of Hertford lies on his sarcophagus with Katherine above him, as a mark of her royal status. The inscription, in Latin, celebrates the lovers, reunited at last:

> *Incomparable Consorts,*
> *Who, experienced in the vicissitudes of changing fortune*
> *At length, in the concord which marked their lives,*
> *Here rest together.*[5]

The new Earl of Hertford never demonstrated any further ambitions for the crown, if, indeed, that is what his marriage to Arbella was about. What he did show after Charles I became King in 1625, was a consistent commitment to the rule of law and constitutional propriety against Charles's increasingly autocratic rule. William Hertford was amongst the signatories of the 'twelve peers petition' that begged the recall of Parliament in 1640, after eleven years of the King's personal rule. As other signatories became increasingly radical, however, William rallied to the monarch's more moderate supporters. In gratitude King Charles raised him to the rank of Marquess of Hertford and, when civil war broke out, he chose the Royalist side, while the Greys took the opposite course.

The family had been restored to Bradgate late in Elizabeth's reign. But four days after King Charles raised his standard at Nottingham on 22nd August 1642, the house was ransacked by Royalist forces. In the battles that followed the head of the family, Henry Grey, Earl of Stamford – a descendant of Lord John Grey of Pirgo – served as a Parliamentarian officer. Tens of thousands died in the fighting, and tens of thousands more of disease. There was mass destruction of property, social upheaval and an explosion of radical ideas, some of which attracted Stamford's son, Thomas, Lord Grey of Groby. When the wars ended with the Royalist defeat and Charles's trial for treason, Thomas was the only elder son of a peer to sign the King's death warrant. His signature 'Tho Grey' appears second, between the names of John Bradshawe and Oliver Cromwell. William Hertford, having tried through the war to mediate between King and Parliament, witnessed Charles's execution on 30th January 1649. Of his people, Charles said on the scaffold:

> *Truly I desire their liberty and freedom as much as anybody . . . but I must tell you their liberty and freedom consists in having of government . . . It is not for having a share of government, Sir, that is nothing pertaining to them. A subject and Sovereign are clear different things . . . it was for this that now I am come here.*[6]

Parliament chose St George's Chapel, Windsor for the King's burial – a place far from London, safely behind castle walls and that would not easily become a Royalist rallying point. On the night of 7th February 1649, William Hertford and three other peers who were to attend his funeral, searched the chapel for a suitable tomb where Charles could be laid to rest. They stamped the floor of the choir in their leather boots and tapped with sticks until they heard a hollow sound. When they opened the tomb they discovered it contained the bodies of Henry VIII and his Queen, Jane Seymour, the marquess's great-great-aunt. The coffins were covered with perfectly preserved velvet cloth and one was described as 'very large'. There could be no doubting whose that was.

Under the will of Henry VIII, backed by Henrician statute, it was William Hertford, the grandson and heir of Katherine Grey, who should have been King, not King James's son, Charles, the decapitated Stuart monarch that Hertford was about to entomb, his head crudely stitched back on to his body in an effort to give him dignity in death. This, however, was where the story of the Tudor succession was to end, and the universe into which Henry Tudor had been born, vanish: with a King tried, executed and buried by his subjects.

The following day, 8th February 1649, was lit with the eerie white of newly fallen snow. It continued thick and fast as William Hertford, walking in step with his fellow peers, held the black velvet pall over the coffin borne by soldiers from the garrison at Windsor. Following behind, Bishop Juxon led a short procession of the King's servants the short distance from St George's Hall to the Royal Chapel. As they entered the chapel the velvet pall was already covered in snow, and witnesses later remembered that Charles had been crowned in white, just as he was now to be buried. As the mourners gathered by the open tomb no words were said. The bishop had been refused permission to read from the banned Stuart Book of Common Prayer. Elizabeth's attraction to a conservative form of Protestantism had gained converts within the English Church by the end of her life, and under the Stuarts they had triumphed over those who had been more forward in religion. But it was the hotter sort, the Puritans, who had proved victorious in the war. It was in silence, therefore, that Charles's coffin was lowered into the tomb to lie with that of Henry VIII and Jane Seymour.

Over the following years there were a number of Royalist conspiracies in support of the exiled Charles II. William Hertford's eldest son was involved in one, taking command of the Royalist 'Western Association' formed in May 1650. Government agents infiltrated it soon after, however, and in April 1651 he was imprisoned in the Tower. His father (formerly imprisoned in the Tower for his marriage to Arbella Stuart) declared miserably that the fortress appeared to have been entailed to his family, 'for we have now held it five generations'. His son was released in September 1651, but never recovered from the experience and died in March 1654. William Hertford lived long enough, however, to be amongst the peers to welcome Charles II back to England to restore the monarchy on 26th May 1660. That September he was made Duke of Somerset, a title last held in the family by his great-grandfather, the Protector.

William, already a sick, old man, died only a few weeks after he had been granted the dukedom, in October 1660. William's younger son, the 3rd Duke of Somerset, died without issue in 1671, leaving

William's daughter, Anne, the heir to Katherine Grey. Her inheritance included 'a rich bed that was Queen Jane Seymour's' – a gift to her father from Charles I.[7] Lady Anne married Thomas, the 2nd Earl of Ailesbury, in 1676. Their descendants remain the senior heirs to the line of Mary Tudor, Duchess of Suffolk.

Of the Greys, Thomas, the regicide, had not lived to see the restoration of Charles II. His father, the Earl of Stamford, had, however, and was included in the general Act of Pardon. He was succeeded as earl by his grandson, another Thomas, who spent time in the Tower for his involvement in the rebellion led by Charles II's illegitimate son, the Duke of Monmouth, against the King's Catholic heir and brother, James II. The family fortunes appeared to change at the so-called Glorious Revolution of 1688, when James II was overthrown and replaced with his daughter, Mary, and her Protestant husband, William of Orange. The earl lavishly entertained William III at Bradgate in November 1694, but the Dutch King (who had been crowned in a dual monarchy that Philip II of Spain would have envied) did not restore the power and wealth of the Greys. The earl was described in 1705 as 'very poor' and under subsequent generations the house suffered fire and abandonment until only the ruins that are there today were left.

Bradgate remains one of the most romantic places in Leicestershire and deeply evocative of its Tudor past. If the house still stood it would be thick with the history of later times: eighteenth-century portraits of bewigged grandees, mementoes of men who died in the Great War, fading photographs of children who have grown. Instead there is little more than the crumbling brick the sisters would have known and the deer picking through the trees in the park, as quiet as ghosts.

Epilogue

In the afterlife of the Grey sisters history has merged with works of the imagination. The Stuarts had no wish for their one-time rivals to the English crown to be remembered and Katherine and Mary Grey have disappeared into ephemera. But the fame of Lady Jane Grey has never dimmed. The Protestant martyr advertised by John Day's press in the year she died, has been cast and recast for successive generations as an ideal of girlhood and the embodiment of innocence offended. Her legend finds its apogee in Paul Delaroche's nineteenth-century historical portrait *The Execution of Lady Jane Grey*, a painting that has all the erotic overtones of a virgin sacrifice.[1] Jane in white feeling blindly for the block represents an apotheosis of female help-lessness: the rebellious and sharp-tongued adolescent of 1554 silenced in art, as she had been in life.

The many fictions about Jane in history begin at her beginning. Her most recent, twenty-first-century biographer[2] Faith Cook, repeats the old falsehood that she was born at Bradgate in October 1537, the same month as the future King Edward. The origins of these details are literary, rather than historical, a means of highlighting Jane's supposed separateness from the worldly court and foreshadowing her fate as a victim of forces outside her control. Born under the same star as Edward, their fates are linked, with Edward's dying decision to name her his heir the cause of all that follows.

The sixteenth-century Jane was a much more interesting and ambivalent figure than the traditional stories allow. As the heir of Henry VIII's royal niece, Lady Frances Brandon, Jane was, in reality, born into the heart of the court, and was raised to be what in the end she became: a leader on one side of a deadly ideological struggle. It was a period and place whose inhabitants were necessarily at once religious and worldly. There was no room for unbelief in Tudor understanding and their universe was strictly hierarchical. The social order on earth reflected the divine order, and Jane was aware from early childhood that she was a significant representative of a great family on the national stage, with the responsibilities that this position carried.

That Jane died a leader, and not merely a victim, became evident shortly after her death when her last letters and carefully choreographed actions were used as the basis of perhaps the most powerful contemporary attack against the reign of Queen Mary, in the pamphlets produced by John Day. By the time Elizabeth's reign began, Jane's words and a description of her death were ready to be immortalised in John Foxe's *Acts and Monuments*, popularly known as his *Book of Martyrs*. But fictional accounts of her life and death were not long coming. These early works, including a ballad printed in 1560 and an elegy in Latin written around 1563, focused on her self-proclaimed innocence, claiming that her death was a consequence solely of her father's actions in 1554 and the cruelty of Queen Mary.[3] The Latin elegy, composed by Sir Thomas Chaloner became particularly influential in the development of the mythology of Lady Jane Grey. Chaloner was a close friend of William Cecil and Walter Haddon, whose brother had been chaplain at Bradgate, as well as Thomas Sackville, the co-author of *Gorboduc*. Chaloner describes Jane as without equal in learning, fluent not only in Latin, Greek, French and Italian, but Hebrew and Arabic, a woman beautiful in body and soul, comparable to Socrates in her steadfastness in the face of death. The reference to Socrates is particularly interesting. It was then too – in 1563 – that Roger Ascham completed his first *Book of the Schoolmaster* in which he recalled finding Jane at Bradgate, reading Plato's *Phaedo* on the death of Socrates. Chaloner may have heard about Jane's interest in Plato's *Phaedo* through their network of friends, but fact and fiction were becoming blurred. A process had begun with the careful pruning of unwelcome facts, the exaggeration of others, and the addition of the occasional outright lie to create 'history as based on actual events'. Most notably, in the elegy, was the claim that Jane was pregnant when she died, which served to emphasise how unnatural and wicked the Catholic Queen supposedly was.

In the seventeenth century, Jane's 'innocence' became equated increasingly with passivity, and the uncompromising Jane of Foxe's *Book of Martyrs* began to be edited out of history. The first abridgements of Foxe made a point of underplaying the erudition and arrogance of Protestant heroines such as Lady Jane Grey, while dramatists such as Thomas Dekker and John Banks turned Jane into a submissive romantic heroine, passionately in love with Guildford, who had been portrayed as her co-victim in the 1560 ballad. Her childlike qualities meanwhile, were emphasised by the invention of the character of the nurse Jacob – sometimes conflated with Jane's lady-in-waiting 'Ellyn' and probably inspired by the nurse in William Shakespeare's *Romeo and Juliet*.

The following century and the age of the Enlightenment remained stubbornly unenlightened about women, with writers and historians continuing to reinforce the acceptable image of Jane as a weak and vulnerable victim. Even the historian David Hume claimed it was only Guildford's entreaties that made her accept the throne. Edward Young's poem 'The Force of Religion; or Vanquished Love' (1714) is suggestive, meanwhile, of the sexual element in depictions of the submissive, chaste Jane, with verses inviting the male reader to imagine the kneeling figure of 'that lovely person' in her private closet and to ponder her exquisite purity.[4]

Come the nineteenth century, Jane had also become enormously popular with a female readership to whom she was held up as an example of 'all that is lovely in domestic life'.[5] The historian Agnes Strickland had the courage to suggest that Jane's education was amongst the attributes worth imitating. But even her Jane remained essentially sweet, gentle and mild. A principal development during this century was the use of the Italian sources that quote a lost letter to Mary, and some dubious variations of it. These were used to add another facet to Jane's victim status, with her now being bullied by her husband Guildford and mother-in-law, as well as her parents and the apostate Duke of Northumberland, on whose ambition Jane's reign has traditionally been blamed.

Parallel to the developing story of Jane as the idealised child-woman has been the reinvention of her mother. From the early eighteenth century, Frances became the archetype of female wickedness whose face is recalled best in the overweight features of Lady Dacre in the Eworth double portrait. Twentieth- and twenty-first-century depictions of Jane, whether in history, film, or fiction, have all drawn on it. In Faith Cook's recent biography, Frances is described as she has been so many times before, as 'a stronger character than her husband. Coarse and domineering [with] ... much of her uncle Henry VIII's determined opportunism'.[6] It is a version of Frances that is very difficult to maintain through the lives of her younger sisters, but Jane's modern biographers only include a few pages on them. For the most part their lives are recalled in books that are long forgotten.

Lady Mary Grey has one work dedicated to her. The author, Flora Wylde, a daughter of Bonnie Prince Charlie's rescuer, Flora MacDonald, composed a fictional memoir in the nineteenth century entitled *The Tablette Book of Lady Mary Keyes*. It is often listed under non-fiction, but its actual origins are apparent in its repetition of myths about Jane. Katherine Grey should have been the most significant of the sisters, as the mother to a royal dynasty, but there were to be no Seymour kings or queens and only a handful of romantic plays, poems and popular histories have been written about the love affair between Katherine and Hertford.[7] The focus of her story, furthermore, is not the significance of her marriage, but the supposed cruelty of Queen Elizabeth, who takes the role that Frances has been ascribed in the life of Jane.

It is striking how the masculine qualities with which the 'powerful' and wicked Frances is associated have also been applied to Elizabeth. In the sixteenth century it was believed that women who exercised power over men could lose their femininity, rendering themselves barren, an idea inspired by the ancient Greek myth of hirsute, masculine women called the Virago. In 1985 a Dr Bakan went so far as to claim Elizabeth suffered from testicular feminisation and was actually genetically male – a diagnosis supported, he argued, by Elizabeth's mental toughness.[8] Thus a story that began with Henry VIII's rejection of his daughter, Mary, as a future ruler of England, continues to reflect our unease with women and power. The old prejudices survive without the ancient beliefs that once sustained them, sometimes justified by 'science' to which so many new myths are attached.

The historical stories of the Grey sisters, stripped of literary debris, remain, meanwhile, as tragic and poignant as any fiction could make them: Jane, a Protestant Joan of Arc, calling up fresh troops to fight against Mary Tudor while her own Councillors betrayed her; Katherine, who made love to 'Ned' in the Tower, leaving him a ring inscribed 'While I Lived, Yours'; and the diminutive Mary, who married her soldier by candlelight and died in a modest house in London, far from the palaces in which the sisters had been raised.

Author's Note

The Sisters Who Would Be Queen is the culmination of eight years' work on the Tudor succession. My curiosity about the Grey sisters arose when I was researching *After Elizabeth*, my book on the struggle behind the accession of James VI and I in 1603. Henry VIII's pursuit of a male heir is well remembered. What is not fully appreciated, however, is the extent to which Tudor beliefs in the inferiority of women shaped events for the remainder of the Tudor period, and the role this played in who we, as a nation, have become.

The old Whig interpretation of history, in which Protestants and liberals fought in the vanguard of progress against the retrograde impulses of Catholics and conservatives, retains a strong hold over our imagination. But no liberal impulses lay behind Henry's break with Rome or subsequent efforts to continue to deny women the absolute power of his crown – efforts that were to sow the seeds of our constitutional monarchy. The Grey sisters and their Tudor cousins, Mary and Elizabeth, were protagonists in the development of a civic consciousness that arose in response to an unwelcome series of reigning queens and proved problematic to the absolutist Stuart kings who followed them.

The Grey sisters were important in the sixteenth century because Henry VIII had excluded the Stuart line from the English throne. Under the terms of his will, Elizabeth's heir in 1603 was the son of Lady Katherine Grey. Her life, like that of her younger sister Mary Grey, was in part a romantic tragedy, a story of lovers divided. It is also, however, one that reveals a forgotten past and an Elizabeth dramatically at odds with the image of the Protestant, nationalist Madonna, with which we are familiar. In beginning to research this book, I hoped that the well-known life of the iconic, teenage Queen,

Lady Jane Grey, would provide an introduction to the since forgotten 'other Grey girls', but suspected there would be little new to say about Jane herself. As I moved from biographies of Jane's life to contemporary sources, however, I realised that I had underestimated the scale of the story and that little that has been written about Jane or her parents could be trusted. Separating myth from truth was a vital process, for the major events of Jane's life had an enormous impact on the culture and politics of not only Queen Mary's reign, but also Elizabeth's, and helps to explain her attitudes to Katherine and Mary Grey, and the consequences of those attitudes.

I reveal also previously unpublished details from love letters and transcripts of interviews concerning Katherine's marriage to Edward Seymour, Earl of Hertford, son of the Protector Somerset, and give new information on Hertford's ties to the authors of the first English play in blank verse, along with its role in efforts to pressure Elizabeth to settle the succession. In this continued struggle, Cecil emerges as far from the dull, loyal servant of tradition, and his efforts to gain control over Elizabeth's decisions on the future of the crown reflect the development of highly significant ideas about royal authority and the importance of Parliament. It was the misfortune of the Grey sisters to remain caught in the net of these great events. Only Lady Mary Grey would, in the end, achieve a measure of freedom from the burden of her royal birth.

The title of this book, *The Sisters Who Would Be Queen*, seems unfair when applied to Mary Grey. Jane would have been crowned if she had not been overthrown, and Katherine was dismayed not to be treated as Elizabeth's heir. Mary, however, never seems to have considered herself a serious contender for the throne. Described as the shortest person at court, she married the biggest – a union that was seen as grotesque and remains easily paraphrased as 'the dwarf who married a giant'. But Elizabeth took the threat this marriage posed seriously, with tragic results for the youngest Grey sister and her husband. Mary was, however, to survive these and that rare discovery – lost manuscripts – lays her story to rest amongst the great kings from whom the sisters were descended and the queens whose rivals they were. Although the least significant of the sisters, she is my favourite.

Where I have quoted contemporary sources I have modernised the spelling so the text reads more fluently for the modern reader. In an attempt to prevent confusion over the many people holding the same names or in instances where the same person changes name, I have used various techniques, for example calling some Katherines (all spelt with a 'K' in the sixteenth century) 'Catherine', and referring to the Lady Mary (Tudor) and the Lady Elizabeth (Tudor) as Princesses, a title that was not in official use in England before the seventeenth century. Finally, I have modernised dates, so that the year begins on January 1st rather than on March 25th, as it did at the time.

I could not even have begun this project without the generous help and advice of scholars such as Kenneth Fincham, whom I would like to thank for his enormous patience in answering my questions, reading the first full draft of this manuscript, as he did the last, and making suggestions as to how the book could be improved. Sue Doran very kindly also read a draft of the Jane section, while working on her own book. Any errors and faults that remain are obviously my own. Other scholars to whom I have turned with bothersome queries include Michael Wyatt and Thomas Mayer, with whom I discussed the Italian sources concerning Jane. I am also very grateful for the help I have had from John Guy, Tom Freeman, Eric Ives, Stephen Alford, David Starkey, Ralph Houlbrooke, Diarmaid MacCulloch, Mark Nicholls, Stephan Edwards, Carole Levin and Penry Williams. I discussed costume with Susan North of the V&A (concerning, for example, the headdress worn by Katherine in bed on her wedding night), and portraits with Katie Coombs of the V&A, Tanya Cooper of the National Portrait Gallery and David Starkey. Medical matters I discussed with Christopher Sutton and Nicholas Lowe (who identifies the Fitzwilliam portrait, said variously to be of Mary I, Jane Grey or Jane Dormer, as a woman of about thirty-eight, which would indicate Mary I).

I had generous help from Robert Yorke, Archivist at the College of Arms and Stephen Freeth, Guildhall Library. I am also very grateful to Rodney Melville of the Chequers Estate, the staff of the British Library and the National Archives, and Christine Reynolds of Westminster Abbey Library. Without the patience and help of the staff of the London Library, in particular Gosia Lawik, I could not have written this book. I would like to acknowledge Nini Murray Philipson for information on the Tilney family; my father-in-law Gerard de Lisle, who generously provided me with transcriptions of manuscripts on which I was stuck; Zia Soothill who kept the flesh from growing too weak; my goddaughter Laetitia Campbell who did useful research on her work experience; and my three historian sons, who also helped. Several friends have advised me on structure and tone. Henrietta Joy and Dominic Pearce offered invaluable opinions on the full draft, as, at an early stage, did my fellow writers and historians Daniel Jones and Rowland Manthorpe. My editor Arabella Pike has always been enthusiastic and very supportive, and I am grateful also to Annabel Wright and Kate Johnson. Above all I am lucky enough to have as my agent, Georgina Capel, with whom it is impossible to have a conversation without feeling happier at the end of it than at the beginning.

Notes

PART ONE: ROYAL CHILDREN

Chapter I: Beginning

1. No portrait of Frances survives and the effigy on her tomb is the only likeness we have of her. A portrait often said to be of Frances and her second husband Adrian Stokes is, in fact, of Lady Dacre and her son.
2. He was known as Harry by intimates, see, for example, Jonathan North (ed.), *England's Boy King*, p. 107.
3. J. S. Brewer (ed.), *Calendar of Letters and Papers, Foreign and Domestic, of the Reign of Henry VIII*, Vol. XIII, p. 280.
4. Ibid., Vol. VI, p. 142.
5. The wardship and arrangement of the marriage of Frances and Dorset, took place 24th March 1533, ibid., Vol. VI, p. 142.
6. Ibid., Vol. VII, pp. 62, 63. Marriages in the sixteenth century were a process rather than a single event. The phrase *per verba de presenti* – I take you now – was used to mark when the process concluded; in the case of the Dorsets it seems to have taken place between 28th July 1533 and 4th February 1534.
7. There have been various suggestions for Jane's birth date. Jane's tutor, John Aylmer, drew attention to her age in a letter written on, or close to, 29th May 1551. In it he describes Jane as being 'just 14' (Hastings Robinson, *Original Letters Relative to the Reformation*, Vol. I, p. 276). Although the dates are guesses by the editor they are inferred by references in the letter to the death of Martin Bucer on 28th February 1551, the arrival in England of Bullinger's fifth *Decade*, which was not published until March, the use of the title Marquess of Dorset (Dorset became Duke of Suffolk in October 1551) and the absence of any comment on the deaths of Jane's uncles, the Brandon brothers, in July. This narrows the dates to between April and July. The reference in the letter to Dorset's client, John of Ulm, who visited Bradgate on 29th May, suggests strongly, however, that it was written around this time. The original letter in Zurich shows some correction on the number '14' but this appears to have been done in Aylmer's hand and it had not – to my mind – been changed from a different number. There is another letter written by Ulm in late April

1550 which also describes Jane as being 'about 14', suggesting she was born in 1536. Ulmer didn't know Jane as well as Aylmer, however, and the 'about' indicates his uncertainty. The letter is more useful in supporting the May timing. Michel Angelo Florio also claimed later that Jane was seventeen when she died, but he was writing after her death, while Aylmer was under the same roof as Jane when he wrote the letter noting her age.

8. Dorset was serving on the treason trials, in London, of the leaders of the Pilgrimage of Grace.
9. John Ponet, *A Shorte Treatise of Politike Pouuer 1556*, in Winthrop Still Hudson, *John Ponet*, p. 134.
10. David Loades, *Politics, Censorship and the English Reformation*, pp. 1, 3, 4, 5. MacCulloch, *Reformation*, pp. 76–87, 99–104.
11. It is possible she also had a daughter, of whom no details survive. Another daughter may have been lost in 1539.
12. For a detailed discussion on this act of Parliament see Eric Ives, 'Tudor Dynastic Problems Revisited'.
13. Royal godparents ran in the family. Frances had herself been named after the French King, Francis II.
14. Eric Ives, *The Life and Death of Anne Boleyn*, p. 44.
15. Charles Wriothesley and William Douglas Hamilton, *A Chronicle of England during the Reign of the Tudors, 1485–1559*, Vol. I, p. 64.
16. Barbara J. Harris, *English Aristocratic Women 1450–1550*, p. 106.
17. Brewer (ed.), *Letters and Papers*, Vol. XII, pt ii, p. 311, also Vol. XIII, pt i, pp. 81, 515, 567; Robinson, *Original Letters*, Vol. I, p. 276. The friend with whom Frances was staying was Lady Derby.
18. Wriothesley and Hamilton, *Chronicle*, Vol. I, pp. 66, 67.
19. Brewer, (ed.), *Letters and Papers*, Vol. XII, pp. ii, 311.
20. Ibid., Vol. XII, p. 340.
21. John Strype, *Ecclesiastical Memorials Relating Chiefly to Religion*, Vol. II, pt I, p. 12; Brewer (ed.), *Letters and Papers*, Vol. XII, pp. 311, 372–4.
22. For a commentary on this speech see Tillyard, *The Elizabethan World Picture*, p. 18.

Chapter II: First Lessons

1. Brewer (ed.), *Letters and Papers*, Vol. XIII, pp. 81, 515, 567. Barbara J. Harris, *English Aristocratic Women 1450–1550*, pp. 115, 116, 281.
2. Wingfield, 'Vitae Mariae Reginae' in Camden Miscellany XXVIII, p. 286.
3. When Katherine Grey was born the King was passionately in love with his fifth wife, the flirtatious teenager Katherine Howard. She had many connections to the Greys and it is probable, therefore, that Katherine Grey was, like Jane, named after a Queen. The young Queen's sister was married to Dorset's cousin and estate manager, Sir Thomas Arundell, and her

favourite lady-in-waiting, Katherine Tilney, was related to the Brandons through her mother, Elizabeth Jeffery. Other possible godparents include Dorset's sister, Katherine Fitzalan, or Frances's stepmother, Katherine of Suffolk – but the Greys had a fondness for royal godparents. Their son Henry was named after the King, Frances after Francis II and Jane after Queen Jane Seymour.

4. It is likely that Mary Grey was named after the Princess Mary. She was born after the Third Act of Succession that restored Mary Tudor in line to the throne and Frances was in a good position to ask her to be godmother since not only were they first cousins, their mothers had been friends and Frances had been a member of her household in 1538.

5. William Shakespeare, *As You Like It*, Act II, scene i.

6. Dorset gave the King two greyhounds as a New Year's gift in 1540.

7. *HMC Salisbury*, Vol. I, p. 131.

8. Sir Thomas Hoby.

9. Charlotte Isabelle Merton, 'The Women Who Served Queen Mary and Queen Elizabeth', p. 236. Houlbrooke, *The English Family 1450–1700*, pp. 140, 141, 144, 145.

10. Harris, *Aristocratic Women*, p. 35. In the 1995 film *Six Degrees of Separation* the protagonist played by Will Smith asks a rhetorical question about the mores of the modern American upper class. 'What do the rich like to give each other as presents?' 'Jam!' he answers. The same was true in Tudor England; Frances left letters to friends thanking them for their conserves.

11. I have found no evidence dating from before 1554 that Jane learned Spanish as was claimed in Thomas Chaloner's *Elegy*. The 'Italian grammar' may have been the book Michel Angelo Florio dedicated to Jane in 1553.

12. Thomas Becon, *The Catechism of Thomas Becon*, p. 348; Lacey Baldwin Smith, *Treason in Tudor England*, p. 72.

13. The word originally existed to describe a group of German princes who drew up a protest against other princes who had supported traditional religion at a diet in 1529.

14. James Kelsey McConica, *English Humanists and Reformation Politics under Henry VIII and Edward VI*, p. 227. The Jesuit was Robert Persons.

15. Sir Richard Morison quoted in Conyers Read, *Mr Secretary Cecil and Queen Elizabeth*, p. 41.

16. Jessie Childs, *Henry VIII's Last Victim*, p. 260.

17. Nicholas Throckmorton in around 1549 married Anne Carew, a cousin of Frances, and a future friend of Jane's. As a widow Carew would marry Frances's widower, Adrian Stokes, and act as a stepmother to Mary Grey.

18. John Foxe/Stephen Reed (ed.), *Acts and Monuments*, Vol. VI.

19. John Bale, who recorded Askew's life, presents a young, gentle woman, totally at odds with Askew's representation as confident, witty, and disputatious. The same fate awaited the fiery Jane, at the hands of her future admirers.

Chapter III: Jane's Wardship

1. In 1524 when Henry VIII faced his friend and brother-in-law, Charles Brandon, Duke of Suffolk, at the joust, it was universally argued that monarchy was instituted by God, and that the King ruled by God's grace for the benefit of the community. His duties, enshrined in his coronation oath, encompassed the defence of the realm, maintaining law and order, issuing justice impartially, and upholding the Church, especially against heresy. He possessed a royal prerogative that was 'ordinary' and 'absolute'. The former were his common law privileges as a feudal lord and included his ability to issue pardons. The latter was his emergency power. He could suspend the law in time of war, to billet soldiers, for example; if a fire was burning a street of houses he could order the demolition of private property; and he could raise taxes. It was largely a self-limiting monarchy: but Henry cast these aside when he broke with Rome. Henry's research team, led by Thomas Cranmer, the Archbishop of Canterbury, had 'rediscovered' the royal supremacy in 'divers sundry old authentic histories and chronicles'. The crucial extract concerned a mythical king, Lucius I, who had converted Britain to Christianity in AD 187. According to Cranmer and his team, Lucius had wanted to know the details of Roman law, but Pope Eleutherius told him that he was 'vicar of God' in his own kingdom and, as he already had the Old and New Testaments, he had everything he needed to make his own laws. From this Henry insisted he was the superior legislator who 'gave' the law and exercised his *imperium* or 'command' over Church and state. His 'absolute' prerogative was no longer confined to war or emergencies. This political theology was proclaimed in the Act of Appeals in April 1533, the month before Anne Boleyn was crowned. John Guy, 'The Tudor Monarchy and its Critiques', www.tudors.org

2. Roy Strong, *Artists of the Tudor Court*, pp. 201–3. Dale Hoak, 'The Coronations of Edward VI, Mary I, and Elizabeth I', pp. 147–9.

3. Wingfield, 'Vita Mariae Reginae', p. 245. Brewer (ed.), *Letters and Papers*, Vol. XIII, p. 81; p. 280; John Gough Nichols, *The History and Antiquities of the County of Leicester*, Vol. III, p. 673.

4. Brewer (ed.), *Letters and Papers*, Vol. XIII, pt I, p. 81; pt II, p. 280. Nichols, *County of Leicester*, Vol. III, pt 2, p. 673. Henry VIII had also denied Dorset the Garter, which he was given in February 1547.

5. G. W. Bernard, 'The Downfall of Sir Thomas Seymour', p. 226.

6. Henry Clifford, *The Life of Jane Dormer, Duchess of Feria*, p. 60. The reference to 'king' suggests, to my mind, a period post-January 1547. Jane Dormer's grandfather, Sir William Sidney, who was first cousin of Frances's father, Charles Brandon, Duke of Suffolk, was Steward of the King's Household in 1547.

7. *HMC Salisbury*, Vol. I, p. 70.

8. Ibid., Vol. I, p. 63; Patrick Fraser Tytler (ed.), *England under the Reigns of Edward VI and Mary*, Vol. I, p. 138.
9. Tytler, *Edward VI and Mary*, Vol. I, p. 138; Samuel Haynes (ed.), *A Collection of State Papers Relating to Affairs in the Reigns of King Henry VIII, King Edward VI, Queen Mary and Queen Elizabeth*, Vol. VI, p. 838.
10. John Gough Nichols, *Chronicle of the Grey Friars of London*, p. 55.

Chapter IV: The Example of Catherine Parr

1. Harris, *Aristocratic Women*, pp. 40, 41.
2. Kate Astley's uncle, Sir Gawain Carew, was the brother-in-law of Jane's grandfather, Charles Brandon, Duke of Suffolk. After Katherine Astley's death on 18th July 1565, John married an illegitimate daughter of Jane's uncle, Thomas Grey, one Margaret Lenton.
3. Clifford, *Jane Dormer*, p. 86.
4. The first volumes were printed in January and the huge number of 20,000 was sold over the next three years.
5. www.oxforddnb.com/Katherine Parr.
6. The Queen's chaplain, John Parkhurst, was previously chaplain to Jane's grandfather, Suffolk and was a friend of her tutor John Aylmer. It is highly likely she read the 'Lamentations'.
7. *CSPS*, Vol. IX, p. 50.
8. Nichols, *Grey Friars*, p. 55.
9. Strype, *Memorials*, Vol. II, p. 13.
10. Haynes (ed.), *State Papers*, Vol. VI, p. 75.
11. Mary Bateson, *Records of the Borough of Leicester*, p. 57.
12. Haynes (ed.), *State Papers*, Vol. VI, p. 100.
13. Strype, *Memorials*, Vol. II, p. 196. The accusation was included in his indictments of 1549.
14. Catherine's biographer, Susan E. James (*Kathryn Parr, The Making of a Queen*), believes this incident took place on Twelfth Night, 6th January. I believe, however, that this is a misreading of the source. Katherine Astley described this incident to Elizabeth's cofferer, Thomas Parry, on 6th January 1549, rather than the incident occurring on this date (see Haynes, ed., *State Papers*, Vol. VI, p. 96).
15. James, *Kathryn Parr*, pp. 412, 413.
16. Strype, *Memorials*, Vol. II, pt I, p. 201.
17. So claimed Katherine Suffolk's spiritual adviser Hugh Latimer. The duchess, who began paying for publication of his sermons that year, may have been his informant.
18. Wriothesley and Hamilton, *Chronicle*, Vol. I, p. 5.
19. For the evangelicals, the Holy Sacraments were not inviolate, so divorce was quite possible. But Somerset feared that allowing it was too progressive a step at this stage. Indeed, England remained in the sixteenth

century the only Protestant country in Europe not to allow divorce. It may not have been coincidental however, in this instance, that Somerset's wife was a cousin of the woman to whom Northampton had been wed as a child and wished to divorce.

20. *HMC Salisbury*, Vol. I, p. 70.

21. Tytler, *Edward VI and Mary*, Vol. I, p. 140.

22. James, *Kathryn Parr*, p. 332.

23. Dorset's cousin and estate manager, Sir Thomas Arundell, who had been Katherine Howard's brother-in-law, was currently Chancellor of Catherine Parr's household, and well placed to find Tilney a position with the Queen dowager. Elizabeth Tilney was the niece of Agnes Tilney, Duchess of Norfolk, and her mother – also called Elizabeth – was related to Jane's mother through the Brandons. See Cyril Bristow's *Tilney Families*.

24. To make ippocras: 'Take of chosen Cinamon two ounces, of fine Ginger one ounce, of Graines halfe an ounce, bruse them all and stampe them in three or fower pints of good odiferous wine, with a pound of suger, by the space of foure and twenty houres, than put them into an Ipocrasse bagge of wollen and so receive the liquor. The readiest and best way is to put the spices with the halfe pounde of suger, and the wine into a bottell, or a stone potte stopped close, and after xxiiii houres it will be ready, then cast a thinne linnen cloth, or a piece of boulter clothe on the mouthe and let in so much run through as ye will occupie at once, and keepe ye vessell close, for it will so well keep bothe the spirite, odour and vertue of the wine and the spices' (quoted in www.tudorhistory.org; see also Agnes Strickland, *Lives of the Tudor Princesses*, p. 96).

Chapter V: The Execution of Sudeley

1. Eleanor had been complaining of blood in her urine as well as pains in her side towards her back. Professor Christopher Sutton suggests it is possible that she was suffering from renal tuberculosis.

2. James, *Kathryn Parr*, p. 48.

3. Haynes (ed.), *State Papers*, Vol. VI, pp. 77, 78.

4. Tytler, *Edward VI and Mary*, Vol. I, p. 133.

5. Haynes (ed.), *State Papers*, Vol. VI, p. 78.

6. Ibid., p. 79.

7. In April 1547 the Council forbad the coining of any more *testons* or shillings, two-thirds of which were alloy. Sharington nevertheless bought up large quantities of church plate from the Somerset villagers, and during May, June, and July, coined it into *testons*. He also made over 4,000 livres in three years by shearing and clipping coins. To conceal his frauds he made false copies of the books of the Mint and destroyed the originals.

8. Tytler, *Edward VI and Mary*, Vol. I, p. 140.

9. *CSPD*, Vol. I, p. 88.

10. Haynes (ed.), *State Papers*, Vol. VI, pp. 68, 95.
11. Anne Boleyn's uncle, Thomas Howard, died in the Tower in 1537 having become betrothed to Lady Margaret Douglas without the King's permission. The following year, 1538, the Earl of Devon was executed for plotting to ally his son, Edward Courtney, with the King's daughter, Mary. The then twelve-year-old Courtney, a descendant of Edward IV, remained in the Tower, perhaps in part because he remained a potential groom for Mary: together they could pose a threat to Edward who, in Catholic countries, was not considered legitimate as he was born when England was in schism with Rome.
12. Strype, *Memorials*, Vol. II, p. 430.
13. Haynes (ed.), *State Papers*, Vol. VI, p. 107. Tytler, *Edward VI and Mary*, Vol. I, p. 141.
14. Strype, *Memorials*, Vol. II, p. 198; Bernard, 'Downfall', p. 150. Simon Adams and G. W. Bernard, 'A Journal of Matters of State', p. 57. The Treason Acts of 1547 had confirmed the 1544 Act of Succession. At the time, however, the Protector still hoped that Mary would conform to her brother's religious decrees, as he had to their father's. This hope had diminished rapidly since. It is therefore possible that her being passed over in the succession was under consideration as a future option – and this may have been what Sudeley was suggesting. The man who commented on the messages was Hugh Latimer.
15. I have taken the date from Nichols, *Grey Friars*. Different sources seem to give a slightly different date.
16. Baldwin Smith, *Treason in Tudor England*, pp. 476, 477, 491.
17. Bernard, 'Downfall', p. 231.

Chapter VI: Northumberland's 'Crew'

1. *CSPD*, Vol. I, p. 110.
2. A. J. Fletcher and D. MacCulloch, *Tudor Rebellions*, p. 11.
3. *CSPD*, Vol. I, p. 131.
4. *HMC Middleton*, p. 519; Alice Friedman, *House and Household in Elizabethan England*, p. 15. There were, however, outbursts of violence. Leicestershire, for example, was convulsed by riots just two years later, in August 1551.
5. Margie Mae Hankinson, 'William Thomas, Italianate Englishman', p. 30.
6. It was with Anne Parr, Lady Herbert, that John Foxe describes Jane Grey escorting Catherine to King Henry's chamber carrying her candle before her.
7. The date of this visit is often given as 1550. This is a misreading of the source. The following February is described as the fourth year of Edward's reign – 1550 – making the previous November 1549 (*HMC Middleton*, p. 520).

8. Giovanni Michieli, Venetian ambassador, 1557 (see www.tudorplace.com.ar/Documents/description_of_mary_i.htm).
9. *CSPS*, Vol. X, 1550–52, p. 6.
10. Ibid., Vol. IX, p. 489.
11. Ibid., Vol. X, 1550–52, p. 6.
12. *HMC Middleton*, pp. 520, 521.
13. Strype, *Memorials*, Vol. II, pp. 485, 486.
14. Nichols, John Gough (ed.), *The Literary Remains of Edward VI*, Vol. I, p. ccxxvii.
15. *CSPD*, Vol. I, p. 163. Cecil's brother-in-law, William Cooke, was married to Frances Grey, daughter of Lord John Grey of Pirgo and first cousin of the Grey sisters.
16. Dorset was paying John of Ulm a pension of 20 crowns per annum from August 1549. The chief sources of religious radicalism in England were the religious exiles – men such as Ulm – and their leading patrons were all close to the Grey sisters. On the Privy Council they were Dorset and Northampton, outside it Katherine Suffolk and Edward's tutors, Sir John Cheke (a former Parr client) and Sir Anthony Cooke, father-in-law of William Cecil and whose son was married to Frances Grey, first cousin of the Grey sisters.

Chapter VII: Bridling Jane

1. Quoted in Baldwin Smith, *Treason in Tudor England*, p. 84.
2. See Plato, *Phaedo*. For 'young and lovely' see letter in Strickland, p. 128.
3. Ascham, *The Whole Works*, Vol. III, pp. 118, 119.
4. Robinson, *Original Letters*, Vol. I, p. 276.
5. Henry Ellis, *Original Letters Illustrative of English History*, Vol. II, p. 430.
6. Heinrich Bullinger, *The Decades of Heinrich Bullinger*, Vol. IV, pp. 528, 544. It was published in March 1551, but Dorset was still in Leicester in April (Bateson, *Records*, p. 65).
7. Bateson, *Records*, p. 68. The wine would have been intended for Lord John Grey's wife.
8. Robinson, *Original Letters*, Vol. I, pp. 9–11.
9. Ibid., pp. 4, 5, 6. Also see note 16, chapter 6.
10. Ibid.
11. Ellis, *Letters Illustrative*, Vol. II, p. 430.
12. Strickland, *Tudor Princesses*, p. 120.
13. Ibid., p. 110.
14. North (ed.), *England's Boy King*, pp. 92, 93.
15. Thomas Wilson, quoted in Cecilie Goff, *A Woman of the Tudor Age*, p. 195.
16. Ibid., p. 197.
17. Dorset appears to have employed Wilson for a time as a tutor for Thomas Willoughby.

Chapter VIII: Jane and Mary

1. www.hrionline.shef.ac.uk/foxe/1563 edition, Bk 12, p. 1746. Foxe – the source of this story – does not give a date for it. The last recorded visit Jane made to Beaulieu was November 1949 and the incident could have taken place then, although the following year, 1550, when her father was on the Privy Council seems more probable.
2. MacCulloch, *The Boy King*, p. 134; Michael Wyatt, *The Italian Encounter with Tudor England*, pp. 83, 84.
3. *CSPS*, Vol. X, pp. 205, 206.
4. Clifford, *Jane Dormer*, p. 63.
5. Edward followed up the Christmas meeting with a letter in which he warned his sister that her closeness to him in blood made her faults all the greater. 'Truly sister,' he wrote in a postscript written in his own hand; 'I will not say more and worse things, because my duty would compel me to use harsher and angrier words. But this I will say with intention, that I will see my laws strictly obeyed, and those who break them shall be watched and denounced' (*CSPS*, Vol. X, p. 212). Evangelicals later averred that Councillors had sometimes to restrain Edward in his determination to put a stop to Mary's Mass. Perhaps so. Thirteen-year-olds like Edward and Jane have few shades of grey in their moral universe; but Edward was always more conciliatory when he was with Mary than when he sent her one of his angry letters. Perhaps not all the Councillors at his side were so very keen to restrain him. There was a notable display of aggression from some of them at Greenwich Palace on 13th February 1550, only a week after Mary received Edward's letter. A group of peasants were brought before the Council accused of disobeying the ordinances on religion. As horrified courtiers and diplomats listened in neighbouring rooms they could hear the men being beaten and threatened. The loudest shouts were recognised as 'my Lord of Warwick [John Dudley] and the two marquesses [Dorset and Northampton]' (ibid., Vol. X, p. 223).
6. Ibid., Vol. IX, p. 407.
7. North (ed.), *England's Boy King*, p. 76.
8. Ellis, *Letters Illustrative*, Vol. II, pp. 176–81.
9. Tytler, *Edward VI and Mary*, p. 3.
10. It doubled the number of dukes in England – the other two being Somerset and the old Duke of Norfolk, who had been in the Tower since the end of King Henry VIII's reign, his crime being that his son had argued that Norfolk's royal blood meant he should be governor during Edward's minority. His son, Henry Howard, Earl of Surrey, was executed for his offence. Frances's father had tried to arrange a marriage for her with Surrey in 1530, but the duke turned him down on the grounds that Frances's dowry was insufficient.

11. 'The pomp of English ladies abated by the Queen's example', John Aylmer, *An harbrowe for faithful and trew subjects*, margin reference.
12. Robinson, *Original Letters*, Vol. I, p. 4.
13. Simon Thurley, *The Royal Palaces of Tudor England*, pp. 48, 74.
14. Nichols (ed.), *Machyn*, pp. 13, 14.
15. Robinson, *Original Letters*, Vol. I, p. 277.
16. Ibid., pp. 285, 286.
17. 'A young Lady's Answer', Aylmer, *Faithful and trew subjects*, margin reference.
18. *CSPS*, Vol. X, p. 453. Tytler, *Edward VI and Mary*, Vol. II, pp. 71, 72.
19. Wyatt, *Italian Encounter*, p. 79.

PART TWO: JANE, QUEEN AND MARTYR

Chapter IX: No Poor Child

1. Florio dedicated to Jane the *Regole de la Lingua Thoscana* in 1553.
2. Strickland, *Tudor Princesses*, pp. 133, 134.
3. Ibid.
4. Sir Thomas Chaloner's 1563 *Elegy* suggested Jane spoke Arabic. This source, however, has to be treated with circumspection. Besides his Arabic translations Biblander was the author of a famous Hebrew grammar and commentaries on the Bible, which may well have been what interested Jane.
5. Strype, *Memorials*, Vol. II, pt 2, p. 39.
6. Skinner, who was a close friend of John Ulmer and Wullocke, also sometimes attended the King.
7. Herbert's first letter to Katherine in 1561 makes clear they were betrothed when 'very young' – i.e. before she was twelve in August 1552 – then married 'at lawful years' and later divorced. See Tanner MS 193, f. 224.
8. The duchess's only recorded words on the subject were to insist how much better she loved her husband than any of her sons (see S. J. Gunn, 'A Letter of Jane, Duchess of Northumberland', p. 1270).
9. On the same day he made Northumberland's intimate, Sir John Gates, Chancellor of the Duchy of Lancaster, Nichols, *Literary Remains*, Vol. I, p. clxv.
10. *CSPD*, Vol. I, p. 254.
11. Chris Skidmore, *Edward VI, The Lost King of England*, p. 235.
12. Strype, *Memorials*, Vol. II, pt 2, p. 30.
13. Foxe quoted in Goff, *Woman of the Tudor Age*, p. 179.
14. Antonio de Guaras, *The Accession of Queen Mary*, p. 89.
15. Ellis, *Letters Illustrative*, Vol. II, pp. 145, 146n. The letter is undated. David Starkey argues it was written around Candlemas (February) (Starkey,

Elizabeth, p. 108). It may even have been marginally earlier (see Tytler, *Edward VI and Mary*, Vol. I, pp. 161, 162).

16. This was a period, in 1547, when it was still hoped that Mary would conform to her brother's religious decrees as she had, eventually, to her father's settlement.

17. S. T. Bindoff, 'A Kingdom at Stake 1553', p. 645.

18. According to one slightly later source, Northumberland consulted Edward's doctors about his prognosis and was told he had a fatal consumption but should live to September (Estienne Perlin, *Description des Royaulmes d'Angleterre et d'Escosse 1558*, pp. iii, iv). He hoped he could have Parliament recalled then to rubber stamp whatever decision the King and Council came to. He also hoped that the decision made in 1551, that the king no longer needed to have documents co-signed by the Council, had, in effect, recognised his majority at fourteen.

19. On the dating of the will see Ives, 'Tudor Dynastic Problems Revisited', p. 14 n56.

20. Goodrich had joined the Council with Henry Grey in 1549.

21. The 'Device' offers no explanation for Edward's decision, but the letters patent drawn later in the summer and minutes drawn up for his will give us some insight into his thinking.

22. According to the contemporary Robert Wingfield, Edward specifically drew attention to Anne Boleyn's adultery and treason as a reason for excluding Elizabeth when he tried to get legal backing for his will (see 'Vita Mariae Reginae', p. 247). This is reflected in Edward's praise of the Grey girls' upbringing and background in the letters patent with its implied suggestion that they were somehow morally superior to both his sisters.

23. The Empress Maud, mother of Henri II, was one such. John Cheke had always maintained that everything he taught Edward was supported by example.

24. Nichols (ed.), *Machyn*, pp. 33, 34.

25. Read, *Mr Secretary*, pp. 94, 95.

26. *CSPS*, Vol. XI, p. 169.

27. In her 1548 letter to Sudeley. Haynes (ed.), *State Papers*, Vol. VI, p. 79. Also see Wingfield, p. 245.

28. The King – Nothumberland and Suffolk's grandson – would be a Dudley.

29. Wingfield, 'Vita Mariae Reginae', p. 245.

30. Malfatti, *Marriage of Mary Tudor*, p. 5. The phrase used by Commendone to describe Jane's resistance to the marriage is identical to Giulio Raviglio Rosso's: '. . . *alla Primagenita del duca di Sofolch, nominata Gianna: la quale ancona che ricusasse molto questo matrimonio, nondimeno et sospinta dalla madre et battuta dal padre* . . . [etc.]': '. . . the first-born daughter of the Duke of Suffolk, Jane by name, who although strongly depreciating such marriage, was compelled to submit by the insistence of her mother and the threats of her father . . .' The later, embellished story that Jane had been

beaten into submission is supposed to have come from a historical tract written by a man called Baoardo (see Strickland, *Tudor Princesses*, p. 136). 'Baoardo' was a Venetian called Badoaro, or Badoer (the name is Anglicised in the Venetian calendar). He was not the author of the work which Strickland attributes to him, however; the volume which she cites is an anonymous, mutilated, and pirated edition of Raviglio Rosso's *Historia delle cose occorse nel regno d'Inghilterra*, published in 1558. Rosso in his preface of 1560 merely says that Badoaro had read his book and approved it.

31. *CSPS*, Vol. XI, p. 35.
32. Strype, *Memorials*, Vol. II, pt 2, p. 117.
33. *CSPS*, Vol. XI, p. 35. Grey of Wilton was a kinsman of Suffolk, he was also the father-in-law of Henry Denny, whose sister was married to John Gates.

Chapter X: A Married Woman

1. The date is almost always given as the 21st but this is drawn from Commendone writing after the event. It was booked to take place on a Thursday (see Albert Feuillerat, *Documents Relating to the Revels at Court*, p. 306) and when I calculated the day from other known dates – e.g. Jane's entry to the Tower – it confirmed my suspicion that it was the 25th.
2. Wingfield, 'Vita Mariae Reginae', p. 245; Feuillerat, *Revels at Court*, p. 306; *CSPS*, Vol. XI, pp. 45, 46.
3. Perlin, *Description*, pp. iii, iv.
4. *CSPS*, Vol. XI, p. 47.
5. E. Harris Harbison, *Rival Ambassadors at the Court of Queen Mary*, pp. 44, 45. For Michel Angelo Florio's book *Storia della vita e della morte di Jane Grey* see www.riforma.net/libri/micheflorio/index.htm, for her relationship with her mother, and father, see p. 19a.
6. *CSPS*, Vol. XI, p. 117.
7. *CSPS*, Vol. XI, p. 53.
8. Ives, 'Dynastic Problems Revisited', pp. 15–16.
9. Ibid., p. 55.
10. De Guaras, *Accession*, p. 89.
11. www.tudorplace.com.ar/documents/EdwardWill.htm
12. David Loades, *John Dudley, Duke of Northumberland*, p. 241.
13. *CSPS*, Vol. XI, p. 70.
14. Nichols (ed.), *Machyn*, p. 34.
15. Wingfield, 'Vita Mariae Reginae', p. 262.
16. *CSPS*, Vol. XI, pp. 77, 106.
17. Malfatti, *Marriage of Mary Tudor*, p. 46.
18. Harbison, *Rival Ambassadors*, p. 45.
19. Chapter 11 deals with the Commendone/Pollini versions of Jane's letter to Mary, on which this is based. The letters are similar but not identical, and appear to be approximate translations of an original written in August

1553 and which Commendone may have seen. They tally closely to details of events in June/July. The Commendone letter refers accurately, for example, to the poisoning at Chelsea recorded at the time in Spanish diplomatic correspondence (*CSPS*, Vol. XI, p. 53). For timings see also *CSPS*, Vol. XI, p. 106.

20. *CSPS*, Vol. XI, p. 106.
21. It says much about our expectations of the sexes that the gentle, kindly Edward has developed an undeserved reputation for coldness, as he was forced into in a position where he had to sign the death warrants of his two closest male relatives, while Jane, who was notably acerbic, is remembered for a kitsch sweetness, of which there is no evidence in her life.
22. This is drawn from Giovanni Francesco Commendone but there is also mention of such an oath and Jane's reluctance to accept the crown in an anonymous chronicle of the period. As Northumberland faces battle with Mary he reminds his fellow Councillors 'of the sacred and holy oath of allegiance made freely by you to this virtuous lady the Queen's Highness, who by your and our enticement is rather of force placed therein than by her own seeking and request' (John Gough Nichols, *Chronicle of Queen Jane*, pp. 6, 7. Also see *CSPS*, Vol. XI, p. 106).
23. Six years earlier the proclamation that had announced Edward's accession had declared that Edward came to the throne 'fully invested and established in the crown Imperial'. No coronation was necessary to confirm this fact (Hoak, 'Coronations', p. 146). Jane was therefore fully Queen.
24. Nichols, *Grey Friars*, p. 78.

Chapter XI: Jane the Queen

1. *CSPS*, Vol. XI, pp. 82, 83.
2. Wriothesley and Hamilton, *Chronicle*, Vol. I, p. 87.
3. Ellis, *Letters Illustrative*, Vol. II, pp. 184, 185.
4. Nicholas Harris, *The Literary Remains of Lady Jane Grey*, p. lxv.
5. BL Harl 611, f. 1A.
6. *CSPS*, Vol. XI, p. 83.
7. Thomas Fuller later commented that Mary I and Elizabeth 'owed their crowns to [Winchester's] counsel: his policy being the principal defeater of Duke Dudley's design to disinherit them'.
8. Malfatti, *Marriage of Mary Tudor*, p. 48.
9. *CSPS*, Vol. XI, p. 113. It is worth noting that this report came immediately after Jane's fall, and may have been an early attempt at buck passing. Suffolk had spent time with Arundel and Pembroke to get their stories straight on this, if they needed to.
10. Ibid., p. 85.
11. Ibid., p. 86.

12. Henry Dudley was also the son of Suffolk's aunt, Cecily, daughter of Thomas, 1st Marquess of Dorset.
13. Harbison, *Rival Ambassadors*, p. 45.
14. Nichols, *Chronicle of the Grey Friars of London*, pp. 119, 120.
15. Nichols (ed.), *Machyn*, p. 34.
16. Wingfield, 'Vita Mariae Reginae', p. 262.
17. Nichols, *Chronicle of Queen Jane*, p. 5.
18. Ibid., pp. 5, 6.
19. Ibid., pp. 6, 7.
20. Ibid., p. 8.
21. Alan Bryson, 'The speciall men in every shere', p. 280.
22. Wingfield, 'Vita Mariae Reginae', p. 265.
23. Harris, *Literary Remains*, p. lvi.
24. Ibid., pp. lvii, lviii.
25. Wingfield, 'Vita Mariae Reginae', p. 265.
26. Anne Carew was an old family friend. Her father, Sir Nicholas Carew, had been an ally to Charles Brandon, Duke of Suffolk, to whom he was related and, as a widow, she would later marry Frances's widower, Adrian Stokes.
27. There is a view current that Sir Nicholas wished to proclaim Mary himself. This is based on his nephew's later claim that Sir Nicholas had always opposed Jane's accession. This seems to me highly unlikely. During Elizabeth's reign Sir Nicholas's support for Jane was an embarrassment and so the nephew had good cause to cover it up. It is worth recalling that his poetic biography of his uncle's life is called *The Legend of Nicholas Throckmorton*.
28. Lord Rich was made infamous by John Foxe for turning the rack on Anne Askew with his own hands, and more recently in Robert Bolt's play, and Fred Zinnemann's 1966 film, *A Man for All Seasons*, as the ambitious young man who betrayed Thomas More and sold his soul 'for Wales'.
29. Loades, *Northumberland*, p. 265.
30. Tytler, *Edward VI and Mary*, Vol. II, p. 207. Rosso, *Historia delle cose . . .* pp. 15, 16.
31. Malfatti, *Marriage of Mary Tudor*, p. 19.
32. Nichols, *Narratives of the Reformation*, pp. 151, 152, 153, 226. Perlin, *Description*, pp. vi, vii. *CSPS*, Vol. XI, p. 113. *CSPD*, Vol. I, p. 344.
33. N. A. Sil, *Tudor Placemen and Statesmen*, p. 86.
34. Julius Ternetianius to Ab Ulmis in Robinson, *Original Letters*, Vol. I, p. 367.

Chapter XII: A Prisoner in the Tower

1. *CSPS*, Vol. XI, p. 113.
2. Nichols (ed.), *Machyn*, pp. 37, 38. Wriothesley and Hamilton, *Chronicle*, Vol. I, pp. 90, 91. Wingfield, 'Vita Mariae Reginae', p. 168. *CSPS*, Vol. XI, pp. 419, 420.

3. Nichols (ed.), *Machyn*, p. 37.
4. Harbison, *Rival Ambassadors*, p. 67.
5. Bateson, *Records*, p. 71.
6. *CSPS*, Vol. XI, p. 151.
7. De Guaras, *Accession*, p. 138n.
8. *HMC Salisbury*, Vol. I, p. 131.
9. Loades, *Mary Tudor, A Life*, p. 196. Nichols, *Chronicle of Queen Jane*, p. 24.
10. Also Northumberland's brother, Sir Andrew Dudley, and Sir John's brother, Henry Gates.
11. Nichols, *Chronicle of Queen Jane*, p. 17.
12. Barrett L. Beer, *Northumberland, The Political Career of John Dudley*, p. 160.
13. This was suggested in the Jane letter, Malfatti, *Marriage of Mary Tudor*, p. 48.
14. Nichols, *Chronicle of Queen Jane*, pp. 20, 21.
15. Beer, *Northumberland*, p. 160. At no point did Northumberland claim the will was all Edward's idea, although it was surely in his interest to do so.
16. De Guaras, *Accession*, p. 107.
17. Nichols, *Chronicle of Queen Jane*, pp. 23, 24.
18. *CSPS*, Vol. XI, p. 168.
19. Ibid., Vol. XI, pp. 168, 169.
20. Sir Miles was also a friend of Edward Underhill, the father of baby Guildford. After Sir Miles's death his goods and chattels had been granted to Henry Gates. It has also been suggested Partridge was Nathaniel Partridge, the Queen's goldsmith, but I can't see why this would be (Richard Davey's *The Nine Days Queen*, p. 291).
21. Several of Jane's biographers refer to her as Ellen Jacob, and describe her as Jane's nurse, but this is to conflate with one real and one fictional character. Jane had another lady-in-waiting called 'Mistress Ellyn' – or 'Allan' in modern English – probably a relation of Jane's uncle, the Earl of Arundel whose family name was Fitzalan, and who might, perhaps, even have been his daughter Mary. Her other lady-in-waiting, Elizabeth Tilney, was a relation of Frances Brandon. The 'nurse' was, it seems, a later invention, possibly inspired by the nurse in Shakespeare's *Romeo and Juliet*. All we can say for certain about the real 'Jacob' is that she had a Jewish name. Since the Jews had been expelled from England in the early middle ages, Jewish names were very unusual. There were several Jews, however, amongst the court musicians and Jane may have met Mrs Jacob in Catherine Parr's household.
22. In the letter Jane informed Mary that she had accepted the crown with many tears, having been assured by the Council that it was rightfully hers, and that thereafter she had been abused by Northumberland and his family, who had pressured her to make Guildford King and tried to poison her, as they had her father. It appears the contents of Jane's letter were

soon being broadcast to Catholic diplomats who were not of the Spanish camp. They included the papal envoy Giovanni Commendone, who met Mary that month, and Venetian diplomats. The letter, recorded by Commendone and Giulio Raviglio Rosso, matches in its details events described contemporaneously, such as the food poisoning at Chelsea. A close version of the Commendone letter, published in the 1590s by Girolamo Pollini, dated the letter to August. The dating is also suggested, however, by Jane's mention of Gates having been the first to suggest to Edward that she be named his heir. (My thanks to Eric Ives for providing me with a translation of the Pollini letter.) Pollini's history was dedicated to Cardinal William Allen who had many contacts in England, and was a close friend of Nicholas Sander, who had in turn been a client of Commendone. Eric Ives will be publishing a critique on the importance of the Pollini letter in 2009.

23. Jane may have known him: he was the patron of the Leicestershire vicarage of Buckminster.
24. Nichols, *Chronicle of Queen Jane*, pp. 25, 26.
25. They also included Sir Nicholas Throckmorton and a kinsman of her mother's, Sir Peter Carew. *CSPS*, Vol. XI, p. 332.
26. Ibid., Vol. XI, pp. 334, 359.
27. This had the ring of truth to the Spanish, who had heard that Suffolk's brother, Lord Thomas Grey, hated Courtney, the English candidate for Mary's hand.
28. J. A. Wagner, *The Devon Gentleman*, p. 164.
29. Ellis, *Letters Illustrative*, Vol. II, pp. 187, 188.
30. Knighton (ed.), *CSPD Mary*, p. 42.

Chapter XIII: A Fatal Revolt

1. Re-established by royal proclamation on 15th December.
2. *Original Letters Relative to the English Reformation*, Vol. I, p. 365.
3. Foxe quoted at www.hri.shef.ac.uk
4. Lord Thomas Grey was later accused of carrying messages to Elizabeth shortly before the revolt and John Harington, the servant who had helped Sudeley arrange Jane's wardship, also did so on Suffolk's behalf, although nothing found incriminated Elizabeth. It is possible that Jane, being out of contact with the rebels, believed, when she learned of the revolt, that her father wished to put her back on the throne. This was what the Marian regime were saying, and before her death she told her sister that if their father had been successful, she (that is, Katherine) would have inherited their father's lands. Jane as Queen would have had royal lands instead. But it is as likely that she said this because she thought that regardless of whether her father won or lost, she would die. If this was the case, she may have believed he was being reckless. Her last letter to her father is

ambiguous on this point. It observed that God had decided to hasten her death at the hands of one 'by whom my life should rather have been lengthened' (Strickland, *Lives of the Tudor Princesses*, p. 176).

5. D. M. Loades, *Two Tudor Conspiracies*, p. 26.
6. Knighton (ed.), *CSPD Mary*, p. 42.
7. Nichols, *Chronicle of Queen Jane*, p. 25.
8. *CSPD*, Vol. I, p. 28.
9. Ibid., p. 44.
10. This was a former close associate of Parr of Northampton, called Robert Palmer.
11. Loades, *Two Tudor Conspiracies*, pp. 28, 29.
12. Thomas Rampton.
13. Merton, 'The Women Who Served', p. 85.
14. Nichols (ed.), *Machyn*, p. 54.
15. H. W. Chapman, *Lady Jane Grey*, p. 190. According to Michel Angelo Florio, Jane wrote three aphorisms in Latin, Greek and English. They were: 'If justice is done with my body, my soul will find mercy with God.' 'Death will give pain to my body for its sins, but the soul will be justified before God.' 'If my faults deserve punishment, my youth at least, and my imprudence were worthy of excuse; God and posterity will show me favour.'
16. Strickland, *Tudor Princesses*, p. 179.
17. Nichols, *Chronicle of Queen Jane*, p. 42.
18. Ibid., p. 49.
19. www.hrionline.shef.ac.uk/foxe. I have modernised the English to make it easier to read.
20. Recorded by the polemicist John Bale.
21. Foxe, Vol. VI, pp. 415, 416, 417. Also www.hrionline.shef.ac.uk/foxe
22. Ponet in Hudson, *Ponet*, p. 134.
23. Nichols, *Chronicle of Queen Jane*, p. 54. Ponet in Hudson, *Ponet*, p. 134.
24. Strickland, *Tudor Princesses*, p. 177.
25. Ibid., pp. 187–9. The letter echoed the language of the letter she had once received enclosing the gift of a book of Basil the Great, and of letters she had sent, notably that to Harding, as well as the lessons of her youth.
26. It may or may not have actually occurred but the story is certainly in keeping with what we know of Jane and Guildford.
27. Malfatti, *Marriage of Mary Tudor*, pp. 48, 49.
28. Nichols, *Chronicle of Queen Jane*, pp. 56, 57; www.bl.co.uk/onlinegallery; Harris, *Literary Remains*, pp. 58, 59. The prayer on this page, which can be seen in the endpapers of this book, is the Te Deum, which in legend was composed by St Ambrose for St Augustine's baptism.
29. Ibid., pp. 58, 59.

PART THREE: HEIRS TO ELIZABETH

Chapter XIV: Aftermath

1. Ponet in Hudson, *Ponet*, p. 61.
2. Ibid., p. 62; Nichols (ed.), *Machyn*, p. 55.
3. Baker, Vol. I, p. 10.
4. Loades, *Two Tudor Conspiracies*, p. 103.
5. Ibid., p. 30.
6. Nichols, *Chronicle of Queen Jane*, p. 60.
7. Robinson, *Original Letters*, Vol. I, p. 305.
8. Such sermons were commonplace at the executions of heretics and religious dissidents in Henry VIII's time. This scene does not appear in the earlier Nichols, *Chronicle of Queen Jane*, however, and what follows concerning the scuffle is drawn from Foxe.
9. www.hrionline.ac.uk/foxe/single/book10/101570_1637 and Nichols, *Chronicle of Queen Jane*, pp. 63, 64.
10. Loades, *Two Tudor Conspiracies*, p. 104.
11. Starkey, *Elizabeth*, pp. 145, 146, 147.
12. Robinson, *Original Letters*, Vol. 1, pp. 304, 365. Translations by John Banks.
13. John Day claimed he had the originals in the printed introduction to the letters.
14. For a fuller account of this story see Elizabeth Evendon, 'The Michael Wood Mystery', pp. 383–94; see also www.hrionline.shef.ac.uk/foxe
15. Loades (ed.), *John Foxe and the English Reformation*, p. 18.
16. Evelyn Read, *Catherine, Duchess of Suffolk*, pp. 99–100.
17. *CPR*, 1553–54, p. 106.
18. Herrick MSS, Leicester, DG9/79, Misc. 4th series, 1980, Vol. 2, p. 215.
19. Merton, 'Women Who Served', pp. 19, 80, 81.
20. A. Carter, 'Mary Tudor's Wardrobe', p. 15; Merton, 'The Women Who Served', p. 67.
21. Nichols, *Chronicle of Queen Jane*, p. 166.
22. The descriptions of Katherine's attendance in Richard Davey's *The Sisters of Lady Jane Grey* are inaccurate – he may have confused sources with those concerning Elizabeth's coronation.
23. Nichols, *Chronicle of Queen Jane*, p. 166.
24. Ibid., p. 169.
25. Malfatti, *Marriage of Mary Tudor*, pp. 85–8. *CSPS*, Vol. XII, p. 297.
26. *CSPS*, Vol. XIII, p. 33.
27. David Loades, *Intrigue and Treason, The Tudor Court 1547–1558*, p. 189.
28. It is possible it was the name of Jane, Duchess of Northumberland, but I incline to Jane Grey, who they knew was to die, and whom they had served loyally as Queen.

29. Frances was staying with Lord Strange's mother when Queen Jane Seymour went into labour with Edward VI. His maternal grandmother was Agnes Tilney, aunt of Jane Grey's lady-in-waiting Elizabeth Tilney.

30. The elder brother, John, died shortly after his release.

31. C. C. Stopes, *Shakespeare's Environment*, p. 254; Alan Young, *Tudor and Jacobean Tournaments*, p. 31.

32. *CSPS*, Vol. XIII, p. 166.

33. Devon Record Office, Petre 123M/TP22, TP24 and TP25–26. Leicester, *Commonwealth*, p. 75 (www.oxford-shakespeare.com/new_files_dec_21/Leicesters_Commonwealth.pdf).

34. The Spanish comment on Frances's possible marriage to Courtney was written on 22nd April 1555. As Renard was very close to Mary the quality of imperial gossip was high and it may well be that Frances was married to Stokes after this date and not in March at all. There is no contemporary manuscript that mentions March 1555 that I have seen, although plenty of secondary sources quote a March date (though they differ on the precise day).

35. Stokes was born on 4th March 1519, and Frances on 16th July 1517. Stokes had served as Marshal of Newhaven in 1546, alongside Lord John Grey, and the following year was plaintiff in a court case for trespass in the Great Park of Brigstock. He made distinguished friends such as the antiquary and Anglo-Saxonist Laurence Nowell, and gained a later reputation for being amongst the hotter sorts of Protestant (*Notes and Queries*, March 2000, p. 28; *Notes and Queries*, 11th series, Vol. V, p. 26).

36. The alleged comments about Frances were, in fact, made about Elizabeth by Catherine de Medici in 1560, when it looked as if Elizabeth might marry Robert Dudley, her Master of the Horse. Elizabeth's only reported comment on Frances's marriage was made in the spring of 1561. 'What,' Elizabeth asked the Spanish ambassador, would King Philip 'think if she married one of her servitors as the Duchesses of Suffolk [Frances and Katherine] and the Duchess of Somerset had done?' (*CSPS*, Vol. I, 1558–67, p. 182). Snobbish comments were made about the Stokes marriage in Leicester's Commonwealth, but this was a Catholic polemic and its authors weren't likely to have anything good to say about Frances. Frances's marriage to Stokes at this time suggests she may have played a role in 1553 in the rumour that Jane had been betrothed to a lowly member of Gardiner's household.

Chapter XV: Growing Up

1. Add MSS 33749, f. 84.
2. Carter, 'Mary Tudor's Wardrobe', p. 18.
3. Sir John Hayward, *Annals of the First Four Years*, p. 7.
4. *CSPV*, Vol. VI, p. 107.

5. The mastermind was Northumberland's kinsman, Henry Dudley, who was actually more closely related to the Greys – he was Suffolk's first cousin.
6. www.tudorplace.co,.ar/documents/Dudley_conspiracy
7. Wyatt, *Italian Encounter*, pp. 122, 123.
8. *HMC Salisbury*, Vol. I, p. 139n, at Christmas 1555.
9. In March 1555.
10. Thomas Stafford's sister, Dorothy, then in exile, is mentioned in Mary Grey's will.
11. The exposure of plots encouraged by agents provocateurs was to be used highly successfully against Catholics later in the century; perhaps the Protestants had learned from their enemies.
12. Up to 18 per cent of the population succumbed to sickness or hunger in 1557/58, the highest death rate recorded in England between 1540 and 1740 (Houlbrooke, *Death, Religion and Family in England 1480–1750*, p. 6).
13. Alford, *Burghley: William Cecil at the Court of Elizabeth I*, p. 80.
14. BL Add MSS 33749, ff. 47, 66.
15. Ibid., f. 47.
16. Clifford, *Jane Dormer*, p. 70.
17. Such images were used even in the funeral of the nobility and of bishops: Stephen Gardiner had one at his funeral.
18. Strype, *Memorials*, Vol. II, pt 2, pp. 141–2.
19. Winthrop S. Hudson, *The Cambridge Connection*, p. 18.

Chapter XVI: The Spanish Plot

1. Wyatt, *Italian Encounter*, p. 123. *CSPV*, Vol. VII, p. 12.
2. Hoak, 'Coronations', p. 131.
3. J. R. Planche, *Regal Records*, p. 35.
4. The advice of Bess of Hardwick's descendant, the Duke of Newcastle, to the restored King Charles II (Andy Wood, *Riot, Rebellion and Popular Politics*, p. 27).
5. *CSPV*, Vol. VII, p. 12.
6. Planche, *Regal Records*, p. 35.
7. *CSPV*, Vol. VII, p. 14.
8. Margaret J. Beckett, 'The Political Works of John Leslie Bishop of Ross', p. 147.
9. Aylmer's *Faithful and trew subjects* was published in April by John Day, the man who had published Jane's writings from his secret press on Cecil's estate in 1554.
10. Hoak, 'Coronations', pp. 139, 140, 141.
11. It is notable also that the Greys were close relations or friends of the leaders of both the invasion attempts during Queen Mary's reign.
12. Loach, 'The Function of Ceremonial in the Reign of Henry VIII', p. 44.
13. *CSPV*, Vol. VII, p. 17.

14. It is believed to have been the same or similar to that revised for Edward VI (Stephen Alford, 'The Political Creed of William Cecil', p. 9).
15. Ibid.
16. *CSPS*, Vol. I, p. 45.
17. *CSPF*, Vol. II, p. 2.
18. *CSPS*, Vol. I, p. 45; *CSPF*, Vol. II, p. 2.
19. *HMC Bath*, Vol. IV, p. 131.
20. Clifford, *Jane Dormer*, pp. 108, 109.
21. *CSPF*, Vol. II, p. 422.
22. Add MSS 37749, f. 83.
23. Ibid., f. 56.
24. Nichols, *The Progresses and Public Processions of Queen Elizabeth*, Vol. I, p. 74.
25. Foxe had been living with their friend Norfolk who was married to Katherine's first cousin, Margaret Audley.
26. Add MSS 37749, f. 57. Stokes recalled it as being in October; it was certainly not March as suggested by Agnes Strickland, Richard Davey and followers (Add MSS 37749, ff. 57, 75).

Chapter XVII: Betrothal

1. *CSPD*, Vol. I, p. 254.
2. Add MSS 37749, f. 75.
3. Add MSS 37749, f. 74.
4. Add MSS 37749, f. 57.
5. *Miscellanea Genealogica et Heraldica*, 4th Series, Vol. 2, pp. 215, 216 (1908). Her will was proved on 28th November.
6. Harris, *Literary Remains*, p. cxvii (note).
7. Roger Bower, 'The Chapel Royal', p. 342; the use of the cross was also allowed.
8. Thomas Harding continued to be a leading controversialist on the Catholic sides of the theological debates in the 1560s, engaging from exile in a war of printed words with John Jewel, his Oxford contemporary. Harding maintained throughout a humanist outlook and his arguments were grounded in Scripture and the practices of the early Church. He even petitioned Rome for English Catholics to be allowed to read the Bible in the vernacular.
9. Nichols (ed.), *Machyn*, p. 217.
10. Arundel, No. 35, ff. 5–9: 'the chief mourner, the Lady Katherine, daughter to the said Duchess, defunct'. It was unusual to have an immediate member of the family playing such a role, but the other royals, Margaret Lennox and Margaret Strange, were both Catholic.
11. Nichols, *The Progresses and Public Processions of Queen Elizabeth*, Vol. I, pp. 80, 81.

12. *HMC Bath*, Vol. IV, p. 178.
13. *CSPS*, Vol. I, 1558–67, p. 122.
14. The civil war was fuelled, in large part, by the desire of the rebel lairds to keep their feudal powers and private armies against the wishes of a centralising monarchy. But Protestantism, which offered a useful tag for some rebels, was a genuine ideological commitment to others.
15. Alford, 'Political Creed', p. 13.
16. Add MSS 37749, ff. 57, 73, 76.
17. *CSPS*, Vol. I, p. 122; *HMC Salisbury*, Vol. I, p. 197.
18. *CSPF*, Vol. III, p. 312.
19. M. Le Baron Kervyn de Lettenhove, *Relations Politiques Des Pays-Bas et de L'Angleterre* . . . , Vol. II, p. 608n.
20. *CSPS*, Vol. I, p. 175.
21. Sir Philip Hoby had crowed when Katherine's father joined the Council in 1549, that it 'puts all honest hearts in good comfort for the good hope that they have of the preservation of God's word'.
22. Thomas Hoby, *A Booke of the Travaile and Lief of Me*, Vol. X, p. 128.
23. *CSPS*, Vol. I, 1558–67, p. 176.
24. Ibid. Cecil tried to lure the Spanish back towards Katherine by suggesting what an excellent idea it would be for them to find her a groom since she 'would succeed by virtue of the will of King Henry'. But de Quadra called his bluff by enquiring if Elizabeth would name Katherine her heir and end all dispute on the matter? 'Certainly not,' Cecil was forced to admit, 'because, as the saying is, the English run after the heir to the crown, more than after the present wearer of it.' This is before Elizabeth's famous 1561 speech on the succession in which she reiterated this saying.
25. The daughter of Sir Peter Mewtas, who had been a keen supporter of Jane's accession in 1553.
26. Add MSS 37749, ff. 58, 49.
27. Add MSS 37749, f. 49.
28. BL Harl 611, f. 1A. Exactly such a ring was listed amongst the jewels Jane Grey had as Queen in the Tower, and these had included many jewels worn previously by the Duchess of Somerset. The particular 'ring of gold with a pointed diamond' may have been returned to her and then passed to her son, Hertford.

Chapter XVIII: A Knot of Secret Might

1. Intriguingly Fortescue was a former servant of Cardinal Pole.
2. Add MSS 37749, f. 40.
3. Halloween was then called 'Allhallowtide'. In Catholic belief it is the feast of All Souls.
4. Barnaby may have been sent to actually fetch the ring, but subsequently not wished to have admitted playing such a direct role in the ceremony.

5. Add MSS 37749, f. 52.
6. Add MSS 37749, f. 43.
7. I am grateful to Susan North of the V&A who helped me make sense of the different references to this headdress in the Hertford/Katherine interviews in the Tower.
8. Add MSS 37749, ff. 41, 50, 58.
9. Norman Jones, *The Birth of the Elizabethan Age*, p. 104.
10. Add MSS 37749, f. 59.
11. Her age is given on the inscription of her tomb – although they do seem to have been a bit haphazard about ages and this does make her very young to have done the work she did after the death of the Queen of Navarre! The funeral address was given by a friend of Cecil, Edmund Scambler, Bishop of Peterborough.
12. Nichols, *The Progresses and Public Processions of Queen Elizabeth*, p. 88.
13. Add MSS 37749, ff. 42, 50.
14. Add MSS 37749, ff. 63.
15. As she recalled in later testimony.
16. *CSPF*, Vol. IV, p. 113.
17. Ibid., p. 299.
18. Ibid., p. 152.
19. John Guy, *My Heart Is My Own*, p. 131.
20. *CSPF*, Vol. IV, p. 159.
21. Jane Seymour had been certain the Queen would not give him a licence.
22. Add MSS 37749, f. 51.
23. *CSPF*, Vol. IV, p. 159.
24. Ibid., p. 160.
25. Tanner MS 193, f. 224. Although dated 1559, the letter appears to be a misdated transcript.
26. Hardwicke, *Miscellaneous State Papers*, Vol. I, p. 172. Add MSS 37740, f. 63.
27. Tanner MSS 193, f. 227.
28. Nichols, *The Progresses and Public Processions of Queen Elizabeth*, p. 96.
29. 'Mistress' usually refers to a married woman but Cecil later insisted that the only people discovered to have known about Katherine and Hertford were maids and their servants. Bess was, furthermore, in sufficient favour at Christmas to exchange New Year gifts with the Queen. There is no mention of her sister-in-law.
30. Sir John Harington, *Nugae Antiquae*, Vol. II, p. 391. Add MSS 37749, f. 83.
31. Add MSS 37749, f. 59.
32. Add MSS 37749, f. 43.
33. Lettenhove, *Relations Politiques*, Vol. II, p. 608n.
34. Haynes (ed.), *State Papers*, Vol. VI, p. 370.
35. Lettenhove, *Relations Politiques*, Vol. II, p. 608n.
36. *CSPD*, Vol. I, p. 184.

Chapter XIX: First Son

1. The orders had been written at Smallbridge, a house near Ipswich that belonged to Queen Mary's former favourite, Sir Edward Waldegrave. Evidently the strain of having to entertain the enraged monarch proved too much for him: he died on 1st September.
2. *CSPF*, Vol. IV, p. 262.
3. Ibid., p. 281.
4. *CSPR*, Vol. I, p. 46; Strickland, *Tudor Princesses*, p. 210.
5. The previous year Sackville had written a sonnet for publication in Thomas Hoby's translation of the *Book of the Courtier*. Hoby, we may recall, was Cecil's brother-in-law and the host of the dinner party to which Hertford and Katherine were invited after Amy Dudley was found dead.
6. Nichols (ed.), *Machyn*, p. 266.
7. Add MSS 37749, f. 43.
8. Hertford Castle was on the site of a Saxon fort built by King Alfred to keep out the Danes and reconstructed by William the Conqueror shortly after 1066 as a motte or bailey. It had been updated by various kings since, but it was not one of Elizabeth's more comfortable residences.
9. *CSPS*, Vol. I, 1558–67, p. 214.
10. Pollen, John Hungerford (ed. and trans.), 'Lethington's Account of Negotiations . . .', p. 39. John Spottiswoode, *History of the Church of Scotland*, pp. 11–30.
11. Ibid., p. 39.
12. Ibid.
13. Nichols (ed.), *Machyn*, p. 267.
14. A Robert Wingfield was a witness to Frances Brandon's will. He may have been from the Midlands Wingfield family.
15. J. E. Jackson, 'Wulfhall and the Seymours', p. 154.
16. *CSPR*, Vol. I, 1558–71, p. 51.
17. Strickland, *Tudor Princesses*, pp. 226, 227.
18. J. H. Baker (ed.), *Reports from the Lost Notebooks of Sir James Dyer*, Vol. I, p. 81.
19. The tourist's name was Gerard Leigh.
20. Nichols, *The Progresses and Public Processions of Queen Elizabeth*, Vol. I, pp. 133, 134, 135, 139.
21. By Vita Sackville-West.
22. Greg Walker, *The Politics of Renaissance Drama*, p. 202; Mortimer Levine, *The Early Elizabethan Succession Question*, p. 43.
23. The list of Hertford's expenses from 10th February to 27th January 1568 includes: 'Th. Norton 6l' (*HMC Bath*, Vol. IV, p. 178).
24. N. Jones and P. W. White, 'Gorboduc and Royal Marriages', pp. 3–16.
25. This is the limning that David Starkey has argued is of Jane. The writing declares the sitter is in her eighteenth year, rather than her seventeenth, as

I believe Jane was when she died. But I do not think this matters much – the date of death on Katherine's tomb, for instance, is out by several years. At least two people who knew Jane slightly thought she was seventeen when she died: John Ulmer and Michel Angelo Florio. Nor do I think it important that she has blue eyes, rather than brown, as Jane was described as having. The likely artist, Lavina Teerlinc, habitually painted her sitters with blue eyes. I find Starkey's arguments about the foliage representing Guildford and Robert Dudley compelling, and this date makes sense of their being linked. The image is therefore posthumous, but it is the nearest image we have to Jane's likely appearance. Teerlinc would have known Jane well – she was a courtier like Jane and she also painted Katherine. She could have based it not only on personal memories of Jane, furthermore, but also on images that may since have been lost. We know that Bess Hardwick owned at least one image of Jane, as did the Earl of Hertford. Arbella Stuart commented on both in 1603. That the one owned by Hertford was a miniature is suggested by the fact Arbella describes it as something easily transportable (see Chapter 24).

26. Haynes (ed.), *State Papers*, Vol. I, p. 378.
27. Alford, *The Early Elizabethan Polity*, pp. 92, 93.
28. Baker (ed.), *Dyer*, Vol. I, p. 82; Longleat PO/I/93.
29. Longleat PO/I/93.
30. Alford, *The Early Elizabethan Polity*, p. 94.

Chapter XX: Parliament and Katherine's Claim

1. *CSPS*, Vol. I, 1558–67, p. 263.
2. The description is reminiscent of the Hoby dinner party that took place after the death of Amy Dudley. A guest at that dinner, the Earl of Arundel, was holding one of these dinner party meetings in 1563 at his house.
3. They were at Sheen, in the care of Sir Richard Sackville, the father of Thomas Sackville, the author of *Gorboduc*.
4. Neale, 'Parliament and the Succession Question in 1562/3 and 1566', pp. 124, 125. Levine, *Tudor Dynastic Problems*, pp. 106, 107. Levine, *The Early Elizabethan Succession Question*, p. 49.
5. *CSPS*, Vol. I, 1558–67, p. 296.
6. Levine, *Early English Succession Question*, p. 28; *HMC Salisbury*, Vol. I, p. 396.
7. Haynes (ed.), *State Papers*, Vol. VI, p. 396. The date of 1562 given in Davey's *Sisters* is incorrect. On Mason's betrayal of Jane Grey, see Chapter 11.
8. Baker (ed.), *Dyer*, Vol. I, pp. 81, 82.
9. By John Tisdale between 22nd July 1562 and 22nd July 1563.
10. He would try to pull off a similar measure to this over twenty years later, in 1584/5.

11. According to de Quadra, Katherine Grey's rivals hadn't liked Cecil's suggestion that they (or their husbands) be members of the Council that would help choose the Queen's heir. They feared that instead of being safe on their country estates, plotting in their own interests, they would be corralled into choosing Katherine and then locked up. Equally they could not afford to be left off such a Council, and leave others in charge of their interests – so no such Council could be permitted.
12. *HMC Salisbury*, Vol. I, p. 294.
13. Ellis, *Letters Illustrative*, Vol. II, p. 285.
14. *CSPS*, Vol. I, 1558–67, p. 313.

Chapter XXI: Hales's Tempest

1. *HMC Salisbury*, Vol. I, pp. 179, 280.
2. Ellis, *Letters Illustrative*, Vol. II, pp. 177, 278.
3. Strickland, *Tudor Princesses*, pp. 225, 226.
4. Ellis, *Letters Illustrative*, Vol. II, pp. 279, 280.
5. Ibid., p. 281.
6. Landsdowne 6, f. 36.
7. Ellis, *Letters Illustrative*, Vol. II, pp. 281, 282.
8. Longleat, Portland, Vol. I, ff. 92, 93: 'No small joy, my dearest Lord, is it to me the comfortable understanding of your maintained health. I crave to God to [give you strength] as I doubt not but he will. You, neither I, have anything in this most lamentable time so much to comfort [us in our pitiable absence from each other] as the hearing, the seeking and countenance [of good health] in us both. Though of late I have not been well, yet now, I thank God, pretty well, and long to be merry with you, as you do with me as when our little, sweet boys in the Tower was gotten either the twenty fifth or twenty ninth of May; even I say no more but be you as merry as I was heavy when you the third time came to the door and it was locked. Do you think I forget old fore ... matters between us? No surely I cannot but bear in memory fare many more than you think, for I have good leave to do so when I call to mind what a husband I have of you, and my great hard fate to miss the viewing of so good a one. Very well, though I write you [are] good, you be my naughty Lord. Could you [not] find [it] in your heart to have pity of me to [have given me] more pains for more brats, so fast one after another? No, [but] I would not only have regard to rest my bones ... I should have remembered the blessing of God in giving us such increase. I [don't] doubt I should rather have been glad to have borne a great deal [more] pain than thought any too much ... to bring them, so much is my boundless love to my sweet bedfellow that I was wont with joyful heart to lie by, and shall again ... Thus most humbly thanking you, my sweet Lord, for your husbandly sending both to see how I do, and also for your money, I most lovingly bid you farewell:

not forgetting my especial thanks to you for your book, which is no small jewel to me. I can very well read it, for as soon as I had it, I read it over even with my heart as well as with eyes; by which token I once again bid you *Vale et semper salus* my good Ned, Your most loving and faithful wife during life, Katherine Hertford'

9. Ellis, *Letters Illustrative*, Vol. II, pp. 283, 284, 285.
10. Lady Knollys was a daughter of Elizabeth's aunt, Mary Boleyn.
11. Landsdowne MS 7, ff. 110, 119.
12. Strickland, *Tudor Princesses*, p. 239.
13. Ibid., p. 241.
14. *HMC Salisbury*, Vol. I, p. 294.
15. Ellis, *Letters Illustrative*, Vol. II, p. 273.
16. Hertford's servant Anthony Penn testified that a man called Thomas Dannet, a cousin of Cecil, had delivered a discourse on the marriage to him, written by Robert Beale, Hales's agent in Europe. Dannet was a veteran conspirator who had been involved in the rising led by Katherine's father in the Midlands in 1554. He told Penn to show the discourse to Hertford's lawyers 'to quicken their wits' (Levine, *The Early Elizabethan Succession Question*, p. 73). Those clients of Cecil who were named included the lawyer William Fleetwood, a friend of the *Gorboduc* author Thomas Sackville. He would be associated in the 1580s with Cecil's plans for a Grand Council on Elizabeth's death. He enjoyed, at this time, the patronage of Sir Ambrose Cave whose daughter and heir was to marry Mary Boleyn's grandson, Henry Knollys in 1565 – the wedding Mary Grey would use as cover for her own marriage. It is worth recalling here Katherine's presents of the stockings to Lady Knollys, Henry's mother in the New Year 1564. Another client of Cecil whose name emerged was that of the evangelical preacher David Whitehead, who had been a chaplain to Katherine Suffolk (Ellis, *Letters Illustrative*, Vol. II, p. 285). Whitehead, whom Cecil strongly supported for a bishopric, was one of a number of Protestant divines who took part in a debate about transubstantiation at his house in November 1551.
17. Lord John's son Henry Grey who was Cecil's godchild – named after his late uncle, one assumes – was made Henry Grey Baron Grey of Groby by James I. His descendants include Henry Grey, 1st Earl of Stamford, whose son Thomas, Lord Grey of Groby, was a regicide.

PART FOUR: THE FINAL TRAGEDY

Chapter XXII: The Lady Mary and Mr Keyes

1. The Knollys wedding did not take place in August or at Whitehall, as stated by previous biographers.
2. *CSPS*, Vol. I, 1558–67, p. 451.
3. Both Lady Arundell and Lady Stafford would be remembered in Mary's will.
4. The brother was called Edward Keyes, the friend Martin Cawsley.
5. Ellis, *Letters Illustrative*, Vol. II, p. 299. It may have struck Elizabeth that Mary Grey's betrothed in 1553, Grey of Wilton, had also been a soldier much older than she. If so she may have asked herself if Mary was, on some level, acting out her parents' former ambitions.
6. He founded the Muscovy Company of London, which held a monopoly on Anglo–Russian trade.
7. Norma Major, *Chequers*, p. 27.
8. Strickland, *Tudor Princesses*, p. 269. *CSPD*, Vol. I, p. 263; photocopy from Chequers estate.
9. The 'Allegations against the Surmised Title of the Queen of Scots . . .', published in December 1565 demanded that Mary Stuart be excluded on religious grounds – an argument that could even justify overthrowing a reigning monarch. Cecil's friend, Sir Thomas Smith, meanwhile, had composed a major work on England's 'mixed monarchy' entitled *De Republica Anglorum*.
10. *CSPD*, Vol. I, p. 277. Strickland, *Tudor Princesses*, p. 271.

Chapter XXIII: The Clear Choice

1. *Notes and Queries*, Vol. I, June 1995, p. 423.
2. Wentworth's only child, Lady Maltravers, was the widow of Katherine's first cousin, Henry Fitzalan, Lord Maltravers (d.1556). He may therefore have been close to her uncle and ally the Earl of Arundel. This suggests he was chosen (possibly by Cecil) as someone who would at least be kind to Katherine. A remodelled Gosfield Hall was later home to the exiled Louis XVIII.
3. Sir John Mason died on 20th April 1566. Hertford was still with his widow on 24th June when he writes 'from my Lady Mason's house in London' (*Notes and Queries*, 1 June 1995, p. 423).
4. Ellis, *Letters Illustrative*, Vol. II, p. 286.
5. Levine, *The Early Elizabethan Succession Question*, pp. 168, 170.
6. Ibid.
7. *CSPS*, Vol. I, 1558–67, p. 589.

8. The letter is dated 16th October and is from Gosfield.
9. J. W. Burgon, *The Life and Times of Sir Thomas Gresham*, Vol. II, pp. 398, 399.
10. Guy, 'Tudor Monarchy and its Critiques', p. 6.
11. Levine, *The Early Elizabethan Succession Question*, p. 176.
12. Sally Kempton, 'Cutting Loose', *Esquire*, New York, July 1970.
13. *CSPS*, Vol. I, 1558–67, pp. 587, 588.
14. Levine, *Early Elizabethan Succession Question*, p. 181.
15. Ibid., pp. 184, 185; Doran, *Monarchy and Matrimony*, p. 87.
16. This time they began with a learned oration for a resumption of discussions from William Lambard, a client of Cecil's kinsman Ambrose Cave. It is worth recalling here Cave's link to the Hales tract.
17. *CSPS*, Vol. I, 1558–67, p. 595.
18. Ibid., p. 596.
19. Cecil was the principal draftsman although he collaborated with half a dozen MPs (Alford, *Early Elizabethan Polity*, pp. 155, 156).
20. *CSPS*, Vol. I, 1558–67, p. 618.
21. Ibid., p. 620.
22. Guy, *My Heart Is My Own*, p. 365.
23. *CSPS*, Vol. I, 1558–67, p. 69.
24. *Notes and Queries*, 8th series, 1895, p. 2.
25. Agnes Strickland (*Lives of the Tudor Princesses*), and modern biographers who have drawn extensively from her, have erroneously said that he was already 'Lieutenant'. However he did not achieve this post until 1570/71.
26. Hopton billed the Privy Council for the stop over, 'one supper and one dinner, fire, lodging and horseman there 7sh 15 d' (*Notes and Queries*, 8th series, 1895, p. 82).
27. *Notes and Queries*, 7th series, 1886–91, p. 162.
28. James A. Yorke, 'A Chest from Cockfield Hall', p. 84. The Tudor north wing of the house is still standing, along with the gatehouse and stables.

Chapter XXIV: While I Lived, Yours

1. *Notes and Queries*, 8th series, 1895, pp. 82, 233.
2. Cotton Titus MS, no. 107, ff. 124, 131.
3. It is, of course, impossible to know how much the deathbed scene owes to Katherine and how much to the writer. Katherine was the Protestant heir and it was important that she was remembered as noble and saintly.
4. Cotton Titus MS, no. 107, ff. 124, 131.
5. Ibid.
6. Ibid.
7. They were present in 1578 at Mary's funeral.
8. Harris, *Literary Remains*, p. cxx.
9. *Notes and Queries*, 8th series, 1895, pp. 82, 83.

10. Harris, *Literary Remains*, p. cxx.
11. *Notes and Queries*, 7th series, 1886–91, p. 161.

Chapter XXV: The Last Sister

1. Not Lincolnshire as stated by Evelyn Read in *Catherine, Duchess of Suffolk*.
2. Read, p. 144; *CSPD*, Vol. I, pp. 294, 297.
3. Ibid., pp. 144, 145; *CSPD*, Vol. I, p. 297.
4. He was a friend and relation by marriage of William Cecil. Thomas Gresham's sister-in-law had married Sir Nicholas Bacon, Cecil's brother-in-law, and his illegitimate daughter Anne married Sir Nicholas's son, Nathaniel. Gresham was also a co-patron of Hertford's favourite poet Thomas Churchyard.
5. The translations of Isocrates may have been inherited. King Edward had been presented with French translations of Isocrates in 1551, and a similar gift could have been made at the same time to Mary's father or sister, Jane (Skidmore, *Edward VI*, p. 212). The Italian grammars may also refer to the book Michel Angelo Florio dedicated to Jane in 1553.
6. Mary Grey's mother had been godmother to the first born, Frances, in 1548, Jane to the second in 1549 – a little girl called Temperance who didn't live long. Her father had been godparent to a son in the autumn of 1553 and Katherine to a daughter in 1555.
7. Thomas Percy, 7th Earl of Northumberland, and Charles Neville, 6th Earl of Westmoreland.
8. J. E. Jackson, 'Wulfhall and the Seymours', p. 195.
9. *CSPD*, Vol. I, p. 377, dated 7th May 1570, from Sandgate Castle.
10. Burgon, *Sir Thomas Gresham*, Vol. II, pp. 349, 350, 351.
11. Brother-in-law of William Parr, Marquess of Northampton.
12. A fact that supports suggestions that Lord Burghley owed them a favour.
13. Burgon, *Sir Thomas Gresham*, Vol. II, pp. 409, 410.
14. Ibid., Vol. II, pp. 410, 444. Elizabeth visited the house in 1576 when a play was put on for her written by Hertford's favourite poet, Thomas Churchyard.
15. *CSPD*, Vol. I, p. 425.
16. Ibid., p. 433.
17. Burgon, *Sir Thomas Gresham*, Vol. II, pp. 144–413.
18. Strickland, *Tudor Princesses*, p. 288.
19. He had died of pneumonia in February the previous year at Leicester's house.

Chapter XXVI: A Return to Elizabeth's Court

1. *HMC Bath*, Vol. IV, pp. 138, 139.
2. Katherine Duport was probably one of the seven children of Mary's executor Thomas Duport and his wife Cornelia.
3. Landsdowne 27, no. 31, ff. 60, 61.
4. *HMC Bath*, Vol. IV, pp. 141, 145, 146.
5. Also important was Mary's father's cousin the Countess of Lincoln, raised at Beaumanor, as Elizabeth Fitzgerald, and immortalised by the poet Henry Howard, Earl of Surrey, as the 'fair Geraldine'.
6. Landsdowne 27, no. 31, ff. 60, 61.
7. Written by the London clergymen, John Field and Thomas Wilcox.
8. In 1579 Knewstub was given the living of Cockfield in Suffolk where Katherine Grey was buried – and would be buried there himself. In 1604 he spoke at the Hampton Court Conference in favour of Puritan ideas (*CSPD*, Vol. I, p. 591).
9. It is possible that Thomas Keyes had a son or nephew who was also later welcomed back at court. There is an intriguing list of 'Presents at Richmond' in *HMC Salisbury*, Vol. II, dated 20th Nov 1578. Various people gifted food, including Hertford and Stokes, but also one Thomas Keyes gave 'a cock of the kitchen, a pullet in grease, one woodcock, 6 plovers, 4 snipes and twelve larks'.
10. Simon Thurley, *Hampton Court*, pp. 86, 87.
11. The idea of the exceptional woman, uniquely qualified to rule, was always evident in treatment of the Virgin Mary, the Queen of Heaven, who became a mother despite also being a virgin, and alone amongst the human race was born without the taint of original sin. It is notable also that on earth while successful male rulers were considered exceptional amongst men, successful female rulers were/are judged exceptional to women.
12. BL Harl 611, f. 1A.
13. A brass in Shepshed Church commemorates Thomas Duport. His estate in Shepshed consisted of 'the manor of Shepshed and 40 messuages, 2 watermills, 3 dove houses, 30 gardens, 500 acres of land, 100 of meadow, 200 of pasture, 200 of wood, 300 of furze and heath, 100 of alders and 13/- rent in Shepshed, Thorp, Long Whatton, Hemington and Charnwood and common of pasture in Charnwood Forest' (see the Rev. Harold Mack, 'Shepshed Parish Church', 1947). I suspect Edward Hall is the same Mr Hall with whom Burghley's errant son Thomas was staying on 25th September 1578, at Grantham on his way to stay with Katherine Suffolk (*HMC Salisbury*, Vol. II, p. 227). He must also have been related to John Hall, the executor to Mary's uncle Henry Willoughby in 1549 whose son Joseph became Bishop of Norwich (*HMC Middleton*, p. 396).
14. Landsdowne 27, reel 10, 31.

15. Mary's burial place is mentioned in Westminster Abbey Muniment 6406 and in William Camden's guide to the abbey printed in 1600.
16. I would like to thank Robert Yorke, Archivist at the College of Arms for his patient, kind and helpful support in this.
17. See MS Dethick's Funerals, Vol. 2: f. 455 recto: things to be prepared; f. 455 verso: fees appertaining; f. 502 verso: rough scheme of procession; f. 503 recto: list of mourners; f. 503 verso: continuation of above (12 poor women only); f. 517 recto & verso: list of mourners; MS R.20; f. 429 recto: list of mourners.

Chapter XXVII: Katherine's Sons and the Death of Elizabeth

1. More literally 'the burdensome female companion of a beggar' (*HMC Bath*, Vol. IV, pp. 190–3).
2. Ibid.
3. There had been no reason for her to prevent Hertford's remarriage earlier, except spite.
4. Demosthenes: 'All speech is vain and empty unless it be accompanied by action.'
5. Nichols, *The Progresses and Public Processions of Queen Elizabeth*, Vol. II, pp. 2, 3.
6. Ibid., p. 5.
7. For more on this see De Lisle, *After Elizabeth*.
8. De Lisle, *After Elizabeth*, p. 113.

Chapter XXVIII: The Story's End

1. Rather like his uncle Thomas, who had died in 1600, William was the younger but also the more ambitious brother. Unlike Thomas he outlived his elder brother, Edward Seymour.
2. The history of depression and associated weight loss, or possible eating disorders, is striking amongst female descendants of Henry VII and Elizabeth of York. Mary Tudor like Jane Grey was notably thin, and her false pregnancies could have had psychiatric origins. Queen Elizabeth and Mary Queen of Scots both also suffered depressive episodes; Elizabeth would stop eating when she was unhappy. Katherine Suffolk reported Mary Grey also stopped eating while depressed.
3. He had married twice since Katherine's death. Frances Howard died without issue in 1598, and three years later he had married a young and beautiful widow called Frances Pranell, with whom he had been unhappy.
4. Katherine's viscera remain at Yoxford, where the spot was marked until the nineteenth century with a black stone.
5. 'Ned' Hertford was remembered in the inscription as 'An ardent champion of religion' and Katherine as 'A woman of exceptional quality, of honour,

piety, beauty, and constancy, The best and most illustrious not only of her own but every age.' Katherine's first husband, Henry Herbert, 2nd Earl of Pembroke, the man who had accused her of being a whore, was also buried in the cathedral, but has no monument.

6. Robert Partridge, 'O Horrable Murder', p. 91.
7. Jackson, 'Wulfhall and the Seymours', p. 163.

Epilogue

1. Nancy Mitford, writing to Evelyn Waugh, confessed the image of Jane on the scaffold was the object of lifelong sexual fantasy: 'I used to masturbate whenever I thought about Lady Jane Grey, so I thought about her almost continually and even executed a fine watercolour of her on the scaffold which my mother still has, framed and in which Lady Jane and her ladies-in-waiting all wear watches hanging from enamel bows as my mother did at the time ... I still get quite excited when I think of Lady Jane (less and less often as the years roll on)', The Letters of Nancy Mitford, edited by Charlotte Mosley, p. 259.
2. Faith Cook, Lady Jane Grey, published in 2005.
3. The ballad was printed by John Tisdale in 1560 and 1562–3.
4. Cook, Lady Jane Grey, p. 21.
5. Strickland, Tudor Princesses, p. 94.
6. Cook, Lady Jane Grey, p. 21.
7. For example see Catherine Grey by G. Linley, a play written in the nineteenth century (BL Add MSS 42942: 6).
8. R. Bakan, 'Queen Elizabeth I: a case of testicular feminisation?', Medical Hypotheses, July 1985. A few years later, in 1992, the Derek Jarman film Orlando saw the part of Elizabeth played by a man, Quentin Crisp.

Bibliography

The following abbreviations are used in the Notes:

CSPD	*Calendar of State Papers Domestic*
CSPF	*Calendar of State Papers Foreign*
CSPR	*Calendar of State Papers Rome*
CSPS	*Calendar of State Papers Spanish*
CSPV	*Calendar of State Papers Venetian*
CPR	*Calendar of the Patent Rolls, Philip and Mary*
HMC Bath	*Historical Manuscripts Commission, Calendar of the Manuscripts of the Marquess of Bath ... Preserved at Longleat, Wiltshire*
HMC Middleton	*Historical Manuscripts Commission, Report on the Manuscripts of Lord Middleton ... Preserved at Wollaton Hall, Notts*
HMC Rutland	*Historical Manuscripts Commission, The Manuscripts of His Grace the Duke of Rutland, KG ... Preserved at Belvoir Castle*
HMC Salisbury	*Historical Manuscripts Commission, Calendar of the Manuscripts of the Most Honourable the Marquess of Salisbury ... Preserved at Hatfield House, Hertfordshire*

UNPUBLISHED SOURCES

Manuscripts

Bodleian Library
Tanner 193 f. 224, 227

British Library
Additional MSS 33749; Add 63543; Add 10617, 195–225v; Add 26748 ff.13v and 15v; Add 35327; Add 35830 f. 104, 183, 185, 189v, 191–191v; Cotton Titus CVII f. 11v and 122; Cotton Titus MS no. 107 f. 124, 131; Cotton Vitellius C XVI (Vol. 2) f. 413, 459–62, 517, 523; Harley 611; Landsdowne 27, 31 (reel 10 of microfilm); Landsdowne 6, 27, 32, 33, 36, 37, 38, 43, 44 (reel 3 of microfilm);

Landsdowne 81/13 f. 108, 109; Landsdowne 8, 43; Landsdowne 102, 62; Landsdowne 103, 1; Landsdowne 104, 1

The College of Arms
Arundel 35 ff. 5–9; MS Dethick's Funerals 2: ff. 455, 502, 503, 517; MS R.20 f. 429; (MS Dethick's Funerals 2: f. 455 recto, things to be prepared [file 1]; f. 455 verso, fees appertaining [file 2]; unnumbered leaf immediately following, painters' or painter's bill [file 3]; f. 502 verso, rough scheme of procession [file 4]; f. 503 recto, list of mourners [file 5]; f. 503 verso, continuation of above (12 poor women only) [file 6]; f. 517 recto and verso, list of mourners [files 7–8]; MS R.20 f. 429 recto, list of mourners [file 9])

Devon Record Office
Petre MSS 123M/TP22; 123M/TP24; 123M/TP25–26

Leicester and Rutland Record Office
Herrick MSS DG9/79

Longleat MSS
Portland papers I ff. 92, 93

The National Archives
C 1/1469/75; SP 46/10; SP 13/E

Warwickshire County Record Office
CR 1998/EB/20

Ph.D. Theses

Beckett, Margaret J., 'The Political Works of John Leslie Bishop of Ross 1527–96' (University of St Andrews, 2002)

Bryson Alan, 'The speciall men in every shere, 1547–1553' (University of St Andrews, 2001)

Hankinson, Margie Mae, 'William Thomas, Italianate Englishman' (Columbia University, 1967)

Harkrider, Melissa Franklin, 'Faith in a Noble Duchess, Piety, Patronage, and Kinship in the Career of Katherine Willoughby, Duchess of Suffolk, 1519–1580' (University of North Carolina at Chapel Hill, 2003)

Merton, Charlotte Isabelle, 'The Women Who Served Queen Mary and Queen Elizabeth' (Trinity College Cambridge, 1992)

Swenson, Patricia Cole, 'Noble Hunters of the Romish Fox, Religious Reform at the Tudor Court, 1543–1564' (University of California, Berkeley, 1981)

Papers

Alford, Stephen, 'The Political Creed of William Cecil: A Paper Read to the Reformation Studies Institute', University of St Andrews, 2 March 2006

Levin, Carole, 'Lady Jane Grey on Film' (for forthcoming publication *The Tudors and Stuarts in Film*, ed. Susan Doran and Thomas Freeman)

PUBLISHED SOURCES

Adams, Simon, 'The Dudley Clientele', in G. W. Bernard (ed.), *The Tudor Nobility* (Manchester, 1992)

——'Favourites and Factions at the Elizabethan Court', in John Guy (ed.), *The Tudor Monarchy* (London, 1997), pp. 253–77

——*Leicester and the Court* (Manchester, 2002)

Adams, Simon and G. W. Bernard, 'A Journal of Matters of State', in Ian W. Archer, with Simon Adams, G. W. Bernard, Mark Greengrass, Paul E. J. Hammer and Fiona Kisby (eds), *Religion, Politics and Society in Sixteenth-Century England*, Camden 5th series, Vol. 22 (London, 2003)

Adams, Simon and Rodriquez-Salgado, M. (eds and translators), *Count of Feria's dispatch to Philip II of 14 November 1558*, Camden Miscellany XXVIII, Camden 4th series (London, 1984), pp. 302–44

Alford, Stephen, *Kingship and Politics in the Reign of Edward VI* (Cambridge, 2002)

——*The Early Elizabethan Polity, William Cecil and the British Succession Crises, 1558–1569* (Cambridge, 1998)

——*Burghley: William Cecil at the Court of Elizabeth I* (New Haven CT, 2008)

——'Reassessing William Cecil in the 1560s', in John Guy (ed.), *The Tudor Monarchy* (London, 1997), pp. 233–53

Archer, Ian W. (ed.), *Religion, Politics and Society in Sixteenth-Century England* (Cambridge, 2003)

Archer, Jayne Elisabeth, Elizabeth Goldring and Sarah Knight (eds), *The Progresses, Pageants and Entertainments of Queen Elizabeth I* (Oxford, 2007)

Ascham, Roger, *The Whole Works*, edited by the Rev. Dr Giles, Vols I–III (London, 1864)

Auerbach, Erna, *Tudor Artists, A Study of Painters in the Royal Service, from the Accession of Henry VIII to the Death of Elizabeth* (London, 1954)

Aylmer, John, *An harbrowe for faithful and trew subjects* (London, 1559; reprinted Netherlands, 1972)

Bakan, R., 'Queen Elizabeth I: a case of testicular feminisation?', *Medical Hypotheses*, July 1985

Baker, J. H. (ed.), *Reports from the Lost Notebooks of Sir James Dyer*, Vol. I (London, 1994)

Baldwin Smith, Lacey, *Treason in Tudor England* (London, 2006)

Bann, Stephan, *Paul Delaroche, History Painted* (London, 1997)

Bateson, Mary, *Records of the Borough of Leicester*, Vol. III (Cambridge, 1905)

Becon, Thomas, *Works* (Cambridge, 1843)

———*Prayers and Other Pieces* (Cambridge, 2004)

———*The Catechism of Thomas Becon* (Cambridge, 1844)

Beer, Barrett L., *Northumberland, The Political Career of John Dudley, Earl of Warwick and Duke of Northumberland* (Kent OH, 1974)

Bergeron, David M., 'The "I" of the Beholder: Thomas Churchyard and the 1578 Norwich Pageant', in Jayne Elisabeth Archer, Elizabeth Goldring and Sarah Knight (eds), *The Progresses, Pageants and Entertainments of Queen Elizabeth I* (Oxford, 2007), pp. 142–62

Bernard, G. W., 'The Downfall of Sir Thomas Seymour', in G. W. Bernard (ed.), *The Tudor Nobility* (Manchester, 1992)

———*The King's Reformation* (London, 2005)

———*Power and Politics in Tudor England* (London, 2000)

Bindoff, S. T., 'A Kingdom at Stake 1553', *History Today*, vol. 3, 1953

Bower, Roger, 'The Chapel Royal, the First Edwardian Prayer Book, and Elizabeth's Settlement of Religion, 1559', *Historical Journal*, 43, 2 (2000), pp. 317–44

Breight, Curt, 'Realpolitik and Elizabethan Ceremony, The Earl of Hertford's Entertainment of Elizabeth at Elvetham, 1591', *Renaissance Quarterly*, Vol. 45, pt I (1992), pp. 20–48

Brewer, J. S. (ed.), *Calendar of Letters and Papers, Foreign and Domestic, of the Reign of Henry VIII*, Vols VI, XII (pt II), XIII (pt I); XIV (pt I); XV, XVI, IX, XX (pt II): XXI (London, 1894–1910)

Brigden, Susan, 'Youth and the English Reformation', in P. Marshall (ed.), *The Impact of the English Reformation 1500–1640* (London, 1997), pp. 55–84

———(ed.), *The Letters of Richard Scudmore to Sir Philip Hoby, September 1549–March 1555,* Camden Miscellany XXX, Camden 4th series, 39 (London, 1990)

Bristow, Cyril, *Tilney Families* (printed and published by the author, 1988)

Bullinger, Heinrich, *The Decades of Heinrich Bullinger, Fifty Sermons Divided into Five Decades Containing the Chief and Principal Points of Christian Religion* (1587 English translation), Vol. IV (Grand Rapids MI, 2004)

Burgon, J. W., *The Life and Times of Sir Thomas Gresham*, Vols I and II (London, 1839)

Burnet, Gilbert, *The History of the Reformation*, 2 vols (London, 1841)

Byrne, Muriel St Clare (ed.), *The Lisle Letters*, Vols III and IV (Chicago and London, 1981)

Calendar of the Patent Rolls Philip and Mary, Vol. I (London, 1937)

Calendar of State Papers Domestic, 1547–1625, 12 vols, edited by Robert Lemon (London, 1856–1872)

Calendar of State Papers Domestic, 1547–53, of the Reign of Edward VI, edited by C. S. Knighton (London, 1992)

Calendar of State Papers Domestic, 1553–58, of the Reign of Mary I, edited by C. S. Knighton (London, 1998)

Calendar of State Papers Foreign, Vols I–VIII (London, 1865)

Calendar of State Papers Rome, Vol. I, 1558–71 (London, 1916)

Calendar of State Papers Spanish, Vol. I, 1558–67 (London, 1971); Vol. IX, 1547–49 (London, 1912); Vol. X, 1550–52 (London, 1914); Vol. XI, 1553 (London, 1916); Vol. XII, Jan–Jul 1554 (London, 1949); Vol. XIII, Jul 1554–Nov 1558 (London, 1954)

Calendar of State Papers Venetian, 1864–98, Vol. V (1534–54), Vol. VI.i (1555–56), Vol. VI.ii (1556–57), Vol. VI.iii (1557–58), Vol. VII (1578–80) (London, 1873–1890)

Carrington, Laurel, 'Women, Rhetoric and Letter Writing', in Molly Meijer Wertheimer (ed.), *Listening to Their Voices, The Rhetorical Activities of Historical Women* (Columbia SC, 1997), pp. 215–32

Carter, A., 'Mary Tudor's Wardrobe', *Costume*, 18 (1984), pp. 9–28

Castiglione, Baldassare, *The Book of the Courtier*, translated by Sir Thomas Hoby (London, 1900)

Chapman, H. W., *Lady Jane Grey* (Boston, 1962)

———*Two Tudor Portraits* (London, 1960)

Childs, Jessie, *Henry VIII's Last Victim, The Life and Times of Henry Howard, Earl of Surrey* (London, 2006)

Clifford, Henry, *The Life of Jane Dormer, Duchess of Feria* (London, 1887)

Collinson, Patrick, 'The Monarchical Republic of Queen Elizabeth I', in John Guy (ed.), *The Tudor Monarchy* (London, 1997), pp. 110–35

———'Religion and Politics in the Progress of 1578', in Jayne Elisabeth Archer, Elizabeth Goldring and Sarah Knight (eds), *The Progresses, Pageants and Entertainments of Queen Elizabeth I* (Oxford, 2007), pp. 122–41

Cook, Faith, *Lady Jane Grey* (New York, 2005)

Crawford, Patricia, *Women and Religion in England 1500–1720* (London and New York, 1993)

Cross, Claire, *The Puritan Earl, The Life of Henry Hastings, Third Earl of Huntingdon* (London, 1966)

Dasent, J. (ed.), *Acts of the Privy Council*, Vol. II, 1547–1550 (London, 1890)

Davey, Richard, *The Sisters of Lady Jane Grey and Their Wicked Grandfather* (London, 1911)

———*The Nine Days Queen* (London, 1909)

Daybell, James (ed.), *Women and Politics in Early Modern England, 1450–1700* (Aldershot, 2004)

De Guaras, Antonio, *The Accession of Queen Mary*, edited by Richard Garnett (London, 1892)

Dickens, A. G. (ed.), *Clifford Letters of the Sixteenth Century* (London, 1962)

Doran, Susan, *Monarchy and Matrimony, the Courtships of Elizabeth I* (London and New York, 1996)

Doran, Susan and Thomas Freeman (eds), *The Myth of Elizabeth* (Basingstoke, 2003)

Dowling, Maria, *Humanism in the Age of Henry VIII* (London, 1986)

Duffy, Eamon, *The Stripping of the Altars, Traditional Religion in England c.1400–1580* (London, 1992)

Durant, David, *Bess of Hardwick* (London, 1999)

Ellis, Henry, *Original Letters Illustrative of English History*, First Series, Vol. II (London, 1825); Second Series, Vol. II (London, 1827); Third Series, Vol. III (London, 1826)

Elton, G. R., *The Parliament of England 1559–81* (Cambridge, 1986)

Erlanger, Philippe, *The Age of Courts and Kings 1558–1715* (London, 1967)

Evendon, Elizabeth, 'The Michael Wood Mystery, William Cecil and the Lincolnshire Printing of John Day', *Sixteenth Century Journal*, XXXV/2 (2004)

Feuillerat, Albert (ed.), *Documents Relating to the Revels at Court in the Time of King Edward VI and Queen Mary* (Louvain, 1914)

Fincham, K. and N. Tyacke, *Altars Restored, the Changing Face of English Religious Worship 1547–c.1700* (Oxford, 2007)

Fletcher, A. J. and D. MacCulloch, *Tudor Rebellions* (London, 1997)

Florio, Michel Angelo, *Historia de la vita e de la morte de l'Illustrissima Signora Giovanna Graia, gia regina eletta a publicata d'Inghilterra* (Middelburgh, Zeeland, 1607)

Foxe, John, *Acts and Monuments*, Vol. VI, edited by Rev. Stephen Reed (London, 1838)

——*Acts and Monuments*, The Variorum Edition, hrionline (Sheffield, 2004); www.hrionline.shef.ac.uk/foxe

Friedman, Alice, *House and Household in Elizabethan England* (Chicago and London, 1989)

Fuller, Thomas, *Church History of Britain*, Vol. IV, edited by J. S. Brewer (Oxford, 1845)

Gardiner, James (ed.), *Letters and Papers, Foreign and Domestic, of the Reign of Henry VIII*, Vols I–XXI (London, 1886)

Giry-Deloison, Charles, 'France and Elizabethan England', *Transactions of the Royal Historical Society*, 14 (2004), pp. 223–42

Goff, Cecilie, *A Woman of the Tudor Age* (London, 1930)

Grafton, Richard, *A Chronicle at Large and Mere History*, Vol. II, edited by H. Ellis (London, 1809)

Graves, Michael A. R., *The House of Lords in the Parliaments of Edward VI and Mary I* (Cambridge, 1981)

Gunn, S. J., *Charles Brandon, Duke of Suffolk 1484–1545* (Oxford, 1998)

——'A Letter of Jane, Duchess of Northumberland in 1553', *English Historical Review*, Nov 1999, pp. 1267–71

Guy, John, *Tudor England* (Oxford, 1998)

——*My Heart Is My Own, The Life of Mary Queen of Scots* (London, 2004)

————(ed.), *The Tudor Monarchy* (Cambridge, 1995)

————'The Tudor Monarchy and its Critiques', www.tudors.org

Hallowell Garrett, Christina, *The Marian Exiles* (Cambridge, 1938)

Harbison, E. Harris, *Rival Ambassadors at the Court of Queen Mary* (London, 1940)

————'French Intrigue at the Court of Queen Mary', *American Historical Review*, Vol. 45, no. 3 (April 1940), pp. 533–51

Hardwicke, Lord, *Hardwicke, Miscellaneous State Papers*, Vol. I (London, 1778)

Harington, Sir John, *Nugae Antiquae*, Vol. II (London, 1804)

Harris, Barbara J., 'The View From My Lady's Chamber, New Perspectives on the Early Tudor Monarchy', in *Huntingdon Library Quarterly*, Vol. 60 (1998), pp. 215–47

————'Women and Politics in Early Tudor England', *Historical Journal*, 33, 2 (1990), pp. 259–81

————*English Aristocratic Women 1450–1550* (Oxford, 2002)

Harris, Nicholas, *The Literary Remains of Lady Jane Grey* (London, 1825)

Haynes, Alan, *Sex in Elizabethan England* (Somerset, 1999)

Haynes, Samuel (ed.), *A Collection of State Papers Relating to Affairs in the Reigns of King Henry VIII, King Edward VI, Queen Mary and Queen Elizabeth From the Years 1542–1570, Left by William Cecil Lord Burghley*, Vol. VI (London, 1740)

Hayward, Sir John, *Annals of the First Four Years of the Reign of Queen Elizabeth*, edited by John Bruce, Camden Society (London, M.DCCC.XL)

Hickerson, Megan L., *Making Women Martyrs in Tudor England* (Chippenham, 2005)

Hickman, Rose, 'The Recollections of Rose Hickman', *Bulletin of the Institute of Historical Research*, Vol. 55 (1982), pp. 94–102

Historical Manuscripts Commission, Calendar of the Manuscripts of the Marquess of Bath ... Preserved at Longleat, Wiltshire, Vol. I (London, 1968); Vol. I (London, 1883); Vol. II (London, 1888); Vol. IV, 'Seymour Papers, 1532–1686', edited by Marjorie Blatcher

Historical Manuscripts Commission, Calendar of the Manuscripts of the Most Honourable the Marquess of Salisbury ... Preserved at Hatfield House, Hertfordshire, Vol. I (London, 1883); Vol. II (London, 1888)

Historical Manuscripts Commission, Report on the Manuscripts of Lord Middleton ... Preserved at Wollaton Hall, Notts (London, 1911)

Historical Manuscripts Commission, The Manuscripts of His Grace the Duke of Rutland, KG, ... Preserved at Belvoir Castle, Vol. I (London, 1888)

Hoak, Dale, 'The Coronations of Edward VI, Mary I, and Elizabeth I, and the Transformation of the Tudor Monarchy', in C. S. Knighton and Richard Mortimer (eds), *Westminster Abbey Reformed* (Aldershot, 2003)

Hoak, D. E., *The King's Council in the Reign of Edward VI* (Cambridge, 1976)

Hoby, Thomas, *A Booke of the Travaile and Lief of Me, Thomas Hoby*, Camden Miscellany X (London, 1902)

————(trans.), *The Book of the Courtier, With an Introduction by Walter Ralegh* (London, 1900)

Houlbrooke, R. A., *The English Family 1450–1700* (London and New York, 1984)

————*Death, Religion and Family in England 1480–1750* (Oxford, 1998)

————(ed.), *English Family Life, An Anthology of Diaries 1576–1715* (Oxford, 1988)

Hudson, Winthrop S., *The Cambridge Connection and the Elizabethan Settlement of 1559* (Durham NC, 1980)

Hughey, Ruth, 'A Ballad of Lady Jane Grey', *Times Literary Supplement*, 7th Dec 1933

Hume, M. A. S. (ed.), *Chronicle of King Henry VIII of England* (London, 1889)

Hutchinson, Robert, *The Last Days of Henry VIII* (London, 2005)

Ives, E. W., 'Henry VIII's Will – A Forensic Conundrum', *Historical Journal*, 35, 4 (1992), pp. 779–804

————'Henry VIII's Will – The Protectorate Provisions of 1546–7', *Historical Journal*, 37, 4 (1994), pp. 901–14

Ives, Eric, *The Life and Death of Anne Boleyn* (Oxford, 2004)

————'Tudor Dynastic Problems Revisited', *Historical Research*, Vol. LXXXI, no. 212, May 2008

Jack, S. M., 'Northumberland, Queen Jane and the Financing of the 1553 Coup', *Parergon*, New Series 6 (1988), pp. 137–48

Jackson, J. E., 'Wulfhall and the Seymours', *Wiltshire Archaeological and Natural History Magazine*, Vol. XV (1875), pp. 140–207

James, Susan E., *Kathryn Parr, The Making of a Queen* (Aldershot, 1999)

James, Mervyn, *Society, Politics and Culture, Studies in Early Modern England* (Cambridge, 1986)

Jones, Norman, *The Birth of the Elizabethan Age* (Oxford, 1995)

————'Elizabeth's First Year', in Christopher Haigh (ed.), *The Reign of Elizabeth I* (London, 1984), pp. 28–53

Jones, N., and P. W. White, 'Gorboduc and Royal Marriages', *in English Literary Renaissance*, Vol. 26 (1971), pp. 3–16

Jordan, Constance, 'Women's Rule in Sixteenth-Century British Political Thought', *Renaissance Quarterly*, 40 (1987), pp. 421–51

Jordan, W. K., *Edward VI, The Threshold of Power* (London, 1970)

————(ed.), *The Chronicle and Political Papers of Edward VI* (New York, 1966)

Leahy, William, 'Propaganda or a Record of Events? Richard Mulcaster's *The Passage of Our Most Drad Souveraigne Queen ...*', *Early Modern Literary Studies*, 9.1, May 2003; www.shu.ac.uk/emls/09-1/leahmulc.html

Lettenhove, M. Le Baron Kervyn de, *Relations Politiques Des Pays-Bas et de L'Angleterre ...*, Vol. II (Brussels, 1883)

Levin, Carole, 'Lady Jane Grey, Protestant Queen and Martyr', in Margaret Patterson Hannay (ed.), *Silent but for the Word, Tudor Women as Patrons, Translators, and Writers of Religious Works* (Kent OH, 1985)

Levine, Mortimer, *Tudor Dynastic Problems 1460–1571* (London and New York, 1973)

———*The Early Elizabethan Succession Question* (Stanford CA, 1966)

Loach, Jennifer, 'A Close League with the King of France', *Huguenot Society Proceedings*, 25 (1989–93), pp. 134–44

———'The Function of Ceremonial in the Reign of Henry VIII', *Past and Present*, 142 (1994), pp. 43–68

———*Edward VI*, edited by George Bernard and Penry Williams (New Haven and London, 1999)

Loades, David, *Politics, Censorship and the English Reformation* (London and New York, 1991)

———*John Dudley, Duke of Northumberland 1504–1553* (Oxford, 1996)

———*Intrigue and Treason, The Tudor Court 1547–1558* (London, 2004)

———*Mary Tudor, A Life* (Oxford, 1992)

———*The Dudley Conspiracy* (Oxford, 2001)

———'Philip II and the Government of England', in C. Cross, D. Loades and J. J. Scarisbrick (eds), *Law and Government under the Tudors* (Cambridge, 1988), pp. 177–94

———(ed.), *John Foxe and the English Reformation* (Aldershot, 1997)

Loades, D. M., *Two Tudor Conspiracies* (Cambridge, 1965)

Loades, John (ed.), *John Foxe, An Historical Perspective* (Aldershot, 1999)

Lodge, Edmund, *Illustrations of British History*, Vol. I (London, 1838)

Lovejoy, Arthur O., *The Great Chain of Being* (London, 1964)

Lovell, Mary S., *Bess of Hardwick* (London, 2005)

MacCaffrey, Wallace, *The Shaping of the Elizabethan Regime 1558–72* (London, 1969)

MacCulloch, D., *Suffolk and the Tudors, Politics and Religion in an Elizabethan County, 1500–1600* (Oxford, 1986)

———*Reformation, Europe's House Divided 1490–1700* (London, 2003)

———(ed.), *The Reign of Henry VIII, Politics, Policy and Piety* (New York, 1995)

MacCulloch, Diarmaid, *Thomas Cranmer, A Life* (New Haven and London, 1996)

———*Tudor Church Militant, Edward VI and the Protestant Reformation* (London, 1999)

McConica, James Kelsey, *English Humanists and Reformation Politics under Henry VIII and Edward VI* (Oxford, 1965)

McLaren, Anne, 'Gender, Religion and Early Modern Nationalism', *American Historical Review*, Vol. 107, no. 3 (June 2002); in www.historycooperative.org/journals

———*Political Culture and the Reign of Elizabeth I* (Cambridge, 1999)

Madden, Frederick, *Privy Purse Expenses of the Princess Mary* (London, 1831)

Major, Norma, *Chequers* (London, 1996)

Malfatti, C. V. (trans.), *The Accession, Coronation and Marriage of Mary Tudor as Related in Four Manuscripts of the Escorial* (Barcelona, 1956)

Malkiewicz, A. J. A., 'An Eye Witness Account of the Coup d'Etat of October 1549', *English Historical Review*, LXX (1955), pp. 600–9

Marshall, Peter (ed), *The Impact of the English Reformation 1500–1640* (London, 1997)

Martin, J. W., *Religious Radicals in Tudor England*, preface by A. G. Dickens (London, 1989)

Matthew, David, *Lady Jane Grey, The Setting of the Reign* (Plymouth, 1972)

Mears, Natalie, 'Courts, Courtiers, and Culture in Tudor England', *Historical Journal*, 46, 3 (2003), pp. 703–22

Miller, Helen, 'Henry VIII's Unwritten Will, Grants of Lands and Honours 1547', in E. W. Ives, R. J. Knecht and J. J. Scarisbrick (eds), *Wealth and Power in Tudor England* (London, 1978)

Miscellanea Genealogica et Heraldica, 4th Series, Vol. 2 (London, 1908)

Moorehouse, Geoffrey, *The Pilgrimage of Grace* (London, 2002)

Mosley, Charlotte (ed.), *The Letters of Nancy Mitford* (London, 1993)

Murphy, J., 'The Illusion of Decline, The Privy Chamber, 1547–1558', in David Starkey (ed.), *The English Court* (London, 1987)

Naunton, Sir Robert, *Fragmenta Regalia*, edited by Edward Arber (London, 1870)

Neale, J. E., 'Parliament and the Succession Question in 1562/3 and 1566', *English Historical Review*, Jan–Oct 1921, pp. 497–519

Nicholls, Mark, *A History of the Modern British Isles 1529–1603* (Oxford, 1999)

Nichols, J. G. (ed.), *Narratives of the Days of the Reformation*, Camden Society 77 (1859)

Nichols, John, *The Progresses and Public Processions of Queen Elizabeth*, Vols I and II (London, 1828)

——*The History and Antiquities of the County of Leicester,* Vol. III, pt 2 (Wakefield, 2002)

Nichols, John Gough, *The Chronicle of Queen Jane and Two Years of Queen Mary* (London, 1850)

——(ed.), *Chronicle of the Grey Friars of London* (London, 1852)

——(ed.), *The Literary Remains of Edward VI*, Vols I and II (London, 1857)

——(ed.), *The Diary of Henry Machyn* (London, 1848)

Nicolas, Nicholas Harris, *The Literary Remains of Lady Jane Grey* (London, 1825)

North, Jonathan (ed.), *England's Boy King, the Diary of Edward VI 1547–53* (Welwyn Garden City, 2005)

Notes and Queries, 5th series, Vol. VIII (London, 1877); 7th Series (London, 1886–91); 8th series, Vols VII and VIII (London, Feb–Aug 1895); 11th series, Vol. V, Jan–Jun (London, 1912); Vol. 240 (London, June 1995), Vol. 245 (London, March 2000)

Ong, Walter J., 'Tudor Writings on Rhetoric', *Studies in the Renaissance*, Vol. 15 (1968), pp. 39–69

Parker, Matthew, *Correspondence* (Cambridge, 1871)

Partridge, Robert, '*O Horrable Murder*', *The Trial, Execution and Burial of King Charles I* (London, 1998)

Perlin, Estienne, *Description des Royaulmes d'Angleterre et d'Escosse 1558* (London, 1775)

Pettegree, Andrew, *Foreign Protestant Communities in Sixteenth-Century London* (Oxford, 1986)

Picard, Liza, *Elizabeth's London* (London, 2003)

Planche, J. R., *Regal Records, or a Chronicle of the Coronations of the Queen Regnants of England* (London, 1838)

Plato, *Phaedo*, edited by C. J. Rowe (Cambridge, 1993)

Plowden, Alison, *Lady Jane Grey* (Stroud, 2003)

Pollen, John Hungerford (ed. and trans.), 'Lethington's Account of Negotiations with Elizabeth Edinburgh in September and October 1561', *Scottish History Society*, Vol. XLIII (Jan 1904), pp. 38–45

Ponet, John, *A Shorte Treatise of Politike Pouuer 1556*, in Winthrop Still Hudson, *John Ponet* (Chicago, 1942)

Prochaska, Frank, 'The Many Faces of Lady Jane Grey', *History Today*, Vol. 35, 10 (Oct 1985), pp. 34–40

Raab, Felix, *The English Face of Machiavelli* (London, 1964)

Read, Conyers, *Mr Secretary Cecil and Queen Elizabeth* (London, 1955)

Read, Evelyn, *Catherine, Duchess of Suffolk* (London, 1962)

Redworth, Glyn, *In Defence of the Church Catholic, The Life of Stephen Gardiner* (Oxford, 1990)

Richards, Judith M., 'Mary Tudor as "Sole Queen"? Gendering Tudor Monarchy', *Historical Journal*, 40 (1997), pp. 895–924

Ridley, Jasper, *Bloody Mary's Martyrs* (New York, 2001)

Robinson, Hastings, *Original Letters Relative to the English Reformation*, Vol. I (Cambridge, 1846–47)

Rogers Forbes, Thomas, *Chronicle from Aldgate, Life and Death in Shakespeare's London* (London, 1971)

Rosso, Giulio Raviglio, edited by Luca Contile, *Historia delle cose occorse nel regno d'Inghilterra, in materia del duca di Notomberlan dopo la morte di Odoardo VI* (Venice, 1558)

Russell, Elizabeth, 'Mary Tudor and Mr Jorkins', *Historical Research*, 63 (1990), pp. 263–76

Rutton, W. L., 'Lady Katherine Grey and Edward Seymour, Earl of Hertford', *EHR*, Vol. 13 (April 1898), pp. 302–7

Sanders, Nicholas, *The Rise and Growth of the Anglican Schism* (London, 1877)

Schutte, W. M., 'Thomas Churchyard's "Doleful Discourse" and the Death of Lady Katherine Grey', *Sixteenth-Century Journal*, 15 (1984), pp. 471–87

Scott-Warren, Jason, *Sir John Harington and the Book as Gift* (Oxford, 2001)

Sil, N. A., *William, Lord Herbert of Pembroke* (New York, 1992)

——*Tudor Placemen and Statesmen* (London, 2001)

Skidmore, Chris, *Edward VI, The Lost King of England* (London, 2007)

Slack, Paul, *The Impact of Plague in Tudor and Stuart England* (London, 1985)

Smith, Richard S., *Sir Francis Willoughby of Wollaton Hall* (Notts, 1988)

Spottiswoode, John, *History of the Church of Scotland* (Edinburgh, 1848–51)

Starkey, David, 'The Court, Castiglione's Ideal and Tudor Reality', *Journal of the Warburg and Courtauld Institutes*, Vol. 45, 1982

——*Six Wives, The Queens of Henry VIII* (London, 2003)

——*The Reign of Henry VIII, Personalities and Politics* (London, 1985)

——*Elizabeth* (London, 2001)

Starkey, David, Bendor Grosvenor et al. (eds), *Lost Faces: Identity and Discovery in Tudor Royal Portraiture* (London, 2007)

Stevenson, Joan and Anthony Squires, *Bradgate Park, Childhood Home of Lady Jane Grey* (Leicestershire, 1994)

Stopes, C. C., *Shakespeare's Environment* (London, 1918)

Strickland, Agnes, *Lives of the Tudor Princesses* (London, 1868)

Strong, R., *Artists of the Tudor Court, The Portrait Miniature Rediscovered, 1520–1620* (London, 1983)

Strong, Roy, *And When Did You Last See Your Father? The Victorian Painter and British History* (London, 1978)

Strype, John, *Ecclesiastical Memorials Relating Chiefly to Religion*, Vol. II, pts 1 and 2 (Oxford, 1822)

——*The Life of the Learned Sir Thomas Smith* (Oxford, 1820)

Throckmorton, Sir Thomas, *The Legend of Sir Nicholas Throckmorton* (London, 1740)

Thurley, Simon, *The Royal Palaces of Tudor England* (New Haven and London, 1993)

——*Hampton Court, A Social and Architectural History* (London, 2003)

Tighe, W. J., 'The Gentlemen Pensioners: the Duke of Northumberland and the attempted coup of 1553', *Albion*, 19 (1987), pp. 1–11

Tillyard, E. M. W., *The Elizabethan World Picture* (London, 1976)

Tudor, Philippa, 'Protestant Books in London in Mary Tudor's Reign', *London Journal*, 15, 1 (1990), pp. 19–28

Tytler, Patrick Fraser (ed.), *England under the Reigns of Edward VI and Mary*, Vols I–II (London, 1839)

Wagner, J. A., *The Devon Gentleman, The Life of Peter Carew* (Hull, 1998)

Walker, Greg, *The Politics of Renaissance Drama* (Cambridge, 1998)

Weir, Alison, *Children of England, The Heirs of King Henry VIII* (London, 1996)

Wertheimer, Molly Meijer (ed.), *Listening to Their Voices, The Rhetorical Activities of Historical Women* (Columbia SC, 1997)

Whitelock, Anna and Diarmaid MacCulloch, 'Princess Mary's Household and the Succession Crises, July 1553', *Historical Journal*, 50, 2 (2007), pp. 265–87

Williams, Penry, *The Later Tudors, 1547–1603* (Oxford, 1995)

Wilson, Derek, *Sweet Robin, A Biography of Robert Dudley Earl of Leicester* (Bodmin, 1981)

——*The Uncrowned Kings of England, The Black Legend of the Dudleys* (London, 2005)

Wingfield, R., 'Vita Mariae Reginae', translated by D. MacCulloch, Camden Miscellany XXVIII, 4th series, 29 (London, 1984), pp. 182–301

Wood, Andy, *Riot, Rebellion and Popular Politics in Early Modern England* (Ebbw Vale, 2002)

Woodall, Joanna, 'An Exemplary Consort, Antonis Mor's Portrait of Mary Tudor', *Art History*, XIV (1991), pp. 194–224

Woolley, Benjamin, *The Queen's Conjurer, The Science and Magic of Dr Dee* (London, 2001)

Wriothesley, Charles and William Douglas Hamilton (eds), *A Chronicle of England during the Reign of the Tudors, 1485–1559*, Vols I and II (London, 1875)

Wyatt, Michael, *The Italian Encounter with Tudor England* (Cambridge, 2005)

Yorke, James, 'A Chest from Cockfield Hall', *Burlington Magazine*, Vol. 128, no. 995 (Feb 1986), pp. 84, 86–91

Young, Alan, *Tudor and Jacobean Tournaments* (London, 1987)

Index